The World of the Golden Retriever

—A Dog for All Seasons—

TS-197

Overleaf: **Bennington Hill's Zachary CD, TT** and **General JD Gold TT**—"Zach" and "Cubby" pose for photographer (and owner) Karen Taylor.

Title page: **Dual Ch. -AFC Tigathoes Funky Farquar, (FC-AFC-CFC Bonnie Brooks Elmer ex Tigathoe's Chickasaw***),** owned by Dottie Mikeska.

The last breed dual champion . . . today's role model for the ideal Golden Retriever. National Derby Champion in 1973. Claimed his field titles in 1975, before four years of age, and qualified for the National Open, the first Golden to qualify since 1942. Bench title in 1979 at eight years of age, thus gaining dual status. Graced his owner's life for many abundant years, as his family shares:

"Friendship is a flower whose beauty touches the lives of those who hold it." *Author unknown*

Quar's accomplishments are a tribute to the intelligence and versatility of the Golden Retriever. Our companion for almost 16 years, he will remain the lasting memory of a friendship that will never die.

Joe, Dottie, Shannon and Greg

© 1993 T.F.H. Publications, Inc.

Distributed in the UNITED STATES to the Pet Trade by T.F.H. Publications, Inc., One T.F.H. Plaza, Neptune City, NJ 07753; distributed in the UNITED STATES to the Bookstore and Library Trade by National Book Network, Inc. 4720 Boston Way, Lanham MD 20706; in CANADA to the Pet Trade by H & L Pet Supplies Inc., 27 Kingston Crescent, Kitchener, Ontario N2B 2T6; Rolf C. Hagen Ltd., 3225 Sartelon Street, Montreal 382 Quebec; in CANADA to the Book Trade by Macmillan of Canada (A Division of Canada Publishing Corporation), 164 Commander Boulevard, Agincourt, Ontario M1S 3C7; in ENGLAND by T.F.H. Publications, PO Box 15, Waterlooville PO7 6BQ; in AUSTRALIA AND THE SOUTH PACIFIC by T.F.H. (Australia), Pty. Ltd., Box 149, Brookvale 2100 N.S.W., Australia; in NEW ZEALAND by Brooklands Aquarium Ltd., 5 McGiven Drive, New Plymouth, RD1 New Zealand; in the PHILIPPINES by Bio-Research, 5 Lippay Street, San Lorenzo Village, Makati, Rizal; in SOUTH AFRICA by Multipet Pty. Ltd., P.O. Box 35347, Northway, 4065, South Africa. Published by T.F.H. Publications, Inc.

Manufactured in the United States of America by T.F.H. Publications, Inc.

The World of the Golden Retriever

—A Dog for All Seasons—

Nona Kilgore Bauer

Author Nona Kilgore Bauer with her precious brood in autumn 1992.

Dedication

For my five Goldens, who sacrificed along with my husband
and children to make this book possible.
Guess what, guys? Now we can train all day again!

Nona

The Golden Retriever: A Dog For All Seasons

Top: **Barley** at three months, owned by Pat and Carol Beaulieu. *Bottom:* **Chiporego Kodi's Gold Mark UDT, WC** and **Ch. Beaulieu Akacia O'Darnley UDTX, JH, WCX, VCX (OD).** Owned by Jeanne von Barby.

Goldens glowing amid new blossoms . . .
Spring is here!

Top: **K-9 High Speed Chaser** at six weeks, owned by Terry and Diane Schoenbach. Photo by Karen Taylor. *Middle:* **Ch. Honor's Bunny Hug (OD),** a therapy Golden, owned by Ann Chase. *Bottom:* **Amber** asleep at seven weeks. Owners Mark and Gail Lore. Photo by Karen Taylor.

The Golden Retriever: A Dog For All Seasons

Top left: **Jenlyn's Hark Halloa** wading for owners Donna Thompson and Jennifer Foster. *Top right:* The aptly named **Honor's Fun in the Sun WC,** for short "Sunny." *Bottom:* The diving **Brandywine's Golden Amaretto** owned by Vicki Rathbun.

We work early morning . . . but in the sun the livin' is easy . . .

Welcome Summertime.

Top: The bouyant **Can. OTCh. Kelly of Queen Island UDT, WCX, TT.** Photographed by owner Susan Kluesner.
Bottom: Keeping his cool, **Spencer** owned by Joan Bell.

The Golden Retriever: A Dog For All Seasons

Top: **Can. OTCh. Brownards Benjamin Brittan,** "Bandit" posing with his retrieve. *Middle:* Photograph by Karen Taylor of a Golden captured in the falling leaves. *Bottom:* **Kona** and **Hilo** in the pumpkin field. Photo by Karen Taylor.

With ease we fall into our work . . .
A Golden Autumn.

Caution—Quickleaves. Photo by Karen Taylor.

The Golden Retriever: A Dog For All Seasons

Top: **Akacia** in the newly fallen snow. Photo by Ron Brown. *Bottom left:* Golden in his wintertime by Karen Taylor. *Bottom right:* The proud hunter, **Chances R This Bud's For Me,** bred by the author, owned by Clary and Lois Busse.

Pheasants and frollicking . . .
the wonders of Winter.

Top left: The von Barby family carolers. *Top right:* Catch! **Ch. Birnam Wood's Show N' Tell CD.** *Middle:* **Am-Can. Ch. Windsor's St. Elsewhere** waiting for a snowball. *Bottom:* Oriana champs in the snow.

Sun-Day's MVP (Ch. Lemier's Sunshine Bear CDX ex Meadowpond Glory Days UD) owned by Dan and Ann Graham. Photo by Karen Taylor.

Contents

Chances R Wisconsin's Big Jake CDX (Marshland's Shotzy MH, CDX,*** ex Chances R Mein Leibschen CDX, WC) bred by the author, owned, hunted and loved by Nick Kuhn, Mukwonago, Wisconsin. Photo by author.

About the Author

When my five children were growing up, I couldn't wait until they took their teenage noise and clutter off to college. Eventually they did just that, and then, to my dismay, moved on into their own new worlds.

Finally, when my last "baby" turned 24, he bent down and kissed my wet cheek, whispered, "Please don't worry, Mom," and drove down our gravel road in search of his identity.

That same day I lost mine.

I rattled around in my new empty nest like a dime in a Salvation Army can. Each room cried out with memories...... echoes of his music, a towel faintly scented with his aftershave, the refrigerator stocked with nine varieties of his favorite mustard, the empty chair post where his jacket always hung.

Each day I asked myself, "What's left?" I searched for another purpose, a reason to justify the next 30 or 40 years.

As I struggled to regain some balance in my life, I turned, as I often did, to my dogs for comfort and support. My two Goldens had been faithful, silent listeners at each child-rearing crisis, always offering wagging tails and unwavering devotion. Now they became my personal therapists, surrogate child-dogs who wiggled deeper into my heart and curled up in the empty spot left by my last child. Therapy for my empty nest. A sure cure for loneliness, and proof that, yes, there is life after children.

My surrogate kids have grown in number from two to five as my need to nurture grew only stronger after the children left home. Fact is, I need them as much as they need me.... to feed them, exercise them, train them, potty them, talk to them, play with them. They've given my life

structure, a new plan, because I can't neglect their basic needs.....or mine.

They've restored the chaos in my life. They squabble over first place, race for the door and scatter the rugs, bang their behinds loudly and happily on the floor waiting for their treats. When

The author Nona Kilgore Bauer with three of her much loved pals.

they get into mischief, I must chase and scold and threaten. In the evening they lie underfoot, stretched across the family room like a hopscotch, and I have to thread my way through their bodies to get to the refrigerator. They hog the bed at night, and after a ritual of push and cramp and shove, I give up and cling to my husband in the small sleeping space they save for us.

They take me for hikes, and when I see them tearing fulltilt across the fields, noses into the wind, their tails red flags streaming behind, running for the pure joy of it, my heart grows full again. As they dive headlong into the lake, splashing and nipping like silly porpoises, I can't help but laugh and throw up my hands in wonder and applaud their happy games.

They keep me company while I work; always a soft, furry body under my desk to curl my toes into, an occasional cold nose nudging at my

Hard-working and faithful to breeder-owner Nona Kilgore Bauer, this is **Chances R Mollie's Geronimo CD.** Photo by Kevin Kilgore.

elbow asking for a rub, a ropy tail thumping on the carpet at just a whispered word.

They are a thousand reasons to smile as they clown and frolic, tease and beg. And love. Such complete and unconditional love is inspiration to write about matters of the heart, motivation to go on when the heart is heavy or sad.

They force me from my cloistered farm life out into the peopled world because they need to learn of life beyond the fields and ridges of the farm. They need to know of children and cats and dogs and friendly outstretched hands besides my own.

With each new pup come memories of Goldens past; of squirming, face-slurping fuzzballs who grew, overnight it seemed, into handsome, loyal partners in my life; of dark loving eyes that peered out of grey-white faces; of low mounds covered with sweet alyssum on our hill, from where my old departed friends must sigh know-ingly as they watch each new Golden puppy steal my heart.

With puppies also come the trade-offs, ex-changes made with a kind of happy resignation; Ken-L Ration for baby food, pawprints for finger-prints, tennis balls for lincoln logs, leashes on the hooks once filled with baseball caps and mittens; housebreaking instead of potty train-ing. The switch from kids to canines isn't easier; it's just exchanging love for love.

There's always an armful of dog or puppy to lick my tearstained cheek or lay an understand-ing muzzle on my knee. Each time I come home, they greet me with squeals and wiggles of delight as if I'd been gone for days instead of hours. When they dig me out from under my warm blankets every morning, they remind me to start the day with zest and vigor and a prayer of thanks for having them around. They snuggle up against my easy chair, wrapping their soft bodies against my stockinged feet, and cuddle when I'm lonely and need something to hang on to.

How, when my daughter calls from miles away, and I ache to reach out and smooth her hair again and hug her close, how can I resist the loving friend who plunks down next to me, mouth wrapped around a bright red raquetball, his brown eyes pleading, looking like a skewered pig? That's therapy, and the very best kind.

That same friend and his partners lie quietly in patient wait while I whip up a batch of fudge to send to a starving son. As my tears drip into the chocolate sauce, they keep their silent vigil, waiting to tell me that they care. More therapy, and you can't get it anyplace but home.

When friends raise eyebrows at my dog tribe, and remind me how peaceful life would be with only one or two or none at all, I just smile my secret dog smile....they'll never understand.

My empty nest is full again, feathered this time around with dog hair. Only "dog people" understand. And best of all, so do my children.

(REPRINTED FROM *AMERICAN KENNEL GAZETTE*.)

The author has been "in" Goldens since 1967, when she got her first Golden. Two years following, in 1969, Nona saw Jolly Again of Ouillmette racing back to his owner with a duck, wings and feathers flying (and the dog was as "jolly" as a clam) and the author became hooked on the field Golden Retriever.

Fortunate to meet many key people in the breed, the author has capitalized on their knowledge and generosity and since has trained her many Goldens for field and obedience, and now hunting tests. The Chances R Goldens are first and foremost companion dogs, then they are hunters...and then they are community service dogs. Several of her dogs are certified therapy dogs, visiting local nursing homes between training and trials.

Over the past 25 years, Nona has bred about a dozen litters. Her program is most select and her selection of owners even more so. She has kept in touch with every puppy through its lifetime (by sending whelpday and Christmas cards). She has owned or bred many obedience Goldens titled through Utility, also many with WC/WCX degrees and several Senior and Master Hunters and Qualified All-Age Goldens.

Nona belongs to the GR Club of Greater St. Louis, the GRCA, the Mississippi Valley Retriever Club, the Delta Society, and the American Dog Owners Association. She writes for the *Golden Retriever News* and is a member of the National Federation of Press Women, Missouri Press Women and the Dog Writers' Association of America, from whom she has won several awards for her newspaper features as well as the DWAA 1992 Public Service Award. Nona also writes for the *American Kennel Gazette*, *Dog Fancy*, *Retriever International* and a dozen other dog publications. Nona has written for other non-doggie publications, focusing on animal welfare and responsible dog ownership. This is her first book, hopefully the first of many to follow!

(ANDREW DE PRISCO, *EDITOR*)

The Farm Fresh Girls plus one. **Farm Fresh Jersey Blue, Farm Fresh Grade A Apple, Bridgton's I'm On CD, Am-Can. Ch. Farm Fresh Apple Pie Ala Mode CDX, MH, WCX, VCX, Farm Fresh Hasty Pudding WCX** and **Farm Fresh Blubery O Bridgton CD.** Owner, Leslie P. Dickerson of Riegelsville Pennsylvania.

Introduction

When my editor approached me with the prospect of a new book on the Golden Retriever, the writer in me echoed the poet Horace's famous *Carpe diem!* What a challenge...what a responsibility ..."Seize the day!"

Had my dog self been my alpha person at that moment, I might have had second thoughts. So much had already been written about the Golden Retriever, its history chronicled more than once, by respected authorities on the breed. Perhaps a half-dozen fine books over the last few decades have recognized the accomplishments and off-

The most accomplished Golden in breed history: **Am-Can. Ch. Heron Acres Sand Castle Am-Can. UDTX, MH, WCX, VCX, UKC HRCH, UD, NAHRA, MHR,***** owned by Betty Dorbac. Photo by Marsha Hunt.

spring of the twentieth-century Golden. One could hardly say it better or offer some new insight or perspective.

However, after minimal research, it soon became apparent that the activities and achievements of this exceptional breed have exploded during the past ten years. Goldens have always had their paws in everything, only now there were more of them doing more than ever before. Thus, the 1990 Golden, the working Golden Retriever who evolved during the decade of the '80s, has become the principal focus of this book.

The past ten years have been the busiest ever for the breed. The growth of the Golden Retriever population during that period was the largest in breed history. By 1990, some 929,081 Goldens had been registered with the American Kennel Club, up from 354,349 registered through 1980, more than double the total population in just ten years. With over 64,000 registered in 1990, they retained their number four position in AKC breed registrations for the fourth year in a row.

Breed activities and accomplishments rose accordingly. Goldens broke their own previous records in the obedience ring, and in 1990 alone they earned 1,369 CD, CDX and UD titles, with 30 Goldens completing their Obedience Trial Championships, more than any other breed. That same year 226 Goldens became Show Champions, an increase of 11.8 percent over the previous year. Of the hundreds of Goldens who competed in field trials from 1980 through 1990, 40 have become Field Champions and Amateur Field Champions and approximately 269 Goldens earned qualified All-Age status. Many more have trained for and qualified at the AKC-licensed hunting tests, with approximately 848 Goldens earning Junior, Senior and Master Hunter titles since the first official test in 1985. More than 890 passed in licensed tracking tests, and about 4,354 earned Working Certificates and Working Certificates Excellent for proving their basic and inherent ability in the field.

Unfortunately that unique combination of talent and trainability that makes such diversification possible also makes the Golden the ideal candidate for dissent and separation within the ranks of breeders and exhibitors. This breed schism isn't new. These same concerns existed 40 years ago; today they're simply more intensified. Particularly during the past two decades, the breed has continued to split and develop into

FC-AFC Mioak's Main Event (AFC Wildfire of Riverview CDX, WCX ex Mioak's Ginger) trained with professional trainer Bill Eckett, who considers Rocky one of the most biddable and talented retrievers he has trained. At home with Cathy Morse of Fullerton, California, he goes duck, goose and pheasant hunting, and hikes, swims, and combs the beach with her four boys.

specific lines bred to excel in conformation, field trials or obedience.

Further, each of these disciplines has become so specialized that many breeders, exhibitors and trainers have lost sight of the "complete and correct" Golden in pursuing the Golden champion of their dreams. Today's competitors frequently breed and promote the type of dog best suited to their particular interest: conformation dogs with heavy bone and still heavier coats who are mentally and structurally unable to spend even a few hours in the field; field dogs bred solely for function who look like poor or distant relatives of the traditional Golden; obedience dogs

with so much go-go-go that they border on the hyperactive, Goldens in every area bred without regard for true Golden temperament or purpose. And the superior talent that has evolved in each discipline has only expanded the market for more specialized Goldens.

According to the breed standard, which is based on the original working dog of years ago, the ideal Golden should be able to win in the show ring after spending the day hunting upland game or waterfowl. The last field champion Golden who proved that possible was Dual Ch.-AFC Tigathoe Funky Farquar, who finished his bench championship in 1979 at eight years of age.

21

The last Golden Retriever to earn his Dual Champion title: **Dual Ch. -AFC Tigathoe Funky Farquar**, at age two, with Dotty Mikeska.

It's not likely the breed will see another dual champion for many years to come. In today's competitive marketplace and sports arena, few hopefuls and competitors have the luxury of enough time or money to pursue more than one goal with their dog....... which may also explain the disappearance of the Dual Champion Golden Retriever. An oversimplification perhaps...but the missing link today may be the dual-purpose Golden Retriever owner.

But despite the overwhelming problems within our ranks, there are still hundreds, in fact thousands, of Goldens who do indeed still do it all: show champion Goldens who still hunt before or after a day of competition; bench-pointed Goldens with obedience and tracking degrees, hunting titles and field trial placements; field trial dogs who hold titles in obedience, hunting tests, and other areas; multiple-titled Goldens whose high-in-trial talent or intensity in the field is handicapped only by their owners' pocketbooks or schedules.

This book recognizes and honors those many dual-purpose dogs. I feel privileged to have been invited into their lives, to share the pride and energy and love that spurred these Goldens and their people to new challenges and goals.

Through it all I was constantly reminded of what Samuel Magoffin, founder and first president of the Golden Retriever Club of America, wrote in 1939 in the September issue of the AKC *GAZETTE*.

"...do not be discouraged if all litters do not turn out to be field trial winners or best in show dogs. What we have in the Golden Retriever is a grand hunting companion for both upland game and waterfowl during the hunting season, and the best companion imaginable for the balance of the year."

So I write "The End" with a mixture of sadness and relief, grateful to be once again in charge of my life, to spend REAL leisure time with my Goldens, to train them without feeling guilty about the manuscript on my desk.

But I will miss the contact with the many people who made this book possible, the hundreds who wrote notes and letters about their special dogs, who trusted me with many irreplaceable pictures of their beloved friends. They wrote this book, and enriched my life. My thanks to all of you for sharing.

I'm especially grateful to the many friends who proofread and edited and offered support and encouragement when I most needed it, and to the experts and authorities who contributed their time and wisdom to the pages of this text...they are too numerous to name. And a special thanks to my eight guest authors and contributors. For my own sake, I list them in alphabetical order, and only wish I had more space to acknowledge all their many contributions to the dog world.

BONITA M. BERGIN, Cotati, California, founder and director of Canine Companions for Independence. Her faith in the spirit of man and the natural ability of the dog has enabled hundreds of Canine Companions to bring dignity and independence to their disabled masters.

W. JEAN DODDS, D.V.M., Albany, New York, named Gaines "Woman of the Year" in 1990 for her years of research on blood diseases in dogs, work which has won her worldwide acclaim. A breeder, teacher, and advocate of rational animal care, she also finds time to write and lecture for dog clubs.

BETTY GAY of Gayhaven Kennels, Rockwood, Michigan, a 40-year breeder of dozens of Golden champions and a 12-year conformation judge. As an officer in GRCA and co-chairman of the Breed Standard committee, Betty has long been the champion of a structurally sound and stable Golden Retriever.

BARBRA GOODMAN, Chicago, Illinois, leading authority on dog obedience, founder of the Illini Obedience Association and mentor of the Gaines Regionals and Classic, winner of the 1988 Gaines "FIDO" (Latin for faithful) award for outstanding contribution to the obedience community, trainer, author, judge and good friend. The sport of obedience is richer for her 30 years of involvement.

CAROLE KVAMME, Alderwood Manor, Washington, Chairman of the GRCA archives and gentle tender of the GRCA historical memorabilia, past GRCA Western Regional vice-president. She searched, sorted, copied, cataloged, mailed and called. The Best of Breed series in this book is a tribute to her devotion to her beloved Goldens.

LUCILLE SAWTELL, Somerset, England, 50-year breeder of the dual-purpose Yeo Golden Retrievers in England and author of *All About the Golden Retriever*, Pelham Books, London, now in the fourth printing of its third edition. In 1977 she was chosen to judge the Golden Retriever class at Crufts.

MARCIA SCHLER, Clinton, Michigan, artist, author of *A Study of the Golden Retriever*, and long-time breeder of Kyrie Golden Retrievers. Co-chairman of the GRCA Breed Standard committee, Marcia is committed to "a Golden that is genetically and physically sound . . . and with truly Golden personality."

CHRIS WALKOWICZ, Sherrard, Illinois, author, breeder and journalist ...co-author of *The Atlas of Dog Breeds of the World* and *Successful Dog Breeding*, both with Bonnie Wilcox, DVM.

This book makes no attempt to offer volumes of statistical information or training techniques that can better be obtained elsewhere. Even minimal training for reasonable household be-

Rohan's Murphmeister, bred by Sherry and Brent Blankenship and owned by Al and Judie Freeland, shows his loving Golden temperament as he baby-sits with his new baby sister. . .

havior would require more detailed instruction than could be presented in a single chapter of a breed book. Excellent training books and manuals abound, and persons interested in any facet of training a Golden should study more than one book on that particular discipline. Clubs and training classes and seminars offer yet another source to plumb for help in working with your dog.

Nor does this book include a list of prominent Golden kennels and breeders. That would fill another book. Location of Golden breeders in any particular area may be obtained from the Golden Retriever Club of America through information included in this book's chapter on GRCA activities.

All the information in this book is true to the best of my knowledge. No dog or its achievements has been deliberately omitted or misrepresented. If there is any fault at all, it lies in the reality of a breed so populous and active that it would take many volumes to credit each and every Golden deserving of an "Atta Boy." There are countless thousands out there quietly achieving in big and small ways in every sport. Each is a credit to the breed. My hat's off to all of them.

A select bibliography delineated chapter by chapter can be located at the end of this book. My own recommended Golden books and those books regarded highly by each of my guest authors are provided to help further every reader's Golden education.

An animal of action. This is Dynamite, officially **Can. Ch. Sunfire's Kinetic Dynamite UD, JH, WCX, Can. UD, WCI.**

Elegant and smart, and never vain, this is **Kona Gold** owned by Jim Taylor. This beautiful portrait was photographed by Karen Taylor of Taylor, Michigan.

A peek at early breed history. *Top:* A historical photograph of the keepers and dogs at Guisachan. *Left:* **"Nous"** and his keeper. *Right:* Golden Retriever bred in 1871 at Guisachan. *Bottom:* Kennel belonging to Col. le Poer Trench, 1901.

Belvedere's Union Jack and **Tex** hunting widgeon near Beaver Lodge, Alberta, Canada, in October 1989. Jack at age 21 months.

Four Goldens immortalized from 1930s' England: **Silence of Tone, Noranby Black-eyed Susan, Ch. Noranby Diana,** and **Noranby Jane.**

The Golden Comes of Age

The world of Golden Retrievers is made up of two kinds of people, those who own Golden Retrievers and people who know someone who does. Outranked by only three other breeds in AKC annual registrations, Goldens in 1990 wiggled their way into over 65,000 new homes. Over 130,000 is probably more accurate, since AKC estimates from litter registration figures that less than half the Goldens born are ever registered. That's a healthy climb in popularity for the youngest of this country's six recognized retriever breeds.

1886: "Sam", the property of Walter, Earl of Kalkeith. Bred by the Earl of Ilchester.

1986: "Buddy," KC's High Times Roll 'n Gold CD, MH, WCX,*** (OS). Bred by Kaye Fuller, DVM.

The Golden is also the infant of retriever breeds in England, dating back to 1868. Despite 40 years of publicity on the origin of the breed, many people still refer to the persistent myth that Goldens descended from a troupe of Russian tracking dogs that traveled with a circus in Brighton England in the mid-nineteenth century. A brief review then, for those interested in or still unaware of Golden Retriever history.

The Golden's true ancestry surfaced in 1952 when *Country Life* magazine published the research of the sixth Earl of Ilchester on the original kennel records kept by his great uncle, Lord Tweed–mouth (the former Sir Dudley Marjorie–banks) at his Gúisachan (Gaelic for place of firs) estate in Inverness, Scotland.

According to those records, Tweedmouth in 1865 acquired a yellow retriever pup named Nous (Greek for wisdom) who was allegedly the only "sport" in a litter of blacks, assumed to be ancestors of today's Flat-Coated Retriever. Two years later Tweed-mouth's cousin gave him a curly-coated, liver-colored Tweed Water Spaniel named Belle. (Liver meaning any shade from sandy or fawn to brown.) Tweed Water Spaniels were hardy, rugged dogs known along the Tweed River and British seacoast for their courage, intelligence and strong retrieving ability.

An avid sportsman and hunter, Tweedmouth held a keen interest for developing a dog capable of retrieving game from the rugged fields and waters of the English coast and delivering those birds to hand. Also an ardent dog breeder, he had a passion for producing a strain of all-yellow retrievers that would do the job.

No surprise then, when in 1868, he bred Belle to Nous. The genes fell into all the right places, and the two produced four yellow pups which he named Ada, Crocus, Primrose and Cowslip. Over the next 20 years, Tweedmouth consistently and methodically linebred on those first four pups,

Harold's boys *(left to right)* **AFC Son of Red** ("Sonny"), **FC-AFC Topbrass Bandit,** and **FC-AFC Sangamo Red**. Harold Bruninga, field trainer from Springfield, Illinois.

Ada, born *1871:* The property of the Earl of Ilchester. She was the daughter of Lord Tweedmouth's original dog.

St. Hubert's Peter, bred by the late Col. the Hon. W. le Poer Trench. This Russian retriever or tracker was afterwards presented to H.M. the late King George V.

Col. D. Carnegie's **Glory of Fyning.**

Noranby Daybreak, dam of Ch. Noranby Daydawn; by Ch. Noranby Campfire ex Noranby Dandelion.

Culham Copper (by Culham Brass), sire of Ch. Noranby Campfire. The property of the late Lord Harcourt.

outcrossed at times, then bred back to that original mating. Occasionally he gave puppies to good friends, who started their own lines of dogs. By the end of the nineteenth century, the Yellow Retriever had become popular in England.

Eventually travelers and hunters took some of those dogs with them on visits to America, and during the 1890s Golden Retrievers were seen in the United States and Canada. Goldens from Great Britain and Canada, the majority of them hunting dogs, were brought to both the East and West coasts in the 1920s and 1930s, with the first AKC registration of a Golden Retriever recorded in November 1925.

Thus from those first four yellow fuzzballs has emerged the twentieth-century Golden, every bit the dog Tweedmouth desired and more, a dog beyond even his imagination.

The Golden Retriever who has evolved over the past one hundred-plus years might easily be called the dog for all seasons. The most versatile of all the retriever breeds, today's Golden offers something for every dog fancier. Still the hunting

Splashdown Emberain Aubrey UD, MH, *(OD),** owned by Edwina Ryska. The first Golden UD!

partner Tweedmouth so carefully developed, he will flush and fetch upland game as well as plunge into icy waters after duck or goose. His nose will follow fur or feather, and in Europe he may track rabbit one day and quail the next.

The modern Golden Retriever contributes more to society than just a pretty face. Used by law enforcement agencies and U.S. disaster teams, that famous "Golden nose" will sniff out hidden drugs or alcohol, or locate people buried beneath snow or earthquake debris.

As charming and persuasive therapy dogs, Goldens have flocked to hospitals and nursing homes to offer a wet nose and wagging tail to the sick and the elderly. Devoted guide dogs for the

Noranby Sandy, by Sandy of Wavertree ex Yellow Nell (bred by William Hall). Grandsire of F. T. Ch. John of Auchencheyne and great-grandsire of Noranby Black-eyed Susan.

OB. Ch., Ch. Leacroft Golden Isla CDX (N.Z. -Aus. Ch. Leacroft Logan ex Moorfield Emma) owned by Pat Greig, Speyside Golden Retrievers, Wellington, N.Z., shows her good form at eight-and-one-half years of age.

blind and hearing impaired, skilled assistance dogs for the physically disabled and the handicapped, loving partners and helpmates in the home . . . Goldens have nosed their way into every facet of the human-animal connection. An overachiever in the obedience ring and a favorite showman in the breed ring, he's still content to plop down and snooze at your feet after a blue ribbon or a high-in-trial. Not bad for a retriever recognized by the AKC a scant 65 years ago.

As guard dog, however, the Golden is a flop, although his bark and size might deter a home intruder. But don't bet on it if the perpetrator is familiar with a typical Golden's "love 'em all" attitude. If you want a bark-protector, praise him when he barks, but don't expect more. Still, tales

abound about the Golden who sensed danger to its human family and took action or stood fast.

On the down side, the very reasons that make the Golden easy to own and love have also become the breed's undoing. In 1987 they soared to number four in breed popularity with over 62,000 registered with AKC, a dubious distinction that serves little to enhance the quality of the breed. Increased popularity within any breed has always caused a like increase in problems.. ...in health, temperament, soundness, and ultimately, heartbreak.

Because of the Golden's high-profile status and marketable characteristics . . . the soft look and loving nature, its never-ending willingness to please . . . puppies-for-profit breeders today

From the turn of the century in England is **Ch. Noranby Campfire**, by Culham Brass ex Noranby Beauty, at age one year.

Honorary Dual **Ch. -AFC Honor's Darado of Spindrift,** bred by Ann Chase and owned by John Sprufe. One of the breed's last dual champions, "Hondo" earned his bench championship in April 1972, and finished his AFC in April 1976.

Noranby Tweedledum, bred by N. Hall, a reversion to original Guisachan type except in size. Tweedledum was a well-known trial dog before 1914.

that of family pet and companion. Despite the broad visibility of the breed's accomplishments, the plain fact is about 95 percent of all Goldens do nothing more than live with and love their humans, thus making a significant contribution to their owners' lives. The majority of these dog-loving people will be moved to propagate the wonderful qualities of their beloved pets.

But just loving your dog like crazy is not enough to produce quality or even decent Golden Retrievers. Without a thorough understanding of the breed or knowledge of the genetics behind the dog, without the expertise to raise a litter of pups in a humane and intelligent fashion, or the experience and patience to educate the future owners of those pups, this well-meaning majority will only propagate the problems of their Goldens' ancestors; poor temperaments and aggressive personalities, health disorders, untypical appearance and structural faults. Eventually our lovely Goldens won't be Golden any longer.

are producing Goldens who no longer personify the gentle, amiable and talented Golden Retriever. Hip dysplasia, heart problems, epilepsy, eye problems, aggressive behavior, elbow and bleeding disorders are all problems which have become too common within the breed due to indiscriminate breeding practices of both the novice and the experienced breeder.

The major role of today's Golden Retriever is

The twenty-first century will be a critical time in determining the future of the Golden Retriever. No doubt it will continue to climb in popularity. Hopefully the efforts of responsible owners and breeders who care about the welfare of the breed will help maintain the great temperament and versatility that make the Golden Retriever the ideal dog for all seasons.

Oil painting reproduction of **FC-AFC Casey Two of Fox Creek MH (HOF)** and mother **Rocky-Vue of Fox Creek*****. Courtesy of Sibby Woods.

In England around 1930, Mrs. Charlesworth with **Noranby Sandy** and **Noranby Balfour**. Sandy was the first breed member to run in field trials in England. She earned a number of certificates of merit. Balfour was the sire of Rory of Bentley and grandsire of Ch. Michael of Morton.

This painting by Nina S. Langley (1934) graced the famous *Hutchinson's Encyclopaedia*.

Understanding the AKC Standard

BY MARCIA SCHLER

Ch. Asterling Wild Blue Yonder (OS, HOF), owner-handled by Mary Burke. "James," as he has been nicknamed, is a spectacular Best in Show Golden of impeccable grace and beauty.

THE AKC STANDARD FOR THE GOLDEN RETRIEVER

The American Kennel Club approved the following revised Standard for Golden Retrievers as submitted by the Golden Retriever Club of America, Inc., effective Jan. 1, 1982:

General Appearance

A symmetrical, powerful, active dog, sound and well put together, not clumsy nor long in the leg, displaying a kindly expression and possessing a personality that is eager, alert and self-confident. Primarily a hunting dog, he should be shown in hard working condition. Overall appearance, balance, gait and purpose to be given more emphasis than any of his component parts.

Faults: Any departure from the described ideal shall be considered faulty to the degree to which it interferes with the breed's purpose or is contrary to breed character.

Size, Proportion, Substance

Males 23–24 inches in height at withers; females 21½–22½ inches. Dogs up to one inch above or below standard size should be proportionately penalized. Deviation in height of more than one inch from the standard shall disqualify.

Length from breastbone to point of buttocks slightly greater than height at withers in ratio of 12:11. Weight for dogs 65–75 pounds; bitches 55–65 pounds.

Head

Broad in skull, slightly arched laterally and longitudinally without

Am-Can. Ch. Lothlorien Edgecombe Gildor (Am-Can. Ch. Birnam Woods Mountin' Ash ex Edgecombe's Winter Wheat), bred by Janet Provenzano, owned and handled by Barbara Kersten, Holbrook, New York.

prominence of frontal bones (forehead) or occipital bones. Stop well defined but not abrupt. Foreface deep and wide, nearly as long as skull. Muzzle straight in profile, blending smoothly and strongly into skull; when viewed in profile or from above, slightly deeper and wider at stop than at tip. No heaviness in flews. Removal of whiskers is permitted but not preferred.

Eyes friendly and intelligent in expression, medium large with dark, close fitting rims, set well apart and reasonably deep in sockets. Color preferably dark brown; medium brown acceptable. Slant eyes and narrow, triangular eyes detract from correct expression and are to be faulted. No white or haw visible when looking straight ahead. Dogs showing evidence of functional abnormality of eyelids or eyelashes (such as, but not limited to, trichiasis, entropion, ectropion, or distichiasis) are to be excused from the ring.

Ears rather short with front edge attached well behind and just above the eye and falling close to cheek. When pulled forward, tip of ear should just cover the eye. Low, hound-like ear set to be faulted.

Nose black or brownish black, though fading to a lighter shade in cold weather not serious. Pink nose or one seriously lacking in pigmentation to be faulted.

Teeth scissors bite, in which the outer side of the lower incisors touches the inner side of the upper incisors. Undershot or overshot bite is a disqualification. Misalignment of teeth (irregular placement of incisors) or a level bite (incisors meet each other edge to edge) is undesirable, but not to be confused with undershot or overshot. Full dentition. Obvious gaps are serious faults.

"Primarily a hunting dog" . . . the breed's last Dual Champion. This is the very talented and beautiful **Dual Ch. -AFC Tigathoe Funky Farquar.**

Neck, Topline, Body

Neck medium long, merging gradually into well laid back shoulders, giving sturdy, muscular appearance. No throatiness.

Back line strong and level from withers to slightly sloping croup, whether standing or moving. Sloping back line, roach or sway back, flat or steep croup to be faulted.

Body well balanced, short coupled, deep through the chest. Chest between forelegs at least as wide as a man's closed hand including thumb, with well developed forechest. Brisket extends to elbow. Ribs long and well sprung but not barrel shaped, extending well towards hindquarters. Loin short, muscular, wide and deep, with very little tuck-up. Slabsidedness, narrow chest, lack of depth in brisket, excessive tuck-up to be faulted.

Tail well set on, thick and muscular at the base, following the natural line of the croup. Tail bones extend to, but not below, the point of hock. Carried with merry action, level or with some moderate upward curve; never curled over back nor between legs.

Forequarters

Muscular, well coordinated with hindquarters and capable of free movement. Shoulder blades long and well laid back with upper tips fairly close together at withers. Upper arms appear about the same length as the blades, setting the elbows back beneath the upper tip of the blades, close to the ribs without looseness. Legs, viewed from the front, straight with good bone, but not to the point of coarseness. Pasterns short and strong, sloping slightly with no suggestion of weakness. Dewclaws on forelegs may be removed, but are normally left on.

Feet medium size, round, compact, and well knuckled, with thick pads. Excess hair may be trimmed to show natural size and contour. Splayed or hare feet to be faulted.

Hindquarters

Broad and strongly muscled. Profile of croup slopes slightly; the pelvic bone slopes at a slightly greater angle (approximately 30 degrees from horizontal). In a natural stance, the femur joins the pelvis at approximately a 90 degree angle; stifles well bent; hocks well let down with short, strong rear pasterns. Feet as in front. Legs straight when viewed from rear. Cow hocks, spread hocks, and sickle hocks to be faulted.

Coat

Dense and water-repellent with good undercoat. Outer coat firm and resilient, neither coarse nor silky, lying close to body; may be straight or wavy. Untrimmed natural ruff; moderate feathering on back of forelegs and on underbody; heavier feathering on front of neck, back of thighs and underside of tail. Coat on head, paws, and front of legs is short and even. Excessive length, open coats, and limp, soft coats are very undesirable. Feet may be trimmed and stray hairs neatened, but the natural appearance of coat or outline should not be altered by cutting or clipping.

Color

Rich, lustrous golden of various shades. Feathering may be lighter than rest of coat. With the exception of graying or whitening of face or body due to age, any white marking, other than a few white hairs on the chest, should be penalized according to its extent. Allowable light shadings are not to be confused with white markings. Predominant body color which is either extremely pale or extremely dark is undesirable. Some latitude should be given to the light puppy whose coloring shows promise of deepening with maturity. Any noticeable area of black or other off-color hair is a serious fault.

Gait

When trotting, gait is free, smooth, powerful and well coordinated, showing good reach. Viewed from any position, legs turn neither in nor out, nor do feet cross or interfere with each other. As speed increases, feet tend to converge toward center line of balance. It is recommended that dogs be shown on a loose lead to reflect true gait.

The ideal gait of the Golden Retriever is smooth and powerful. This dog is retrieving a bird and running uphill at full speed. Although the camera makes him appear uncoordinated, the dog remains in complete control.

from standard either way.

2. Undershot or overshot bite.

Approved October 13, 1981

Temperament

Friendly, reliable, and trustworthy. Quarrelsomeness or hostility towards other dogs or people in normal situations, or an unwarranted show of timidity or nervousness, is not in keeping with Golden Retriever character. Such actions should be penalized according to their significance.

Disqualifications

1. Deviation in height of more than one inch

Am-Can. Ch. Heron Acres Sandcastle Am-Can. UDTX, MH, WCX, VCX,***, UKC HRCH, UD, NAHRA MHR. Owner, Elizabeth Drobac of Okemos, Michigan.

BEST OF WINNERS
MONROE
KENNEL CLUB SHOW

BY MARCIA SCHLER

Topography

1.	occiput	9.	croup	16.	forearm	24.	thigh
2.	frontal bones	10.	tail	17.	knee	25.	hock joint
3.	stop	11.	shoulder	18.	front pastern	26.	point of hock
4.	flews	12.	point of shoulder	19.	ribs	27.	rear pastern
5.	cheek	13.	forechest	20.	tuckup	28.	second thigh
6.	crest of neck	14.	brisket	21.	stifle	29.	feathering
7.	withers	15.	upper arm	22.	flank	30.	ruff
8.	back	15a.	elbow	23.	loin	31.	muzzle

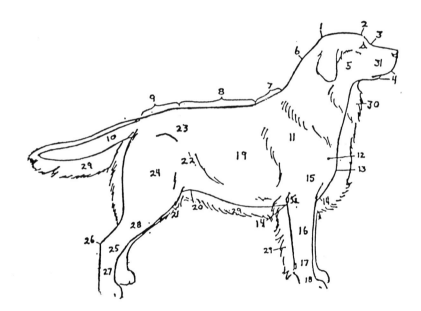

Over-all appearance

The opening paragraph of the breed standard states:

"Over-all appearance, balance, gait, and purpose to be given more emphasis than any of his component parts."

This means that the dog's general unity of structure, his harmony of proportion (balance), the functioning of this structure in movement (gait), and the rightness of all features of the breed's intended uses (purpose) are of greater importance than any factors considered separately—in short, that the dog as a whole is greater than just the sum of its various parts.

The quality called "breed character" is not easily described. It is the sum of everything most typical to the Golden and which makes the Golden distinct from other breeds. It is a most important quality.

The head perhaps more than any other part of the dog expresses the character of the breed. The Golden head in its chiseled, clean-cut appearance reflects the sturdiness, balance, workmanlike qualities, and the intelligent, kindly, responsive mentality typical of the true Golden.

When at rest, the ears fall softly close to the head and neck. At attention, they are drawn up and forward, the inner edge of the flap or leather close to the head. Eye rims, nose, and lips ideally jet black: some will go "smudge" brown in the winter. Eyes from mid-brown to very dark brown,

with tight-fitting lids for protection in the field, moderately deep-set, very expressive.

Body Structure and Rib Cage

A. The rib cage must be capacious to provide maximum volume for heart and lungs, shaped to allow for efficient use of forelegs and proper attachment of muscular systems. The loin area consists of very strong muscles of the spinal "bridge" connecting front and rear, and the abdominal area containing many vital organs.

The rib cage (R) is both deep and long, with prominent forechest, depth at brisket, and depth at the rear part ("rib carried well back"). The loin (L) is comparatively short from rib to hip, deep, wide when seen from top, with heavy musculature. The flank (F) is deep with a slight tuckup and strong muscular abdomen.

B. This dog has adequate depth at the elbow, but compared to A is decidedly lacking in depth at the last ribs giving less internal capacity. He is too "cut up in the flank," with a rather long loin (long-coupled), too much arch, giving a rangy, racy look. This dog is actually the same height and length overall as both A and C.

C. This dog gives an appearance of greater length, due to a foreleg assembly set far forward on a short rib cage (forechest has disappeared); loin is long, lacking strength and firmness. These factors result in a soft backline. The lack of proper muscle tone is also evident in the soft, paunchy abdomen. Such weaknesses in mid-section prevent efficient transmission of power from hindquarters and contribute to fatigue and susceptibility to injury.

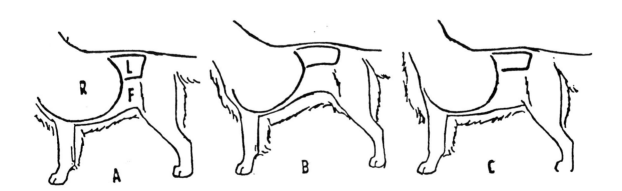

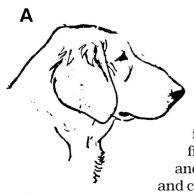

A

HEAD FAULTS

A. Prominent occiput and frontal bones giving bumpy skull. Roman nose—convex line between stop and tip of nose instead of straight profile. Nose too pointed and projecting. Ears large and carried too far forward. Throaty.

B. Inadequate skull for long muzzle. Eyes too open and large, with droopy "houndy" lids, poor expression. Wrinkles. Ears too large, long and curling like a hound's. Missing premolar at "a."

B

C. Too round in skull; cheeky; muzzle snipey and doesn't fit well onto skull. Nose pink. Eyes too small and slanting. Eye rims too light. Overtrimmed "flyaway" ears.

D. Coarse; dish-faced (concave line between stop and tip of nose). Stop too pronounced. Eyes pale in color, giving hard untypical expression. Lower jaw seems to project; this dog is likely to be undershot.

C

D

BITE

A. Scissors bite. Desired as strongest and least wearing. The inner surface of the upper

A

incisors contact the outer surfaces of the lowers. There is a relatively tight meshing of the incisors and canines (eyeteeth). The small premolars do not touch; this is "carrying space."

B. Even, level, or pincers bite. The direct edge-to-edge meeting of the incisors is quite wearing.

B

C. Overshot. The incisors of the upper jaw

C

overlap and fail to contact the incisors of the lower jaw. "Pig jaw." There is often a noticeable space at "a."

D. Undershot. A forward set or extra length of lower jaw causes the incisors of the lower jaw to overlap or project beyond the incisors of the upper jaw when the mouth is closed. Generally

D

there is a more or less considerable space at "b."

In both undershot and overshot jaws, the condition is often noticeable in the incorrect meshing of molars and premolars as well.

E. Misalignment of teeth of lower jaw. Central incisors markedly out of line, forward of the rest of the lower teeth. This in itself does not constitute undershot bite. Undershot or overshot mouths may or may not have misaligned teeth.

E

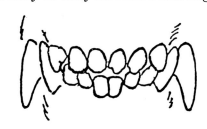

FRONT ASSEMBLY

Note the straight vertical column of bones from the point of the shoulder (a) down to the footpads. The ribs are well sprung from the spine, then drop with moderate curve, allowing easy movement of the leg assembly beside the rib cage. The shoulder blades (scapulae) lie snugly upon the rib cage. They should be long and fairly close together at the withers.

The "bone" of the forelegs should be straight and sturdy, never fine or delicate, nor should it be heavy and coarse like a draft-horse's. Muscling should be well developed throughout, but a bulging, 'loaded' appearance of the shoulder is not desired.

The well-developed chest affords heart and lung capacity for endurance, and buoyancy and stability when swimming. Deepest part of the chest reaches to the level of the elbows; the sternum comes well forward in front to help form a full forechest, thus providing for even more volume within the rib cage and also anchorage for various muscles of neck and forequarters.

Due to the Golden's dense coat and featherings, all visual examination should be verified when possible by the hand.

A. Front too wide, feet turned in. Such a dog will move clumsily. Often a too-round rib cage (barrel-bodied) will result in such a front, or it may be due to an actual bowing of the forelegs.

B. "French front" or "fiddle front." Loose shoulders and turned out feet may be caused by inherently weak or poor structure,

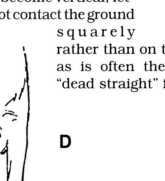

or broken down by activity such as excessive jumping before full growth.

C. Far too narrow, lacking in both depth and width of chest. Due to the lack of chest the elbows are held too close ("tied in") turning the feet outward and resulting in an "east and west" front quite different from B's.

D. A good front. There is a very slight sideways sloping of the pasterns. When the feet converge in gaiting, the pasterns will become vertical, letting the foot contact the ground squarely rather than on the outer edge as is often the case with a "dead straight" front.

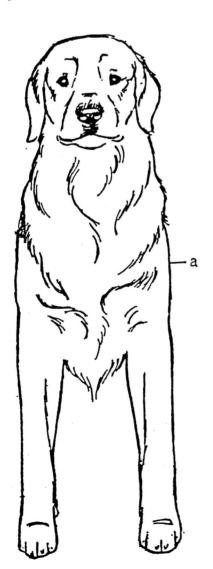

FOREQUARTERS

A. Good fore- quarter assembly. The layback of shoulder blade and its angle with the humerus (up- per arm) allows for greatest length of reach in move- ment, best muscu- lar development of shoulder assembly and, with slightly sloping pastern, greatest shock ab- sorbency. With the point of support (foot pads) directly beneath the shoulder blades, this front is well balanced, ready for action, but at ease. Note the strong neck running well back and strongly united with the back and shoulders.

B. Poorly angulated forequarter, with short upright scapulae lim- iting stride; their for- ward position forces the blades far apart at the withers and weak- ens what should be a strong, smooth merg- ing of neck into shoul- ders and back.

C. "Terrier front." The blade is of fair length and well laid back, but the upper arm is much too vertical and pastern is too upright and rigid. Such a dog may lift the forefeet quite high in order get suffi- cient stride, but it is wasted motion. Many setters have this type of front, with ex- aggerated front action.

A

B

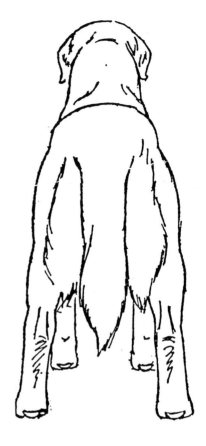

HINDQUARTERS

In the rear as in the front, note the straight line of bones from hip joint to foot pad, allowing most efficient transmission of power in movement. Because the rear limbs supply the drive and "push," they are particularly important. Except in swimming, when they provide a major motive force, the forelimbs serve primarily for support and absorption of impact. A dog may be able to make some compensation for inefficient fore- quarter structure, but if the rear is bad, the dog simply "hasn't got it," and no excellence in front can supply that thrust and power.

A wide pelvis provides for better development and attachment of musculature. The rear can scarcely be over-muscled; it should never seem weak or too small for the front assembly.

The tail reaches to the hock joint in bone. It is the dog's "rudder" and balancing device, as well as indicator of emotion, and should be quite heavily muscled, particularly at the base. A somewhat short, thick tail is preferable to a whip-like or long one. It should hang straight or slightly curved when at rest, and be very densely coated overall, with a thick, rather rounded appearance, not a setter-like thin flag.

C

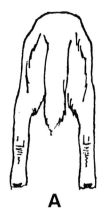

A. This rear is undesirable because of the lack of muscle development, which may be only a result of poor condition, or may not. If so, it is probably to be preferred over the others shown here. The tail is too short.

B. Out at the stifles. The straight line from hip to foot is lost. This is not quite the same as cowhocks since the rear pasterns are parallel, even though the toes turn out.

C. Cowhocks. A common expression of weakness of the rear assembly, either inherited or environmental. Such a dog cannot move well. Some cowhocked dogs may be better

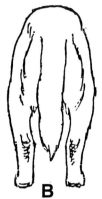

in stifle than this, but convergence of the hock and splay of the rear pasterns is a severe fault. Poor tail.

D. Bowed rear. The opposite of cowhocks, but no less a fault even if less common. The tail is ringed (faulty), lessening its usefulness.

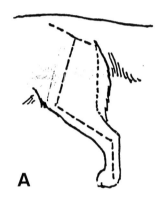

REAR QUARTERS

A. Desirable rear. Proper angulation throughout allows for greatest length of thigh and second thigh and long strong muscles for optimum reach and power with endurance.

B. Overangulated rear. It is impossible to get musculature to support such extreme angulation in a breed the weight of a retriever. The angled-under rear pasterns ("sickle hocks") do not straighten when moving and any advantage supposedly gained by the extreme angle is lost.

C. Too straight rear, lacking proper angulation. Although the leg appears longer than "A," the bones are shorter. Short second thigh and lack of angulation at stifle and hock limit stride and leverage. This dog may show great height in action, but little length of stride.

FRONT MOVEMENT

A. Proper front, moving. The straight column of bones from foot to point of shoulder provides most efficient transmission of power. The feet converge in order to stay under the centerline of gravity, but never interfere with each other. The faster the trot, the more the feet will converge. A dog is single-tracking when the feet are set down directly ahead of one another on the line of travel. This is NOT a fault—unless the legs interfere with each other. Because of the well-developed chest, a retriever should not be expected to move as smoothly in front as some other breeds; but he must move easily and efficiently. (Single-tracking as a result of some structural fault is of course undesirable.)

A

B

B. Too wide. Dog will tend to "roll" as weight shifts slightly from side to side trying to stay over the point of support.

C. Bowed front. Feet turn inwards. Dog will probably tire easily and be subject to injury due to unnatural stress upon the leg.

C

D. Too narrow. This dog may move very smoothly and look quite good from the side, because he has no chest to limit his front action. This lack of chest is highly undesirable.

E. Paddling or winging. Feet thrown sideways as they are brought forward, denoting some weakness in shoulder-elbow assembly.

E

D

REAR MOVEMENT

A. Desirable rear, moving at the trot. As the feet converge with increased speed, the straight line from hip to foot is maintained. Convergence allows the dog more easily to keep his center of gravity over the point of support.

B. Bowed rear. This subjects the leg and foot to undue stress. Note weight on outer side of foot.

A

B

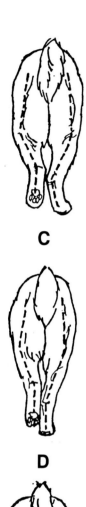

C

D

E

C. Cowhocks. May be due to faulty bone structure or to muscular weakness. The dog tracks widely yet his hocks interfere. Some dogs will show hocks that twist inward only as they take on the weight of the body.

D. Moving too closely. Tracking closely with the rear pasterns parallel makes the dog more likely to interfere.

E. Crossing over. Again, this renders the dog much too likely to interfere, especially on an irregular surface. The dog often lacks proper timing and moves clumsily.

GAIT

Here is a good moving dog, plenty of reach and a powerful drive of hindquarters. His gait looks effortless and graceful. A minimum of exertion is needed to gain fullest advantage of his most efficient structure. Level backline indicates good transmission of thrust from the rear through the back to the fore part of the body without unnecessary sway or bobbing.

Note the great length of stride made possible by the long-boned, properly angulated limbs, and the "opening up" of the shoulder and stifle assemblies. At full speed of the trot, the best moving dogs will actually have an instant's suspension when none of the feet are contacting the ground. The forefoot has left the ground in time for the rear foot of the same side to land on the same line or track without striking the forefoot. Without this timing, the dog would have three alternatives in order to avoid hitting his forefeet: move the rear feet to the side (sidetracking or crabbing); move wide behind, or else shorten his stride considerably.

GAIT FAULTS

A. The choppy mover. His limited stride may look very busy and active, but he needs too many

A

steps to cover ground. His action is stilted and mincing; he cannot "open up" and move smoothly.

B. Hackney action. Short neck and upright shoul-

B

ders, mismatched with a stronger rear, can result in an attempt to gain reach. A tight lead which raises the dog's head can have a similar effect. Tail carriage is faulty as well.

C. Pacing. The pace is often used by tired or out-of-condition dogs. It is an easy gait that

C

requires minimum exertion. In the pace, right fore and rear and left fore and rear move in pairs. Thus, there is less chance of interference between front and rear feet due to poor timing or short middlepiece. This dog also shows a roached back, perhaps indicating fatigue or tension.

FEET

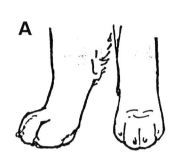

A

A. Desirable fore-foot. Deep thick pads for sturdiness, nails short and strong, toes well arched and held compactly together for endurance and strength. The slightly sloped pastern allows for "spring" and shock-absorbance. Medium size. Tiny feet indicate unwanted fineness and less support area; over-size feet may be so because they are splayed, or due to coarse and clumsy bone.

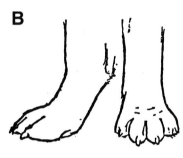

B

B. Open, splayed foot, thin pads, weak pastern. Such a foot "gives" too much with impact and is much more susceptible to injury than a tight foot.

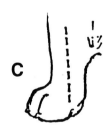

C

C. Terrier foot. Ultra-tight with vertical pastern, has no "give" to it and does not absorb shock, but transmits it to the higher parts of the leg.

D. The terrier foot which has knuckled over in the pastern. This is definitely not a strong or enduring foot, since each

D

impact will tend to force the knee farther over; it is extremely difficult to maintain stability.

COAT

The Golden's coat provides protection from cold, wetness, and heavy cover. A very thick, soft wooly undercoat from one-half inch to one and one-half inches in length underlies a longer topcoat of hair which lies close to the body to form a weatherproof jacket. Outer coat has good body, being neither softly silky as a setter's, nor stiff and hard as a short-coated dog like the pointer. The proper coat will be oily enough and flat-lying to enable rain to run off easily, firm enough to resist tangles and burrs. Texture, density and oiliness of undercoat prevent wetness from penetrating to the skin. Undue length of coat which would interfere with the Golden's function as a field and water dog is not desired.

Straggling hair on paws may be trimmed to show natural contour of feet. Other than this, trimming should be kept to an absolute minimum, retaining a natural appearance.

It is permissible to remove whiskers (vibrissae) from face for show purposes, but such is not preferred. Whiskers are tactile sensors which serve a definite function, especially in a dog working afield.

A. Straight coat, moderate length, clean-cut outline. Sometimes too soft, but when of proper texture and undercoat, this is a very easy-to-care-for coat, requiring a minimum of grooming,

practically self-cleaning, and excellent for field work. It should be very dense, with good body ("firm and resilient") and thick undercoat.

B. Wavy coat is equally as acceptable as the straight coat. Of more importance is that any coat be of proper lie, texture, length, and under-

coat. The topcoat with a definite wave, which lies paralleling the surface of the body to form a clean outline, should not be penalized. Some "break" over the shoulders and hips is a normal pattern. The sort of wavy coat illustrated is usually of good texture, water-resistant, with good undercoat, and easy to care for.

C. Soft, silky, dead-straight coat, and too much of it. Undesirable because it is not water-

resistant, mats too easily, picks up burrs and tangles, and generally lacks proper undercoat. Length of coat on this dog is excessive; it spoils his outline and destroys the balanced, functional appearance a Golden should have. While very "flashy" in the ring, this is *not* a correct retriever coat. Too much like a setter or spaniel coat.

45

The Kennel Club Standard for the Golden Retriever

General Appearance: Symmetrical, balanced, active, powerful, level mover; sound with kindly expression.

Characteristics: Biddable, intelligent and possessing natural working ability.

Temperament: Kindly, friendly and confident.

Head and Skull: Balanced and well-chiselled, skull broad without coarseness; well set on neck, muzzle powerful, wide and deep. Length of foreface approximately equals length from well-defined stop to occiput. Nose preferably black.

Eyes: Dark brown, set well apart, dark rims.

Ears: Moderate size, set on approximate level with eyes.

Mouth: Jaws strong, with a perfect, regular and complete scissor bite, i.e., Upper teeth closely overlapping lower teeth and set square to the jaws.

Neck: Good length, clean and muscular.

Forequarters: Forelegs straight with good bone, shoulders well laid back, long in blade with upper arm of equal length placing legs well under body. Elbows close fitting.

Body: Balanced, short coupled, deep through heart. Ribs deep, well sprung. Level topline.

Hindquarters: Loin and legs strong and muscular, good second thighs, well-bent stifles. Hocks well let down, straight when viewed from rear, neither turning in nor out. Cowhocks highly undesirable.

Feet: Round and cat-like.

Tail: Set on and carried level with back, reaching to hocks, without curl at tip.

Gait/Movement: Powerful with good drive. Straight and true in front and rear. Stride long and free with no sign of hackney action in front.

Coat: Flat or wavy with good feathering, dense water-resisting undercoat.

Colour: Any shade of gold or cream, neither red nor mahogany. A few white hairs on chest only, permissible.

Size: Height at withers: Dogs 56-61 cms (22-24 ins); Bitches 51-56 cms (20-22 ins).

Faults: Any departure from the foregoing points should be considered a fault and the seriousness with which the fault should be regarded should be in exact proportion to its degree.

Note: Male animals should have two apparently normal testicles fully descended into the scrotum.

English Golden Retriever owned by Mrs. Pounds Longhurst. Photograph by Robert Smith.

Coloration of dogs in England often adheres to the "blonde" side. Field dogs may tend to exhibit richer tones of the Golden colors. Although some may fuss over the intensity of coloration, soundness and working ability must be considered foremost. Photo by Robert Smith.

Forty Years of Best of Breed

BY BETTY GAY

1951 Golden Retriever Club of America National Specialty
Left: **BOB Ch. Golden Knoll's Shur Shot.** Owned by Mrs. Russell Peterson.
Right: **BOS Ch. Golden Knoll's Ladybelle.** Owned by Ralph Bates.

Part of the problem in reviewing some of the National Specialty winners are the pictures themselves. I have had the opportunity to see most of these winners "in person," many at the time of their big win, but we all know that not every picture is truly representative of the dog itself.

One kennel (Sprucewood of Wisconsin owned by Bud and Maureen Zwang) was a dominant force in the 1950s. Many champions came from this kennel, and the foundation bitch, Ch. Chee-Chee of Sprucewood, was lovely. She went Best of Breed at my first National in 1953 and remains a positive memory for me. Her children, all sired by Ch. Golden Knoll's King Alphonzo, were sound, well-bodied and usually good moving individuals. Some differences in head characteristics might have been desirable in occasional instances.

The picture of 1963 Specialty Winner, Eng-Am. Ch. Figaro of Yeo makes this very handsome dog appear straight in front.

Compare to the forepage of Section II in the GRCA yearbook to see him at his best.

Although the Cheyenne kennels did a good bit of breeding within its own family, there was not much use of the line by other breeders.

The rather poor picture of 1966 Specialty Winner, Ch. Cheyenne Golden's King John, does, in fact, show a well-structured dog of overall good balance and quality.

During the '60s and '70s there were many winners from the Sun Dance kennels owned by Bill and Shirley Worley in Indiana. A couple of my favorites were Sun Dance's Sayonnara, which went Best of Opposite Sex from the puppy class in 1961, and Ch. Sun Dance's Contessa, which took Best of Opposite Sex in both 1971 and 1973. Neither of Contessa's specialty pictures do her justice, but she was a quality bitch....maybe "biggish" for her day, but certainly attractive in many respects.

As we get into the '70s, the first Best of Breed winner was Connie Gerstner's Ch. Malagold Beckwith Big Buff CD, a darker Golden whose picture makes him appear somewhat straight in angulation. My recollection of him does not bear this out. He was a well-balanced, well-angulated dog, solid and good moving.

Another nice picture is that of Ch. Gold Rush's Great Teddy Bear, the 1978 Best of Breed winner, owned by Diane Smith and Ann Johnson. I remember this to be a huge Specials entry, at least for that time, 75 entries, and while I thought Teddy Bear may have been a bit overdone, his structure and general qualities were very nice.

No one can look back into the '80s without remembering Sylvia Donahey and "Brook," 1983 Best of Breed winner, Ch. Asterling's Tahiti Sweetie. Moving into the era of the "picture dog," Brook was always beautifully presented and had a great deal of personality and charm to go with her physical qualities

One of the Pepperhill winners whose picture I find to be very attractive is of 1984 Best of Breed, Ch. Pepperhill East Point Airily, owned by Daniel Flavin. A lovely neck into level backline and nice balance all around. The trim on her foreassembly makes her appear a bit straight in front.

In 1986 Mrs. Gerstner also handled another Specialty Best of Breed winner, Ch. Toasty's Royal Mercedes, owned by Jerry Oxendale and Pam Monthei. This was really a good moving bitch with good angulation and body development. Some might have criticized her very strong head properties for her sex, but the planes of her head and expression were very nice.

Mrs. Gerstner had the distinction of winning the National again in 1988 (as well as Group First at the AKC Centennial show in 1984) with Ch. Libra Malagold Coriander. Cory's grandfather, Ch. Colacove Commando di Sham, won the Specialty in 1971, and his daughter, Ch. Carlin Happy Holidays, was Best of Opposite Sex to his Best of Breed in 1988. All handsome individuals.

Recent available Specialty pictures from 1989 show two really excellent, workmanlike representatives of the breed. I have seen them on numerous occasions and really appreciate the breed character which they represent. Best of Breed Ch. Alderbrooke's Rush Hill Rebel Am-Can.TD. Owner, M. and T. Struble. Best of Opposite Sex Am-Can. Ch. Beaumaris Timberee Tessa Ann UDT, WC, Can. CD (HOF). Owner, Sandy Fisher.

The Golden Retriever Club of America National Specialty Best of Breed

1940	Beavertail Gay Lady
1941	Ch. Beavertail Butch
1942	Ch. Goldwood Pluto ***
1943	Stilrovin Chiang
1944	Lord Goeffrey
1945	Ch. Highland Chief
1946	Ch. Noranby Balloo of Tara Mar
1947	Ch. Czar of Wildwood
1948	Am-Can. Ch. Des Lacs Lassie CD
1949	Am-Can. Ch. Des Lacs Lassie CD
1950	Ch. Golden Knolls Shur Shot
1951	Ch. Golden Knolls Shur Shot
1952	Am-Can. Ch. Chee-Chee of Sprucewood
1953	Am-Can. Ch. Chee-Chee of Sprucewood
1954	Am-Can. Ch. Golden Knoll's King Alphonzo
1955	Ch. Sprucewood's Chore Boy
1956	Ch. Rusina's Mr. Chips
1957	Am-Can. Ch. Sprucewood's Chinki
1958	Am-Can. Ch. Sprucewood's Chocki
1959	Ch. Sundance's Bronze CD
1960	Ch. Sprucewood's Chore Boy
1961	Ch. Prince Royal of Los Altos
1962	Ch. Cheyenne Golden's King
1963	Eng-Am. Ch. Figaro of Yeo
1964	Am-Can. Ch. Beckwith's Copper Coin
1965	Ch. Sundance's Bronze CD
1966	Ch. Cheyenne Golden's King John
1967	Ch. Lorelei's Fez-Ti Za-Za
1968	Am-Can. Ch. Sun Dance's Vagabond Lover CDX
1969	Beckwith's Malagold Flash
1970	Ch. Malagold Beckwith Big Buff CD
1971	Ch. Colacove Commando di Sham
1972	Ch. Wochica's Okeechobee Jake
1973	Ch. Cheyenne Golden's Son of James
1974	Am-Can. Ch. Cummings Gold Rush Charlie
1975	Ch. Wochica's Okeechobee Jake
1976	Ch. Sun Dance's Rarue
1977	Ch. Wochica's Okeechobee Jake
1978	Ch. Gold Rush's Great Teddy Bear
1979	Ch. Russo's Pepperhill Poppy
1980	Ch. Gold Rush Copper Lee
1981	Ch. Tempo's Frontier Bronco
1982	Ch. Laurell's York
1983	Ch. Asterling's Tahiti Sweetie
1984	Ch. Pepperhill East Point Airily
1985	Ch. Wingsong Maker's Mark
1986	Ch. Toasty's Royal Mercedes
1987	Am-Can. Ch. Windsor's St. Elsewhere
1988	Ch. Libra Malagold Coriander
1989	Ch. Alderbrooke's Rush Hill Rebel Am-Can. TD
1990	Ch. Sassafras Batterys Not Incl'd
1991	Ch. Sassafras Batterys Not Incl'd
1992	Ch. Asterling's Wild Blue Yonder

1955 Golden Retriever Club of America National Specialty
BOB Ch. Sprucewood's Chore Boy. Owned by Mrs. Henry Barnour

1955 Golden Retriever Club of America National Specialty
BOS Am-Can. Ch. Sprucewood's Chinki. Owned by Miller Zwang.

1960 GRCA National Specialty
BOB Ch. Sprucewood's Chore Boy. Owned by Mrs. Henry Barbour.

1960 GRCA National Specialty
BOS Ch. Vickersby Ferlach. Owned by Miss. Eleanor H. Burr. Handled by Virginia Hardin.

1961 GRCA National Specialty
Left: **BOS Sun Dance's Sayonnara CD.** Owned by Wayne and Irene Petty. *Right:* **BOB Ch. Prince Royal of Los Altos.** Owned by Oliver and Janet Wilhelm.

51

1963 Golden Retriever Club of America National Specialty
BOB Eng-Am. Ch. Figaro of Yeo. Owned by Mrs. Charles W. Englehard.

1964 Golden Retriever Club of America National Specialty
BOS Finderne Gypsy of Nerrisside. Owned by Frances Hargrave.

1965 Golden Retriever Club of America National Specialty, winner BOB 1959.
BOB Ch. Sundance's Bronze CD. Owned by Opal Horton.

1965 Golden Retriever Club of America National Specialty
BOS Ch. Sun Dance's Vivacious Sock. Owned by George and Gretchen Abbott.

1966 Golden Retriever Club of America National Specialty
BOB Ch. Cheyenne Golden's King John. Owned by Cheyenne Golden Kennels.

1966 Golden Retriever Club of America National Specialty and 1967 winner BOB
BOS Ch. Lorelei's Fez-Ti Za-Za. Owned by Reinhard Bischoff.

1968 Golden Retriever Club of America National Specialty
BOB Am-Can. Ch. Sun Dance's Vagabond Lover CDX. Owned by V. Topmiller and L. Ellis.

1968 Golden Retriever Club of America National Specialty
BOS Duckdown Tuffy of Buckskin CD. Owned by Judith Anne Collins.

1969 Golden Retriever Club of America National Specialty
BOB Beckwiths Malagold Flash. Owned by Carole Kvamme.

1969 Golden Retriever Club of America National Specialty
BOS Ch. Brackenhollow Sherry. Owned by Gary Arnold.

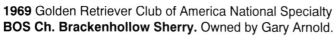

1970 Golden Retriever Club of America National Specialty
BOB Ch. Malagold Beckwith Big Buff CD. Owned by Connie Gerstner.

1971 Golden Retriever Club of America National Specialty
BOB Ch. Colacove Commando di Sham. Owned by John and June Mastracola.

1971 Golden Retriever Club of America National Specialty
BOS Ch. Sun Dance's Contessa. Owned by Lisa Klein.

1972 Golden Retriever Club of America National Specialty
BOB Ch. Wochica's Okeechobee Jake. Owned by Susan Taylor.

1972 Golden Retriever Club of America National Specialty
BOS Ch. Goldsprings Miss Muffet. Owned by Catherine Welling.

1973 Golden Retriever Club of America National Specialty
BOB Ch. Cheyenne Golden's Son of James. Owned by Cheyenne Golden Kennels.

1973 Golden Retriever Club of America National Specialty
BOS Ch. Sun Dance's Contessa. Owned by Lisa Klein.

1974 Golden Retriever Club of America National Specialty
BOB Am-Can. Ch. Cummings Gold Rush Charlie. Owned by R. Clark and L. Johnson.

1974 Golden Retriever Club of America National Specialty
BOS Ch. Valhalla's Amber Kate. Owned by Kathy and Lawrence Leibler.

1975 Golden Retriever Club of America National Specialty
BOB Ch. Wochica's Okeechobee Jake. Owned by Susan Taylor.

1976 Golden Retriever Club of America National Specialty
BOB Ch. Sun Dance's Rarue. Owned by Shirley and William Worley.

1976 Golden Retriever Club of America National Specialty
BOS Ch. Foxy Lady of Loch Wil-lin. Owned by Linda and Willard Hall.

1977 Golden Retriever Club of America National Specialty
BOB Ch. Wochica's Okeechobee Jake. Owned by Susan Taylor.

1977 Golden Retriever Club of America National Specialty
BOS Ch. Golden Glo's Valentine. Owned by Donald and Marilyn Sturz.

1978 Golden Retriever Club of America National Specialty
BOB Ch. Gold Rush's Great Teddy Bear. Owned by Diane Smith and Ann Johnson.

1978 Golden Retriever Club of America National Specialty
BOS Ch. Russo's Pepperhill Poppy. Owned by Barbara and Jeffrey Pepper.

1979 Golden Retriever Club of America National Specialty
BOB Ch. Russo's Pepperhill Poppy. Owned by Barbara and Jeffrey Pepper.

1980 Golden Retriever Club of America National Specialty
BOB Ch. Gold Rush Copper Lee. Owned by W. Wingard and A. Johnson.

1981 Golden Retriever Club of America National Specialty
BOB Ch. Tempo's Frontier Bronco. Owned by H. Arzman and V. Wright.

1981 Golden Retriever Club of America National Specialty
BOS Ch. Sutter Creek Cloverdale Erin. Owned by Richard and Jane Zimmerman.

1982 Golden Retriever Club of America National Specialty
BOB Ch. Laurell's York. Owned by Thomas and Laura Kling.

1982 Golden Retriever Club of America National Specialty
BOS Ch. Skilfor Butterblac Bisque. Owned by Francine Shacter.

1983 Golden Retriever Club of America National Specialty
BOB Ch. Asterling's Tahiti Sweetie. Owned by Sylvia Donahey and Mary Westenberg.

1983 Golden Retriever Club of America National Specialty
BOS Ch. Goldwing Blues Boy CDX. Owned by Haney, Davis and Dove.

1984 Golden Retriever Club of America National Specialty
BOB Ch. Pepperhill East Point Airily. Owned by Daniel Flavin and H. Geary.

1985 Golden Retriever Club of America National Specialty
BOB Ch. Wingsong Maker's Mark. Owned by Susan Heinl.

1985 Golden Retriever Club of America National Specialty
BOS Meadowpond Diamond Lady. Owned by Jim and Heather Heyboer.

1986 Golden Retriever Club of America National Specialty
BOB Ch. Toasty's Royal Mercedes. Owned by Jerome Oxenberg and Pam Monthei.

1986 Golden Retriever Club of America National Specialty
BOS Ch. Donner's Gold Rush Jake. Owned by D. and Norma Shipman.

1987 Winner of the Golden Retriever Club of America National Specialty
BOB Am-Can. Ch. Windsor's St. Elsewhere. Owned by Bob and
Connie Adams.

1988 Golden Retriever Club of America National Specialty
BOB Ch. Libra Malagold Coriander. Owned by P. and T. Haines and C. Gerstner.

1988 Golden Retriever Club of America National Specialty
BOS Ch. Carlin Happy Holidays. Owned by K. Mortensen and C. Chapley-Rasmussen.

1989 Golden Retriever Club of America National Specialty
BOB Ch. Alderbrooke's Rush Hill Rebel Am-Can. TD. Owned by Mark and Tonya Struble.

1989 Golden Retriever Club of America National Specialty
BOS Am-Can. Ch. Beaumaris Timberee Tessa Ann UDT, WC. Owned by Sandy Fisher.

1990 Golden Retriever Club of America National Specialty
BOS Ch. Mardovars Savannah Star. Owned by Janeen Rice.

1991 Golden Retriever Club of America National Specialty
BOS Am-Can. Ch. Peppercreek Sweetest Taboo. Owned by Paul and Kathleen Scoggin.

1990 and **1991** winner of the Golden Retriever Club of America National Specialty
BOB Ch. Sassafras Batterys Not Incl'd. Owned by Lorraine Rodolph.

1992 Golden Retriever Club of America National Specialty
Winner of BOB was Ch. Asterling's Wild Blue Yonder, owned by Mary Burke. *See* page 79 for photo.
BOS Am-Can. Ch. Golden Pine Tres Cherrybrook. Owned by Nancy J. Kelly and Eileen K. Oshiro.

Ch. Lizzie's Gold Rush Echo (OS, HOF) owned by Jill and Gary Stone and Ann Johnson, Beverly Hills, California, was the Number One Golden Retriever and Number Eight Sporting Dog in 1985-1986. A member of the Show Dog Hall of Fame and a GRCA Outstanding Sire, Echo has sired hundreds of litters and produced many titled offspring.

In The Conformation Ring

BY BETTY GAY

When we look back on the world of conformation in the last dozen years and compare it to the many more years prior to that, we find a vast difference in the purpose which dog shows are filling these days. The original reason that dog shows came into being was to compare the physical structure of animals best suited to do the job for which they were being developed, and to help in the selection of breeding stock most likely to produce such animals. Unfortunately, this criteria no longer seems to be the primary focus of modern shows. The selection of superior working/breeding stock has taken a back seat to the beauty pageant.

The attitude about showing has become much more commercial and exploitive in nature, and these negative influences are certainly not confined to this breed alone. However, since the Golden Retriever is one of the most popular breeds, it may well be one of those most seriously affected. There is a market out there, and many puppies are produced with no other concern except to fill it. If it's cute and fluffy, it sells!

The word "conformation" has its root in the word "conform." Conform to what? The breed standard, of course, and the breed standard is a written guide describing a dog physically most capable of doing its work. In the breed standard of the Golden Retriever, there is virtually nothing included which merely describes a "pretty dog."

The Golden is a handsome animal, without doubt, but we surely don't want him to be only that. We hear the comment from time to time that

"if we don't hunt with our dogs, what difference does it make if they are changing?" We know that many breeds are no longer used for the purpose

Ch. Asterling's Wild Blue Yonder, "James," is owned, bred and handled by Mary Burke of Milwaukee, Wisconsin. James won the 1992 Purina Invitational, taking Best in Show over 350 of America's top AKC show dogs.

for which they originated, but it is these variances of use which distinguish breeds, and even groups, of dogs into their different categories. Certain characteristics exist in the sporting breeds as a group, but they are modified by the kind of work each breed was developed to do. It was by selection for these variations that the original breeders made one sporting breed different from another.

The primary divisions in the sporting breeds are those physical attributes that separate the pointing (speed) families from the flushing (stamina) families on land and the water retrievers. A breeder/exhibitor/judge who doesn't understand the basic sructure necessary for these various styles of work can hardly be expected to make correct decisions in choosing breeding stock, exhibits, or proper placements.

Let us examine some of the changes which we have observed in recent years, and even while considering the breed ring in detail, keep in mind that the dogs we see there are but a very small percentage of the whole Golden population. Any faults or virtues that Goldens have ever had still exist in the breed today, but because of the fact that most exhibitors know that certain problems will preclude them from winning, many dogs with these faults are just not presented for judgment.

We can begin with some obvious modifications seen now with regard to color. Coat color is much more in the middle range than it has ever been. We seldom see white feet or chest or head splashes. While some of this may be due to artful cover-up, which is against the show rules, white markings have become less prevalent due to their obvious nature. Eye coloring in the ring is certainly better, and although we still see some smudgy pigmentation on eye rims and lips, this characteristic is much improved.

Also missing from the show ring are dogs with blatant structural problems, e.g., severe cowhocks, flat splayed feet, swayed backs, very crooked legs . . . weaknesses which, over a lifetime, might well disable an animal.

We look instead to the more subtle changes in the breed, and because Goldens are of generally better quality and more artfully presented, it takes a more thorough understanding of the

Ch. Libra Malagold Coriander (OS, HOF), owned by Patricia Haines and Connie Gerstner, DeForest, Wisconsin, claimed highest honors at the 1988 GRCA National Specialty when he took Best of Breed.

breed, as well as a discerning eye, to find the truly desired characteristics that are so valuable. And, while we often hear comments about "judges' education," it is the breeder and the exhibitor who make the first selections.

There is no doubt that heads have improved overall, but we still see very few that are really correct in most aspects. There are certainly fewer of the obviously poor heads, and many might be considered "pretty" or pleasant, but still lacking the true nobility of the quality Golden head.

Even when we see dogs with eyes "set well apart," they frequently have a hollowness below the eyes which does not give a smooth blend into what is supposed to be a wide and deep foreface. Good strength of muzzle and chin, without being flewsy, and the blend between muzzle and head really distinguish the good head.

Often the temple area above the eyes is also not well filled, and the eyes themselves are often poorly shaped or set. None of these shortcomings lends itself to the warm, sensitive, friendly expression so desired in the Golden. In addition there is the houndy appearance caused by low-set and/or large-sized ears seen much too often.

Ch. Copper Lee Gold Rush Apollo (OS, HOF), owned by Judy Bruer, Glen Mills, Pennsylvania and always handled by his best friend, Janet Bunce. GRCA Outstanding Sire and Show Dog Hall of Famer, Apollo was known for his wonderful temperament, head type and soundness . . . what more could one ask of a once-in-a-lifetime Golden? . . .

Dentition is better in many regards. The bite with dropped lower, middle incisors is less and less common. Alignment of all incisors is much better. Some bite problems, being disqual–ifiable, are obviously absent from the ring. There are still a number of dogs shown with missing premolars, and while the absence of the small, first premolar cannot be considered a serious fault, lack of any of the larger back teeth must be. Complete dentition is important in a breed that uses its mouth in its work, and any missing teeth should be faulted according to their location. Occlusion of the molars is sometimes difficult to determine in a brief ring examination, but it is the key to evaluating the mouth as a whole.

Bone and substance have improved over the years, and we see very few slight, weedy individuals in the ring. In fact, for a time, the term "good bone" was carried to extreme, with the additional phrase "but not to the point of coarseness" often overlooked. In the '90s it appears that the trend towards this excess is diminishing.

One of the subtle faults we do see is the selection of tiny feet with virtually no toenails and almost upright pasterns. None of these characteristics is workman-like, and the standard specifies a "medium" foot and "slightly sloping" pasterns. Those that are so very upright cannot absorb the initial shock from the foot, and that unabsorbed shock then moves into the elbow and other joints of the front assembly.

Because of selection for shorter hocks, we are seeing more and more Goldens which are really short in the leg as well, lacking length in the second thigh and not in balance in their height/ length proportions. Remember that a good rule of thumb regarding height is that half of the Golden's height should be at his elbow. While the standard tells us that a Golden is not to be "long in the leg," neither is the opposite condition desirable. Dogs with

Ch. Krishna's Ja-Jim Extra Special (HOF) (Ch. Camelot's Noble Fella CDX ex Krishna's E Z Taffy), called "Extra," is owned by Jerome Oxenberg. His owner admits that Extra was a once-in-a-lifetime dog who became the keystone for all future breeding successes. A noble and magnificent animal, he sired the Oxenbergs' National Specialty winner Ch. Toasty's Royal Mercedes, as well as numerous other Group-winning champion get and High-In-Trial offspring.

less and less daylight under them, a combination of long body hair and short legs, do not have the athletic balance needed for jumping or scaling fences, nor even enough leg for efficient swimming.

A discussion of angulation and movement might easily take up a whole book, and many good ones have been written on the subject. Suffice it to say that balance of angles is very

Ch. Aspengold's Par Excellence, bred by Linda Atwell and co-owned by Inge Whiting and Linda. "Chip" has multiple Group placements from the classes.

important to sustain movement; that elbows should be located vertically below the tip of the shoulder blade with good layback of both bones; and that timing and an equal length of stride in both quarters are of great importance. Over-reaching under the body, kicking-up either with front or back legs are all evidence of poor construction, and side action in the dog is a primary consideration. Evaluation and selection of good front assembly continues to be a major problem in this breed, and probably one of the most difficult to solve.

In discussing body properties, we must keep in mind the importance of a deep and long rib cage. We see various examples of shallowness, flat ribs without sufficient spring, or short ribs combined with too long a loin. Most of the length of a Golden's body should be in his ribbing, with a relatively short loin making up the rest.

In discussing movement, we cannot stress the phrase "shown in hard working condition" strongly enough. Good, natural musculature is seldom seen in the show ring today. Upon examining dogs outside the ring, the owner may say "he's in really good condition . . . has his Senior Hunting title . . . work him every day," and we find

him in fairly decent condition, but no where close to the natural musculature found in many field-line individuals.

How many breeders of show dogs even consider inherited musculature as part of their criteria in selecting mates for breeding? It is indeed inherited and then maximized by conditioning. In a world which spends millions on sweatsuits, sport shoes, health clubs, and exercise machines, we not only show our dogs fat and flabby, we often do so deliberately to try to cover some structural faults.

Also contributing to the problem is the "rush to maturity" used in raising puppies on too much food and supplements. They do not have the chance to develop the strong framework and early muscling needed to support what will ultimately be a fairly large animal. These early bloomers are frequently the ones who fade the fastest. Stop making the excuse that this is "puppy roll" and realize that a dog of any age will move truer, sounder and more efficiently if he is fit and trim.

We are seeing the same kind of excess in the selection for coat, not only in the amount of coat but in the texture as well. The standard describes a proper coat as "firm and resilient" and "lying close to body," not long, fluffy or open. The obvious reasons for this coat description pertain to resistance to cold water and the ease of cleaning field debris out of the coat after hunting work, but even in the show ring, a moderate amount of good-textured coat will give the dog a neat and more powerful appearance, which in itself would be desirable in a winning exhibit.

As with the use of weight to cover faults, the selection for too much coat serves the same purpose. The barbering techniques used to deceive the observer do not

Ch. Honor's Goldstorm Party Girl JH, "Savannah," bred by Ann Chase and adored by Diane Mueller, New Brunswick, Texas.

make the dog a better Golden, and the breed would be well served if more effort were put into developing better dogs instead of merely better tricks.

We also cannot stress the word "moderate" strongly enough when talking about the desired Golden Retriever. Any of the excesses seen in the show ring (size, bone, coat, even "showmanship" in some cases) all carry what should be good characteristics to undesirable extremes.

We must not miss the opportunity to discuss the Golden temperament. Always one of his most

fact, have never seen a game bird except in the lovely art prints won at dog shows.

This is not to say, however, that many Goldens no longer possess the instincts to work, and those in the hands of the all-purpose owner are proving this at the many working and hunting retriever tests. These tests, in addition to existing field trials, have become available during the 1980s. The Golden Retriever Club of America has recently approved a Versatility Award which provides recognition for the multi-purpose Golden. Generally, it is not the dog who is

Ch. Pepperhill East Point Airily (HOF), bred by Barbara and Jeffrey Pepper and owned by Daniel Flavin of Wainscott, New York. A member of the Show Dog Hall of Fame, this lovely lady was a multiple Best of Breed and Best-in-Show winner, and culminated her dazzling career by taking Best of Breed at the 1984 GRCA National Specialty.

endearing qualities, it must not be lost to selection for "up," hard-going, highly competitive individuals for show, field or obedience. Remembering that most Goldens that we breeders sell must live with someone, their sweet, stable, willing attitude is paramount.

While many aspects of the Golden have certainly improved, we are still beset with many genetic problems. We must also face the fact that the character of the breed has also changed. No longer is he "primarily a hunting dog." Many, in

limited, it is the owner. Goldens should be capable of doing so many activities and yet many owners do not make the effort to achieve more than one of them; by using an all-purpose criteria many much desired qualities could be retained even in families which do not appear to be multi-developed.

It is always discouraging to hear field trial or obedience people say they aren't interested in conformation. It may be that they aren't interested in conformation competition, but some

Right: A handsome obedience dog who turns heads whenever he enters the ring, **OTCh. Meadowpond Keepin' in Stride (OS, HOF)** has been trained by owner Terry Arnold, Sansea, Massachusetts. Stride surely keeps pace with the best of 'em!

Below: Doing what comes naturally, **FC-AFC Mioak's Main Event (OS, HOF)** performs at field trials to the callname "Rocky." Owner Cathy Morse and trainer Bill Eckett acclaim this Golden for his natural talent and stamina.

The first Dual Champion in Golden Retriever breed history: **Dual Ch. Stilroven Nitro Express** was bred by Ben Boalt and owned by Ralph Boalt. This fantastic dog was born on January 2, 1940, received his Field Championship in October 1942 and his conformation title in July 1947.

consideration to the structure of the working dog described in the breed standard benefits breeders of any competitive dog.

A consistent choice for the top levels of field or obedience competition is an athletic dog, muscular, with fairly high energy levels, and stable enough in temperament to take difficult training.

In the field trials, we have always seen many Goldens which are smallish, wiry, and fast. The character of the American field trial tends to put a lot of emphasis on speed, which is not really a primary consideration for a good upland hunting dog . . . a purpose more consistent with the development of the breed and of its use in present times. A ground-working stamina dog is built in a more stocky manner than most of the trial dogs.

So we find that selection of field trial dogs is made to meet the demands of the tests, which are different from original breed use, without enough consideration given to soundness and staying power. One cannot help but wonder if many of the really good field trial or obedience dogs might not have been even better had they possessed more of these qualities.

I well remember the Best of Breed at the 1965 Golden Retriever National Specialty, a dog named Ch. Rusina's Mr. Chips owned by Van Holt Garrett, Jr. He was a wonderful dog, lovely head,

powerful body and outstanding coat . . . all that a good retriever should be, as he proved the next day with a merit award in the Qualifying and later becoming a qualified field trial dog with points in Amateur tests.

I'm sorry we do not have a picture of him, but we do have one of Dual Ch. Stilrovin Nitro Express. Yes, this picture is over 40 years old, but in many respects he shows the qualities desired in the conformation Golden even today (angulation, solid musculature, balance, excellent body properties, and moderate coat of good texture). Granted, his head isn't wonderful and he is pretty dark, but certainly extremely workman-like and athletic. He also surpasses virtually any of the dogs seen in field trials today. *A Dual Champion!!* Will we ever see one again?

There are so many in the breed now whose knowledge and appreciation for the breed do not even extend a dozen years. They may think that all there is to the Golden Retriever is what they themselves have experienced, and tend to relegate anything before that to ancient history. We cannot know where we are going, or how the breed is changing, if we don't know where we've been. There must always be more to the appreciation of the Golden Retriever than just conformation for its own sake.

Top left: **Am-Can. Ch. Colabaugh's Going Magical Can. WC.**
Middle: **Can. Ch. Colabaugh's The Chase Is On.**
Bottom left: **Am-Can. Ch. Colabaugh's Ali Kazam CD.** Colabaugh dogs owned and bred by Janine Fiorito of Croton-on-Hudson, New York.
Top right: **Am-Can. Ch. Beckwith's Bit-O-Honey** was a Top-20 Golden USA in 1987 and '88. Honey has six generations of Beckwith breeding behind her.
Bottom right: **Am-Can. Ch. Tri Valleys Doc Holiday Am-Can. CDX, WC,** owned by Carole Kvamme of Alderwood Manor, Washington.

Top: **Evergrace Original One** ("Adam") by Am-Can. Ch. Miramichis Pier Connection ex Ch. Whisper's Stowaway Gracie. Owned by Stephen G. Leehy; bred by Jane Love. Here Adam is nine months old.
Middle: **Am-Can. Ch. Colabaugh's Fire Bear Houdini** owned by Laurie Berkowitz.
Bottom left: **Am-Can. Ch. -OTCh. Meadowpond Simon Sez UDT, JH, WC, VCX, TT, Can. CDX (HOF)** ("Simon") at two years finishing his Canadian title. Simon is by Ch. Meadowpond Crowd Pleaser CDX ex Meadowpond Tango Dancer. Owned by Judy Super-Borton of Plymouth, Massachusetts.
Bottom right: **Ch. Aspenglo's Coors Lite Delite (HOF)** owned by Charles M. Rogers, MD, of Sandy, Utah.

87

Top left: **Ch. Malagold Summer Encore** owned by Connie Gerstner of Deforest, Wisconsin.

Middle left and bottom left: **Ch. Toasty's Royal Rolls Royce CD (HOF).** "Rory" is a high-scoring obedience dog, gaining his CD at 17 months of age and won both his conformation majors at specialties. Rory was sired by Ch. Krishna's Ja-Jim Extra Special ex Cloverdale's Delta Dawn. Owner, Pam Monthei.

Top right: **Musicur's Tango in the Night** with Samantha Spring Wilson winning the Novice Junior Class.

Middle right: **Goldwing Gala Lalique** bred by Leslie Dove, owned by Suzanne Russ.

Top and Bottom left: **Am-Can. Ch. Asterling's Jamaica Verdict (OS, HOF)** (Ch. Goldrush's Judgement Day ex Am-Can. Ch. Amberac's Asterling Aruba) bred by Mary Wuestenberg, owned by Bill and Kathy Voegel of Chandler, Indiana. "Dust" carries extraordinary family credentials, as son of the top-producing bitch in breed history, and littermate to the top-winning bitch in breed history. He is himself a one-in-a-million dog . . . in 1985, shown for only four-and-one-half months, he defeated over 6,000 dogs, accumulated three all-breed BISs, one BISS, multiple Group placements, and finished Number Four Golden in the nation without being shown the last eight months of that year, statistics which may also be a breed record for that brief period of showing. Known for his outstanding movement, ring attitude, and loving personality, he is also extremely loyal and enthusiastic.

Bottom right: **Ch. Laurell's Brodie Mountain** by Ch. Birnam Wood's Douglas Furr ex Ch. Laurell's Travlin' My Way. Owner, Charles M. Rogers of Murray, Utah.

89

Top: **Ch. Rosewind's Ashford Murphy (OS, HOF)** the Number Two Golden in the US in 1988 is by Ch. Asterling Austin-Healey ex Am-Can. Ch. Rosewind's Rebel Rose CD. Owned by Colette and Jack Agresti, handled by Tom Tobin. *Bottom left:* **Ch. Krishna Ja-Jim Extra Special** winning Veterans Dog at the 1987 Eastern GRCA Regional Specialty. *Bottom right:* **Evergrace Enticing One** ("Eve") at 18 months, bred by Jane Love; owned by Bruce and Donna Thompson. Eve is by Ch. Miramichi's Pier Connection ex Ch. Whisper's Stowaway Gracie.

Top left: **Am-Can. Ch. Windsor's St. Elsewhere,** bred, owned and loved by Bob and Connie Adams of Allegany, New York. After completing her Canadian and American championships, "Elsa" walked off with Best of Breed at the 1987 GRCA National Specialty. Elsa loved snowballing and chasing rocks down the creek with Bob, but her all-time favorite pastime was snatching apples when the Adams' apple trees were full of fruit. This beautiful life ended tragically at age three and one-half from an adverse reaction to sedation for a routine x-ray. Elsa lives on in the loving memories she left with Connie and Bob.

Bottom left: Ever so humble, this is **Windfall's Royale Frolic CD** (or "Magnum") by Ch. Amberac's Casino Royale ex Morning Sage Windfall's Charm.

Top right: **Cougar** at three taking one of many BOBs.

Middle right: **Am-Can. Ch. Clark Sunfire's Bullseye JH, CD, WCX, Can. CD, WCI** . . . or simply "Winchester" taking a wonderful Best in Show at Oromocto Kennel Club. Owned by Sunfire.

Top left: **Ch. Rosewind's Ashford Murphy (OS, HOF)** by Ch. Asterling Austin-Healey ex Am-Can. Ch. Rosewind's Rebel Rose CD, owned by the Agrestis. Murphy is a multiple BIS and BISS winner, ranking among Top Ten Goldens for 1986–1988.

Bottom left: **Ch. Honor's Pucker Up** ("Kiss") is owned and breeder-handled by Paige Chase McBride. Kiss was Number Three in the whole smackin' US in 1990!

Top right: **Ch. Laurell's Brodie Mountain** with owner Charles M. Rogers, MD.

Middle: **Ch. Malagold Disco Duck (HOF)** bred by Connie Gerstner and Mary Hopkins, owned by D. and J. Pabst. Best-in-Show and Group winner in 1989 had amassed 97 Hall of Fame points and was the Number Four Golden that year.

Bottom right: **Ch. Aspenglo Telluride,** bred and owned by Charles Rogers, MD.

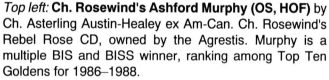

Top left: **Ch. Pekay's Lizzy Borden CD, JH, WC,** owned by Pat Klausman and better known as "Pat's Brat," is a competent obedience and hunting dog who is also a conformation diva. Her Novice obedience scores averaged 196+. Lizzy was sired by Ch. Beaumaris Pekay's Kilowatt ex Pekay's Up and Coming Lady. Owner, Pat Lodge. *Top right:* **Am-Can. Ch. Thornfield Lark O'Meadowpond** has won BOB many times. Sire was Ch. Freedom's Celebration ex Ch. Thornfield Skylark. Bred by Kathy Heisler, owner Cherie Berger. *Bottom left:* **Ch. Birnam Wood's Show 'N Tell CD** ("Chelsea") by Ch. Birnam Wood's Douglass Furr ex Ch. Asterling Lana Lalenia CD. *Bottom right:* **Can. Ch. Meadowpond Diamond Lady** by Ch. Jungold Legend of Golden Pine ex Am-Can. Ch. Cimaron's Dazzle Dust CDX, TD, WC, owned by J. Heyboer. Here she is winning BOS at the GRCA 1985 Specialty from the Veterans Bitch Class.

Top left: **Ch. Aspenglo's Guiness Stout,** "Duke" has honored "Ruffie," his dam and his littermate, Coors, by taking Best of Breed and multiple Group placements from the classes.

Top right: **Ch. Aspenglo Telluride (HOF),** bred, owned and handled by Charles Rogers, MD, Murray, Utah, was a Top Ten Golden in 1989 and 1990. "Rider" has five champion littermates, and is himself a multiple Best-in-Show winner and GRCA Hall of Fame Golden.

Bottom: **Ch. Toasty's Royal Mercedes (OD, HOF),** owned by Pam Monthei and Jerome Oxenberg.

Top: **Ch. Asterling Austin-Healey, (OS, HOF),** (Ch. Beaumaris Pekay's Kilowatt ex Am-Can. Ch. Amberac's Asterling Aruba) bred by Mary Wuestenberg, owned by Susan and Donna Nyberg of Canyon Country, California, and Mary Burke, multiple Best-in-Show and Group winner and placer, looks as good at eight years of age as he did at two.

Bottom left: **Am-Can. Ch. Heron Acres Sandcastle MH, Am-Can. UDTX, MH, WCX, VCX, ***, UKC HRCH, NAHRA MHR** winning Veterans at the GR Central Regional Specialty in 1990.

Bottom right: **Ch. Asterling Lanai Lalenia CD (OD)** at eight years of age taking BOS from Veterans in Los Angeles. Owner, Suzanne Wilson.

Top left: **Ch. Pekay's Ready Aim Fire . . .** just say "stack!" *Bottom left:* **Ch. Birnam Wood's Show 'N Tell CD** by Ch. Birnam Wood's Douglas Furr ex Ch. Asterling Lanai Lalenia CD. Bred by Sylvia Donahey and owned by Bruce and Donna Thompson of St. Louis, Missouri.
Top right: **Ch. Sutter Creek Laurell Ruffian,** bred by Laura Ellis Kling, owned by Charles Rogers, MD, Murray, Utah. "Ruffie" is a Best-in-Show and Hall of Famer, the foundation bitch of Aspenglo Golden Retrievers, and the dam of Ch. Aspenglo's Coors Lite Delite.
Middle: **Ch. Beckwith's Phortune Cookie** owned by Ludell Beckwith has many Breed and Group wins.
Bottom right: **Am-Can. Ch. Musicur's Pardon My Brass** owned by the Thompsons. Prowler takes the Breed at 21 months.

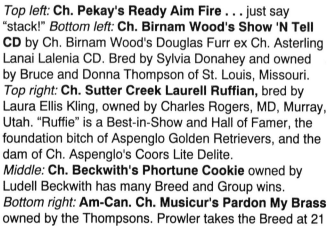

Top left: **Am-Can. Ch. Whipaly's Colabaugh Senna UD, SH, WCX, TT, Can. UD, WC** owned by Janine Fiorito.

Top right: **Am-Can. Ch. Tri Valley's Doc Holiday Am-Can. CDX, WCX,** owned by Carole Kvamme. Photo by Jerry Vavra.

Bottom: **Am-Can. Ch. Llanfair's Yankee Doodle UD, WCX, VCX, Can. CD,** bred by Emily and David Burgess and owned by Jacquie and John Jansky of Bethel Park, Pennsylvania. "Bruiser" was Jacquie's first dog, her beloved brat and best friend, and they learned everything together. Despite being one of those exceptional bench champions to also achieve a UD, Bruiser nevertheless did everything "his way," usually running the bank with his duck and shaking off on the judges whenever possible. During his last two years he roared his way through nine surgeries for a localized tumor and continued to place in Veteran conformation and obedience classes during that time. He retrieved his last duck in a working test just six weeks before he died.

Top left: **Ch. Beckwith's Justa Tuckerbear (HOF)** took 32 BOBs in 1984 and 24 Group placements. Owned by the Beckwiths. *Top right:* **Ch. Whisper's Stowaway Gracie,** owned by Jane Love, East Carondelet, Illinois, shown with her owner-handler after taking Best of Breed at the White River GRC Specialty. *Bottom:* BISS **Am-Can. Ch. Asterling Jamaica Verdict (OS, HOF)** looking regal and relaxed.

Top left: **Ch. Freedom's Celebration (OS),** bred by John Freed and Laura Ellis Kling, and owned by Judy Glasgow of Athens, Ohio. "Rally" was the Number One producing Golden Retriever sire for an amazing four consecutive years . . . 1986, 1987, 1988 and 1989. He has sired multiple BIS and Group winners, SDHOF Goldens and Specialty BIS winners. Through 1990 he had sired 54 AKC champions of record.

Middle: **Ch. Malagold Hail Victoria (HOF),** "Tory," bred by Connie Gerstner and Cheryl Blair, owned by Patricia Haines and Vivian Wright, Amelia, Ohio, was a Best of Breed winner and a Top Ten Golden in 1987.

Bottom left: **Ch. Aspengold's Glamagorn Storm,** bred by Linda Atwell and owned by Kelly Holmes. Handled by Linda Atwell.

Top right: An Outstanding Dam, **Ch. Asterling Lanai Lalenia CD,** "Layla" at age four years. By Ch. Goldrush's Judgement Day ex Am-Can. Ch. Amberac's Asterling Aruba. Owned by S. Wilson.

Bottom right: **Musicur's Clairvoyant** (Am-Can. Ch. Musicur's Pardon My Brass ex Birman Woods Barely Legal). Owned by the Thompsons.

Top: **Am-Can. Ch. Trumpet's Tijac Twister Am-Can. CDX, JH, Am-Can. WCX** ("Dexter") by Am-Can. Ch. and Can. OTCh. Amanda's Pacific Whirlwind Can. UDT, WCI, TT, Am. CDX, TD, JH, WCX, VCX ex Am-Can. Ch. Pepperhill GldnPine Trumpet CDX, SH, WCX, Can. CD, WCX, owned by Tim and Jackie O'Brien and Anita Lee; bred by Charlotte Gaynor.

Bottom left: **Trumpet's Ratfaced McDougal CDX, SH, WCX, Can. CDX, WCX** . . . that's "Scrapper" for short . . litter brother to Dexter. Owned by Charlotte and Peter Gaynor of San Francisco, California.

Bottom right: **Am-Can. Ch., Can. OTCh. Amanda's Pacific Whirlwind Can. UDT, WCI, TT, Am. CDX TD, JH, WCX, VCX (OS)** (Am-Can. Ch. Trowsnest Whirlwind, UD, WC, Can. CDX, WC (OS) ex Am-Can. Glenallens Amanda) owned by Anita Lee, Vancouver, British Columbia. When Anita threw puppy "Jaimie" his first bird wing, and he ran around the yard with his entire litter hot on his heels, she knew at once, he was "the one." Appropriately named, his whole career has been a whirlwind. A Canadian champion in his first three shows, American and Canadian obedience titles with placements in every class, all titles . . . tracking and field in Canada and the US. . . . on his first try. He flies through his obedience routines and was second highest scoring dog in trial three times in the Open B class. In 1988 and 1989 he was awarded the GRCC J. P. Crawley Memorial Trophy for the Grand Champion Golden who continues to excel and achieve in all fields of competition.

Jaimie just loves to be doing ANYTHING, and always with enormous enthusiasm and a smile on his face . . . Anita's once-in-a-lifetime Golden.

Jaimie has passed the same zest and reliability on to his kids. His litter out of Am-Can. Ch. Pepperhill Gldn Pine Trumpet CDX, SH, WCX, Can. CD, WCX (OD) earned a total of 23 titles at 28 months of age through 1991, with most of them owner-trained and handled.

Right: Head study of **Ch. Smithaven's Jazz Jeneration,** owned by Debi Hanson and June Smith of Alamo, California.

Bottom right: **Ch. Elysian's Lil Leica Reprint CDX, TD, JH, WCX, VCX** owned by Jeanne von Barby.

Bottom left: **Am-Can. Ch. Whipaly Sierra Zip 'N Zachary CDX, JH, WCX (OS)** (Am-Can. Ch. Ambertrail's Flatbush Flanagan CD ex Topbrass Razzle Dazzle Rose CD, TD, WCX), owned by Michele Andavall, Hendersonville, North Carolina. What began as an obedience career blossomed into success in the show ring as well, when Zach matured into a handsome young performer. He won his Canadian bench title handily, in one three-show weekend, with a Sporting Group First two days in a row. Zach claimed high-scoring champion awards on his way to his CDX, and surprised the hunt test judges with his drive and speed in the field. A battle with cancer interupted his UD and SH pursuit, but he still chases his tennis ball with boundless energy and enthusiasm.

This page: **Am-Can-Mex-Int-Dom-S. Am. Ch. U-UD Beckwiths Main Event UDT, JH, WCX, VCX Can. UDT, WCX, VCX, Mex. PC, Dom. UD** (Am-Can. Ch. Smithhavens Benchmark Caper CD (OS, HOF) ex Am-Can. Ch. Beckwiths Whirlaway Dust) owned by Caroline McCormick, Bellevue, Washington.

"Ryan" earned 27 titles on his way to this impressive string of bench, obedience and working accomplishments. He is believed to be the record international title holder in the United States. Additionally, he has more than half the required AKC OTCh. points, and has points as a NAHRA Started Retriever. The Mex. PC stands for *Perro Campañero,* or Companion Dog. His Mexican titles were earned with a Group placement and a HIT.

Ryan gained his full International Champion title when he passed an instinct/working test held in Mexico City. Competing dogs must retrieve a live, shackled duck in swimming water, after a shot by the bird thrower; dogs must be steady to the shot. Tests are for pure-bred dogs only; two other Goldens competed. Setters and spaniels also participated in their own working areas.

Instinct tests are rarely held in the Western Hemisphere due to the expense, and the scarcity of uncontaminated water in which the dogs can safely swim. The previous test was in the early 1980s.

Despite his extraordinary achievements, Ryan's most outstanding feature is his incredibly Golden temperament and personality. He loves to do everything, go everywhere, and adores everyone. His energy and enthusiasm belie his eight years . . . he leaps onto the porch railing to pick apples from the apple tree, charges out to the bird feeder several times a day to check for leftover bread crumbs, and goes wild to retrieve anything, preferably birds, and will stuff as many birds as he can get into his mouth. When he's finally worn out, Ryan sleeps on his mistress's bed, head upon her pillow, a place he and Caroline agree he has earned.

Top: **Ch. Gold-Sun's Hurricane Cajun UD, SH, WCX, VCX,** owned and trained by Terry Thornton, Carrollton, Texas, one of the few Goldens to hold a bench championship, a Utility degree and Senior Hunter title.

Bottom left and Bottom right: **Am-Can. Ch. Bardfield Boomer Am-Can. UDT, WC, (OS, HOF)** owned by Cherie Berger. Sitting *left*, Boomer at fourteen and competing in veterans obedience, outdoing the regular class with his age-old style. Boomer was the "last pick" from his litter.

Top left: **Ch. Beaulieu's Akacia O'Darnley UDTX, JH, WCX, VCX (OD) (**Ch. Kachina's Kamiakin O'Darnley CD, WC ex Ch. Beaulieu's Printa WC). Photo by Ron Brown. Owner, J. von Barby.

Top right and Bottom: **Am-Can. Ch. Timbereee's Tenacious Token UDT, WCX (HOF)** is a multiple specialty show winner with multi-HITs. His progeny enjoy his field and obedience prowess as well. Owners, Bob and Sandy Fisher.

This page: An English import and Canadian Obedience Champion, this is **Can. OTCh.Brownards Benjamin Brittan UD, JH, WCX, TT, Mex. PCE, TT, GRCC Ob (HOF) . . .** called "Bandit" by his owner Brenda Radcliff of Orangevale, California. Bandit has 16 HITs to his credit earned in North America, and has two Novice Dog World awards, two Open Dog World awards and has placed in the Gaines competitions and the Detroit Windsor World Series. Bandit approaches the challenge of hunting with gusto and good GR humor. As an obedience dog, Bandit scores range from 194 to 199.5, with the average at 197.5 or better. Sire was Sandyne Casanova ex Colesburg Coarl Maid. Born on March 31, 1981, he was the first male import to earn JH in October 1988.

Can. OTCh. Hickory-Dickory Zachary UDT, JH, WCX, (OS), owned by Andrea Johnson, Minneapolis, Minnesota, shown with dumbbell and clearing the bar jump with spectacular style and grace.

Goldens in Obedience

BY BARBRA GOODMAN

Glamour dog of the eighties, companion of presidents, kings and queens, favorite of celebrities, the Golden Retriever continues to ride its crest of popularity through the '90s.

Its handsome countenance photographed from every angle is as likely to be found on the pages of *Vogue* magazine as it is adorning the cover of the *American Kennel Gazette.*

Even best-selling author Dean Koontz, whose books are avidly read the world over, gets into the act. In his highly suspenseful novel *Midnight*, the lovable hero is an astounding Golden Retriever that has been scientifically endowed with remarkable powers.

The Golden Retriever has even invaded the television commercial industry. Goldens, Goldens and more Goldens playfully lope at the seashore, happily chasing a ball or splashing in the surf. And do you get the feeling that every new car comes equipped with a Golden Retriever? Well it seems like there is always a Golden joining the family as they joy ride in their shiny new station wagon or sedan.

And who among us hasn't viewed the youths of this country guzzling their favorite drink as a graceful Golden soars high in the air in quest of a Frisbee?

The American public first became even more aware of the breed when President Gerald Ford shared the television camera with his Golden, Liberty. Like wildfire, the breed captured the fancy of people everywhere.

Even in the sport of obedience, where they have for some time enjoyed a modicum of appreciation, it appeared that the breed had been rediscovered. Goldens began turning heads everywhere as they danced effortlessly through their obedience routines.

This was especially true when a team was known for their high-scoring accomplishments. And how those teams did flourish, once the challenge of the coveted Obedience Trial Cham-

OTCh. Meadowpond Keepin' in Stride (OS, HOF) (Ch. Meadowpond Crowd Pleaser CDX ex Heron Acres Meadowpond Gofer CD,*) bred by Cherie Berger, owned, trained and treasured by Theresa Arnold, Swansea, Massachusetts. Stride's record is in itself a breed record, and speaks for the superb talent of this extraordinary obedience champion. Over a dozen 200 scores, five awarded by judges who had never before credited any dog with a perfect score, 75 HITs and 35 High Combineds, winner of 1991 Gaines Classic Super Dog, four Regional Super Dog titles, five Godsil awards "200" at the Gaines Classic, Gaines Superdog second and fourth places, set record for the highest Superdog average score with 198.917. Small wonder crowds gathered to watch Terri and Stride when they entered the ring, to marvel at Stride's obvious adoration and complete attention riveted on Terri. Yet through it all, Terri credits Stride most with being the perfect best friend and companion.

pionship was instituted by the American Kennel Club in 1977!

Abbreviated to OTCh., only dogs that had earned a Utility title would be eligible to vie for this award. Once attained, owners could then proudly display the initials in the dog's name.

In order to attain the OTCh., the AKC devised a system whereby dogs needed to amass 100 points. That could be achieved by having won three first places in Open B and Utility under three different judges.

The very first dog to claim the award was Golden Retriever OTCh. Moreland's Golden Tonka, owned by Russ Klipple of Pennsylvania.

All the more remarkable was that his owner, a very special gentleman, was well into his sixties when he accomplished this feat. Russ and his beloved Tonka continued to dominate East-coast competition and the Gaines/Cycle events for many years.

Fanned by the spirit of competition, two very prestigious tournaments, The World Series in Detroit, Michigan and the Gaines/Cycle Regionals and Classics provided other challenges in which the breed was destined to excel.

Throughout the '80s, a steady procession of

198.5. He attained a breed championship at just 16 months old. Still going strong at his very last trial in Duluth, Minnesota in July of 1982, Duster scored a 198.5 under Judge Sharon Fulkerson. Duster died on June 3, 1989 at 13 years of age.

Bernie's next challenge was OTCh. Tanbark's Bristol Creme. At the very first trial, at 13 months of age, Bristol scored a 200! In 1990 Bristol won the First and Foremost, the Delaney System and the Ken-L-Ration Dog of the Year. He was shown 79 times, qualifying 75 times in Utility and 71

OTCh. Meadowpond Especial One UDT, SH, WCX (OD, HOF) (Am-Can. Ch. Laurell's Especial Jason UDT, WC ex Am-Can. Ch. Chafa Honeybun of Jungold CDX, TD, WC) owned by Glenda Brown, Santa Barbara, California.
Her career included Dog World awards in Novice and Open, being the first Golden to hold an OTCh., SH, and TD titles. Always willing, and always at Glenda's side, "Sprite" epitomized Glenda's ideal Golden, beautiful both inside and out. She earned her final, champion-quality score, 199½, in Veteran's Open, at ten years old, just five months before she died.

Golden Retrievers continued to make their mark in the world of obedience breaking an astounding number of records along the way.

High on the list of achievers through the later part of the 1970s and early '80s was Ch., OTCh. Meadowpond Dust Commander, owned and trained by Bernie Brown of Lake Villa, Illinois. This obedience superstar led all dogs in the number of OTCh. points in 1981 with 1,159. In 1979, 1980 and 1981, "Duster" was the top obedience dog in the country and the Ken-L-Ration Dog of the Year. During the time that Duster was being shown, his achievements were numerous. Added to his impressive credentials were a career-high 94 High-In-Trial awards and fifth in all-time OTCh. points with 2,476.

When Duster was shown for the very first time at 13 months of age at the International Kennel Club under Judge Harold Maloney, he scored a

times in the Open class. In addition, this team accumulated some 1,472 OTCh. points, which is the most earned in a single year by anyone. Bristol, earned over 100 High-In-Trials through 1991.

1990 marked the passing of a captivating dog whose career accomplishments spanned more than 12 years, including a perfect score of 200 at the grand old age of 11. OTCh. Topbrass Ric O Shay Barty WCX came on the scene like a rocket in the early 1980s.

Winner of the Ken-L-Ration award in 1982 and 1983, Ric and his owner Sharon Long rode the winning trail with a dazzling 150 High-In-Trials and over 3,400 lifetime OTCh. points. Standing at ringside watching this team gracefully move through their paces, one sensed a mutually shared devotion.

As a GRCA Outstanding Sire, a member of the

Can. Ch., U-UD Amberac's Gaety at Honeycomb Am-Bda-Can. UD, SKC-CDX, JH, Am-Can. WC, TT, CGC (Am-Can. Ch. Amberac's Ramala Rougue, Am-Can. CD ex Ch. Amberac's Yul B Ritzi) bred by Ellen Manke, owned by Patricia O'Brien, Lakewood, New Jersey. "Gae" is Pat's soulmate and, after visiting three countries to complete a whopping 21 titles, obviously Pat's once-in-a-lifetime dog. In 1991 Gae earned her fifth UD, breaking her own record of the most UD titles in breed history. Better yet, Gae is also a registered therapy dog and charms the residents of two nursing homes on a regular basis. A true ambassador for the breed.

Obedience Hall of Fame, and the sire of six OTCh. dogs, Ric will long be remembered for the heart and desire he showed in every performance.

It is interesting to note that many of the obedience handlers of today's record-breaking Goldens were converts to the breed. And who could blame them? There are few breeds that show more and more desire, willingness and adaptability to obedience training than a Golden Retriever. Teach it sit, come, give it a cookie or a big hug and you've found a dog who will please you from the tip of its tail all the way down to its big, bursting heart full of love. What more could anyone ask of a dog!

In the case of Sue Mayborne of Roscoe, Illinois

and OTCh. Shoreland's Big Harry Deal, obedience training competition was not part of their original game plan. Sue and Harry started out running licensed field trials in 1980. Harry sparkled at this, winning the Derby Stake at the Golden Retriever National Specialty that year in New York. He had even placed in several Licensed Qualifying Stakes before the age of two. For someone who is starting a family, anyone can tell you that the time spent training and trialing can be very time-consuming. Sue decided obedience would be much more convenient and less demanding on her time.

Harry and Sue had found their niche. By ten years of age, Harry had more than found his sea legs. The twosome won the 1989 Ken-L-Ration Dog of the Year, and for the second year in a row, Harry captured first place in Super Dog at the Gaines/Cycle Central Regional. They also won the Top Dog title at the World Series. At that time Harry also broke the record for the most OTCh. points accumulated in one year, raking in some 1,321 points. That same year he had 26 High-In-Trials and two perfect scores of 200.

Sadly this great dog passed away in 1990. On his epitaph it surely must say, "He lived his life on the fast track."

The Gaines/Cycle Regionals and Classics is a tournament that was established in 1975 by the Illini Obedience Association. In order to qualify for the Regionals, which move to different cities each year, dogs must have attained three scores of 193 or better in their individual classes.

There is an Eastern Regional, a Central Regional, a Western Regional and the finale, which is referred to as the Gaines/Cycle Classic. Winners of each Regional then compete at the Classic at the end of the year in a different city each year.

The World Series is an on-going tournament formed by the Detroit Windsor Association in

OTCh. Tanbark's Bristol Creme (HOF) took owner Bernie Brown on his second trip to the top. By 1990 the two had accumulated a record 5,989 OTCh. points, one for every dog defeated in competition under the Delaney System of rating obedience dogs. In 1991, Bristol's record, 1,472 points earned in a single year, won him the Ken-L-Ration Dog of the Year award, and pushed him into fourth place for lifetime points, passing Bernie's previously fourth-place Duster, who was a tough act to follow. Bernie didn't care, as long as Bristol was his dog, too.

OTCh. A Case of Love (HOF), (Ch.-OTCh. Meadowpond Dust Commander ex Lake Tahoe's Princess) owned by the late Ed Kniep, Big Rock, Illinois.

1970. While the format is similar to that of the Gaines/Cycle events, this prestigious tournament is held in July each year in Detroit, Michigan.

The pride of accomplishment is apparent if you have a moment to speak to Michael McDonald of Ohio. His pride and joy is OTCh. Altair's Sardaukar Sadie, and she didn't come to him in her formative first few months. She was already 18 months old when she arrived at the McDonald household. Although she has had a star-studded career, Mike thinks Sadie's greatest accomplishment was her one and only litter of eight puppies. Incredibly, five of these pups have earned their OTCh. titles and are in the Golden Retriever Obedience Hall of Fame. In 1990, Sadie's puppy, Rocky, won the Superdog division at the Gaines/Cycle Western Regional and was second at the Classic, tying with his father "Reggie."

Sadie has achieved "stardom" in her own right. To date she has earned over 1,600 OTCh. points and 68 High-In-Trials along with three perfect scores of 200 from the Open B class.

Sadie has a unique little trick which makes her easily recognizable. If she has won a High-In-Trial and is asked to put on a demonstration, at the end of the demo she expresses her happiness by jumping right into Mike's arms!

For a dog to earn *all* of its OTCh. points in just seven weeks is nothing short of remarkable. Yet OTCh. Stardust Ruby Slippers accomplished this feat with relative ease. Owned and handled by Laurie Rubenfeld of Monsey, New York, this young bitch provided some breathtaking performances that held audiences in rapt attention. To date Laurie and Ruby have accumulated 29 High-In-Trials, two perfect scores of 200 and three Gaines Superdog placements. In 1988 Ruby captured the Gaines/Cycle Classic in Las Vegas.

Just mention the name "Arthur" in obedience circles and you find instant recognition even from people who don't necessarily own Goldens. When a dog is shown on the average of 60 times a year over a five year period and that dog qualifies 95% of the time in Open and Utility, it becomes something of a legend.

Formally, Arthur is known as Am-Can.OTCh. Glorybee Amber Arthur's Honor and has been owned and lovingly handled by Deborah Platt of Omaha, Nebraska. Arthur is a dignified charmer who has surmounted horrendous obstacles that would surely have defeated a lesser team. As a puppy, he was, to quote Debbie, "just a little country bumpkin from off the farm who was afraid of everything—objects, noises, new people, etc." It was through patience, love and a careful socialization and training program that Arthur

OTCh. Shoreland's Big Harry Deal (OS, HOF) (Chances R Cool Hand Luke CDX, MH,*** ex Shoreland's Somday Shahasta) bred, owned and trained by Suzanne Mayborne, Roscoe, Illinois. The 1988 and 1989 Gaines Central Regional Super Dog, 1989 World Series Top Dog, two 200 scores, and at ten years of age, when most dogs have retired, the 1989 Ken-L Ration Dog of the Year with a record 1,321 OTCh. points!

Here's **Harry**!

eventually matured into a solid, steady canine citizen.

At his very first show, Arthur went High-In-Trial from a Novice A class with a score of 198.5, and went on to finish his CD with all first places. In May of 1985 Arthur and Debbie finished their OTCh. within three weeks and nine shows.

In 1986, 1987 and 1988, this twosome captured the first place OTCh. and Ken-L-Ration award. Not content with only those accolades, Arthur won a career-dazzling 173 AKC High-In-Trials and accumulated over 4,500 OTCh. points at his retirement in 1989. Debbie proudly adds that Arthur became an official "Canine Good Citizen" in 1989 also.

Until his death in 1992, Arthur accompanied the Platts to the shows, entrenched in a plushly appointed bed upon which rested a very gray, but very wizened old muzzle.

A modest, unassuming man, Fred Einhorn of Chester, New York, and his stylish dog, OTCh. Meadowpond Stardust Reggie rank high among the great dogs of the '80s. In fact, Reggie at the age of nine continued to astound onlookers, having won the coveted Gaines Cycle Classic Super Dog Division in 1990 for the third time.

Reggie's talent for winning is not his only accomplishment. His offspring, whose numerous accomplishments are too vast to list, reads like a "Who's *Who*" in Goldens. His daughter, OTCh. Stardust Ruby Slippers and owner Laurie

Rubenfeld are but one of many who have graced the winners circle frequently.

Remarkably, Reggie has sired over 20 OTCh. dogs. This team's dazzling credits include over 50 High-In-Trials, 15 perfect scores at AKC trials, and two perfect scores at Gaines events.

Are you wondering how these high achievers made it to the top? The answer is through hard work, dedication, discipline and love. Golden Retrievers seem to thrive on a steady regimen of hard work, which is why they rarely ever burn out even at the age of ten or 11.

A large percentage of these handlers started by joining an obedience club or school. Some started with private instruction. Many began early training in puppy kindergarten classes which are a unique and highly enjoyable experience for both handler and pup.

After a bit of research, you should be able to locate classes in your area. Check with your local veterinarian for the names of clubs and schools

Deborah Platt and **Arthur** making it look effortless!

Am-Can. OTCh. Glorybee Amber Arthur's Honor CGC (HOF), (Ch. Glorybee's Bobby G CD ex Glorybee Tamarc Holly) bred by Jean and Ralph Madsen, owned by Deborah and Gary Platt, Omaha, Nebraska; trained, handled and spoiled by Debbie. Ranked Number One in OTCh. lifetime All-Breed points for four consecutive years, three-time Ken-L-Ration award winner, over 4,500 OTCh. points . . . a tough act to follow, but Arthur has done it . . . in other extraordinary ways.

HIGHEST SCORING DOG

that teach obedience. Vets are generally familiar with the dog activities that are conducted in the area. Pet shops and the local humane society are often excellent sources of this information.

Most handlers first honed their skills in very basic obedience classes. Some of these students were undoubtedly urged by their instructors to continue on with more advanced training. Many have been bitten by the bug as they watched these advanced classes. Dogs who are climbing the level of difficulty are required among other things to retrieve dumbbells, perform high and broad jumps, remain in a group Sit, then Down position for a period of time while the owners are out of sight. But this is getting ahead of the game, so let's start at the beginning.

Once a beginner thinks his dog is ready for obedience trial competition, he has options as to which organization to register his dogs. American Kennel Club obedience trials are held all over the United States on any given weekend of the year. The majority of dogs exhibited in obedience are registered with the AKC. Other registering bodies include the United Kennel Club based in Kalamazoo, Michigan and the States Kennel Club.

Though this is definitely oversimplifying the requirements, there are three levels of obedience classes which an exhibitor may enter at an American Kennel Club trial.

Level number one where you must start, which

you might equate with the human version of grammar school, is called "Novice." These are very elementary exercises. Dogs are required to heel on and off leash, execute what is called a "Stand For Examination," perform an exercise known as the "Recall," in which the dog must come running in promptly to the handler from a distance of about 30 feet. Finally dogs must take part in Group exercises. With other dogs in the class they must sit in place for one minute while their handlers stand across the ring from them. Once that is completed the dogs must do the Long Down for three minutes in the same manner.

At the next level, which is noticeably more difficult, dogs who have met the Novice qualifications may then be exhibited in the Open class. Here you might say the dogs have entered the high school level. These dogs must perform the Heel Off-leash, a Drop On Recall, a Retrieve on Flat, a retrieve of the dumbbell over the high jump and finally they must clear a broad jump. These advanced dogs must do a three-minute Group Sit and a five-minute Long Down with their owners out of sight.

OTCh. Meadowpond Stardust Reggie (OS, HOF) (Am-Can. Ch. Meadowpond Sugarbear Hondo CDX ex Nyland's Gandy Dancer) bred by Jeff Nyland, owned and trained to stardom by Alfred Einhorn, Chester, New York.

Reggie continues to set records . . . the second dog in history to win Super Dog and the sterling silver dumbbell three times, fifteen 200 scores, his winning offspring . . . the world of dog obedience is vastly richer for Reggie's contributions to the sport.

As you would expect, the last leg of the ladder, which we "dog folks" equate with college, is the most difficult level. In this class which is called "Utility," it becomes awesome as the dogs are put through their paces. For one exercise they will be worked without any voice commands and solely on hand signals.

Part of the regimen which puts their keen sense of smell to the test is the Scent Discrimination exercise. Dogs must go to a pile of small leather and metal dumbbells, of which there are nine on the floor. They must retrieve one article in the pile which has been scented by the handler. This is done twice. At large dog shows which draw vast numbers of spectators, this exercise never fails to elicit excited "ohhs" and "ahhs" along with hearty applause when the dog sniffs out the correct article and returns with it proudly to his handler.

Next on the agenda is the Directed Retrieve exercise. Handler,

Am-Can. OTCh. Meadowpond Angelic Abbey TD, WCX (OD, HOF) (Am-Can. Ch. Bardfield Boomer UDT,*, Can. UDTX ex Laurell's Jaunty Jinn-Jinn CDX), 1974–1987, bred by Cherie Berger, owned, loved and missed by Renee Schulte, Fair Haven, Michigan. As a World Series competitor, Abbey placed first four years in a row in consecutive classes, a record still standing through 1990.

using the left arm, point to one of three gloves dropped about 18 feet away. The dog must take the direction from the handler in retrieving one of the gloves that has been designated by the judge.

Then there is the Moving Stand. Handler is ordered by the judge to walk a dog into a Stand position. It is then given a hands-on examination by the judge, whereupon the judge orders the handler to call the dog. The dog must then trot smartly in to heel position.

The last exercise, the Directed Jumping, often tries the patience of both dog and handler. For many it is regarded as a tough exercise to teach. The dog is commanded to run out between a High Jump and a Bar Jump, going a distance of approximately 40 feet. It must be done twice, once jumping the High Jump on the handlers command, followed by the same procedure this time jumping the Bar Jump.

Getting back to the Golden Retriever achievers

of the 1980s, it is necessary to take note of Am-Can. OTCh. Meadowpond Angelic Abbey TD, WCX. This was Renee Schulte's first obedience dog, though you would never know it to watch this team in person. Abbey was a graceful, accurate worker who obviously enjoyed every step she took in the obedience ring. During the time she was campaigned, she easily made it to the GRCA Obedience Hall of Fame. With a career total of 25 High-In-Trials, the two placed in Gaines Cycle Tournaments, had four firsts in a row in the Top Ten Goldens and All-Breed obedience dogs in the 1979 Delaney System.

To many, Pauline Czarnecki and her animated, enthusiastic Goldens epitomize the style and panache that so many people associate with the breed. Following in the winning ways of her first great OTCh. Topbrass Cisco Kid, OTCh. Topbrass Windjammer finished his OTCh. on November 14, 1982. Jammer was a multiple

114

High-In-Trial dog who attained three perfect scores of 200. He was a first-place winner at the World Series and the Gaines/Cycle Regionals and Classics.

Miraculously finishing still another Golden only one month later on December 18, 1982 Pauline strutted along with OTCh. Meadowpond Strut, who enjoyed almost the same stellar career as his kennelmate Jammer. Strut was also a multiple-High-In-Trial dog who chalked up three 200 scores. He was also a first-place winner at all the tournaments.

Pauline's next dog Ch. Topbrass Break 'Em Up UD finished in the breed ring in 1986. Breaker also landed in the Hall of Fame as a multiple-High-In-Trial dog and an Outstanding Sire. In addition, he placed first in Novice at the Gaines/Cycle Regional in Nashville in 1986.

The uniqueness that Pauline brings to the annals of Golden Retriever fanciers is that she's one of the few exhibitors showing successfully in both obedience and conformation. In the past nine years, she has owner-handled three of her dogs to breed championships and obedience titles.

Husband and wife team Lynn and Joe Heidinger of Tinley Park, Illinois, had different breeds of dogs before Goldens entered the picture in 1980. Nowadays they often share the spotlight in the obedience ring. On more than one occasion, they laughingly find themselves in run-offs (ties) against one another.

Joe, who is a popular obedience judge, exhibited OTCh. Meadowpond's Autumn Blaze until 1983 attaining five HITs and 151 OTCh. points.

Ch. Topbrass Break 'Em Up UD (OS, HOF) (Am-Can. Ch. Kachina Twenty Karat ex Topbrass Dazzlin' Daisy Slade) bred by Judy Slayton and Jacquelyn Mertens, owned by Pauline Czarnecki, Chicago, Illinois, accumulated multiple HITs on his way to a breed championship.

OTCh. Topbrass Windjammer (OS, HOF) (Topbrass Knuckles CD,*** ex Ch.Topbrass Dazzlin' Daisy Slade) bred by Judy Slayton and Jacquelyn Mertens, and owned and trained to stardom by Pauline Czarnecki, Chicago, Illinois. Over thirty HITs, three perfect scores of 200, Top Dog at the World Series and Super Dog at the Gaines Classic . . . "Jammer" did it all and did it in grand style.

At the same time, Lynn's OTCh. Meadowpond's Roller Coaster was busy making a name for himself. When he was retired in 1988 with 949 OTCh. points, he had 23 High-In-Trials, placed in 1982 and 1985 at Gaines events, won the Open division of the World Series in 1984, then went on to win the Top Dog Division of the World Series in 1986.

While recovering from a bout with cancer in 1988, Lynn's courage was awe-inspiring during the time that she was campaigning her new Golden Meadowpond's High On Chemo. Born in October 1988, Chemo attained the coveted OTCh. just seven months from the time he was first shown in Novice! And all before the age of two! At three years of age, Chemo has over 26 High-In-Trials and 13 High-Combined scores.

It would take an entire chapter to list the accomplishments of Judith A. Myers of Hercules, California, whose Goldens have made

A trio of over-achieving obedience Goldens, owned, loved and trained by Joe and Lynn Heidinger, long-time exhibitors and judge from Tinley Park, Illinois.
Bottom: **OTCh. Meadowpond's Autumn Blaze (HOF)** (Am-Can. OTCh. Meadowpond Tackle ex Meadowpond's Lady Ginger) bred by Cherie Berger. Retired in 1988, Joe's first and always special obedience Golden.
Top left: **OTCh. Stardust Circus Time (HOF)** (OTCh. Meadowpond's Stardust Reggie ex Meadowpond Stardust Mist) Joe's succeeding obedience Golden and good friend.
Top right: **OTCh. Meadowpond's Roller Coaster (HOF)** (OTCh. Meadowpond's Happy Valentine ex Laurell's Jaunty Jinn-Jinn CDX) Lynn's retired competition Golden, World Series Top Dog in 1986, and Lynn's Top Dog forever.

folks sit up and take notice. In two years of showing, Am-Can. OTCh. Culynwood's Buckthorn Taiga TD, WC, earned over 350 OTCh. points, 33 first places and 12 High-In-Trial awards in the US and four HITs in Canada. She placed in the Open division of the 1983 Gaines/Cycle Classic and ranked among the top ten Goldens according to all national ranking systems in 1984 and 1985. She is a member of the GRCA Obedience Hall of Fame.

Her next Golden, Am-Can. OTCh. Culynwood's Miss Mindy II, or Karma as she is known to her admirers, earned over 165 OTCh. points, 23 first places, and nine High-In-Trial awards in the US and four High-In-Trials in Canada. Karma placed at the 1987 Western Gaines/Cycle Regional, fourth at the Classic, sixth at the 1988 Western Gaines/Cycle and third in 1988 in Open. She is a member of the GRCA Obedience Hall of Fame.

Four OTCh. relatives shown with their winnings at the 1988 Norcal GRC Winter Specialty. *Left to right:* **Am-Can. OTCh. Culynwood's Buckthorn Taiga TD, WC (HOF),** "Taiga," owned by Judy Myers; **Am-Can. OTCh. Splashdown Tess of Culynwood WCX (HOF),** "Tess," owned by Dee Dee Anderson; **OTCh. Culynwood's Field Mouse Can. CD** "Minnie"; **Am-Can. OTCh. Culynwood's Miss Mindy II (HOF),** "Karma," owned by Judy Myers. The judge was Luane Vidak.

One of the top competitors in Southern California is Karen Price, whose beautifully trained Goldens emphasize the keen working ability of the breed. OTCh. Sunfire Spontaneous Combustion JH, WCX or "Flash" is her second OTCh. and her second dog that has reached the GRCA Obedience Hall of Fame. An engaging and enticing fellow who is bold and brash one moment, then mellow and mindful the next, Flash and

Karen continue to impress all who watch them perform. Thus far in his career Flash has 150 OTCh. points, 13 High-In-Trials, nine High Combined scores, one AKC 200 score and another 200 in the California State Obedience Competition.

Showing OTCh. Hi-Point's Skip Off The Ol' Block TDX, WC (OS, HOF), Judy Lee of Illinois enjoys every moment that she shares with "Blockie." In Judy's own words she says, Blockie is one of those truly special, once-in-a-lifetime dogs. His combination of characteristics—gentle, loving and devoted, and yet full of enthusiasm for

Am-Can. OTCh. Culynwood's Buckthorn Taiga TD, WC (HOF), "Taiga." Owner, Judith A. Myers. (Splashdown Sky-Lab Syndicate*** ex Am-Can. Ch. Culynwood's Spirit of America CDX, WCX, Can. CDX).
In two years of showing competitively, Taiga earned over 350 OTCh. points, 33 first places, and 12 High-In-Trial awards in the US and four High-In-Trials in Canada. She placed in the Open Division of the 1983 Gaines Classic and ranked among the Top Ten Goldens according to all national ranking systems in 1984 and ranked among the top ten of all breeds according to the Shuman System in 1985. She is a member of the GRCA Obedience Hall of Fame. She is shown winning High In Trial at the 1985 Norcal GRC Summer Specialty.

Am-Can. OTCh. Culynwood's Miss Mindy II (HOF), "Karma." Owner, Judith A. Myers. (Culynwood's Rough Rider WCX, **, ex Am-Can. OTCh. Splashdown Tess of Culynwood WCX). Karma earned over 165 OTCh. points, 23 first places, and nine High-In-Trial awards in the US and four High In Trials in Canada. In Gaines competition, Karma placed seventh at the 1987 Western Regional and fourth at the 1987 Classic in Novice and sixth at the 1988 Western Regional and third at the 1988 Classic in Open. She is a member of the GRCA Obedience Hall of Fame. She is shown winning High In Trial and High-Combined at the Sacramento Kennel Club Show in 1989.

his work—has allowed him to excel in obedience, tracking, and field. Like his father, Judy's OTCh. Rocky Mtn. Skipper puts his heart into everything he does..."

His record certainly proves what Judy claims: 48 High-In-Trials, nine High-Combined awards, second place Novice division 1986 World Series, third place, Novice 1986 Gaines/Cycle Regional and second place Novice at 1986 Gaines/Cycle Classic, first place Open division, 1987 Gaines Cycle Regional, 10th place Open division, World Series, Sixth place Open division, 1987 Classic and sixth place, Top Dog 1990 World Series.

1990 was not a great year for Nancy Patton of Lilburn, Georgia. Not that her great dog OTCh. Locknor B Fifty-Two Bomber let her down. He didn't. Nancy, who had more than her share of severe problems with rheumatoid arthritis, also underwent some very serious surgery. If it bothered her, you'd never know, because her courage, fortitude and determination turned 1991 into a banner year.

By the end of 1991, this tremendous team had captured an incredible 57 High-In-Trials, and 1,462 OTCh. points in '91 alone. A feat which earned Bomber the prestigious 1991 Ken-L-Ration Obedience Trial Champion of the Year award. Altogether Bomber has a career high of 134 High-In-Trials.

Nancy and Bomber have three 200 scores and ranked ninth All-Breed in 1990, though only shown for four months that year. They have placed in Gaines/Cycle events eight times, placing tenth in Superdog at the 1990 Classic.

Bomber is that special dog in Nancy's life. Jokingly she notes that she feels they are bonded at the hip. "I didn't realize," she said, "how close we were until I came home from the hospital after my

illness. Before that time Bomber always slept in the hall at our bedroom door. From the moment that I returned, he has slept at the side of my bed. Two or three times during the night, I feel his cold nose on my face as though he's checking to be sure I'm still there."

This is but one small trait that endears the Golden Retriever to its owners everywhere. The caring and sensitivity that are manifested by these marvelous creatures 365 days a year lend an almost human quality to their bearing.

OTCh. Hi-Point's Skip Off the Ol' Block TDX, WC (OS, HOF) (OTCh. Rocky Mtn. Skipper ex Wynwood's Yuletide Tallie CDX) bred, owned and trained by Judy Lee, Pleasant Plains, Illinois. "Blockie's" great enthusiasm for his obedience work is best expressed by his prancing heeling gait, the speed with which he works the exercises, his absolute, undivided attention, and his frequent "woof" between or finishing the exercises. His ability to combine this eagerness with remarkable accuracy makes him a truly exceptional obedience competitor.

If you are curious as to how Golden Retrievers have fared as they attained their various titles, the following statistics will definitely interest you:

YEAR	CD	CDX	UD	OTCh.	TD	TDX
1992	824	308	129	32	61	14
1991	831	335	118	26	70	16
1990	895	341	133	30	70	11
1989	814	370	127	20	55	8
1988	954	267	104	24	73	9
1987	934	272	91	24	64	8
1986	846	293	86	20	57	9
1985	1050	313	110	43	83	17
1984	869	265	99	9	65	10
1983	1041	298	97	19	59	9

OTCh. Locknor B Fifty-Two Bomber (HOF), owned by Nancy Patton, Lilburn, Georgia. A spec tacular obedience team, Bomber and Nancy have eight Gaines Classic placements and three enviable 200 scores. In 1990 they competed for only four months, yet placed ninth in the all-breed obedience rankings with an amazing 1,123 OTCh. points. In 1991 they surged forward again, with 1,125 of OTCh. points and 57 HITs, for a career record-breaking 134 HITs. For that year, they also placed first in the Delaney System with 7,095 points (scoring higher than over 7,000 dogs). This team has the rare distinction of winning both the Delaney and First and Foremost Systems.

Right: **Ch. OTCh. Pekay's Deliverance TD, WCX** (Ch. Misty Morn's Sunset CD, TD, WC ex Honor's High Stakes) owned by Nancy Patton of Lilburn, Georgia, and Kitty Cathey. "Banjo," one of only ten Ch.-OTCh. Goldens, Nancy's first Golden, is the one who showed her how to "do it all."

Below: **Windfall's Quantock Joshua CD, Can. CDX** owned by Eileen Bohn of Zimmerman, Minnesota.

Above: **Malcairns Brass Fanfare UD, SH, WCX, ✳✳** is owned by Julie Cairns of Arcata, California.

Below: **Chances R Wizard of Wonders UD, WCX** (Bonnie Brook's Mortimer ✳✳ ex Chances R Milady) "Butch," bred by the author, owned, trained and missed by Bridget Carlsen, Sandwich, Illinois. The Midwest obedience world remembers well this flashy, high-powered Golden and his diminutive, 16-year-old trainer. He adored her.

Ch. Dasu's Better Mousetrap UD, WC (Am-Can., OTCh. Sunstreak of Culynwood TD, WCX, Can. CD ex Ch. Dasu's Champagne Edition CDX) bred, owned and trained by Dave and Suzi Bluford, Carmel, California. "Trapper's" flashy, high-stepping footwork was his trademark, and won him many fans in obedience as well as in the breed ring.

Facing page and This page: **OTCh. Altair's Sarduakar Sadie (OD, HOF)** (Ch. Sun Destiny's Echo CDX ex Meadowpond Cherokee Sunday Am-Can. UD) bred by John and Nancy Janoch, owned, trained and pampered by Michael MacDonald. Sadie's sterling obedience record and star-studded litter of obedience over-achievers is enough to thrill any Golden owner. But her survival and recovery in 1989 from an emergency spleen removal is the win that pleases Michael most. As Sadie entered surgery, thoughts of first place, HIT or High Combined were no longer important . . . all Mike wanted was for her to be okay and come back home. Now they show just to have fun, and do very little training, an arrangement that Mike and Sadie both enjoy.

Siverado's Emmet UD owned by Marsha Ross Dandridge, Sacramento, California, is a perfect role model for both Golden obedience dogs and service dogs. Before this win, they earned a Dog World award in Open, and two HITs, one with a 199.5 score in Open A!

A super win for **"Sadie"** and Michael MacDonald, taking second at the 1987 Eastern Regional Gaines Competition.

Terri Arnold and the incomparable **OTCh. Meadowpond Keepin' in Stride (OS, HOF)** winning Super Dog at Gaines Regional.

Stride and Terri Arnold winning a perfect "200" under Dick Chirst, the first ever awarded by this judge in 25 years.

A rare and special occurrence. Four Goldens place first through fourth, win HIT and High-Combined in the Open B class at an all-breed show. All four are Tess's kids, three are sired by Thumper. *Left to right:* First place and HIT **DD's Little Joey,** owner-handler, Gloria McGrath; second place **OTCh. DD's Calaveras Sparklin' Gold WC,** owner-handler, Janet Naylor; third place **OTCh. Culynwood's Miss Mindy II,** owner-handler, Judy Myers; fourth place and High-Combined **OTCh. DD's Culynwood Cotton Lace,** owner-handler, Lisa Hall.

At the GRCA National 1986, this unique team of Beckwith Champions includes: **OTCh. Beckwith's Hennessy Five Star TDX, Can. WC; Am-Can. Ch. Beckwith's Normandee Rose CDX, Can. WC; Am-Can. Ch. Beckwith's Easter Celebrity UDT, WCX;** and **Am-Can. Ch. Beckwith's Main Event Am-Can. UDT, JH, Can. WC.** Breeder of these obedient victors, Mr. and Mrs. R. E. Beckwith of Snohomish, Washington; Photo by Fox and Cook.

A bench champion-UD Golden is every breeder/owner's dream. But three of them in one family is a fairy tale come true. The Ronnie Bizer household in Maple Park, Illinois, is home to these three very special Golden Retrievers. They joined the family while the Bizers were living in Alaska.

Top: **Ch. Amberac's Aurora Sunshine Am-Can. UD,** "Sunny." (Ch. Amberac's Casino Royale ex Amberac's Brandy Wine Rose UD) bred by Terry Rademaker. While still in the whelping box, Sunny "picked" Ronnie, and went on to prove herself worthy of Bizer Golden versatility. A multiple-HIT and Group placer, she is solidly entrenched as one of the Bizer foundation bitches.

Bottom left: **Ch. Meadowpond Aurora Chugach Am-Can. UD,** "Chinook," (Ch.- OTCh. Gold-Rush Wild Trout ex Meadowpond Tango Dancer) bred by Cherie Berger, became a champion with three consecutive five-point majors, and completed his CDX with a first place the same day he finished his championship. By age two he had earned his Canadian UD, in three consecutive trials, as well as his American UD, placing in each of the US trials.

Bottom right: **Am-Can. Ch. Laurell's Aurora Daybreak Am-Can. UD,** "Hope." (Ch. Amberac Tackled Mybowser ex Laurell's Sunn Do and Sunn Don't) bred by Laura Ellis Kling. Hope fit right into the busy Bizer schedule. She became a multiple-HIT bitch, and a Group winner from the classes. She placed first in Open B on the same day she took the Group.

OTCh. Topbrass Ric O Shay Barty WCX (OS, HOF) (AFC Holway Barty ex Ch. Sunstream Gypsy of Topbrass) bred by Jacquelyn and Joseph Mertens, owned, trained and forever missed by Sharon Long, El Paso, Illinois. An obedience mega-star, Ric was the ultimate showman. Accustomed to being photographed for his many wins, whenever Ric spotted the show photographer, he would leap up onto the nearest table, thrust out his chest and pose, assuming that every camera lens was for him. Also the ultimate teammates , he and Sharon were always in sync, both in the ring and in the heart.

Left: **Ch.-OTCh. Gold-Rush Wild Trout, WC (OS, HOF)** (Am-Can-Bda. Ch. Cummings Gold-Rush Charlie ex Ch. Jungold's Gold-Rush Hope), 1977–1990, bred by R. Ann Johnson and Larry Johnson, owned and trained by Joan and Tony Jung, Lancaster, Texas. One of only ten Ch.- OTCh. Goldens in breed history. Despite Trout's success in the breed and obedience rings, his first and strongest love was retrieving birds. Joan broke several leads while teaching him to honor. On one occasion, while tied to a rowboat, Trout pulled the entire boat into the water when he saw Joan working another dog!

Am-Can-Bda. Ch. Bargello's Cymbidium Am-Can. CD (OS) bred by Barbara Tinker of Katonah, New York. Cymbi is five years old in this photograph. His talented offspring are bench champions who also sport CDX, JH, and WCX titles.

Am-Can. Ch. Ambertrail's Flatbush Flanagan Am-Can. CD, (OS), bred by Mike and Val Ducross and owned by Barbara Tinker.

Barbara Tinker with **"Just"** at age three. Formally this is **Am-Can. Ch.Bargello's Fair and Square Am-Can. CDX, Am-Can. WCX.**

Rocky Mountain Gold XXVII CDX, JH, WC owned by Rita Robins, Dallas, Texas. Rocky came to Rita at age four from an abusive home . . . her first Golden, her first obedience dog, her trial-and-error dog. Always willing to learn and eager to please, he coerced her into the obedience ring and proved that, yes, you can teach an old dog new tricks.

Above: **Am-Can. Ch.-Am-Can.OTCh. Gold Country's Timber Flash (HOF),** (Sham-O-Jets Luv-a-Mike ex Rainbow's Tupelo Honey), owned by Bill Kopecko, Minocqua, Wisconsin. "Tim" was a beautiful, intelligent dog, an important family member and an excellent hunter.
Below: **Mekin's Gold Satin Dancer UD, WC, Can. CDX,** owned by Janet Dupree of Elmira, New York. Janet's first Golden and Utility Dog.

OTCh. Pekay's Rocky Mtn. Skipper (HOF) (Ch. Captain Neil's Goldstorm CD, WCX ex Pekay's Pawprint CDX), owned and trained by Judy Lee, Pleasant Plains, Illinois. Skipper's tremendous joy and enthusiasm in his work always captivated spectators at the obedience ring. He garnered 16 HITs and top ten placings in the Gaines Regional and World Series. His heeling on the "fast" was so exuberant, Judy often struggled just to keep up with him.

Am-Can. OTCh. Meadowpond Angelic Abbey TD, WCX (OD, HOF) owned by Renee Schulte, with just one litter of pups produced four OTCh., two UD, one TDX, CDX, and WCX. Her battle with cancer at seven years of age was Abbey's greatest victory; she died in 1987 at almost 13 years of age.

Yes, my name is "Stitch". Bred by Mike and Val Ducross, **Am-Can. Ch. Ambertrail's Bargello Stitch Am. UDTX, WCX, Bda. UDTX (OD)** is a multi-talented Golden who has sewn up many impressive titles. Owned by Barbara Tinker. Photograph by Paul Korker.

OTCh. DD's Cher (OS, HOF) (OTCh. DD's Tagalong Thumper TD, JH, WC, Can. CDX ex Am-Can. OTCh. Splashdown Tess of Culynwood WCX) bred by Dee Dee and Billy Anderson and Lynn Fletcher, trained and handled by Billy, and owned by Richard Wejmar and the Andersons.

DD's Tagalong Thumper TD, JH, WC, Can. CDX (OS, HOF) (Culynwoods Courageous WCX ex OTCh. DD's Nuggett of Gold TD, WCX, Can. CDX) bred, trained and handled by Dee Dee Anderson. This was Dee Dee's best friend—above all he protected and loved his mistress.

OTCh. Topbrass Supercharger WC (HOF) owned by Bonnie and Lew Baker of Tomball, Texas.

Am-Can. OTCh. Culynwood's Miss Mindy II (HOF) and **Am-Can. OTCh. Culynwood's Buckthorn Taiga TD, WC (HOF)** owned by Judith A. Myers of Hercules, California.

OTCh. Topbrass Supercharger WC (HOF) (AFC Wildfire of Riverview CDX ex Topbrass Butter Up) bred by Joseph and Jackie Mertens, owned by Bonnie Baker, Tomball, Texas. Bonnie has always felt Charger could do almost anything. With Dog World awards in Open and Utility, a hefty 28 HITs, one perfect score of 200 and Gaines Regional and Classic wins to his credit, Charger apparently agrees with her.

Am-Can. Ch.,-OTCh. Meadowpond Simon Sez UDT, JH, WC, VCX, TT, Can. CDX (Ch. Meadowpond Crowd Pleaser CDX ex Meadowpond Tango Dancer) bred by Cherie Berger, owned and trained by Judy Super-Borton, Plymouth, Minnesota. Already a superstar in the '80s, in 1991 Simon entered Golden Retriever breed history when he captured HIT at the GRCA National Specialty, to become the tenth bench champion to also hold an OTCh. title. Simon is the first Golden to achieve that elite status at a National Specialty event . . . a special occasion . . . for a special dog.

The superstars from the Heidingers: **Timer, Blazer** and **Coaster** for short enjoying a fisherman's afternoon.

Am-Can. OTCh. Splashdown Tess of Culynwood UD, WCX (OD, HOF) (NAFC-FC Topbrass Cotton ex Splashdown Culynwood Spirit) bred by John Cavalier and Cynthia Williams. 1981–1988. Tess earned her CD, CDX, UD, WC and WCX, by 20 months of age, the youngest Golden to earn those combined titles. Top Obedience Golden in 1985, number two all-breed in OTCh. points, Gaines classic winner, the youngest dog . . . and Dee Dee the youngest handler . . . ever to win. Multiple HITS, awards and wins. Tess' biggest win . . . her get from three litters includes five OTCh. and five UD.

OTCh. Culynwood's Field Mouse WCX, Can. CD (Culynwood's Rough Rider WCX,** ex Am-Can. OTCh. Splashdown Tess of Culynwood UD, WCX) bred by Dee Dee Anderson, owned by Lynn Fletcher, Billy and Dee Dee, trained and handled by Billy.

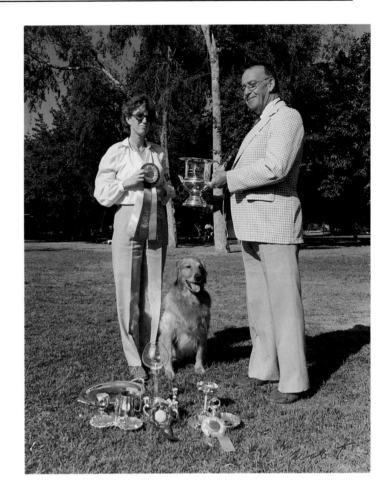

OTCh. Ciders Golden Bear (HOF), owned by L. Williamson, has won ten High-In-Trial awards, as well as a third place Super Dog (Gaines Regional) and High-Combined score awards. Bear entered the GRCA Hall of Fame in 1982 and earned his obedience title in 1983. The Williamsons live in San Bernadino, California.

Below: **Ch. Daystar Small Craft Warning** (Am-Can. Ch. Trowsnest Whirlwind UD, *, Can. CDX ex Am-Can. Ch. Gosling Daystar's Dawn CDX, WC) bred by Zelia Bohsen, owned by Pauline Czarnecki, Chicago, Illinois.

Am-Can. Ch. Candlewick's Magic Cahain CDX, WC, JH, Can. CD, WC (OD) owned by Janine Fiorito, Croton, New York. A high-stepping, very attentive heeler, Magic took three HITs while going for her Canadian obedience title.

Dynamite—**Can. Ch. Sunfire's Kinetic Dynamite UD, JH, WCX, Can. UD, WCI.** (Ch. Captain Neil's Goldstorm CD, WCX ex Sunfire's Kinetic Ruffian CD, WC). Breeder: Barbara F. Biewer and Susan A. Simmons. Owners: Michael A. Book and Barbara F. Biewer.

Ritz—**Am-Can. Ch. Comstock Sunfire O'Hillcrest UDT, MH, WCX, VCX, Can. CDX, WCI.** (Can. Ch. Comstock Caramel Nut UDTX, SH, WCX, Can. UD, WCX ex Sunfire's Breila of Bristol CD, JH, WCX, **. Breeder: Jean Loveland. Owner: Kathryn Eddy VMD, M.A. Book and B. F. Biewer. One of two dogs in breed with Ch.-UD-MH; trained and handled in field and obedience by Kathy Eddy McCue.

Am-Can. OTCh. Splashdown Tess of Culynwood UD, WCX (OD, HOF) taking HIT. Owners, Dee and Billy Anderson.

FC-AFC Tigathoe's Kiowa II (OS) (FC-AFC-CFC Bonnie Brook's Elmer ex Tigathoe's Chickasaw ***) owned by Pat Sadler, Sandy Hook, Connecticut and bred by Mrs. George Flinn. Kiowa was born at his owner's house . . . at three weeks old, he picked Pat for his very own. She hardly noticed Ki's brother, destined for Retriever stardom . . . Dual Ch.-AFC Tigathoe's Funky Farquar. Kiowa was a "good" Golden, as often overheard in the field trial gallery, and taught beginner Pat the field trial game from the ground up. Only now that he is gone, and Pat has trained many other dog's, does she truly understand and appreciate Ki's amazing natural marking ability, his regal and unflappable personality, and his "whatever you want, I'll do it for you" attitude. A once-in-a-lifetime dog.

The Field Trial Golden

This chapter on the field trial golden is enhanced by contributions from several experienced and long-time Golden Retriever breeders and field trainers. My sincere appreciation to the following people (in alphabetical order) who graciously shared their time and experience with me.

Bruce Curtis, Alma, Wisconsin, has specialized in training young retrievers since 1979. During his apprenticeship under professional trainer Jim Kappes, Bruce developed a four-month program to teach novice dogs basic field skills and build a solid foundation for more advanced training. Forty-five to 50 dogs a year from the Midwest and East and West coasts attend "boot camp" at the Curtis Kennel in Alma, Wisconsin. About 30 of the dogs who began their trial careers under Bruce went on to earn field championships under other trainers and handlers.

Mrs. George H. "Torch" Flinn, Jr. Greenwich, Connecticut, bought two Goldens in 1947 and has been running Goldens in field trials ever since. Of the 24 Goldens she has owned and campaigned over the past 40-plus years, eight became bench champions, five became FC-AFC, one an AFC, one Can. FC, and one FC-AFC, Can. Dual Ch., 18 reached qualified All-Age status, and several others earned over 20 Derby points. Additionally, under the Tigathoe prefix, she has bred at least a dozen field champions, as well as the last Golden in breed history to earn a dual championship, Dual Ch.-AFC Tigathoe's Funky Farquar. She has an outlook enriched by four decades of living and working with field trial Golden Retrievers.

Professional trainer **Michael Lardy,** Montello, Wisconsin, grew up with the famous Handjem Golden Retrievers. Under the watchful eye of his father, Handjem founder Henry Lardy, Mike handled his first Golden puppy to second place in a puppy trial when he was nine years old. A professional trainer since 1981, he has trained and titled over 30 field champions and has been instrumental in the careers of at least three Golden Retriever field champions. His experience training Goldens as well as Labradors adds another dimension to his perspective on today's field trial Golden.

Jackie Mertens of Topbrass Goldens, Elgin, Illinois, is best known for having bred and campaigned NAFC-FC Topbrass Cotton, the only Golden Retriever to achieve a National Amateur Championship. Cotton is also the all-time High Point All-Age Golden Retriever. Through 1992 Jackie had bred and trained eight field champions and has owned and trialed several others. Topbrass Goldens have been the foundation dogs for several other successful lines of Goldens in the field and obedience rings.

Mickey Strandberg, Dousman, Wisconsin, has bred, raised and trained field trial Goldens under the Mioaks prefix for some 20 years. She bred AFC Mioaks Raincheck, and bred and trained FC-AFC Mioak's Main Event and CFC-CAFC Mioak's Shake N'Jake through their basic training programs and into qualifying placements. She has also bred and/or trained over two dozen qualified All-Age Goldens and many Derby list Goldens (ten or more points), including three of the top ten all-time High-Point Derby Goldens.

"Torch" Flinn and **FC-AFC Chips of Sands,** field-trial star of the '70s and '80s.

FC-AFC Tangelo's Sidekick "Pardner" (OS, HOF) (Sungold Sandkicker *** ex Troymar Shahasta Spring WCX) bred by Ted and Pat Gross, owned by Bill and Terry Woods, Fresno, California. Multiple National qualifier, top ten high point All-Age Golden, yet Bill and Terry are proudest that, despite his ability and accomplishments, Pardner is truly a nice guy.

Four of the seven Goldens on the 1990 Derby list carried the Mioaks kennel name.

Valerie Walker, Medford, Oregon, was born into a Golden Retriever field trial family and went to her first field trial at six years old. She founded her Sungold line in 1965 with her first Golden, FC-AFC Misty's Sungold Lad CDX, the all-time High Point Golden until 1986, and still the Golden with the highest number of points per trial run. When Val married in 1971, her husband had Labradors; somehow Sungold didn't fit. They devised their own kennel name of Trieven for their Goldens and their blacks. Val's Sungold lines are still behind many of the leading field trial and hunting test Goldens today.

Terry and Bill Woods, Fresno, California, have trained field trial Goldens since 1970 and breed them under the Tangelo prefix. Like most amateurs, they train their own dogs with little professional assistance. Bill and Terry trained AFC Sungold T-Bill Sunsplasher MH and FC-AFC Tangelo's Sidekick to their field titles and have bred and trained seven other qualified All-Age Goldens.

The purpose of a Non-Slip Retriever field trial, paraphrased from the *AKC Field Trial Rules and Standard Procedure* manual, is to determine the relative merits of purebred retrievers in the field. The tests therefore are designed to simulate as nearly as possible the conditions encountered in an ordinary day's shoot. The dogs are tested on both land and water on marked and blind retrieves.

The function of a Non-Slip Retriever (non-slip meaning one who does not move or go until sent) is to find and retrieve "fallen" game under all conditions when ordered to do so. He should walk at heel and sit quietly on command, and when sent, should retrieve briskly and deliver gently to hand. Marking is of primary importance, and the dog that marks the fall of a bird, uses the wind, follows a strong cripple, and takes direction from his handler is of great value.

Dogs are judged for their natural abilities, including memory, intelligence, attention, nose, courage, perseverance and style, as well as for their abilities acquired through training, including steadiness, control, response to direction, and delivery, and the ability to retrieve any type of game bird under all conditions. The dog must not injure the game, retrieve decoys or retrieve without having been ordered to do so.

A blind retrieve is a bird hidden from view of the dog, where only the handler knows the placement of the bird. On a blind retrieve the dog must obey his handler by taking a line to the bird, by stopping to the whistle to take direction to the right or left, back or return. The handler of the dog is also under judgement and must not touch his dog or exhibit unsportsman-like conduct.

The regular official stakes at a Retriever trial are Derby, Qualifying (minor stakes) and Open All-Age, Limited All-Age, Special All-Age, Amateur All-Age and Owner-Handler Amateur All-Age (major stakes).

The Derby stake is open to dogs under two years of age. Tests consist of single or double marked retrieves on land and water and/or a combination of both.

The Qualifying stake is open to dogs of any age who have not won two first places in the Qualifying stake, or a Judges Award of Merit (JAM) or higher in any Open stake, or fourth place or better in an Amateur stake. Dogs are tested in two land series and two water series consisting of multiple marked and blind retrieves. Dogs who place first or second in a Qualifying stake earn qualified All-Age status.

Placements in the major stakes earn championship points. Open points apply toward a Field Championship (FC) and Amateur points apply toward an Amateur Field Championship (AFC).

The Amateur stake is open to amateur handlers or amateur owner-handlers. Tests include multiple marked and blind retrieves on land and in water at a greater level of difficulty than found in minor stakes.

The Open stake is available to professional as well as amateur handlers and involves land and water series similar to the Amateur, but often with a greater level of difficulty.

Complete details on rules, procedures and eligibility can be found in the official AKC registration and rule book for Retriever Field Trials.

The field trial Golden has been a source of controversy for longer than most arbiters recall. Questions raging over Goldens as an endangered field trial species have persisted since 1939, the year Paul Bakewell's FC Rip made Golden field trial history when he became the first American Golden Retriever Field Champion.

In those early field trials, Labradors outnumbered and outran most Goldens. They still do. Less than 10 percent of trial dogs today are Goldens, slightly less than the figure 50 years ago. Indeed, in Mrs. W.M. Charlesworth's 1947 book *The Golden Retriever,* she recalls that in 1931, the first year for AKC-licensed field trials, 18 Goldens won in trials compared to 153 Labradors on that year's winners' list.

Today there are also more Labradors born than Goldens. In 1989 and 1990, AKC-regis-

tered Labs outnumbered Goldens by over 26,000 and 31,000 respectively. That numerical superiority also translates into an advantage in any field of competition.

From 1980 through 1990, 40 Goldens earned Field Champion or Amateur Field Champion status, equal the number of titles gained during the 1970s. Yet despite keeping pace with the previous decade, the retriever world is less than optimistic about the prospect for Goldens in the field trial of the future.

Sorting through those questions and possible solutions has become a favorite pastime of both

AFC Sungold's T-Bill Sunsplasher (HOF), "Splash," (Amber's Diablo Rock *** ex Sungold Black Velvet) bred by Valerie Walker, owned by Mike Lauderdale and Bill Woods. Shown here with Terry Giffen Woods.

Sungold Shilo SH, owned by Valerie Walker, Trieven Retrievers, Medford, Oregon.

creasingly difficult. Today's trials are more intense, the competition even more so. Today's field trial Labrador is evolving into a breed unto itself and tougher than ever to beat.

Training techniques have also affected the progress of the Golden in the field. So much so that many trialers send their young Goldens to professional specialists to instill the solid foundation in basic training necessary to persevere through several years of complex field trial work.

Bruce Curtis sees little difference in the Goldens he trains today from those he worked with a dozen years ago. "I've had some very intense young Goldens, with a desire level equal to the Labs," he related, "and most of them are just as trainable as the blacks." Bruce emphasized, however, that he trains *each* dog differently, Labs as well as Goldens, according to its personality. "I don't do anything different because it's a Golden," Bruce said. "I just adapt the training to suit the dog." Bruce feels that problems with the field trial Golden may be more obvious simply because there are so few of them, and so many more Labs.

Training techniques such as those developed by Bruce and other professionals have also impacted the progress of the Golden in the field. Jackie Mertens observed that the caliber of today's training methods is superb. "The quality of the dog a professional trainer produces is hard for the average amateur to compete with unless he is very dedicated and has a truly talented dog. It's much harder to train for this level of difficulty unless you have a spectacular animal," she said.

Recalling the tests she and FC-AFC Topbrass Mandy ran in their first National in 1980, Jackie said, "They would be easy Amateur tests today, and some might even be considered tough Qualifying tests."

Mike Lardy described a typical '90s' Open water test as a quad (four marks), with two retired guns, (guns that are hidden after the fall of the bird), that takes 20 minutes for each dog to complete. By the time the dog returns to the line with the third bird, it has to remember what happened 18 minutes ago. "While pinpoint

the field-trial fancier and critic. Observations on the breed and sport abound: today's field trials hardly simulate an "ordinary day's shoot"; today's Golden is softer than its field-trial ancestors; it lacks the intensity or drive necessary to survive the '90s' tests . . . the '90s' Golden is too intelligent....or not smart enough; Goldens are better amateur dogs....conversely, a good one will work willingly with a good pro; it's moodier, worries too much, thinks too much; a good dog is a good dog, regardless of the breed, and the counter-claim.....good, yes, but still different.

Yet overall, the field trial community agrees that Goldens haven't really changed that much. Although physically the field Golden of today is smaller, finer boned and faster due to the intensive linebreeding of the past two decades, the greater change is in the field trial work itself, which has become much more precise and in-

Mioak's Golden Torch (OD) (AFC Wildfire of Riverview CD ex Mioak's Ginger ***) bred and owned by Mickey Strandberg. Full-sister to FC-AFC Mioak's Main Event, dam of one AFC, over ten qualified All-Age and Derby List dogs.

marking is a natural ability in a dog," he said, "as the marks become more difficult, marking becomes a function of trainability."

Mike also feels the trial dogs of the Poika (Poika of Handjem) and Elmer (FC-AFC-CFC Bonnie Brook's Elmer) generation were tougher mentally and better able to withstand the pressure of field trial training. "The old Goldens had a more aggressive reaction to pressure, and some would go after the owner or trainer when things got rough," he recalled. "Today's dog gets nervous and worries a lot and doesn't handle the pressure as well."

Mike finds that nervous reaction to training pressure is unique to most of today's highly successful AFC Yankee's Smoke'N Red Devil strain of field dogs. He also feels the electronic collar method of training is superior for this type of dog because the dog understands it better, and it's less personal and more humane than the older methods of physical correction.

HR Ch Trieven's Magic Marker MH, a Mighty Mo daughter, bred by Val Walker, owned and trained by Tony Dotson.

Mickey Strandberg agrees the field trial Golden is more sensitive to pressure, a little softer than it used to be, and attributes that difference to breeding practices which have failed to pursue a variety of lines from which to breed. "It's not a matter of more intelligence or less drive," she said, "just less ability to take pressure. A Golden worries so much more about getting a correction. It's a more complex dog, so you just have to adapt your training to this type of dog and be more patient, use a little more psychology."

Mickey also finds that Goldens respond better to collar training because it's less physical and more indirect. "But it's not a wonder tool," she warned. "It's just another training tool and has to be used carefully. If it's used by people who don't know what they're doing or have poor timing, it will be no more effective than anything else."

Torch Flinn is equally emphatic about cautious use of the electronic collar. "In ignorant hands, it can be a menace," she said. "It's so easy to just press a button. I think anyone who buys one should be required to take a short course on its use and misuse."

Does the Golden train and perform better for its amateur owner than for a professional trainer?

AFC Gold Mark Bicentennial Blue, (FC-AFC Kinike Chancellor ex FC-AFC Tigathoe's Magic Marker) owned by Helen and Harvey Phillips. Helen mused . . . "I wish we could have him again at age one. Positively the best marker we have ever seen . . . he would have been unbeatable if trained by today's methods."

Jackie believes a talented field Golden is no different than a Lab. "All of the early titled Goldens were pro-trained. My titled Goldens have all been with a pro at one time or another and have done very well, and there are some pro-run Goldens today that also perform well."

Torch agrees. "A good dog is a good dog," she said. "Of all the dogs I've had, all but one were happy to work for whomever took them out of the crate to train them. A dog who is training one-on-one with an amateur may be very happy and mark well, but tucked in the back of that little dog's mind is a lack of respect for someone who has not *made* him do things he didn't want to do."

However, Mickey believes the Golden owner has the edge when training his own dog. "The Golden is so people-oriented and has a more diversified personality. He needs more affection and has so much of it to give, so he thrives under more personal attention. In the Labrador, just the joy of working is all it needs. The Golden also likes to work, but he likes to climb in your lap when he's done. I've had a lot of Goldens who don't do as well with a pro as they do on a one-to-one basis."

Val Walker agrees the one-on-one association is important, especially for the Golden puppy and adolescent because it is usually more sensitive and responsive. "A Lab retrieves for itself, and a Golden retrieves and works for its handler, so the early socialization and foundation is very important with a Golden."

Val has found the Golden grows in style and drive as it matures, and said in the past she washed out youngsters who later developed into very competitive dogs.

Mike feels that may be one of the reason some amateur-owned and trained Goldens endure and make it to their titles. "Goldens are slower to mature, and through patience and putting-up-with, an amateur trainer will persist in cases where a pro may give up sooner."

And that may be the most significant fact about the working Golden and its person. "Perhaps more Golden people are one-dog oriented," Mike observed, "and if the dog doesn't make it, they will live with the dog anyway. In a typical scenario, people keep the dog and adjust their sport to suit the dog's ability."

That scenario is true at Tangelo Goldens in California. Terry Woods feels she and Bill usually adjust their goals to suit the dog. "We've been lucky because we've had "Pardner" (FC-AFC Tangelo's Sidekick) who's done very well for us, but we also have "Bruin" who is five and has only earned one second place in a Qualifying. But he's such a fun little dog with a great sense of humor,

A "Kiowa" son photographed by Hamilton Rowan, an AKC vice president in charge of field trials. This dog owned by Pat Sadler appeared on the front cover of the *AKC Gazette* in October 1979.

In 1988 there were over 10,000 retrievers running field trials, and 100 retriever clubs hosting almost 200 trials that year. An estimated 8,000 to 10,000 dogs were in regular training, and the odds were less than one in 25 of becoming a field champion. With 80 to 100 dogs competing in some major stakes, and only four placements awarded, it's no surprise some trialers call it a loser's game.

The road to winning field trials has never been an easy one, regardless of the breed, but now a field trial hopeful almost certainly needs professional assistance in order to be competitive in the sport. There is no other discipline in the sport of dogs today that demands the time and energy, degree of difficulty or complexity of training as Retriever Field Trials.

The training of a trial dog is a full-time commitment and involves much more than a few people throwing plastic bumpers. City and suburban developers have gobbled up available training grounds; yesterday's fields and ponds have become today's shopping malls and "Quik-Stop" shops. Serious field trainers travel many hours every week to find training space and partners, a variety of terrain with land hazards and unusual water or ponds, plus a supply of live and dead birds. Thus the quality of any retriever's field trial

AFC Yankee's Smoke 'N Red Devil (OS) (FC-AFC Northbreak's Kinike Sir Jim ex Yankee Fluff ***) bred by Carl Thurman, owned by Paul and Darlene Corona, Mission Viejo, California. Sire of multiple FC-AFC and qualified All-Age dogs, Red was unaware of his notoriety and played the part of the clown at home, stalking the mounted ducks on the wall, or stealing gloves and rakes during yard work. Red was also a sucker for Oreo cookies, often sharing a bedtime Oreo routine with good friend and frequent trainer/handler, Janie Bsharah. Quivering with anticipation, Red would gently accept her Oreo gift, then just as gently, lay the cookie in the middle of the carpet, take noticeable aim, and throw his entire body onto the cookie, rolling it into the rug. He then meticulously snorkled the tiny crumbs of Oreo out of the rug. Hardly fitting behavior for a field trial star. Friend Janie still misses Red's funny little tricks.

FC Windbreaker's Razzmatazz (OD) (AFC Holway Barty ex Nutmeg's Harvest Gold Heather **) bred by Rachel and Jeff Lee. Owned by Pat DeNardo, Grass Valey, California. Bred four times to AFC Yankee's Smoke 'N Red Devil, Razz became an Outstanding Dam when those litters produced three FC-AFC and two Canadian FTCh-AFTCh., and at least eight qualified All-Age dogs.

and he runs like the wind. Sometimes our personal goals are not the dog's goals at all, and sometimes the dogs cannot do what we expect. If I set goals that were unreachable (for my dog), I'd be setting myself up for a lot of disappointment, and it would take a lot of the fun out of this game for me. As much as I want to win, I do love these little dogs too."

Someone once asked Terry just how long she lived with her field trial Goldens. She smiled, "Would you believe . . . forever?"

According to some experts, setting reasonable goals and "forever" Goldens may be a mixed blessing for the breed. "It's not necessarily a bad trait in Golden Retriever people," Mike observed. "It just won't help the future of the field trial Golden."

Maybe not. But the Golden world appears united in their loyalty to the dogs they breed, own and train. That's what they feel sets them apart in the retriever world. Perhaps Terry said it best. "If winning were the only thing, I guess we'd all have black dogs."

career is enhanced or limited by the amount of time, energy and money invested by its owner.

Small wonder Mickey said ". . . you had better start with a good dog. This is such an expensive sport and so competitive. If you're in the game to make a field champion, you have to do it with the best caliber animal you can find."

Yet these field trial trainers still agree the Golden will prevail; that serious trialers will maintain the Golden in the field and breed to keep the field instinct alive and strong.

And therein lies one more dilemma. The most common lament of the '80s has been the shrinking gene pool of field trial Goldens from which to breed. Continued use of the same successful and prepotent sires has reduced the number of available dogs on which to build a strong and healthy pedigree, yet still ensure the talent and stability of the whelp. Intensive and repeated linebreeding also magnifies and/or produces extremes in health and temperament problems which are detrimental to any breed and every discipline in dogs. To curb the declining health and behavior in some of today's field trial stock, some experienced field breeders are seeking good old-fashioned hunting dogs with solid pedigrees to incorporate into their lines.

Many of the successful trial dogs of the recent decade are descendants of AFC Yankee's Smoke'N Red Devil (OS) (FC-AFC Northbreak's Kinike Sir Jim ex Yankee Fluff***) who produced outstanding field talent from breedings to over a dozen bitches. . . six FC-AFCs, one AFC, three Canadian FTCh.-AFTCh., and over three dozen qualified All-Age dogs. The most successful offspring came from the mating of Red to FC Windbreaker's Razzmatazz (OD) (AFC Holway Barty ex Nutmeg's Harvest Gold Heather**), a breeding which was repeated four times, producing three FC-AFCs one AFC, three Canadian FTCh.-AFTCh. Goldens, and at least eight qualified All-Age dogs.

Red's talent and production record is a tribute to his English import grandsire, AFC Holway Barty (OS, HOF), owned and trained by Barbara Howard of Longmont, Colorado. Sire of eight FC or AFCs (many of whom also became outstanding producers), over 50 qualified All-Age dogs, at least three OTCh. and many UD dogs, Barty's influence on the American field and working Golden is unequaled. The flashy style and speed of many of today's field dogs can be attributed to the appearance of Barty in their pedigrees, with the smaller size and finer boned structure more directly attributable to Red. The most successful of the Red offspring are doubled up on Barty.

Barty also produced the only Golden Retriever to win a National Amateur Retriever Champion-

Harold Bruninga of Springfield, Illinois, is an ideal role model for Golden Retriever field trainers. In 1989, at 70+ years old, Harold finished his fourth home-trained FC-AFC Golden Retriever, proof that a Golden and his amateur trainer can succeed with love, tempered with a generous amount of patience and persistence. Harold has trained his Goldens without professional assistance, often sitting in the middle of his kitchen floor, tossing tiny bits of hotdog to give his Golden puppies their first casting lessons. Where professionals advised him not to waste his time, he persisted out of faith in the dog he loved. Harold acquired his first Golden, **Bonnie Brooks Red**, from breeder Richard Kerns. Red and Harold learned the field trial game together and earned Red's FC and AFC in 1976. Red died of heatstroke in 1977 at 8 years old, leaving a huge Golden void in Harold's world. Thinking he had no more challenges left, Harold just "plugged along" with one of Red's sons, and, proof that patience pays, in 1982 "Sonny" became AFC Son of Red. Still in search of mountains, Harold acquired Topbrass Bandit from Jackie Mertens. He "fooled around" with Bandit, and they amassed 29 Derby points before Bandit was two years old. Bandit became an FC-AFC in September 1987. Two years later Harold reached yet another plateau with Red's grandson, Sangamo Red, and he completed Red's FC-AFC in 1989. "I don't buy the idea that Goldens are second-class citizens in field trials," Harold insists. He credits Bonnie Brooks Red for his love for Goldens and the field trial game. Isn't it just like a Golden to do that?

ship. In 1985 at Hugo, Minnesota, NAFC-FC Topbrass Cotton and his breeder/co-owner Jackie Mertens bested 79 Labradors and seven other

FC-AFC Right-on Dynamite John, Willie Win *** and **Right-on Rocky High *****, John's son out of Poppygold Ready-to-Go, owned and trained by Elaine Klicker.

Goldens for the National Amateur Championship title.

Jackie had given Cotton as a puppy to Jeff and Beverly Finley, who trained and handled Cotton to both of his field titles. She then acquired a co-ownership in 1983 to continue Cotton's progress. It was a good career move. At retirement in 1988, he had qualified for 13 Nationals in a row and was a finalist three times.

"Cotton fulfilled my every dream as a breeder," Jackie said. "Best of all, he's been a great friend and the best house rug you could want." When he retired, Cotton returned to the Finleys to assume the role of full-time fur rug in their home.

To become a GRCA Outstanding Sire, Cotton sired three field champions, four Candian field champions, three obedience-trial champions, two Master Hunters, and 26 qualified All-Age dogs. He also holds the breed record for Combined Open/Amateur points earned with 274 points, and the record for lifetime Amateur points with 195.

The Barty/Red-ex-Razz influence claimed several other positions among the top ten High Point All-Age Goldens, and the pedigrees of several top ten Lifetime Point holders include Barty in one or more generation. By 1990 FC-AFC Windbreaker's Smoke'N Zig Zag MH (OD) (Red ex Razz, 11-06-80) owned and trained by Jackie Mertens, had earned 84.5 combined points, and FC-AFC Windbreakers Mighty Mo (OS, HOF) (Red ex Razz, 3-

Left: **AFC Deerhill Iditarod ***** (AFC Yankee's Smoke 'N Red Devil ex AFC Ben's Enchanted Glory) poses with her Amateur first place trophy from the Women's FTC at Ocean City, Maryland in October 1990. Owners, Judy Rasmuson and Ron Wallace.

28-83), owned by the late Stan Heiner of Salt Lake City, Utah, had collected 94.5 combined points.

Jackie recounts a less obvious fact about field trial genetics, that most of the present successful field Goldens share a common gene pool similar to Red and Razz. Their ancestors are among those few special breedings that also "clicked" over the past 20 years. Poika of Handjem, when bred to Shenandoah of Stilroven CD,**, produced four FC-AFCs . . . Kinike Coquette, Kinike Chancellor, Northbreak Kinike Sir Jim and Kinike Rojo De Oro; the mating of FC-AFC-CFC Bonnie Brook's Elmer to Tigathoe's Chickasaw** produced four more field stars, FC-AFC Tigathoe's Magic Marker, (the all-time High Point Golden bitch), Dual Ch.-AFC Tigathoe's Funky Farquar, (the breed's last dual champion), FC-AFC Tigathoe's Kiowa II, and FC-AFC Tigathoe's Tonga. Later, when Barty was bred to Ch. Sunstream Gypsy of Top brass CD,*, the Golden world was blessed with Cotton, OTCh. Topbrass Ric-O-Shay Barty WCX, and FC-AFC Topbrass Mandy.

When these titled offspring were later bred, they continued the star-studded breeding saga and produced yet another generation of great producers.

FC-AFC Misty Sungold Lad CDX also enters into the genetic picture as the grandsire of FC Windbreaker's Razzmatazz. Another Lad grandson, FC-AFC Tangelo's Sidekick (Sungold Sand Kicker *** ex Troymar Shasta Spring), bred by Ted and Pat Gross and owned by Bill and Terry Woods, earned his place among the top ten High Point All-Age Goldens with 130.5 combined Open and Amateur points. Lad's 212.5 Open/Amateur points still holds a secure second place on the breed's High Combined Points list.

Other 1980s' dogs who blazed their way into the top ten High Point Goldens through 1989 were FC-AFC Pajim's Klondike with 99.5 combined Open/Amateur points, and three outstanding bitches; FC-AFC Windbreakers Smoke'N Zig Zag, 84.5 points; FC-AFC Topbrass Mandy, 62.5 points; FC-AFC Stony-Brooks Gold Digger with 47 points, although these hard-working la-

dies still trailed the remarkable FC-AFC Tigathoe's Magic Marker, who captured a record 117 Open and Amateur points during her 1970s field trial career.

In addition to Cotton and Pardner among the top ten lifetime Amateur point holders, FC-AFC Benjamin Rajah Frisbie had collected 70 points and FC-AFC Tigathoe's Tonga, 69.5 through 1981, and FC-AFC Pajim's Klondike, 67 points through 1985.

From 1984-1990, six Goldens joined the exclusive "Double Header" club....that group of dogs who have achieved a trialer's wildest dream by winning both major stakes, the Open and the Amateur, at the same licensed field trial. Until 1983, only four Goldens in breed history had accomplished this rare feat, making the decade of the '80s rich in double-header talent.

FC-AFC Casey Two of Fox Creek MH (Champagne of Fox Creek ex Rocky-Vue of Fox Creek ***) bred and owned by Sibby Wood, Camden, South Carolina, at the National Amateur in 1988. Tractable, always willing, Casey also works in school education programs to teach children how to treat dogs. The kids get to brush him, and he loves it!

The most distinguished of the group, NAFC-FC Topbrass Cotton and his co-owner Jackie Mertens, won their double header at the American Amateur Retriever Club trial in September 1983. One month later Mean Joe Green of Rocky-Vue ***, owned by Bill Wandalear, won the Amateur and Open stakes at the October GRCA National Specialty. The previous year AFC Wild Fire of Riverview CDX, owned by Kathleen Daniels and handled by her husband Lew, won both stakes at the Buckeye RC spring trial.

In April 1985, Smoke'N Red Raider *** handled by co-owner Marge Meegan, won both Amateur and Open at the Missouri Valley RC trial.

The year 1990 set a record for double headers in the breed, when two Goldens topped their careers with double headers during the same year. Stan Heiner's FC-AFC Windbreakers Mighty Mo won the Sagehen RC Amateur and Open stakes in February, and FC-AFC Valhaven Smoke'N Vindaloo, handled by co-owner Judy Rasmuson, won her double header in June at the Maine RC trial. This victory also gained "Lulu's"

AFC and qualified her for the 1990 National Amateur Stake.

"Lulu" is the first bitch in breed history to win a double header at an all-breed trial. Only one other bitch, the talented FC-AFC Tigathoe's Magic Marker, had won the prized double header, but claimed her victories at the 1975 GRCA National Specialty.

The 1990s' crop of outstanding canines demonstrates great promise for the future for field trial Golden Retriever. The 1991 and '92 GRCA National Specialties showcased an overall caliber of working Golden superior to those of recent years. Blessed with larger entries in the major stakes, the field trial gallery admired handsome dogs who earned applause and rave reviews with their style and precision performance, talented newcomers who soon may challenge their parents for a piece of the trial, experienced old-timers still running strong and producing well, Goldens who even sparked the interest of the conformation crowd. These field trial Goldens obviously aren't leaving anything to chance.

The spectacular **FC-AFC Windbreaker's Mighty Mo (OS, HOF)** (AFC Yankee's Smoke 'N Red Devil ex FC Windbreaker's Razzmatazz), owned by Stan Heiner, Salt Lake City, Utah. In addition to his impressive career record, Mo's dynamic style in the field never fails to thrill the field trial gallery. FC and National Open Finalist at three years of age . . . Top Open Golden in 1987, 1988 and 1990, Finalist again at the 1988 National Open, and the career topper . . . double header winner in 1990 . . . and still going strong.

FC-AFC Topbrass Windbreaker Zap (OS) (AFC Yankee's Smoke 'N Red Devil ex FC Windbreaker's Razzmatazz) is owned by Sam Silverman of Teserque, New Mexico. Zap's career record is outstanding. He was the top Derby Golden in 1986 with 34 points, also had two qualifying wins before two years of age and qualified for his first National Amateur at two-and-one-half. He completed both his FC and AFC as a three year old, and qualified for three more Nationals. Zap's kids proved Poppa proud. Daughter "Rose," Mistfield Red Zinger ***, owned by Sam and his wife Jane, claimed the top Derby Golden spot in 1989 and 1990, collecting 32 Derby points and a qualifying win, Mioak's Bustin' Luce earned 18 Derby points in 1990 plus two qualifying wins and an Open second, and Mistfield Top Gun has All-Age placements. Zap also sired Topbrass Mioak's Bingo MH, the youngest Golden to become a Master Hunter. Zap died of cancer in 1992.

FC-AFC Valhaven Smoke 'N Vindaloo shown with her double header trophies won at the Maine RC in June 1990. "Lulu" is the only Golden Retriever female to have won a double header at an All-Breed field trial. Owners, Judy Rasmuson and Ron Wallace.

Approximately 269 Goldens earned qualified All-Age status from 1980 through 1990. The following Goldens attained field championships during this same period.

FC-AFC Pajim's Klondike (HOF) (Yankee's Rebel *** ex Lad's Golden Kolleen) bred by James McClellan. Owned by Pattie Harper. March 1980.

AFC Tigathoe's Choptank Child (FC-AFC-CFC Bonnie Brook's Elmer ex Tigathoe's Sister Susie) bred by Mrs. George Flinn Jr. Owned by Ray Earnest. March 1980.

FC-AFC Topbrass Mandy (OD, HOF) (AFC Holway Barty ex Ch. Sunstream Gypsy of Topbrass) bred and owned by Jacquelyn and Joseph Mertens. AFC, April 1980 FC, November 1980.

FC-AFC Firebird of Rocky-Vue (FC-AFC Bonnie Brook's Red ex Holway Joyful***) bred and owned by Carma Futhey. FC, August 1981; AFC, August 1982.

AFC Riverview's Hawk Kiowa CD (FC-AFC Tigathoe's Kiowa II ex Riverview's Nettles CDX) bred by James and Sally Venerable. Owned by William and Martha Lamar. September 1982.

AFC Son of Red (FC-AFC Bonnie Brook's Red ex Holway Joyful**) bred by Carma Futhey. Owned by Harold Bruninga. October 1982.

FC-AFC Wyngate's Sungold Sundance (Wyngates Sungold King** ex Wyngates Tuff Enuf **) bred by Francis Clest, Jr. Owned by Kenneth Gootee. FC, October 1982; AFC, March 1985.

FC-AFC Cherryhill's Rowdy Rascal (HOF) (AFC Holway Barty ex Cherryhill Hawtdaugh***) bred by Catherine Shives. Owned by Darlene Corona. AFC, November 1982; FC, February 1983.

AFC Huntrail's Wailin Willie (FC-AFC Kinike Chancellor ex Huntrail's Cinnamon Sue) bred

FC-AFC Windbreaker Smoke 'N Zig Zag and **NAFC-FC Topbrass Cotton**, shown with son **Topbrass Dustbuster FC-AFC** from their first litter.

AFC Northbreak's Brier (OS) (FC-AFC Northbreak Kinike Sir Jim ex Ch. Topbrass Ad-Lib's Bangor CD***) bred by Joseph and Jacquelyn Mertens. Owned by Joan Morter. September 1981.

NAFC-FC Topbrass Cotton (OS, HOF) (Holway Barty ex Ch. Sunstream Gypsy of Topbrass) bred by Joseph and Jacquelyn Mertens. Owned by Jeff and Beverly Finley and Jacquelyn Mertens. AFC, September 1981; FC, May 1982; NAFC, June 1985.

AFC Wild Fire of Riverview (OS, HOF) (Riverview Kinike Rocket*** ex Riverview's Nettles CDX) owned by Kathleen Daniels. April 1982.

AFC Goldmark's Magic Rug (FC-AFC Kinike Chancellor ex FC-AFC Tigathoe's Magic Marker) bred by Joseph Wattleworth. Owned by Thomas Mundorff, MD. May 1982.

and owned by Diane Voigt. May 1983.

AFC Gold Mark Bicentennial Blue (FC-AFC Kinike Chancellor ex FC-AFC Tigathoe's Magic Marker) bred by Joseph Wattleworth. Owned by Helen and Harvey Phillips. June 1983.

AFC Kiowa's Holiday Joy (AFC Holway Barty ex Kiowa's Satucket Sioux***) bred by Mrs. Robert Sadler. Owned by Ken and Kathleen Gootee. June 1983.

AFC Sportin' Kelty CD (AFC Holway Barty ex Meghin Leygore Deerflite) bred by Bill and Barbara Alldridge. Owned by Judy Bly. August 1983.

AFC Topbrass Gatsby (AFC Holway Barty ex Ch. Topbrass Ad-Lib's Dynamite) bred by Jacquelyn Mertens and Charles Libberton. Owned by Jeff and Beverly Finley. August 1983.

AFC Topbrass Gifford of Valhaven (AFC Holway Barty ex Ch. Topbrass Ad-Lib's Banger CD), owned by Mary Maurer, retired from field trials after he titled in March 1990. No argument from "Giff," . . . he spends hunting season with a hunting guide, and now at ten years of age, feeling great, he's the top duck and goose guide dog on the Texas Katy Prairie, sometimes picks up 50 birds a day.

FC Windbreaker's Razzmatazz (OD) (AFC Holway Barty ex Nutmeg's Harvest Gold Heather**) bred by Rachel and Jeff Lee. Owned by Pat DeNardo. September 1983.

FC-AFC Windbreakers Smoke'N ZigZag (OD, HOF) (AFC Yankee's Smoke'N Red Devil ex FC Windbreaker's Razzmatazz) bred by Pat DeNardo. Owned by Jacquelyn and Joseph Mertens. AFC, April 1984; FC, August 1984.

AFC Ben's Enchanted Glory (OS, HOF) (FC-AFC Benjamin Rajah Frisbie ex Misty's Enchanted Sun Dance) bred by Vera Frisbie. Owned by Brian Pashina. July 1984.

AFC Yankee's Smoke'N Red Devil (OS) (FC-AFC Northbreak's Kinike Sir Jim ex Yankee Fluff***) bred by Carl Thurman. Owned by Paul Corona. September 1984.

FC AFC Shalimar of Thorn Run (FC-AFC Tigathoe's Kiowa II ex Dinah of Rocky-Vue) bred by Ann Walters. Owned by Helen and Harvey Phillips. AFC, September 1984; FC, September 1986.

FC-AFC Stony-Brooks Gold Digger (HOF) (FC-AFC Tigathoe's Kiowa II ex Stony-Brooks Fools Gold***) bred and owned by Carol and Robert Lilenfield. March 1985.

FC-AFC Tangelo's Side Kick (OS, HOF) (Sungold Sand Kicker*** ex Troymar Shasta Spring WCX) bred by Ted and Patricia Gross. Owned by Bill Woods and Terry Giffen. AFC, May 1985; FC, September 1986.

AFC Sungold T-Bill Splasher (HOF) (Amber's Diablo Rock*** ex Sungold Black Velvet) bred by Valerie Walker. Owned by Mike Lauderdale and Bill Woods. June 1985.

FC-AFC Sun Fire's XX Buckshot (OS) (AFC Wildfire of Riverview CDX ex Sun Fire's Dyno of Chances R) bred by Kathleen and Lewis Daniels. Owned by James Morgan. April 1986.

This page: A genetic jumping style and water entry is apparent in these photos of **Houston** *above* and his sire *(left)* **Sky Skylab Argus of Belvedere *** WC**, "Gus." Gus earned his WC at 12 years and ten months old, a record for a Golden earning that title.

FC-AFC Topbrass Bandit (NAFC-FC Topbrass Cotton ex Woodridge's Hannah) bred by Joseph and Jacquelyn Mertens. Owned by Harold Bruninga. September 1986.

FC-AFC Windbreakers Mighty Mo (OS, HOF) (AFC Yankee's Smoke'N Red Devil ex FC Windbreaker's Razzmatazz) bred by Pat DeNardo. Owned by Stanley and Geraldine Heiner. FC, September 1986; AFC, May 1989.

FC-AFC Mioak's Main Event (OS, HOF) (AFC Wildfire of Riverview CDX ex Mioak's Ginger***) bred by Mickey Kendrigan. Owned by Teddy Woodhouse and Jacquelyn Mertens. Currently owned by John and Cathy Morse. AFC, October 1986; FC, September 1987.

FC-AFC Casey Two of Fox Creek MH (HOF) (Champagne of Fox Creek ex Rocky-Vue of Fox Creek***) bred and owned by Mrs. Maxwell Wood. FC, November 1986; AFC, September 1987.

AFC Cranwood's Chill Factor MH (OS, HOF) (AFC Yankee's Smoke'N Red Devil ex Handjem's Cranwood Rox**) bred by Shanda Waller and Michael Lardy. Owned by Mrs. George Flinn Jr. April 1987.

FC-AFC Topbrass Windbreaker's Zap (OS, HOF) (AFC Yankee's Smoke'N Red Devil ex FC Windbreaker's Razzmatazz) bred by Pat DeNardo. Owned by Sam Silverman. AFC, September 1987; FC, October 1988.

FC Topbrass Ace in the Hole (NAFC-FC Topbrass Cotton ex Woodridge's Hannah) bred by Joseph and Jacquelyn Mertens. Owned by Mrs. George Flinn Jr. October 1987.

FC-AFC Sangamo Red (HOF) (AFC Son of Red ex Ben's Enchanted Micalaub) bred by David Frisbie. Owned by Harold Bruninga, AFC, April 1988; FC, May 1989.

FC-AFC Lee's Rocky Marshwinds (OTCh. Sungold Duke of Brookshire WCX ex Goldbriar's K.T. Did CD, WCX) bred by Mark Taube. Owned by D. Lee Courey. May 1988.

FC-AFC Stony-Brooks' Jersey Devil (HOF) (AFC Yankee's Smoke'N Red Devil ex Stony Brooks Fools Gold***) bred by Robert and Carol Lilenfield. Owned by Robert and Margaret Meegan, later co-owner Jacquelyn Mertens. May 1988.

FC Gian Carlo of Fox Creek. (NAFC-FC Topbrass Cotton ex Rocky-Vue of Fox Creek***) bred and owned by Mrs. Maxwell Wood. October 1988.

FC-AFC Topbrass Dustbuster (NAFC-FC Topbrass Cotton ex FC-AFC Windbreakers Smoke'N ZigZag) bred by Joseph and Jacquelyn Mertens. Owned by Barbara Howard. September 1989.

AFC Topbrass Comet (NAFC-FC Topbrass Cotton ex FC-AFC Windbreakers Smoke 'N Zig Zag) is Mary's second field trial Golden. Like "Giff," "Halley" is completely owner-trained and handled. She won her first Amateur stake in summer 1990.

Above: **AFC Topbrass Tyonek** (NAFC-FC Topbrass Cotton ex FC-AFC Windbreakers Smoke 'N Zig Zag) and **AFC Deerhill Iditarod.** (AFC Yankee's Smoke 'N Red Devil ex AFC Ben's Enchanted Glory) bred by Brian Pashina, owned and trained by Judy Rasmuson and Ron Wallace. "Ty's" kennelmate, "Dede," not to be outdone, won the Open stake the following week at the 1991 GRCA National Specialty. Photo by author. *Below:* **AFC Mioak's Raincheck** (Frisbie's Olympia Gold ex Mioak's Golden Torch) and his owner Betty Winkinson of Herald, California, ran their first field trial together when "Check" was ten months old. He never found the first bird because he came upon some old bones and proceeded to roll on them . . . a real confidence-builder! He redeemed himself, however, and 17 months later he won his first Amateur stake.

FC-AFC Right-On Dynamite John (Duke of Handjem *** ex Autumn's Aspen Gold Kandy), Jan. 1974–Jan. 1989, shown with owner Elaine Klicker of Billings, Montana, after first Amateur win at the NWRC trial. Completely amateur trained and handled, John accumulated 87 All-Age points during his field trial career. Every fall he and Elaine took three months off from training to hunt ducks, geese and upland game. John slept at his mistress's bedside every night from seven weeks old until he died at 15 years of age. He retrieved his last goose two weeks before he died.

"Glory" . . . **AFC Ben's Enchanted Glory (HOF)** (FC-AFC Benjamin Rajah Frisbie ex Misty's Enchanted Sundance) (1977–1988). Owned by Barbara and Brian Pashina, Long Lake, Minnesota, was Brian's first dog and will always be remembered. One of Glory's outstanding traits was her ability to run an absolutely straight line, regardless of obstacles in her way. At her first Amateur win, during the last series water triple, her flier landed *directly behind* the gunners. When Glory retrieved that bird, she went "straight," which included *under* the chair of one gunner *to* and *from* the bird. That's really "taking a line!"

Midas Belvedere Houston WCX, *** (Skylab Argus of Belvedere ****, WC ex Holway Dinar) bred by Julie Jellis, owned by Mercedes Hitchcock.

KC's Jeep Cherokee MH, *** (FC-AFC Mioak's Main Event ex Topbrass Spice of Valhaven ***) bred by Mary Maurer, owned by Tom Kitchens and Kaye Fuller, Austin, Texas, poses after winning the qualifying stake at the 1991 GRCA National Specialty. Photo by the author.

AFC Topbrass Gifford of Valhaven (AFC Holway Barty ex Ch. Topbrass Ad-Lib's Bangor CD ***) bred by Joseph and Jacquelyn Mertens. Owned by Mary Maurer and Kim Martin. March 1990.

FC-AFC Valhaven Smoke'N Vindaloo (HOF) (AFC Yankee's Smoke'N Red Devil ex Topbrass Spice of Valhaven***) bred by Mary Maurer and Fred Phillips. Owned by Ron Wallace and Judy Rasmuson. AFC, June 1990; FC, September 1990.

While not 1980–1990 finishers, these 1991 Field Champions deserve recognition in this line-up of outstanding Golden Retriever achievers!

AFC Mioak's Raincheck (Frisbie's Olympia Gold** ex Mioak's Golden Torch) bred by Mickey Strandberg. Owned by Robert and Elizabeth Wilkinson. February 1991.

AFC Topbrass Super Trooper (NAFC-FC Topbrass Cotton ex Pacapooches Pandemonium) bred by Robert and Sandee Peterson. Owned by Darrell Frisbie. August 1991.

FC-AFC Topbrass Tyonek (NAFC-FC Topbrass Cotton ex FC-AFC Windbreakers Smoke'N Zig Zag) bred by Joseph and Jaquelyn Mertens. Owned by Ron Wallace and Judy Rasmuson. October 1991.

FC-AFC Mioak's Main Event (AFC Wildfire of Riverview CDX, WCX ex Mioak's Ginger ***) is definitely the main event in the life of his current owner Cathy Morse of Fullerton, California. Rocky and Cathy ran National Amateur Stakes in 1988, 1989 and 1990. Rocky was the high-point Open Golden on 1989. As a youngster, he finished fifth on the National Derby List with 40 points at the hand of his breeder, Mickey Kendrigan. Sold at age two-and-one-half to Teddy Woodhouse and Jackie Mertens, Rocky completed his AFC in 1986 and his FC the following year. He is presently in training with the professional trainer Bill Eckett, who considers Rocky the most biddable and talented Golden he has trained. At home with Cathy, he hunts duck, goose and pheasant, and hikes, swims, and combs the beach with her four boys.

Left: **HRCh. Scarlet O'Hara of Belvedere ***** (Holway Gillie *** ex Sky-Lab Belvedere Baby Doll ***). Photo by the author.
Right: **FC-AFC Topbrass Tyonek** bred by Joseph and Jackie Mertens, owned and trained by Ron Wallace and Judy Rasmuson, Clinton, Connecticut. "Ty" completed his FC-AFC by winning the 79-dog Open stake at the Kansas City RC All-Breed trial October 18, 1991, one week before the GRCA National Specialty.

Sky-Lab Belvedere Baby Doll *** (OD), "Dolly," (AFC Holway Barty ex Sky-Lab Gandy Dancer WCX) owned by Mercedes Hitchcock.

KC's Sparkle Plenty MH *** (OD) AFC Holway Barty ex Ch. Jungold's Fleetwood Fantasia CD, **) bred, owned and trained by Kaye Fuller, Round Rock, Texas. Sparkle became a GRCA Outstanding Dam for her first litter of only six pups by English import Holway Vodka ***. Three qualified All-Age, four Master Hunters, . . . not bad, old girl.

167

Above left: An old-timer and one of those special dual-titled Goldens . . . AFC-Ch. Honor's Dorado of Spindrift, "Hondo," and owner John Sprude, Keokuk, Iowa. When training, John always cut off Hondo's long chest feathering before he ran. *Above right:* **Topbrass Abilene (NAFC-FC Topbrass Cotton ex Tali's Nugget of the Yukon)** bred by Robert Pfisterer, at the 1991 GRCA National Specialty with her owner, Mrs. George "Torch" Flinn Jr. The last of the dedicated Golden field trialers from the '40s, Torch would surely top today's list of Who's Who in the world of the field trial Golden Retriever.

Below left: **FC-AFC Lee's Rocky Marshwinds,** owned by D. Lee Courey, Sterling, Michigan, shown with Lee at the Wolverine RC trial the day he won the Open to complete his FC-AFC. *Below right:* **Maggie Happydaugh UD, WCX, *** (OD)** (Martdaugh*** ex Cayenne's Happy Thought), owned by Ann and Jeff Strathern of Frederick, Maryland, won the Amateur All-Age stake at the GRCA National Specialty and finished her UD all in the same year. Bred once to AFC Holway Barty, she became an Outstanding Dam from the pups from that one litter.

Right: **NAFC-FC Topbrass Cotton (OS, HOF)**...Retrieving at its finest! The first Golden Retriever National Amateur Field Champion! Cotton was owner-bred by Jackie Mertens of Elgin, Illinois. NAFC-FC Topbrass Cotton's dazzling field trial career includes spectacular statistics...46 Derby points in 19 trials; became FC-AFC at three years of age; in 1981, the youngest dog to ever run the National Open; Double Header winner in September 1983; 1985 National Amateur winner...First Golden ever to win that stake; Qualified for 15 Nationals; High-Point Golden of all-time with 274 points. Number 10 All-time High Point, all breeds; over 30 Qualified All-age offspring, plus several OTCh. and MH get; three field-titled offspring in the United States and three in Canada.

At the 1980 National Amateur in Maine, *(right)* **FC-AFC Tigathoe's Tonga** (FC-AFC-CFC Bonnie Brooks Elmer ex Tigathoe's Chickasaw ***) owned by Ray Earnest and *(left)* **FC-AFC Tigathoe's Kiowa II**. Owned by Pat Sadler.

A "three-star quad" of Goldens. Four descendants of AFC Yankee's Smoke 'N Red Devil who became qualified All-Age in 1987. *Left to right:* **Topbrass Tyonek***** ("Ty"), **Mioak's Hotshot***** ("Skeet"), both Devil grandsons, and **Deerhill Iditarod***,** ("Dede") and **Valhaven Smoke 'N Vindaloo***** ("Lulu"), two Devil daughters. Skeet and Lulu made the Derby list that same year. Lulu finished her FC-AFC in 1990 and qualified for the 1990 National Open and Amateur Stakes. Dede followed closely at her heels, with an Amateur win at the Women's Field Trial Club in Maryland in October 1990. These four over-achievers are owned by Judy Rasmuson and Ron Wallace, Clinton, Connecticut.

A line-up of superstars at the 1991 GRCA National Specialty field trial. Shown *left to right:* **FC-AFC Topbrass Windbreaker Zap** and **FC-AFC Windbreaker's Mighty Mo** with Zap's owner Sam Silverman; **FC-AFC Topbrass Tyonek** and co-owner Ron Wallace; **FC-AFC Valhaven Smoke 'N Vindaloo** and co-owner Judy Rasmuson; **AFC Topbrass Super Trooper** and owner Darrel Frisbee; **FC-AFC Stony Brook's Jersey Devil** and co-owners Jackie Mertens and Marge Meegan; **FC-AFC Topbrass Dustbuster** and owner Barbara Howard. Photo by author.

Ch.-AFC Honor's Darado of Spindrift, bred by Ann Chase, won the Open stake at the GRCA National Specialty in 1976, and as a member of the Field Dog Hall of Fame, claimed 26 and one-half points during his field trial career. The luxurious coat on "Hondo's" chest was always clipped when he was running in the field.

AFC Sportin' Kelty CD (AFC Holway Barty ex Meghin Leygore Deerflite) owned by Judy Bly, Spokane, Washington, at ten years of age. Proof that a Golden improves with age, three months before completing his AFC with an Amateur win, and at nine years old, grey-faced Kelty amazed the obedience audience when he finished his CD with a High-In-Trial in Novice A with a 247 total entry.

AFC Northbreak's Brier (OS) (FC-AFC Northbreak's Kinike Sir Jim ex Ch. Topbrass Ad-Lib's Bangor) owned by Joan Morter, Milwaukee, Wisconsin. Brier was completely amateur-trained, with Joan's emphasis on the *amateur*. As a city dog, Brier had most of his lessons in the vacant fields and water holes of Milwaukee. One of his blinds was over a series of railroad tracks, and when the flatbed cars moved in, Brier would simply run underneath them to stay on the line to the blind.

FC-AFC Sunfire's XX Buckshot (OS) (AFC Wildfire of Riverview CDX, WCX ex Sunfire's Dyno of Chances R) owned by James Morgan, Gary, Indiana. Buck was a precocious youngster . . . won his first licensed Derby at just ten months old, going on to earn 30 Derby points as the 1983 high-point Derby Golden. He achieved his FC-AFC with an Open win at the Maumee Valley RC trial in April 1986. That year he also won the Open at the GRCA National Specialty, and qualified for the 1986 National Amateur. Rounding out his career, Buck also has a four-point Major Reserve on the bench.

FC-AFC Misty's Sungold Lad CDX, a famous sire of the 1960s owned by Valerie Fisher (Walker.)

FC Windbreaker's Razzmatazz *('nuff said)* and Pat Denardo.

FC-AFC Stony Brooks Gold Digger (FC-AFC Tigathoe's Kiowa II ex Stony Brooks Fool's Gold), owned by Pat Sadler and Carol Lilenfield, shown here with co-owner Pat at the National Amateur Retriever Championship in Batavia, New York.

"Check" won back-to-back Amateurs in February 1991, also placing third in the Open. The first win finished his AFC and qualified him for the 1991 National Amateur. **AFC Mioak's Raincheck**. Betty Wilkinson, owner.

FC Gian Carlo of Fox Creek (HOF) (NAFC-FC Topbrass Cotton ex Rocky-Vue of Fox Creek ***) bred and owned by Sibby Wood, Camden, South Carolina, after one of his Open wins.

Argus Sheba of Belvedere MH (Sky-Lab Argus of Belvedere WC, *** ex Belvedere's Joie de Vivre) bred by Mercedes Hitchcock, owned, trained, and missed by Harris Greenwood, Houston, Texas. The first Golden Retriever to become a Master Hunter died just before his tenth birthday in March 1992.

Retriever Hunting Tests and the Hunting Golden Retriever

When first introducing the hunting test program for retrievers and other Sporting breeds, the AKC was prepared for major participation from the hunting and working retrievers. What it did not expect was the tidal wave of response from the bench and obedience community. In addition to attracting traditional and hopeful hunting types, the hunting tests also opened up an exciting new world of activity for hunting dogs who had never hunted or retrieved a duck or pheasant.

The original hunting test concept was not devised by AKC. Credit goes to the North American Hunting Retriever Association, NAHRA, a Vermont-based organization founded in 1983 by nine East Coast hunting enthusiasts who were determined to keep the hunting in the retriever.

NAHRA's purpose, as stated in NAHRA vice-president Richard Wolters' book *Duck Dog*, was to offer the hunter an alternative to field trials. The goals of the new game were a trained retriever for conservation, a hunter who knew how to train a hunting dog, and furthermore, a national gene pool of working hunting stock to preserve the retriever's hunting ability.

The hunting tests were unique because, unlike field or obedience trials, they were totally noncompetitive. They were devised as an opportunity for retriever owners to prove and enjoy their dogs' natural ability in the field without the elimination process associated with competition. The dogs are judged against a set standard of performance and need not outperform other exhibitors in order to qualify or pass. The intent, however, is the same as that of trials—to evaluate the qualities of the hunting dog in a simulated hunting situation.

Hunter's Moon Jedfoord (FC-AFC Windbreaker's Mighty Mo ex Meadowpond Scotch Mist CD, TD, WCX), another of the Foord's young hopefuls.

NARHA's board of directors presented its idea to AKC, and in mid-1984, the two organizations sponsored several jointly run hunting tests. Later that year, however, NAHRA broke away to continue its program, independent of AKC. AKC then developed its own non-competitive testing program for the hunter and his dog.

AKC and NAHRA programs differ very little in basic concept. While both test and evaluate the dog, NAHRA places more emphasis on hunting attire and actual simulated hunting situations. Testing guidelines also differ slightly in the requirements a dog must meet. Hopefully, for the hunting retriever owner, both clubs will help broaden the base of qualified hunting dogs for breeding purposes.

The AKC hunting test program has expanded faster than even AKC ever imagined. Since the first AKC-licensed retriever hunting test in Wichita, Kansas, on June 8, 1985, which was the first AKC-licensed hunting test for *any* breed, the program has grown from only 13 retriever hunting tests with 681 starters in 1985 to 202 tests with 16,188 starters in 1992. That is an increase of over two thousand percent in dog participation, far exceeding the growth rate of any other dog sport in the past decade.

The AKC tests are designed for all three types of Sporting dog: retrieving, pointing and flushing. Each provides a Junior, Senior and Master stake to test the dog's ability on three levels: basic, moderately difficult and very challenging. Most tests attempt to simulate some type of hunting situation, and test procedures at each level include certain hunting requirements.

Scoring is also unique from other dog events. Retrievers are judged on a set of AKC-established standards: marking, style, perseverance and trainability. Dogs receive a numerical score of 0 to 10 in each category. To qualify or pass a dog must receive an overall average of 7.0, based on scores from two judges, with an average no lower than 5 for each characteristic.

had earned Junior Hunter titles, about 231 were Senior Hunters, and 120 Goldens had attained the title of Master Hunter.

As the Master Hunter titles piled up at AKC over the past half-decade, murmurs of "What now?" and "What's left?" reverberated through the hunting retriever crowd. In response, AKC in 1991 offered yet another carrot, the first annual licensed Master National Hunting test. To qualify, a dog must have earned four qualifying master scores during the previous designated 12-month period.

Ninety-eight retrievers ran the first National test held in Glasgow, Delaware in September 1991, thirteen of whom were Golden Retrievers, and two Goldens were among the 26 dogs who

HRCh. Belvedere Ring of Fire (HRCh. Holway Vodka *** ex HR Scarlet O'Hara of Belvedere ***) bred by Mercedes Hitchcock, owned by Gary Hodges of the Colorado River Retriever Club.

A Junior Hunter title (JH) requires four qualifying scores, or "legs," while the Senior Hunter (SH) must pass five times, and the Master Hunter (MH), six. A dog who has already earned a Junior title needs only four legs to qualify for Senior, and a Senior dog needs only five to earn a Master title. Dogs need not earn a lesser title before entering a Senior or Master stake. Once earned, an AKC hunting title appears as a suffix after the dog's registered name.

Through 1992 approximately 1,068 Goldens

finished the week-long event.

In NAHRA Hunting Retriever Field Tests, dogs are tested in four categories based on ability: Beginner and Started, (no title, only points), Intermediate (Working Retriever/WR); Senior (Master Hunting Retriever/MHR), and Grand Master (Grand Master Hunting Retriever/GMHR).

The *NAHRA Field Procedures* manual states its purpose is to educate the public in the use of purebred hunting retrievers "as conservation animals" and to promote the field testing of

AFC-NAHRA WR Glenhaven Devil's Advocate UDT, MH, WCX, owned by Glenda Brown of Santa Barbara, California, was the first Golden to earn all three hunting titles. "Luke" might well be called a canine over-achiever. In addition to his hunting title records, he completed his Amateur Field Championship in 1992.

retrievers in simulated hunting situations.

By 1990, NAHRA had 80 clubs in North America, including several in Alaska, and one in Mexico. Over 2,000 retrievers had earned points as Started dogs, about 500 had WR titles, between 200 and 250 had MHR titles, and 65 to 70 retrievers had become GMHR. Of these numbers, 14 Goldens held the MHR, and two were titled GMHR.

The NAHRA Invitational is the annual plum offered to the 30 top Senior dogs in the country. Handlers who have accumulated the highest number of points during the calendar year are invited to an all-expense-paid, two-day field test held in May of the following year. The dogs still work against the NAHRA standard, and those dogs that pass at the Invitational are named to the NAHRA All-American Team for that year.

The United Kennel Club (UKC), the second largest U.S. breed registry, followed NAHRA's lead in retriever hunting tests. In 1984 their new affiliate Hunting Retriever Club, Inc., (HRC) launched the first UKC hunting tests offered for retrievers. The purpose, as stated in the HRC preamble, is to develop the hunting retriever to fulfill its intended purpose in life—hunting. Using guidelines similar to those described for AKC hunting tests and NAHRA field tests, HRC officials judge dogs against a set standard of performance on a pass-fail basis.

HRC/UKC Hunts (termed hunts rather than tests) are designed for three levels of ability: Started, similar to Junior, earning points only, no title; Seasoned (Hunting Retriever/HR), and Finished (Hunting Retriever Champion/HR CH), similar to AKC's Master. Points earned at the Started and Seasoned levels accumulate toward the 100 necessary to become a Finished Retriever.

HRC/UKC also offers the Grand Hunting Retriever Champion title (GR HR CH) requiring an additional 100 points. Grand Hunts may be held in conjunction with regular HRC/UKC hunts, and each passing score earns 25 points.

Hunting tests serve an important need in the world of sporting dogs. Both hunters and non-hunting owners of hunting dogs now have a chance to prove the working abilities of their dogs. Additionally, as retriever field trials have grown more competitive and more expensive over the years, a great many middle-class trialers have found they no longer can afford the time and money required to maintain a competitive field trial dog. The new tests give them one more opportunity to enjoy a sport based on their dogs' hunting ability. Hunting tests also encourage the conformation and obedience competitor to demonstrate the dual purpose of their dogs.

Conversely, for some participants, hunting tests have inspired them to venture into the intimidating world of field trials. Thrilled with the sight of their own, or someone else's Golden, flying through the tests with style and speed, and working head to head with Labrador owners, has kindled a competitive spirit heretofore unknown. Now some of them want *more . . .* bigger challenges, tougher tests, a better dog. In either event, field trials and hunting tests will benefit each other, and more importantly, both will serve the Golden Retriever in the field.

As in any new sport, especially one involving dogs, the tests and test results have generated observations and opinions as diverse as the many dogs participating. Some say tests are too easy, others too hard, often depending on the region or the judge. The pass-fail basis of the tests can sometimes diminish the fact they are still tests and must evaluate not help the dog, nor merely provide a stepping stone to yet another title.

Most of the judges at the AKC tests are long-time retriever owners, former field trialers and hunters. Those interviewed for this chapter agree that their experience in field trialing has been invaluable in both judging and participating in the tests. Phil Berger, St Cloud, Minnesota, is a lifelong professional trainer who trains retrievers, spaniels and pointing breeds for hunting, field trials and hunting tests. Phil's 19 years on the field trial circuit provide a broad base for his observations as a judge at the AKC hunting tests.

In Arcata, California, Julie Cairns and her husband, Tom, started in Goldens and field trials in 1977. One of the few husband-wife judging teams, they judged together at the original AKC/NAHRA hunting tests through 1990. Tom has judged over a dozen Master Hunting tests, and Julie has judged about 13 tests, most of them at the master level. She has trained one Master Golden, and has two others with Master legs.

Tom Colstad, Irma, Wisconsin, has a Master Hunter Golden who has qualified at the Master level 14 times, and was one of the 26 retrievers who finished the 1991 Master National test in Delaware. Tom has been in Goldens since 1973, in field trials since 1977, and has judged several Master Hunting tests.

Kevin Marks of Wichita, Kansas, has hunted with retrievers since he was eight years old. He joined the field trial circuit in 1977 and has been judging hunting tests from their inception. His current dog is a Master Hunter who is also qualified All-Age. Kevin judged at least eight Senior and 12 Master tests through 1990 in Kansas, Nebraska, Missouri and Oklahoma.

Hamilton Rowan, New York City, is a former 25-year AKC executive and 15-year director of

As alert and ready as ever is **Am-Can. Ch. Comstock's Sunfire O'Hillcrest UDT, MH, WCX, VCX, Can. CDX, WCI** (Can. Ch. Comstock's Carmel Nut UDTX, SH, WCX, Can. UD, WCX ex Sunfire's Breila of Bristol CD, WCX, ✱✱✱), owned by Kathy Eddy McCue, VMD, Ancramdale, New York, Barb Biewer and Michael Book, was quite colorful in the hunting tests . . . at one memorable Master test she stood up on her hind legs to see where the bird was in high cover when the guns went off.

field trials and hunting tests for all breeds. Now retired, he is still involved with the hunting tests as a participant and judge.

Sonny Robertson, Lenaxa, Kansas, has hunted over retrievers all his life and is also a former field trialer. He began judging hunting tests in 1986, has judged about a dozen Master tests in four states, and was one of the three judges at AKC's 1991 first annual Master National Hunting Test in Delaware.

"Scenario" is one of the by-words of the hunting tests. "We're on an early evening dove hunt . . . walking around the lake waiting for the birds to come in . . .," or "Your hunting buddies are already in the duck blind, they've downed some birds, and you just arrived with your dog."

Most of these judges agreed the use of a hunting "scenario" is compatible with testing, adds to the color of the test, and the contestants enjoy the hunting flavor of scenarios. However, Kevin Marks questioned some of the scenarios he's seen.

"A lot of so-called scenarios are created with a 'this-*could*-happen-in-hunting' attitude. That may be so, but everything that happens in hunting doesn't automatically make it a good test or prove anything about the dog. A hunting test is just that...a test. I need to see clearly if the dog can mark, is trainable, uses his nose, etc." Kevin will give a scenario if asked, but prefers to spend more time explaining what the test is about and what is expected of the dog.

Sonny Robertson agreed a hunting-test judge should take the time to be explicit in his instructions to the handlers. "I always tell the handlers we are not in an adversarial position," Sonny said. "I want to make sure the dog has a fair chance against the test, which is, after all, the only thing he is running against."

What do judges look for in a Master dog? Like the prance and pizzazz that identifies an exceptional obedience dog, a Master Hunter must have style, style, style! "Very, very important," Sonny and Kevin both said. They want to see a dog who loves what he is doing. Sonny will hit hard for a dog that slinks or sulks.

"An animated dog who really loves to work," Tom Colstad said. "I look for a dog who would be a blast to hunt over."

"Without style," Phil Berger said, "everything else is irrelevant."

Style, or a lack of it, can cause the biggest problem in the Junior stake, perhaps because some novice handlers don't understand what it is or why it is important. A Junior dog is being evaluated for certain traits and abilities that could be *developed* into an excellent hunting dog. A judge wants to see a pup who gets excited and looks out eagerly for bird, and races out to hunt the area of the fall. A perfect job is not essential, but the desire to do the job has to be there.

A dog who sits without interest or emotion, trots slowly and/or compliantly out to the fall, then plods about and stumbles upon the bird, does not display the qualities necessary in a good hunting dog, and will seldom find favor with the judge, even if he does find the bird.

"In Junior, many handlers are upset because Fluffy can't or doesn't want to do the test," Julie Cairns said. Like all other judges, she sets certain standards, and expects the dog to meet or exceed them. Dogs at every level are expected to like and enjoy the game.

Style was never a problem in the Junior stake for Ch. Gold Country Bandana MH (Ch. Windfalls' Mr. Murphy CD ex Ch. Gold Country's Calamity Jane). "Echo" was the first bench champion of record to earn an AKC hunting title when she became a Junior Hunter in July 1986, and later pushed ahead in grand style to become the third show champion to add the big MH. Echo's lovely show coat has never stopped her from plowing through the mud and cattails in the marsh. Her owner, Joan Kipping of Forest Lake, Minnesota, stresses that Echo is a show dog *and* a hunting dog, who goes from the duck blind one weekend into the show ring the next.

Joan writes, "Her love for birds is incredible, and training twice a day is not enough for her. Several times a day she drags the training gear and check cords from the closet to the front door to inform me it is time to train . . . RIGHT NOW!

Ch. Gold Country Bandana MH, owned by Joan Kipping of Forest Lake, Minnesota, proved that "show dogs can do it, too." "Echo" was the first Golden Retriever bench champion to earn an AKC hunting title with her JH and the third bench champion Master Hunter. No big surprise to Joan, who has hunted over her home-bred Goldens for years. The tests just gave her and Echo one more goal and another reason to train as well as hunt.

Then there is her little trick of releasing the pigeons from the pen in hopes they will fly over the pool, so she can make a grand dive into the water. Echo's style (there's that word again), beauty and perseverance won her several parts in the AKC hunting film, *Love 'em, Hunt 'em, Test 'em.* She is a very special dog . . . "

Methods of testing and judging at the hunting tests have evolved and changed since that historic June day in Wichita, Kansas. With a better understanding of what they want to do and where they want to go, today's judges are setting up their tests accordingly. "A Master dog should be capable of doing field trial Qualifying tests," Phil Berger said. "You can't expect these dogs to thread the needle on a water blind at 200 yards."

On the other hand, . . . "You could take a field trial dog and blow him away with a field full of birds at close range and all the guns and commotion," Sonny Robertson said. He stipulated, however, that with a little training, a good field-trial dog could easily qualify as a Master Dog, a point of unanimous agreement among all six judges.

The switch from field trials to the hunting tests is a breeze if your dog knows what the retrieving game is all about. Chances R Cool Hand Luke MH, CDX, *** (OS) (Bonnie Brook's Mortimer ** ex Chances R Milady) came out of field trial retirement when AKC introduced the hunting tests. Luke easily barreled through his Master tests, despite his 11 and one-half years of age. He is believed to be the oldest Golden known to earn the Master Hunter title.

Owned by John and Nancy Miner of Yorkville, Illinois and bred by this author, Luke had been a master of the hunt long before AKC invented hunting titles, and was renowned as the best duck dog along the Fox River in Illinois. As a two-year-old, Luke made the Derby list, and became qualified All-Age at 28 months of age when he received a JAM in a licensed open stake. The hunting tests gave him one more chance to do what he excelled at and loved best. Luke's legacy to Goldens is his many offspring shivering patiently next to their owners, waiting for the ducks to fly over the blind.

While a Master test today should equal a tough qualifying test, Ham Rowan said that AKC is fostering harder, not easier, tests, although the level of difficulty in the hunting tests nationwide appears to be determined by regional standards. That difference will become more obvious in the quality of Master dog work from various regions of the country when these dogs compete at future National Tests.

"Because of the new National, more dogs will be running Master tests to qualify every year," Ham Rowan said. "We'll also be seeing not better dogs, but better trained dogs, with more ad-

Casey delivers a pheasant, **FC-AFC Casey Two of Fox Creek MH (HOF),** bred and owned by Sibby Wood.

vanced dogs entering at the Master level."

That's precisely what Kevin Marks has been observing for the past two years. "I'm seeing dogs who ran Senior tests two or three years ago running in the Master now, and their work is much improved," he said. "Some of these dogs are looking good."

Julie Cairns's own test performance with her dogs illustrates Kevin's point. "My own work in the hunt tests has improved, not only due to the training but because I started hunting with my husband," Julie said. "Quite a few dogs are run by women like myself who had never hunted before."

That's one of the more subtle benefits of the hunting tests: a number of women handlers have joined their husbands in the duck blind. Running hunting tests has changed the lives of conformation people, coming out of the show

Chances R Cool Hand Luke CDX, MH, * (OS)** (Bonnie Brook's Mortimer ** ex Chances R Milady) bred by the author, owned and trained by John and Nancy Miner, Yorkville, Illinois. Photo by author.

world to work with their Goldens, thrilling to their dogs' excitement at the guns, and to the sight of their dogs racing back with pheasant wings streaming in the wind. The owners are richer for it, and all the sporting breeds will benefit by getting the dogs and people out into the field. Kevin Marks, a past Kansas Regional Director for the American Chesapeake Club, spoke for all the "minority" hunting breeds. "The Golden Retriever people are just like the Chessie people. We've been told for years that we can't do it. The hunts are one of the best places we can go without that kind of pressure." Kevin said he has judged some fine performances by good-looking Goldens, along with the smaller, working-type dogs. "The Goldens I see are about 50-50 bench and field types," he said.

Sonny Robertson also sees an increase in the show-type Golden running Master hunts, dogs

Quoteal's Northwoods Bucyrus and Ray Klassen hunting Blue Grouse near the Bridger Mountains. Bred by Susan Hartzheim of Bozeman, Montana.

with more coat and bone than previous Master dogs. And that type of dog is a surprise to AKC.

"AKC got in to serve the hunting dog owner with one dog, the person who needed to know how to evaluate a good hunting dog or how to find one when it's time to breed," Ham Rowan said. AKC felt these folks might want to prove their dog is a good hunter or to put a title on their hunting dog.

But many hunters who wanted real hunting camaraderie found they had to mingle with show and obedience people at the hunting tests. Some felt the AKC events were strictly an agenda thing for people who just wanted to put a title on their show dog or prove their show dog could also hunt.

In effect then, AKC did not find the one-dog owner who has never been involved in an organized dog game. Instead they have tapped a market they never anticipated, show and obedience dogs who may never have picked up a dead or wounded bird. Nevertheless, the hunts have already served the retriever breeds. People who have never seen a field trial are thrilled to discover their show and obedience dogs actually do have hunting ability.

That discovery may encourage breeders to incorporate more hunting ability into their future breeding plans. Owners running hunting tests just for fun with their older dogs may later acquire a better quality dog because they would like to excel in the hunt test program, or because they were impressed by dogs they admired at the hunts. They see a dog with superior intensity and drive, a real passion for the game, and promise themselves a dog "just like that one" next time. The potential benefits of the hunting tests on the retriever owner and the breed are vast.

The oldest Golden to become a Master Hunter was just doing what came naturally. **Chances R Cool Hand Luke CDX, MH, *** (OS)** owned by John and Nancy Miner of Yorkville, Illinois, and bred by this author, had hunted waterfowl with John as soon as he was old enough to share a duck blind. Known to hunters up and down the Fox River, strangers often knocked on John's front door to ask if Luke lived there or if there were any Luke pups. Photo by author.

Hunting test hopefuls who are reluctant to tackle this new sport might be inspired by those Golden owners who paved the way for others in the breed. Their positive can-do attitudes led them to "Creative Training 101," new horizons to march into, and new adventures with their dogs.

The first Golden Retriever to earn the Master Hunter title is proof that research and "retriever resourcefulness" will produce Golden results. Argus Sheba of Belvedere MH (Sky-Lab Argus of Belvedere*** ex Belvedere's Joie De Vivre) was an urban hunter who received 98 percent of her training on the suburban streets of Houston, Texas. Owned by Harris Greenwood and bred by Mercedes Hitchcock, she was a city Golden who hunted only three or four times a year and trains "in the country" even less. Sheba was Harris's first Golden and first hunting dog, and Harris claims she is proof that a smart Golden can overcome a not-so-smart owner/handler who has never before trained a dog. The following is Harris's account of Sheba's unconventional training and hunting test career.

"I grew up hunting ducks and doves on the Texas prairie and had to retrieve all my own birds as well as my dad's for many years. I admired or envied hunters who had a four-footed friend, and secretly longed for the day that I would own and train my own retriever.

"Living in a nice residential area near downtown Houston, I didn't own a farm or ranch, and was too busy to spend time traveling to and from rural training grounds. I read Richard Wolters' *Water Dog*, James Lamb Free's *Training Your Retriever*, and William Koehler's *Dog Training,* but was most impressed with Lamb Free's statement, "If you can't teach your dog everything it needs to know in 10 minutes a day, you need a new dog." Accordingly, I spent a year and a half searching for, and finding, the 'perfect' Golden litter at Mercedes Hitchcock's Belvedere Kennels from which to pick my Sheba.

"Having read the books and selected the right dog, I spent 10 minutes a day in my front yard, back yard, neighbor's yard, school grounds, flood control easements, golf course, swimming pool

and reflection ponds....in and around my house, neighborhood and town. Every morning, first thing, Sheba got her 10 to 15 minutes of retrieving, 10 to 12 dummies thrown as sight blinds, from corner to corner in all of my neighbors' various yards, up and down the block, both sides of the street. (It helps to have cooperative neighbors.) Front yard, side yard, back yard, my dog ran through the azaleas, over the hedges, across the driveways, around the yard men, past the old ladies, by the postman, between the cars and back again.

"I found that people, stray dogs, squirrels, cats, motorcycles, cars, lawn mowers, civil defense sirens and other routine city noises and objects were wonderful distractions to improve

"Sheba," for short, takes a long flying leap!

concentration. Ten minutes a day, every day, didn't miss a day (or night), right at home, before work, after work, on a lunch break, whenever . . . it was never a problem and never an imposition. . . .it was a lot of fun, and it led us to the Rice Creek Retriever Club outside Little Falls, Minnesota on September 6, 1986, where Sheba completed the sixth out of the six licensed hunting tests she had entered, to become the first Golden Retriever Master Hunter in the world, and more importantly, the first Master Hunter of any breed in Texas . . . and I promise you we couldn't have done it 'where we done it and how we done it,' with any dog other than a Golden."

The first Golden bench champion to become a Master Hunter is another shining role model for Golden versatility. "Cassie" has achieved more diverse goals than any other Golden in breed history entering the decade of the '90s. Am-Can. Ch., MHR, HR CH, Heron Acres Sandcastle Am-Can. UDTX, MH, WCX, VCX, ***, TT, UKC-UD (OD) (Ch. Lochinvar's Hey U Sun Bear ex Sonja of Sylvan Glen WC), owned by Betty Drobac of Okemos, Michigan, is deservant of much recognition for her many talents and true Golden spirit.

Cassie earned the sixth and final leg of her Master Hunter title at the June 14, 1987, Northern Flight Hunting Retriever Association test in Hugo, Minnesota. She had already entered Golden breed records in 1984 when she became qualified All-Age by placing second in the GRCA spring all-breed trial, thus becoming the seventh Golden bitch breed champion in breed history to also claim qualified All-Age status. She is also the last breed champion to accomplish this.

Two years later she won the Qualifying stake at the Inland Retriever Association trial in Canada, thereby reaching All-Age status in Canada as well.

No stranger to record setting, Cassie had become the first Golden bench champion to earn an advanced tracking degree when she earned her TDX as a two-year-old in 1982.

It takes a very special team to set records such as these and excel in almost every discipline offered in the sport of dogs. Betty explained that their goals evolved naturally as they worked together in response to Cassie's enthusiasm and aptitude. Cassie's titles speak for themselves as well as for Betty's dedication to her Golden's versatility and potential.

Her training has had its practical applications as well. Cassie has, on command, "tracked" and found a set of car keys lost in a field at a trial, and located Betty's glasses dropped one day in the woods. At home her passion for tennis balls, especially catching two at the same time, exceeds every other interest or desire. She once persuaded a house guest to play this game for four straight hours and was disappointed when he lost interest so quickly!

At 11 years old, Cassie is more active in retirement than most dogs at the peak of their careers. She began an informal career as a therapy Golden at the local extended care facility where she is welcomed by one and all; she tags along on tracking sessions for a refresher course after the youngsters run their track; she is official pick-up and re-bird dog at field training outings; she provides the ultimate in distractions during obedience training class, sitting amid the scent articles or on the path to go-outs. After all these years, Cassie is not about to be left behind!

Topbrass Mioak's Bingo (FC-AFC Topbrass Windbreaker Zap ex Mioak's Golden Torch) proved that kids can do it too. Bingo became a Master Hunter at just 18 months of age and is believed to be the youngest Golden Retriever to earn that title. Owned by Brian Hartfield of Larsen, Wisconsin, and bred by Mickey Kendrigan, Bingo is "a vision that had come true...."

A professional gun dog trainer, Brian had acquired Bingo for a client who later declined to

Emberain Bay to Breakers UD, MH, WCX, * (NAFC-FC Topbrass Cotton ex Splashdown Emberain Aubrey UD, MH, ***), owned by Ed and Edwina Ryska, has his mom's same funny personality and zest for life.**

purchase the dog. Convinced that Bingo was too special to let go, Brian purchased her for himself. His letter about Bingo follows.

"Bingo's ability to mark and to grasp concepts is uncanny. A more willing dog I have never owned, and she has always given me her very best effort. She completed her Master Hunter requirements in five straight tests between September 17, 1989 and November 12, 1989, having already earned her Senior Hunter title. Bingo later became a qualified All-Age dog at 22 months of age in her very first trial, placing second in the Qualifying stake at the Mobile Alabama Retriever Club. Three weeks later she won the licensed Derby stake at Mississippi Valley R.C. at Weldon Springs, Missouri.

"Bingo has five littermates who have placed in licensed Derby and Qualifying stakes. My thanks to Mickey Kendrigan for breeding a line of Goldens that can do the work!"

For AFC, WR Glenhaven Devil's Advocate UDT, MH, WCX, *** (Smoke'N Red Apache ex OTCh. Meadowpond Especial One UDT, SH, WCX) earning obedience, tracking and field titles wasn't enough. Owned by Glenda Brown of Santa Barbara, California, "Luke" also became the first Golden in the nation to earn all three hunting tests titles. He was also the first Golden and third dog in California to earn a NAHRA Working Retriever title, as well as the youngest Golden in California to become a Master Hunter.

During his hunt test career, Luke had also competed in licensed field trials, earning an Amateur first and fourth, an Open fourth and six JAMs through 1990. Finally, after more placements, in February 1992 the plum... his AFC with an Amateur first place at the Southern Arizona RC trial. He has been completely trained by his owner, probably his biggest handicap, Glenda said.

Field trial judges often suggested that Glenda put Luke with a professional trainer to finish his titles. Her response was typical of many owners of working Goldens: "That's not why I'm in the game with him." Luke is Glenda's full-time house dog and is always ready to play or work at any game she offers him.

OTCh. Fox Creek Topper MH (HOF) (NAFC-FC Topbrass Cotton ex Rocky-Vue of Fox Creek***) is yet another first; through 1990 she was the only OTCh. Golden to also hold a Master Hunter title. Owned by Carla Naylor of Lubbock, Texas, Topper worked on her obedience career while competing in field trial Derbies. Retrieving dumbbells one weekend, ducks the next, she earned High-In-Trials at each level of CD, CDX, and UD, with many High-Combineds along the way.

After Topper earned her obedience championship, Carla wanted her to enjoy the new AKC hunting tests. She had been a constant hunting companion to Carla's husband, so with the real thing as her training foundation, she bypassed the Junior and Senior levels, and headed for the top.

Topper completed six successive Master tests with the same skill and determination she put into obedience competition. Carla felt her obedience training was an as-

AFC, WR Glenhaven Devil's Advocate UDT, MH, *, WCX,** owned by Glenda Brown of Santa Barbara, California, was the first Golden to earn all three hunting titles. "Luke" might well be called a canine over-achiever. After gaining his AKC hunting titles and his NAHRA WR (Working Retriever), he surged forward with field trial placements, and finally earned the coveted AFC! In obedience, he earned his CD...etc. he earned his CD with two first places and two seconds, and earned his CDX and UD from the "B" classes. When going for his tracking degree, he went so fast, the judges couldn't keep up with him. Whatever Luke does, he obviously tries his hardest every time . . . especially lying on his back to get a chest rub.

set in many of the hunting test situations.

Despite accomplishing the ultimate in two disciplines, Carla said Topper's most important quality is her true Golden disposition. Through her, Carla has a world of new friends across the country. A typical Golden, Topper has never met a stranger.

Am-Can. Ch. Comstock's Sunfire O'Hillcrest UDT, MH, WCX, VCX, Can. CDX, WC (Can. Ch. Comstock's Carmel Nut UDTX, SH, WCX, VCX, Can. UD, WCX ex Sunfire's Breila of Bristol CD, WCX,**), owned by Kathy Eddy McCue, VMD, of Ancramdale, New York, and Barb Biewer and Michael Book, earned her Master Hunter title along the busy road to her many other accomplishments. Born in February 1985, "Ritz" earned her American and Canadian CD, CDX, WC, American WCX, and finished her Canadian bench championship undefeated during 1986. Still bouncing from the bench into the field, the following year she passed her TD and JH, and gained her American championship in two months with three majors, including a five-point Best of Winners.

Kathy taught Ritz handling over the winter of 1987–88, using the D.L. Walters method from his book. Once she had claimed her final Senior Hunter leg, she rushed back into the obedience ring and earned her UD less than two months later. In 1990 Ritz finished her Master Hunter title after taking time off to raise a litter of pups—and all when she had just turned five years old. What's left? More Canadian titles and an American TDX, if Kathy will let Ritz have her way.

The outstanding Goldens portrayed here are representative of many Goldens running hunting tests today. Some actually hunt with their owners, and some do not.

Additionally, there are many Goldens who regularly hunt with their owners, but have never seen a field trial or a hunting test. Indeed, why should they? say their owners. Their dogs are proving they can get the bird as well as any field trial or hunting test retriever. Who needs simulated tests when their guys do the real thing every hunting season?

As the NAHRA principle attempts to illustrate, there is a vast difference between the field dog and the field trial dog, and now not to mention

the hunting test dog. Although one dog may be all three, the field trial dog and/or hunting test dog is the training partner and investment of the specialist who may or may not hunt, while the field dog is the hunter's pal and hunting buddy.

The hunter's world lays claim to unknown numbers of field Goldens who have never run a hunting test or trial. Many are pets and family companions who prefer a duck blind to the couch and race wildly for the door at the lift of an orange hunting cap. Some are conformation and obedience competition Goldens who gait around the ring one day and chase pheasants in the field the next. Some could probably outhunt a trial dog who may have never spent a single day afield.

While the actual numbers of such dogs may

The youngest Golden to earn a Master Hunter title, **Topbrass Mioak's Bingo MH** did it at 18 months of age. Four months later she became qualified All-Age. Bingo is out of a star-crossed litter, with five littermates who have also placed in licensed Derby and Qualifying stakes. Owned by Brian Hartfield of Larsen, Wisconsin, and bred by Mickey Kendrigan.

not be great or even in respectable proportion to the numbers of Golden champions and companions in the country, the fact is, they are out there contributing to the hunting pleasure of their owners and the hunting future of the breed.

Hugh Atwell of Albuquerque, New Mexico, Aspengold Golden Retrievers, has never run a hunting test or field trial, but he did hunt regularly with his Golden hunting partner, Ch.

Aspengold's Semi-Tough CD. (September 1982-May 1992) While not bred for field trials or hunting tests, Guv has served Hugh admirably in the field for all of his nine years. And Hugh's wife, Linda, has spent many a patient hour brushing out the mud and burrs Guv had collected in the field the day before a show. Neither wife nor dog had ever complained a bit, Hugh said. Guv proved hunting and the show ring could be compatible when he amassed 15 Show Dog Hall of Fame points while he was hunting in the field with Hugh.

"Guv may not have been a field trial dog," Hugh said, "but he has never lost a bird, never. Whether a clean kill or a cripple, and whether he marked the fall or not, he has never lost a bird. During one dove season, when I 'got lucky' and shot my first triple in a field covered with thick, chest-high sunflowers, Guv found all three birds in less than five minutes." A thrilling feat for any Golden hunter, regardless of his bent.

With Golden Retriever hunting dogs a quiet minority, and the hunting test Golden slowly making itself known, the rest of the would-be Golden hunting world might find a grain of truth in Mike Lardy's comments on the hunting retriever and the field trial dog: "Field trials are not unto themselves," he said. "The qualities you look for in a good trial dog are the same ones you need in a good hunting dog. If those qualities disappear, then good hunting dogs will also disappear. I have hunted over field trial wash-outs, and their inadequacies showed up in their hunting ability.

"Some people may be satisfied with a less-than-great hunting dog, and there's nothing wrong with that, but it's not true that you can produce great hunters but not great field trial dogs. The two are not unrelated. People will plan a breeding program with mediocre dogs to produce good hunters but not good trial dogs. That may produce adequate hunters, but you cannot produce exceptional dogs unless the parents have what it takes to start with."

Steady for the flush, here's **HR Quartermoon Kermit MH**, **WCX** doing his thing. Owned by Quartermoon Goldens of Berthoud, Colorado.

OTCh. Fox Creek Topper MH (HOF) owned by Carla Naylor of Lubbock, Texas and bred by Mrs. Maxwell Wood, had been hunting with Carla's husband, Mark, throughout her obedience career. But it was Carla and Topper's strong teamwork that led the two of them through six successful Master Hunter tests. The new hunting tests were the perfect sport to test her natural skills. She entered at the Master level and successfully completed six straight tests to become the first OTCh. to earn the Master Hunter title. Like many city-trained field dogs, Topper sometimes trains on large puddles and ponds in subdivisions and backyards.

Am-Can. Ch. Comstock's Sunfire O'Hillcrest UDT, MH, WCX, VCX, Can. CDX, WCI, owned by Kathy Eddy, VMD, Ancramdale, New York, Barb Biewer and Michael Book, was a stud fee puppy that "caught Kathy's eye" at six weeks old. "Ritz" has been very consistent in her working career, earning all her obedience legs with placements, all firsts in Canada and two High-In-Trials.

Marshland's Shotzy CDX, MH, * ** (AFC Wildfire of Riverview CDX ex Marshland's Lucky Trick (OD)), owned by Earl and Helen Dillow of Winthrop Harbor, Illinois, is an accomplished field-trial competitor as well as a Master Hunter. He has points toward his Amateur Field Championship, with an all-breed win, placements, and numerous JAMs in both Open and Amateur stakes. He is qualified All-Age in the U.S. and Canada. Shotzy earned his Master Hunter title with six straight qualifying scores. He finished the Master Invitational in 1990 with 21 marks and no handles, the only dog to finish without handling on a mark. His obedience career is equally colorful. He earned a Dog World award in the Novice class and sailed through his CDX. Utility? Now that was a different matter. Earl related Shotzy's brief Utility career. As a force fetched field-trial retriever, Shotzy wanted to put something in his mouth *instantly*. With some reservations, Earl entered four obedience shows. Shotzy sailed through the jumps like a champ. The gallery applauded . . . who was this new "masked man" in the obedience world? On to scent discrimination. Article scented, he was sent and grabbed the correct article with the speed of sound. The judge gasped and asked, "Is he always this fast?" Came article number two, again with the speed of sound, snatched it up. The rest is history. The next three days, with the speed of light, "all the wrong articles," despite perfect work on the rest of the exercises. End of Utility career.

This picture was taken on the last day of duck season with the temperature a balmy -10°F. Although there was heat inside the boat **Heidi Goose Tumbles Am-Can. UD, MH, WCX** refuses to come in except on command and then won't stay very long. In this picture she has just come back from a retrieve, delivered to hand, and then returned to her place on "Duck Watch." At this point her hair is all ice covered and when she leaves the deck to make another retrieve she leaves clumps of hair frozen to the deck. Owned by John L. Marchica, of Lincoln, Vermont. Heidi is by Porters Samuel Companion ex Heather Lea Jaws.

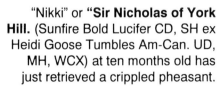

"Nikki" or **"Sir Nicholas of York Hill.** (Sunfire Bold Lucifer CD, SH ex Heidi Goose Tumbles Am-Can. UD, MH, WCX) at ten months old has just retrieved a crippled pheasant.

193

This page: **Ch. Aspengold's Semi-Tough CD** (Ch. Amberac's Aristocrat CD, WC ex Desert Gold's Country Lass) with breeder-owner Hugh Atwell hunting doves on the Albuquerque prairie. "Guv" was a true dual-purpose Golden, retrieving doves or pheasants one day, showing in the ring the next, and doing both with style and panache! He hunted his heart out through his very last year.

This page: **Pine Run's End of the Rainbow CD, JH, WC,** owned by his hunting partner, Gerry Badesso and wife Karen. In the above photo "Bo" wanted the pheasant so badly that . . . all four paws cleared the three-foot-high cover . . . . Bo's ears are up in the air, indicating he was on his way down, and thus had jumped even higher than this photo. Now that's an eager retriever! Finally *(left)* . . . Bo with his prize. Thank goodness Gerry made the shot.

195

Left: "Tai," **Lord Taikimus CDX** shows off his Blue Grouse. Owners, James and Susan Hartzheim. *Below:* **AFC, WR Glenhaven's Devil's Advocate UDT, MH, WCX,** "Luke," waiting for the birds to come, climbs back into the boat after a retrieve. Owner, Glenda Brown.

Above: Tom Colstad's **Superior's Chevas CD, MH, ***** (Handjem's Quick Sand *** ex AFC Ben's Enchanted Glory) started his career in field trials. He became qualified All-Age at two-and-one-half years of age and had several Amateur JAMs when he first entered hunting tests. Chevas became a Master Hunter in September 1989. He was one of two Goldens among the 26 dogs out of 98 starters who finished the first Master National in Delaware in 1991. *Below:* **Quoteal's Sportin' Wild Rose** (AFC Sportin' Kelty ex Quoteal's Right-on Electra CD, TD) and **Quoteal's Northwoods Bucyrus CD, TD** (Ch. Libra Malagold Coriander ex Quoteal's Auralee Jessie). Owners, James and Susan Hartzheim.

Ring bred by Mercedes Hitchcock.

**Riverbend's Ragamuffin MH, WCX, ** owned by Julie and Tom Cairns, Arcata, California. Her reason for living is hunting, and finding and retrieving birds.

Above left: **Foordmore's Smok'n Mist CD, MH, WCX, ***** (AFC Yankee's Smoke'N Red Devil ex Meadowpond Scotch Mist CD, TD, WCX), owned by Alan and Nancy Foord, Walnut Creek, California, started his field career with eight Derby points before moving up to become a qualified All-Age dog before three years of age. Nancy describes "Andy" as a gentle and loving dog, yet a whirlwind of energy and high spirits who is exciting to train and watch. Life is never dull with "Andy!"
Above right: **Duncan's Half Brother CDX, MH, WCX, ***** (Happy's Sir Winston*** ex Cayenne's Sinjin Rose**) owned by Ann and Jeff Strathern of Frederick, Maryland, was Jeff's hunting companion and ran in Gun Dog stakes and pheasant and duck shoots before the hunting tests arrived. Because of his previous training, and at eight-and-one-half years old, Brother entered at the Master level and passed in six straight tests, becoming the second Golden, and third retriever, to earn the Master Hunter title.

Sungold Fortune of Foordmore CDX, MH, WCX, ** (AFC Holway Barty ex Sungold Naughty Pine), owned by Alan and Nancy Foord of Walnut Creek, California, became a Master Hunter at 10 ½ years old. She earned her two-star status with a third place in the Qualifying at the 1986 National Specialty, and completed her obedience titles between field trials. Fortune has also spent three years visiting a local nursing home, holding "hands," smiling and retrieving toys for her many friends.

This page: **MHR, HR CH Bama Bran Muffin CDX, WC** (Golden Will Rodgers WC ex Emberain Smoke'N Bama Belle), owned by Tracy Sanders of Tyler, Alabama, won her first puppy test at six months old, and . . . same old story . . . Tracy was hooked! Muffin started running hunt tests at three years of age, and eighteen months later had a UKC Hunting Retriever Champion title and a NAHRA Master Hunting Retriever title, picking up her CD, CDX and WC during the same time. The next time you see Muffin's name, it should have a UD behind it!

This page: **HR Quartermoon Kermit MH, WCX** (Quartermoon Rage'n Cajun CD, WCX ex Quartermoon Dixie Lilly MH, **) bred by Bobbie Christensen, and owned and hunted by Doug Koeppel, Evergreen, Colorado. Hunting Companion, not "dog," according to Doug. Kermit barks at him when he misses a shot.

Above: **Can. Ch. Comstock's Caramel Nut UDTX, SH, WCX, VCX, Can. UD, WCX** (Bainin of Caernac CD, *** ex Gandolf's Comstock Euphoria CD, ***) owned by Kathy Eddy McCue, VMD, Ancramdale, New York, set a precedent for his daughter, "Ritz." He earned seven Canadian High-In-Trials and is a member of the Canadian Hall of Fame. "Jazz" finished his Canadian championship undefeated and had ten American points, including a Sporting Group first and fourth. *Below left:* **Emberain Taken by Storm CD, MH, WCX, ***** (AFC Yankee's Smoke'N Red Devil ex Splashdown Emberain Aubrey UD, MH, ***), owned by Ed and Edwina Ryska, has been a field-trial dog all his life, had Derby points and two Qualifying wins before his third birthday. *Below right:* **Culynwood's Miss Sunshine UD, WCX** (Ch.-AFC Honor's Darado of Spindrift ex Ch. Tangelo's End of the Rainbow CD, WC), owned by Alan and Nancy Foord, made her mom an Outstanding Dam when she earned her UD title. Although crippled with arthritis, "Missy" still loves to retrieve and be included in the training sessions.

Above: **Mylinda of York Hill Am-Can. CDX, SH, WC**. (Crangold Mighty Maxx JH ex Heidi Goose Tumbles Am-Can. UD, MH, WCX). *Below:* **GMHR WR RockErin Willorun Tyree** (Willorun Nifty Budweiser ex Willorun Mocha) owned by Joseph McCann and Maria Di Gregorio, Stillwater, Oklahoma, is the first Golden MHR and GMHR in NAHRA history, and the only female Golden GMHR in NAHRA in 1991. "Ty" qualified at the NAHRA National Invitational in 1989 and 1990. Ty is pictured with fellow **GMHR The Gamekeeper of RockErin**.

Above: **Emberain Le Pyramid UD, SH, WCX, ** (OD)** (AFC Northbreak's Brier ex Wilaco's Eclipse of Emberain UD, WCX) owned by Ed and Edwina Ryska, Petaluma, California, left home as a puppy, but returned untrained at 14 month of age. Making up for lost time, "Lacey" earned her CD, CDX and UD between field trials, placed third in a Qualifying, and raised three litters of pups between titles. She took a four-year semi-retirement before going on for her Senior Hunter. Her most important job, however, is still that of stick dog, retrieving every little twig for anyone who stands still. *Below:* **Wilaco's Eclipse of Emberain UD, WCX (OD)** (Dual CH-AFC Ronaker's Novato Cain CD ex Ronakers Tara Queen) October 1976–April 1988, owned by Ed and Edwina Ryska. A devoted mother, "Clipper" would steal other bitches,puppies and mother them, even getting in milk. The other moms always gave in and shared the whelping box with her. No wonder she became an Outstanding Dam…

Above: Three generations of ODs, GRCA blue-ribbon Outstanding Dams from the Ryskas of Petaluma, California. They are **Emberain Le Pyramid UD, SH, WCX, ** (OD), Wilaco's Eclipse of Emberain UD, WCX (OD)**, and **Splashdown Emberain Aurbrey UD, MH, *** (OD)**. *Below left:* **Glenhaven Devil May Care UDT, JH, WCX** (Smoke'n Red Apache WCX, *** ex OTCh. Meadowpond Especial One UDT, SH, WCX) a Luke sister also owned by Glenda Brown is following in her brother's pawprints. On her way to her UD she earned three Novice first placements, a High-In-Trial, and a Dog World award. She's ready for her TDX, if Luke will just spare her a little time out from field trials and hunting tests. *Below right:* **Emberain Pacific Storm UD, JH, WXC** (Emberain Taken by Storm CD, MH, WCX, *** ex Emberain Le Pyramid UD, SH, WCX, **), owned by Ed and Edwina Ryska, is the image of his grandmother, "Clipper."

Am-Can. Ch. Pepperhill Golden Pine Trumpet CDX, SH, WCX, VCX, Can. CD, WCX (OD) (Ch. Beckwith's Justa Tuckerbear ex Ch. Pepperhill Golden Pine Irish WC) was the first Golden bench champion to earn a Senior Hunter title. She was trained and handled to her hunting titles by her owner Charlotte Gaynor of San Francisco. While Trumpet was training and working toward her hunting titles, she was also being shown to her bench championship by her co-breeder Nancy Kelly. One typical "Trumpet weekend" included earning a WCX on Thursday, winning Reserve Winners Bitch on Friday, and retrieving in a hunting test on Saturday. A GRCA Outstanding Dam, Trumpet has passed her versatility on to her multiple-titled offspring, who have many bench, obedience and hunting titles to their credit. Photo by Fox & Cook.

Working Certificate Tests and Working Certificate Excellent Tests

The GRCA established the Working Certificate program to encourage the use and development of those natural abilities for which the Golden Retriever was originally bred.

There are many non-hunters who own retrieve-a-holic Goldens, and, due to limitations on their time or space or a variety of other reasons, they are unable to fulfill their dogs' potential in the field. The WC/WCX program offers a reasonable platform for those owners with limited field knowledge, and provides an opportunity for the dogs to realize a bit of their destiny by retrieving "the real thing" instead of a tennis ball or frisbee.

Conversely, there are just as many field-type people who own Goldens less talented on the retrieving end of the breed. Pledged to their dogs for life, these folks can enter WC/WCX tests and enjoy a retrieving adventure with their dogs on a more casual and non-competitive level.

Over 3,400 Goldens had earned the WC through 1989, and 925 had earned their WCX. In multititled Goldens the WCX is one trademark of the versatile retriever who can achieve in all the sporting disciplines. Almost every Golden who boasts a trail of titles after his name has earned a WCX, many more than once.

The WC/WCX is open to all dogs, even those who have already earned their title, and owners often enter just to give their dogs the thrill of the field as a reward for other jobs well done.

The WC/WCX tests are hosted by GRCA member clubs with the approval of the parent club. Manpower and grounds are essential ingredients, and those clubs with access to public wildlife areas or suitable grounds often hold annual WC/WCX tests, some in conjunction with a regional specialty or other club-sponsored event.

At the minimal level the WC tests are designed to demonstrate the dog's memory and marking ability, style, intelligence, nose, perseverance, trainability and desire to retrieve; they are not intended to test the degree of the dog's training, as with the field trial competitor. The tests are non-competitive, and may be held in conjunction with any AKC-licensed retriever field trial or any event held in the name of the GRCA. Dogs must be at least six months old to enter and have an AKC, foreign or ILP registration number.

The WC is judged under the Derby rules as described by AKC Field Trial rules with three exceptions: (1) Artificial decoys may not be used. (2) Dogs may be brought to line on leash and held, but may not be sent until their number is called. (3) Hand delivery of birds is not necessary, but the dog must deliver the bird to the area of the line.

Ch. Elysian Sky-Hi Exposure UDT, MH, WCX, ** (Ch. Wingwatcher Reddi to Rally CD, WC ex Ch. Beaulieu's Akacia O'Darnley UDTX, JH, WCX), owned by Sandy Whicker, Fort Collins, Colorado, and bred by Jeanne von Barby. "Expo" is a littermate to Leica, and another tribute to his mother Kacia's talent for passing Golden versatility on to her get. Expo earned his TD at seven months, WC at 14 months, and his CD at 22 months, with two first placements. He earned his first Senior Hunter leg the day after he finished his JH title. Expo topped his career with a Qualifying JAM at the 1991 National specialty. He's also gone *BOB!*

Requirements (paraphrased) for a WC are:

(1) The retrieving of two (a double retrieve) previously shot upland game birds (pheasant, pigeon or other native game bird) on land in moderate cover, with the birds approximately 40 to 50 yards from the line, and the falls at least 90 degrees apart. This test demonstrates the dog's ability to mark, remember and retrieve a double fall.

(2) The retrieving of two freshly killed ducks in swimming water as back to back singles approximately 25 to 30 yards from the line. This will demonstrate the ability to swim and to retrieve waterfowl and a willingness to re-enter the water.

The dog may be held on a leash or slipcord until he is sent by his handler, but no voice command or hand signal is permitted while the dog is working. When the dog returns with the first bird of the land double, the handler may speak to the dog and give heel, sit or stay commands to ready the dog for the second bird.

He may gently touch the dog to direct him, but may not manhandle or pull the dog by the collar or neck into position.

After the second retrieve, the handler may hold the dog's collar to lead him off line. In each water single, he may hold the dog until his number is called by the judge.

The WCX is designed for dogs trained beyond the Working Certificate, but not to the competitive level of AKC field trials. It is judged under AKC field trial rules for the Qualifying stake and carries the following requirements!

(1) The retrieving of three upland game birds on land as a triple in moderate cover, with two dead birds and the last bird a flier. Falls must be not less than 60 yards or more than 100 yards from the line, not less than 60 degrees apart, and must fall at a 45-degree angle back from the guns. The order of the falls can be left to right or vice-versa. Bird throwers should be in light-colored shirts or jackets.

(2) The retrieving of two freshly killed ducks in water as a double retrieve with an honor. Falls must be 45 to 60 yards from the line, not less than 60 degrees apart at a 45-degree angle back from the guns, and at least one bird must fall in swimming water. The memory bird should be in moderate cover, not visible from line, and the other bird should be fully visible in open water. The diversion may be a shot flyer, with the fall not less than 50 yards from the running dog or the honoring dog. Two to four artificial decoys should be used, but planted away from the line of the falls.

The handler must bring his dog to line off-leash, without a collar and under control, and is not allowed to touch the dog at any time during the test. The dog must be steady and not sent until the judge calls his number, and must deliver each bird to hand and relinquish it readily. At the water double, the dog can leave the line when released by the judge after the completion of the hono̅. As in the WC, voice or hand signals are not permitted.

These test descriptions are paraphrased from the "GRCA WC and WCX Rules and Regulations." A complete set of rules, judging requirements, guideline explanations and supplement can be obtained from the GRCA.

Can. Ch., Can. OTCh. Trumpet's Ratfaced McDougal UD, SH, WCX, Can. UD, WCX, owned and trained by Charlotte Gaynor, San Francisco, "Scrapper," is whizzing through his titles in true style. He is on his way to his Master Hunter title.

Am-Can. Ch. Trumpet's Tijac Twister Am-Can. CDX, JH, Am-Can. WC is Anita's Golden boy out of Jaimie and Trumpet, co-owned with Tim and Jackie O'Brien in Chelan, Washington. Anita Lee works on "Dexter's" Canadian titles after the O'Briens complete them in the U.S.

The Canadian Kennel Club offers to all retrievers, Irish Water Spaniels and Standard Poodles its own Working Certificate program that consists of testing on three levels: the Working Certificate (WC), Working Certificate Intermediate (WCI), and Working Certificate Excellent (WCX). The program is developed, run and recognized by the CKC, in contrast to the programs offered by each retriever breed club in the U.S., where titles earned are recognized only by the parent club.

The Canadians use only dead birds and blank ammunition, and the tests resemble hunting tests rather than the basic field trial tests used in the American WC. Ducks, pigeons and pheasants are used on land, and ducks only in the water.

The WC test is designed to test the dog's natural abilities as a retriever and consists of back to back singles on both land and water. Dogs may not wear a collar, but may be held and must deliver to hand. Land singles should be approximately 50 to 75 yards from line in light to moderate cover with not less than 90 degrees between falls. The water singles should also be no less than 90 degrees apart and 35 to 40 yards away in open water. One gunner should be positioned about 10 yards from the dog, with his bird thrown at an angle back and out into the water. No decoys are used.

Aureo Kyrie Touf Acto Follow UD, JH, WCX, Can. UD, WC (Am-Can. Ch. Kyrie Legendarian, Am-Can. CDX, TD, WC ex Richland Kyrie Liberty Belle Am-Can. UD, WCX, Can. WC) owned by Neida Heusinkvelt Bopp, Prairie Village, Kansas. Happy-go-lucky, rowdy retrieve-a-holic, "Bruiser" is a multiple-HIT dog well on his way to his OTCh. His most significant accomplishment has been as the first-ever recipient of the Nan Gordon Memorial Trophy for triple purpose achievement, awarded at the Canadian Golden Retriever National Specialty in 1983 when Bruiser won first in Bred-By-Exhibitor Dog class, first in Open A obedience and his WC the same weekend. At age ten, he's enthusiastically training for his TD.

hunter. Dogs must be off-lead at all times. Tests consist of a walk-up test with a land double or land/water double, an honor on the walk-up, a water double, land double and a water blind.

The walk-up tests must include a 15-yard walk-up for both the working and honoring dogs. The first bird is thrown about 50 yards, the second about 100 yards in moderate to heavy cover with about a 90-degree angle between. One bird can land in water and one on land, with the closer bird at 50 yards.

The water double falls should be up to 50 yards in swimming or wading water, landing with a splash in natural cover about 90 degrees apart. Single decoys should be planted away from a direct line to the falls. The handler must fire the gun for one of the marks (unless he is without a hunting license, whereby a second qualified person will stand

The WCI tests are intended to evaluate the dog's natural ability and value as a hunting partner. They consist of one land and one water double with an honor on the land test. The land falls should be not less than 90 degrees apart and approximately 75 yards long in moderate to moderately heavy cover. The working dog must be steady and under control, come to line off-lead and deliver to hand. The honoring dog must remain staunch until the working dog has reached the area of the first fall.

In the water double, the birds should be not less than 90 degrees apart and land with a visible splash 40 to 50 yards from the line. One bird must land in cover; single decoys may be anchored centrally between the two marks.

The WCX should prove the dog is a steady, reliable worker who would be an asset to the

Flash—**OTCh. Sunfire's Spontaneous Combustion UD, JH, WCX (HOF).** (OTCh. Heelalong Cracklin Sunfire UDTX, WC ex Am-Can. Ch. Clark's Easter Bonnet UD, WCX, Can. CDX, WC. Breeders, Michael A. Book and Sydney C. Waller. Born: November 6, 1985. Owner, Karen Price.

nearby to fire as necessary).

The land blind should be about 50 yards through moderate cover with some natural obstacle such as a ditch, small hedgerow or standing water about 15 feet from the line. The handler must fire as in the first test. The water blind should be a maximum of 50 yards, the water's edge no more than 15 feet from the line, with a direct, not an angle, entry.

These rules are excerpted from "Canadian Working Certificate Program Rules and Regulations," which can be obtained from the Canadian Kennel Club, 2150 Bloor St. West, Toronto Ontario, M6S 4V7.

Tanya Du Shanka Am-Can. CD, WC (1971-1982). Owner, Michael A. Book. Tanya was the foundation dam for Sunfire, and is a GRCA Outstanding Dam with three UD, WCX offspring (including Cascade with MH).

Known as "Jaimie" to his friends, this is **Am-Can. Ch., Can. OTCh. Amanda's Pacific Whirlwind Can. UDT, WCI, TT, Am. CDX, TD, JH, WCX, VCX (OS)** (Am-Can. Ch. Trowsnest Whirlwind UD, WC, Can. CDX, WC ex Am-Can. Ch. Glenallens Amanda) owned by Anita Lee, Vancouver, British Columbia. When Anita threw puppy Jaimie his first bird wing, and he ran around the yard with his entire litter hot on his heels, she knew at once, he was "the one." Appropriately named, his whole career has been a whirlwind. A Canadian championship in his first three shows, American and Canadian obedience titles with placements in every class, all titles...tracking and field in Canada and the U.S....on his first try. He flies through his obedience routines and was second highest scoring dog in trial three times in the Open B class. In 1988 and 1989 he was awarded the GRCC J.P. Crawley Memorial Trophy for the Grand Champion Golden who continues to excel and achieve in all fields of competition. Jaimie just loves to be doing ANYTHING, and always with enormous enthusiasm and a smile on his face...Jamie has passed that same zest and reliability on to his kids. His litter out of Am-Can. Ch. Pepperhill Golden Pine Trumpet CDX, SH, WCX, Can. CD, WCX, (OD) earned a total of 23 titles by 28 months of age, with most of them owner-trained and handled.

This page: **Am-Can. Ch. Whipaly's Colabaugh Senna Am-Can. UD, SH, WCX, TT, Can. WC** (Am-Can. Ch. Ambertail's Flatbush Flanagan Am-Can. CD ex Topbrass Razzle Dazzle Rose CD, TD, WCX) has been a dream come true for her owner, Janine Fiorito of Croton, New York. Senna is a retriev-a-holic whose first love is retrieving anything, preferably birds. When an injury interfered with her field career, she made up for it on her CD…two firsts, two seconds, and back-to-back HITs. She worked on her CDX and WCX while scoring in the breed ring, and on one proud day, took Best of Breed and a third place with 195 in Open B at the same show. Still doing it all at once, she earned a Senior Hunter leg and qualified in Utility on the same weekend. With 22 OTCh. points and one leg on her Master Hunter, Senna was on her way again. A bout with breast cancer interrupted her momentum…but only briefly, if Senna has her say. At eight years old, she has informed Janine she's just too young to quit!

OTCh. Altair's Dune Mirage TDX, SH, WCX, Can. UDT (OS) (Ch. Sun Dance Destiny's Echo CDX ex Meadowpond Cherokee Sunday UDT, WC, Can. UD) is owned and adored by Rosemary Chase of Bedford, Ohio. Dune is truly a multi-purpose Golden with talent and titles in obedience, tracking and field, as well as five points in the breed ring. Three Dog World awards, a Gaines Super Dog placement, and multiple HITs *and* a perfect score of 200 in the Open B class attest to his strength in the obedience ring.

Dune's eye contact in obedience is superb...very natural, and required almost no training at all.

Dune is always up for anything. While staying at a motel in Pennsylvania to run a hunt test, Rosemary taught him to go down the slide. He loved it, and wanted to do it again and again!

Can. OTCh. Kelly of Queen Island UDT, WCX, TT owned and lovingly photographed by her owner Susan Kluesner, Lakeville, Minnesota. Kelly is shown here in full tracking harness in the field.

Tracking

Blind faith . . . that intangible quality that binds the tracking handler to his dog. The dog is pulling on a 40-foot lead, leading you through fields and hedgerows, across streams and over fences . . .

Complete confidence. You've trained in rain and mud, in sleet and snow and gale-force winds. Now you have to believe in your dog . . . the dog will sense it, feel it in the lead.

Unswerving trust...the deep gut feeling that takes the tracking team a bit beyond the edge of

sible and wonderful, and prize the TDX as the most treasured of all titles. Owners of multi-titled dogs often claim that tracking with their dogs is the ultimate bonding experience.

Rosemary Chase, owner of OTCh. Altair's Dune Mirage TDX, SH, WCX, Can. UDT, speaks for many in the sport. "The bond you form is incredible," she said. "It's just you and the dog alone out there, the dog leading you through woods and fields. The dog has to know that you believe in him completely."

Dune was one of 97 Golden Retrievers who earned the TDX title during the 1980s. Since the introduction of the TDX in 1980, Goldens every year have earned more tracking titles than any other breed except the German Shepherd.

That's not surprising, since the Golden's nose is one of its most famous parts. Breed historians credit the Golden's scenting powers to early outcross breedings to the Bloodhound. In the 1947 *Book of the Golden Retriever,* author W.M. Charlesworth notes that after the Bloodhound cross was made, Lord Tweedmouth gave away certain dogs and puppies to a few relatives and friends.

Hutchinson's *Dog Encyclopaedia* supports Mrs. Charlesworth, stating, "After some years Lord Tweedmouth introduced a Bloodhound cross to retain the wonderful tracking powers produced by Nous and his descendants, as they were used chiefly in the forest for tracking deer."

Many hundreds of Goldens have gained their

other sporting thrills. All you can do is follow . . . the dog knows, you both know . . .

No wonder experienced trackers describe the pursuit of the TDX as at once terrifying, impos-

Tracking Dog title since the first AKC-licensed tracking test in 1940. The first UD Golden to earn that tracking degree was Featherquest Trigger who earned the UDT in 1950. Bred by Dr. Mark

D. Elliott and owned by Marjorie Perry, Trigger was a credit to his sire, Goldwood Toby UD, the first Golden Retriever to earn an obedience Utility degree.

Later, in 1954, Ch. Holly of Claymyr UDT (Flyer of Taramar ex Tulchard Merrilass UD), owned by Clayton Hare, proved a bench champion could follow her nose as well as gait precisely around the show and obedience rings. She earned her TD in November of that year and completed her UDT the following month.

However, the real bonus in U.S. tracking oc-

Earning a TDX title requires an exceptional dog and a dedicated, tracking-crazy owner. Not every dog has the determination, drive or mental capacity to press on. The only motivation for the tracking dog is the strength of understanding and communication with its handler.

Trackers apparently are up to the challenge, as the number of tracking tests has quadrupled since 1980. Over 700 dogs representing 66 breeds have earned TDX titles since that year. In 1990 alone, from the 122 Tracking Dog and 103 Tracking Dog Excellent tests conducted nationally, 71

At eight weeks old, the future **Coronet Goldust Sugr Maple TD** starts to show his propensity for tracking (or perhaps just gloves). Sugr was sired by Am-Can. Ch. Asterling Cntryside Bristol ex Coronet's Angel Mine. Owners, Pam German and Sue Baumgartner of Belvedere, Illinois.

curred in 1980 when AKC added the Tracking Dog Excellent (TDX) title for tracking devotees. Canada has offered the TDX since 1964, and prior to 1980, many Americans traveled into Canada to pursue advanced tracking degrees with their dogs.

Goldens earned their TD and 11 earned the TDX.

Two Goldens earned the first breed TDX titles during that first year it was offered, and paved the track for the many who would follow. Mountain Ridge's Secret Agent CD, TDX, owned by Lowell Stouder, passed the test on April 12,

1980, at Sandia, New Mexico. Later, on November 16, Golden Yoke Awendaw Amber CD, TDX, owned by B. Glazebrook, passed in Concord, Maine.

Six more passed the following year, with Helen Phillips's Meadowpond Son of a Gun UDTX, and Karen Johnson's Heelalong Cracklin' Sunfire CDX, TDX, finishing their OTCh. titles later in their working careers. In September 1981, Can. OTCh. Bonnie Island Dynamite Am-Can. UDTX, (later WCX, Can. WC, Mex. PC) became the first UD Golden to add a TDX. Bonnie's owners, John and Roberta Anderson of Oak Harbor, Washington, also owned the oldest Golden to earn TDX status; their Bonnie Island Antique Bronze, Am-Can. CDX, TDX, WC, claimed her TDX on September 10, 1983 at a hearty 11 and one-half years of age.

The Andersons and their Goldens have an obvious love and talent for their dog sport of choice. That same September day, the Anderson's Bonnie Island Carla's Lady Luv CDX, Can. CD, TD, also added a TDX to her list of working achievements, later earning a JH, WC, Can. CDX, Mex. PC and GRCA OD.

1982 and 1983 saw 21 Goldens gain a TDX. Four of these were show champions, proving the working nose and versatility inherent in a proper Golden. Am-Can. Ch. OTCh. Bonnie Island Gold-Rush Carla WC, Am-Can. UDTX, WC, also owned by the Andersons, in 1982 was the first Golden UD/bench champion to achieve the TDX.

Carla's tracking career began as a puppy, just days after her arrival at the Anderson farm. She loved it!...and passed her first tracking test at barely seven months of age. Much later, with the introduction of the TDX, Carla taught owner Roberta more about tracking, and their tracking adventures aided Roberta in her judging career. Carla topped her many other accomplishments when she became the first conformation champion and UDTX Golden in the U.S. several years after attaining those titles in Canada.

The following year, Ch. Cimaron's Dusty Dawn UDTX, ***, owned by Connie and Betty Drobac, proved that a field dog's nose will follow something besides feathers, when he became the first qualified All-Age Golden Ch-UDTX.

In 1982, Am-Can. Ch., Can. OTCh. Ambertrail's Bargello Stitch Am-Can. UDTX, WCX, owned by Barbara Tinker of Katonah, New York, completed her TDX and continued on to later earn her BDA, CDX and TD.

Showing off all the articles he tracked and found to earn his TDX at the 1989 GRCA National Specialty, this is **Honor's Cogan in the Rockies UDTX, WC, TDI**, owned by Ron Buksaitis.

For many years Stitch held the prominent position of most-titled Golden in the history of the breed in the United States. Of all her many prestigous titles, her TDX is the one most treasured by her owner. Barbara and Stitch spent two and one-half years pursuing their U.S. TDX. Through eye surgery that left scar tissue over Stitch's right eye, one litter of puppies with Stitch nursing between tracking sessions, and her affinity for checking out every deer, rabbit and squirrel that had crossed her track, Stitch finally passed at the Taconic Hills TDX test. As with each of her many achievements, Stitch's great heart and eager attitude always carried her through.

That same year Am-Can. Ch. Heron Acres Sand Castle CDX, WCX, Can. CDX, owned by Betty Drobac, earned her TDX. She later added her UD and MH, UKC HRCH and UD, NAHRA MHR, Can. UDTX, plus three-star All-Age Qualified status in the U.S. and Canada, nudging past

Stitch to become the most accomplished Golden Retriever in breed history.

Two Goldens who earned their TDX in 1982 also number among the oldest of the breed to do so. Can. OTCh. Kyrie Genever Am-Can. UDTX, Am-Can. WC, owned by Ed and Marallyn Wight, was ten years and almost eight months old when she became the first Golden to earn a TDX at a GRCA National Specialty. "Gena" was the Wight's first Golden, and her enthusiasm for the sport of

Making it all look easy, this is **Am-Can. OTCh. Culynwood's Buckthorn Taiga TD, WC**, owned by Judy Myers.

tracking has been their tracking inspiration across the U.S. and Canada for almost 20 years.

Gena was involved in the experimental testing which led to the development of the American TDX format. During one experimental test, while running a track with Ed, she plunged through some high cover and out of Ed's view. Ed followed, and discovered Gena's end of the lead had disappeared into the ground! Gena had fallen into a six-foot-deep skeet-throwing pit buried under the heavy brush! Ed jumped in and lifted her out to the judges, and they quickly determined she had escaped serious injury from the fall. Then Gena, a true sport in every sense, led Ed down the rest of the track to complete the test.

Gena was also the inspiration for the Ann Arbor Dog Training Club's "Order of the Muddy Sneaker." Marallyn says that trackers of all the tracking breeds throughout the United States and Canada now wear the OMS patch signifying that they belong to that tracking fraternity. The original OMS trophy, an old gilded, worn-out tennis shoe mounted on weather beaten wood, is awarded annually to a member of the club.

Ed and Marallyn's Can. OTCh. Anthea of Setherwood Am-Can. UDTX, followed Gena's example when she earned her TDX at ten years and six months of age. "Thea" had opened the advanced tracking gates for Goldens in 1974 when, at two years old, she became the first of the breed to earn a Canadian TDX. Both Thea and Gena continued to track for the sheer enjoyment of working until their deaths in 1987 and 1988.

In 1984 a total of 14 Goldens joined the ranks of TDX-titled dogs. Bonnie Island Gold Rush Piper CDX, TDX, WC, Can. CDX, TD, WC lived up to the Anderson tradition and became the fifth Anderson TDX Golden. Altair's Dune Mirage CD, TDX, owned by Rosemary Chase, went on to earn her OTCh., WCX, SH and Can. UDT, after her 1984 TDX.

In October that year, another Obedience Trial Champion was bitten by the tracking bug: OTCh. Wynwood's Two Double Zera, owned by Lockie Treanor, also earned a TDX. Beckwith's Five Star Hennessy UDTX (a very busy Golden, later achieving his U-UD, Am-Can. OTCh., Am-Can. TDX, WCX, TT, Can. WC) owned by Nancy Light, proved more Golden versatility when he earned his TDX.

In 1986, eight Goldens claimed a TDX, with a sixth Anderson TDX, Bonnie Island Olympia Gold CD, TDX. 1987 witnessed eight more TDX Goldens, including one obedience champion, OTCh. Harvest's Golden Thunder UDTX, owned

Can. OTCh. Kelly of Queen Island UDT, WCX, TT photographed by owner Susan Kluesner of Lakeville, Minnesota.

by David Gannon, and one show champion, Ch. Beaulieu's Akacia O'Darnley UDTX, JH, WCX, owned by Jeanette von Barby. Another versatile Golden who tracked to her TDX that year was Can. OTCh. Comstock's Carmel Nut UDTX, owned by Kathryn Eddy, VMD, who later added a Canadian bench championship, MH, WCX, and Can. WCX.

The next two years produced 16 new TDX titleholders. Of the 11 TDX Goldens in 1990, OTCh. Hi-Point's Skip Off the Ol' Block UDTX was also bred by his owner-trainer Judy Lee. Kyrie Arcane Shane Am-Can. TDX became Ed

and Marallyn Wight's fourth AKC TDX Golden. That year Roberta Anderson kept busy and added the Can. TDX to Bonnie Island Thumper TDX.

Tracking is intimately related to search and rescue as both disciplines require proficient use of the dog's scenting powers. In Snowmass, Colorado, Aspen Highlands Ski Patrol member Ron Buksaitis's two Avalanche Rescue TDX Goldens use their scenting ability to locate people buried under snowslides.

As a puppy Honor's Cogan in the Rockies UDTX, WC, TDI, instinctively used his nose in the snow before he understood the tracking

219

game, and Honor's Who's on First CDX, TDX, SH, WCX, TDI ("Courage") began simple scenting games at only eight weeks old. Ron's training philosophy: keep it simple; keep it fun; most importantly, have faith in your dog.

Apparently it works. In less than one year Ron and Cogan earned their TD, a *Dog World* award, placed in nine of eleven obedience trials on the way to their UD, and culminated their career at the 1989 GRCA National Specialty when Cogan passed the TDX on his first try. The following year Courage followed his big brother's example and earned his TD and TDX in his first attempts.

"A lot goes into tracking, a lot of work, a little or a lot of luck, and finally a lot of prayers," Ron said. Apparently thay all worked for Ron and his Goldens. Four tries, four titles. That's quite a record in the tracking game. And no one deserves it more than a pair of Avalanche Goldens waiting to rescue a snowbound skier.

The purpose of a tracking test, as defined under official AKC regulations, is to demonstrate the dog's ability to recognize and follow human scent, a skill that is useful in the service of mankind. Tracking tests demonstrate the dog's willingness and enjoyment in

Meadowpond Spectacular Beau CDX, JH, TD, owned by Judy Melrose, and son, **Can. OTCh. Hickory-Dickory Zachary UDT, JH, WCX (OD)**, owned by Andrea Johnson, showing off their gloves after earning their TD at the 1989 GRCA National Specialty.

its work, and should always represent the best in sportsmanship and camaraderie by the people involved.

The fundamental feature of the Tracking Dog / TD Test is the dog's ability to follow a track, a path walked by a stranger, under a variety of conditions and over moderate terrain, and retrieve a glove or wallet dropped by that person at the end of the track.

The dog wears a harness and a 20- to 40-foot leash. The handler must follow his dog at least 20 feet behind and may use vocal encouragement, but cannot use commands or body language to guide or influence the dog's direction. The dog and his nose are on their own.

Each test must be conducted on virgin ground. In the TD Test the track must be 440 to 500 yards long and include a total of three to five turns, with at least two turns at right angles or 90 degrees. The scent of that track-laying stranger must be 30-minutes to two-hours old.

Growing up beautifully at 15 months, here's Sugr! This is **Coronet Goldust Sugrmaple TD** at the Glen Bard All-Breed Obedience Club Tracking Test in Barrington, Illinois. Owners are Pam German and Sue Baumgartner.

Terrain and obstacles can vary, with the weather always an unpredictable factor; tracking dogs work in drizzle, wind and freezing rain, and if they're lucky, track on balmy, sunny days as well.

To enter a TD test, a dog must first be certified by a tracking judge over a regulation tracking course. If successful, the handler is issued four certification statements, good for one year, one of which is to be submitted with each entry to a licensed TD Test. If the dog fails four TD tests within that year, he must be recertified to try again. A dog must first be a qualified TD dog to enter a TDX test.

The Tracking Dog Excellent / TDX Test presents more difficult challenges. The intent is to show unquestionably that the dog has the ability to discriminate scent and possesses the stamina, perseverance and courage to do so under a variety of conditions.

The restrictions and minimum requirements for a TDX track are longer, tougher and more complicated. The track must be 800 to 1,000 yards long, with five to seven turns, and at least three right-angle turns. The scent must be three to five hours old.

The TDX track also contains two cross tracks, laid an hour and 15 minutes to an hour and 45 minutes after the original track, at specified points, to further challenge the dog's ability to discriminate scent. Terrain is often more difficult

Can. OTCh. Kyrie Genever Am-Can. UDTX, Am-Can. WC owned by Ed and Marallyn Wight of Clinton, Michigan.

and complex: plowed fields, streams, gullies and woods. The TDX dog must find and indicate or retrieve four personal and dissimilar articles deposited by the tracklayer, a sock, scarf, shoe or hat, perhaps, with only the last article being a glove or wallet.

Whereas the TD track has two starting flags, thirty yards apart, which indicate the track's direction, the TDX track has only a single starting flag; the dog not only has to follow the track but he first has to find the correct direction from that flag.

Challenging? Exhilarating? You bet. Tracking buffs will tell you there's no other feeling like it.

Canadian Kennel Club tracking rules are similar to those of AKC with a few minor variations. The book of regulations is less specific than AKC, being a fraction of the size.

The Wights' TDX Goldens *(left to right):* **Kyrie Arcane Shane Am-Can. TDX, Parabens Cinnamindy Am-Can. CDX, Am. TD, Can. TDX, Parabens Tovë Can. CD, Am-Can. TD, Kyrie Brenjo Sloan The Sleuth Am-Can. CDX, TDX, Can. OTCh. Kyrie Genever Am-Can. UDTX, Am-Can. WC** and **Can. OTCh. Anthea of Setherwood Am-Can. UDTX.**

TD Chart Information

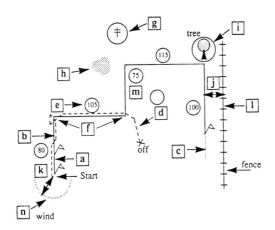

a) 30 yds. between the two starting flags

b) At least 30 yds. beyond the 2nd starting flag to the 1st turn

c) The tracklayer proceeds straight/ahead for 30 yds., after dropping the article.

d) Indicate dogs path with dasher (may use red)

e) Circle distances between turns

f) Must have both right turns and left turns: at least two right angle turns well out in the open

g) Telephone pole used to indicate direction of leg

h) Rock used to indicate location of turn

i) Tree used to indicate direction of leg and location of turn

j) At least 15 yds. from boundary or fence

k) Keep spectators 50 yds. from the start

l) Indicate major features such as fences, roads, hills, slopes vegetation, etc.

m) Legs must be at least 50 yds. long

n) Direction of wind at start

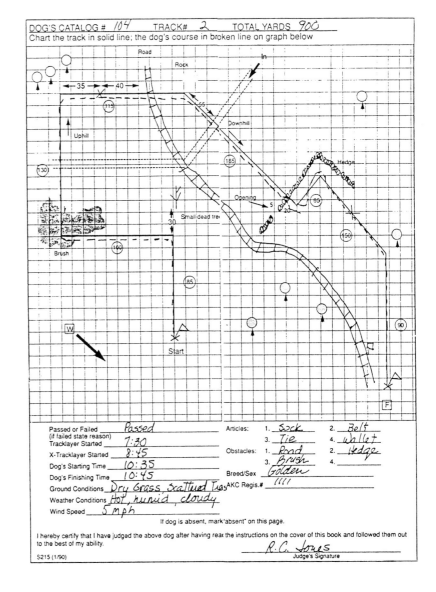

DOG'S CATALOG # _104_ TRACK# _2_ TOTAL YARDS _900_

Chart the track in solid line; the dog's course in broken line on graph below

Passed or Failed _Passed_
(if failed state reason)
Tracklayer Started _7:30_
X-Tracklayer Started _8:45_
Dog's Starting Time _10:35_
Dog's Finishing Time _10:45_
Ground Conditions _Dry Grass, Scattered Trees_
Weather Conditions _Hot, humid, cloudy_
Wind Speed _5 mph_

Articles: 1. _Sock_ 2. _Belt_
3. _Tie_ 4. _Wallet_
Obstacles: 1. _Pond_ 2. _Hedge_
3. _Brush_ 4. ___
Breed/Sex _Golden_
AKC Regis.# _1111_

If dog is absent, mark "absent" on this page.

I hereby certify that I have judged the above dog after having read the instructions on the cover of this book and followed them out to the best of my ability.

R. C. Jones
Judge's Signature

S215 (1/90)

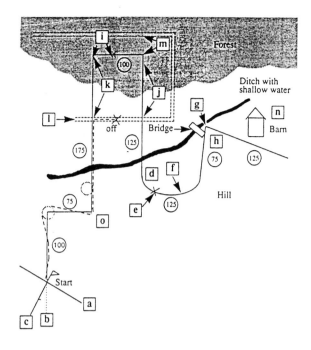

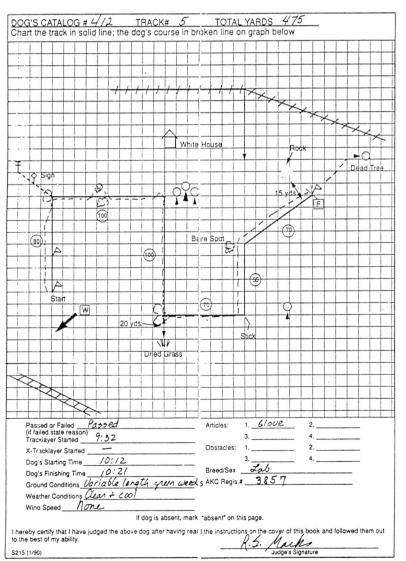

a) 180° arc possible for start
b) 30 yd. straight approach to start flag for tracklayer
c) Handler and dog approach at less than 90° to the direction of the tracklayer
d) Turn just before obstacle
e) Articles: Drop articles at widely separated points on the tracks
f) Curved legs are permissible
g) Turn just before obstacle
h) Non severe acute angles: use only if necessary
i) Article and turn separated by more than 30 yds.
j) Obstacles and cross tracks separated by more than 30 yds.
k) Turns and cross tracks separated by more than 50 yds.
l) Indicate direction of cross tracks
m) Cross tracklayer stay at least 50 yds. from the track
n) Show major features
o) Markers for location of corners and direction of leg should be shown on chart

Ch. Pinehurst Traveling Goldust CDX, WC, VCX crossing-over for owner-handler Janet Schaadt of Quincy, Illinois.

Red Eagle Nickie Fox on the Run UDT, JH, WCX and Beverly Weaver of Overland Park, Kansas, practicing on the weave-poles for an agility match.

Agility

In the 1980s agility was simply an extra attraction at AKC dog shows and obedience trials. Exhibition dogs would race through tunnels and over barriers and hurdles while the spectators roared and cheered them on. The excitement spurred the dogs on, and they would sail faster and higher down the course. The crowd would howl their approval—the dogs loved every minute of it.

Any dog activity so frenetic and exciting is bound to captivate the dog fancy, so it was only natural that agility would blossom into a full-blown and self-sustaining event unto itself. It frequently has been called the sport for all dogs because it allows both pure-bred and mixed-breed dogs to compete. Some breeds of dogs, however, because of their builds, are not well suited for the sport of agility.

The key ingredient to agility's burst of success lies in the sport itself—it's FUN. The handler and his dog race through a timed obstacle course, and both dog and handler have a breakneck good time.

Two national non-AKC-affiliated organizations offer agility fans more than just a good time. Both sponsor competitive agility events and confer titles on successful qualifiers, proof that a good time can be its own reward.

The first and larger organization, the United States Dog Agility Association, Inc. (USDAA), was organized in 1986 and rapidly has become the nation's leading organization for the sport. During its first five years, USDAA spawned 17 member clubs across the country.

Founded by a group of dog agility enthusiasts who promoted the use of international standards for agility in the States, USDAA adopted the same rules and regulations used in Great Britain and throughout Europe. It uses a simple objective scoring system based on faults, as in equestrian jumping events.

A USDAA-approved course contains over a dozen obstacles for the dogs to scale up and down, crawl through or under, balance on, jump over, snake in and out, and otherwise navigate. Obstacles include the A-frame, flexible weave poles, pause box, table, seesaw, dog walk, crossover, pipe and collapsed tunnels, and assorted jumps and hurdles. The jump group numbers seven, which includes a broad jump, tire jump, brush jump, high jump, bar jump, double bar jump, and spread bar jump. Although local

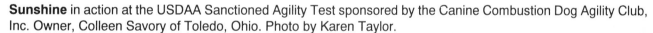

Sunshine in action at the USDAA Sanctioned Agility Test sponsored by the Canine Combustion Dog Agility Club, Inc. Owner, Colleen Savory of Toledo, Ohio. Photo by Karen Taylor.

groups and individuals have devised other obstacles, such as the sway-bridge, hoop jump and log hurdle, USDAA has focused on national standardization in order to foster widespread competition rather than merely the development of new obstacles.

Jump heights are divided into four classes, with a maximum of 30 inches. The dog's height at the withers determines if it is to jump 12, 18, 24 or 30 inches.

The USDAA offers titles to recognize a dog's ability on three levels of performance. To become an Agility Dog (AD), a dog must qualify in Starters or Novice, similar to Novice A and Novice B in obedience, by completing the course in a prescribed time with a clear round. A clear round means no faults with a perfect score of 200. Typical faults are taking the wrong jump or jumping off too soon from a contact zone, such as the dog walk, the seesaw or A-frame table.

To become an Advanced Agility Dog (AAD), a dog must qualify three times under two different judges on a tougher course, where the distance between the obstacles is shorter or longer and the course time is shorter. As in the Novice class, a clear round with a 200 score earns a qualifying leg.

A Master Agility Dog (MAD) must perform at the highest level of difficulty, running a much tougher course at much faster times. A Master Dog must also earn qualifying scores in three non-regular or novelty agility classes as well, with one of those classes a pair relay or team game to demonstrate good sportsmanship with a teammate. Through 1990 no Master title had been earned, and the USDAA had 32 Starter dogs, 20 Novice and five Advanced Agility Dogs.

The crown jewel of the agility world is the USDAA's annual national championship tournament, the Pedigree® Grand Prix of Dog Agility, held in conjunction with the AstroWorld Series of Dog Shows, an exciting three-day event held at

Red Eagle Nickie Fox on the Run CDX, JH, WCX, TD practices a tire jump in preparation for an agility trial.

the Houston AstroArena adjacent to the Astrodome. Supported by Pedigree® dog food, the fourth Grand Prix in 1990 drew 85 finalists and over 3,000 spectators.

Qualifiers for the Grand Prix must compete and qualify in one of 18 regional events held in 15 states across the country and sponsored by the USDAA member clubs. In addition, dozens of other non-member clubs offer agility classes simply for the pleasure and exhilaration of the sport.

The National Club for Dog Agility was born in 1987 as "The National Committee for Dog Agility," in the hope that AKC might approve and adopt the rules. It reorganized as NCDA in 1991 under its founder Charles Kramer, Professor of Biology at Kansas State University.

NCDA sponsors agility trials held by clubs which are approved to hold a qualifying trial. For approval, the club must provide assurance of satisfactory equipment and have arranged for certified or provisional judges. By 1991 NCDA had judges certified in a dozen states and had held about 15 approved agility trials.

The NCDA course contains obstacles similar to the USDAA, and scoring is also based on time and faults with a perfect 200 necessary to qualify. NCDA titles include Agility I, Agility II and Agility Trial Champion. Through 1991, about 50 dogs had earned qualifying scores, and several had two legs at the Agility II level.

While the USDAA maintains a position of complete separation from AKC, NCDA still hopes to obtain AKC and UKC acceptance for its agility program and titles. However, both NCDA and USDAA will authorize AKC show-giving clubs to offer approved agility trials as exhibition in conjunction with an AKC member or licensed show or sanctioned match.

Goldens represent about one-third of the dogs participating in the sport of dog agility, according to Beverly Weaver, who founded the USDAA-affiliated Love Dog Agility Club in Kansas City. Beverly said the Golden athlete is a natural for dog agility. "Goldens are such clowns...they really love this sport. They're beautiful to watch because they are so fast and are such easy jumpers. They bend their bodies well and move like snakes around and between the weave poles. More Goldens are getting involved in agility all the time."

Beverly emphasized a dog must have good hips for the demands of jumping and running an agility course. She also felt agility was good for a dog's obedience work and attitude. "Some people worry that agility might ruin an obedience dog, but the opposite is actually true," she said.

Beverly competes with her female Golden, Red Eagle Nickie Fox on the Run UDT, JH, WCX, in obedience and hunting tests as well as in agility. She and Nickie received Dog World awards for six consecutive first place wins on the way to their obedience titles. Nickie was also one of the six Goldens finalists at the 1990 Grand Prix event in Houston

Agility offers dog lovers and sportsmen everywhere a chance to demonstrate the athletic prowess of their dogs and to enjoy the special teamwork unique in the working relationship of the handler and his agility dog. And because it's available to every dog regardless of its parentage, for a change even the family pet can have a good time too.

Nickie and Beverly work on the cross-over.

This is no rehearsal! Beverly and **Nickie** competing at the agility finals in Lincoln, Nebraska in June 1990. Nickie is working the A-frame.

Above: Agility ring set-up at the USDAA 1990 Pedigree Grand Prix of Agility at the Houston Astrodome.
Below: **Nickie** at Lincoln finals 1990 working the weave-poles.

Above: **Dust Devil** owned by Carrie Blair over the wall at the USDAA Sanctioned Agility Test, sponsored by the Canine Combustion Dog Agility Club, Inc. Photo by Karen Taylor. *Below left:* **Ch. Pinehurst Traveling Goldust CDX, WC, VCX** on the A-frame. Owner assisting, Janet Schaadt of Quincy, Illinois. *Below right:* **Nickie** step by step and tip by tip from owner Beverly Weaver.

Top: **Sunshine** on the A-frame at a USDAA test. Owner, Colleen Savory.
Bottom: **Dust Devil** owned by Carrie Blair being judged on the cross-over by judge Lori Schulz. Carrie and Dust Devil live in Temperance, Michigan. Photograph by Karen Taylor.

Top: **Dust Devil** making it through the tire!
Bottom: **Sunshine** teetering the seesaw.
Photographs by Karen Taylor.

Helping Paws Service Golden **Alpha** follows her owner Jenny Peterson into the elevator.

Goldens as Assistance Animals

BY DR. BONITA M. BERGIN

Close to 50% of all service dogs, 20% of all dog guides, and a significant percentage of dogs involved in pet-facilitated therapy are Golden Retrievers. An occasional Golden Retriever hearing dog can even be heard of. These are impressive figures when the entire scope of assistance dog work is taken into consideration: hearing dogs, guide dogs, service dogs, and dogs involved in pet-facilitated therapy programs. And even more impressive when one considers that of the 130+ breeds listed with the AKC, the Golden has assumed such a prominent place in assistance-dog work.

How has the Golden Retriever laid claim to such an impressive statistic? By being a naturally compliant, willing partner, and sincere friend of man. The qualities that have made the Golden an outstanding field-trial dog, top obedience champion, and popular pet contribute to its role in assistance-dog work.

What has this marvelous animal contributed to the field of assistance dogs? Certainly he is unparalleled in the arena of *service* dogs. This unique assistance animal works primarily with individuals who have a physical disability. Tasks performed by service dogs include retrieving dropped or out-of-reach items, turning lights on and off, opening doors, and pulling wheelchairs.

These dogs also contribute to the social well-being of the disabled individuals with whom they are partnered. Frequently, being disabled, being in a wheelchair, means being invisible. People intentionally or inadvertently avoid interacting with this population. This dynamic is completely reversed with the presence of a dog, particularly a Golden Retriever, at work beside a disabled individual.

Individuals with these dogs find themselves the center of attention everywhere they go. They are besieged with questions about the dog, its purpose, its capability. These interactions with the general public quite naturally lead to the occasional, more individual interpersonal communications resulting in some meaningful and long-lasting relationships.

The psychological benefits are equally impressive. For many disabled individuals, the increased capability available through the dog's workmanship parallels an increase in self-esteem, along with a great acceptance of the disability. Studies have shown that individuals with these dogs are, quite simply, happier.

In service work, the dog must comply with the request of the disabled individual who has a minimal ability to correct inappropriate behavior. The Golden is uniquely suited to this work since it has a pronounced desire to please. In addition, physical agility and strength are a part of the service role, again qualities readily attributable to Goldens.

In order to manipulate light switches, open doors, and grasp awkward items from hard-to-access places, daily tasks required by many of the disabled individuals for whom these dogs work, it is necessary that these dogs possess a pronounced body awareness and physical agility. The gentle willingness of the Golden lends itself favorably to these tasks, while the body sensitivity ensures a non-destructive approach to the intricacies required in certain maneuvers.

No mention of the Golden's role as a service dog can minimize the value of its sweet disposition. This loving nature is a significant part of the social and psychological benefits brought to this work by the breed. The seemingly non-judgmental love that so attracts man to dog is magnified in the relationship between the disabled individual and the Golden service dog. As long as the disabled person shows him/herself to be in charge, the Golden accepts the person totally. Amputees, quadriplegics, individuals with spastic movements or speech, or able-bodied people—acceptance is equal.

The Golden's amiable nature has shown a unique capability to balance the strongly bonded relationship with its disabled partner, with an ability to maintain friendly relations with others in the household and in public. This balance occasionally tips to one side or the other and may need management by the disabled partner, but generally, with minimal effort, the balance is maintained.

Problems do exist, and a careful breeding program is necessary to ensure that these qualities, so identified with the Golden, are fostered. However, as this breed has become more popular, many of the endearing Golden traits are being exaggerated, threatening the role it has the potential to play in assistance-dog work.

As its gentle willingness gives way to hyperresponsiveness, as its interest in retrieving game is upgraded to intensive competitiveness and fierce determination, and as its gentle disposition bends to the pressure of popular demands, protectiveness and heightened sensitivity result. The Golden that was known to handle stimuli without overreacting is becoming harder to find.

Given the remarkable qualities of service to mankind this breed has made available, it is imperative that Golden breeders and owners stay in touch with the characteristics that gave this breed its unique place in history.

In the last century the role of the dog has diminished. In the last two decades, that trend has begun to reverse itself as new uses for the dog have been found of value in modern society. For that trend to continue, dogs that can serve in those useful roles need to be available—and that requires careful nurturing of capabilities that are in tune with modern society. The Golden has won itself just such a place; lets keep it there.

Desert Guide Kirby CDX, Bda. CD leads owner Ed Eames across the street. Kirby and Ed live together in Fresno, California.

THE STORY OF A SERVICE DOG

Nine-year-old John Bismark received his service dog, Glory, in 1986. Glory helped to transition John's life in ways few could have imagined. John had been diagnosed with Duchene's Muscular Dystrophy several years before. The gradual weakening of his muscles had put John in a wheelchair by the time he came to school to get his service dog.

His parents, agonizing with the knowledge that their beloved son's lifespan would not last much beyond his teenage years, had promised themselves that he would have the *best* life possible for those years remaining. And Glory, a two-year-old Golden Retriever, was the *best.*

John attended Canine Companions for Independence's training program along with 11 other students ranging in age from 16 to 45. The disabilities of these students were equally diverse. Spina bifida, quadriplegia from a motorcycle accident, post-polio syndrome, deafness and cerebral palsy were just a few of the disabilities of the students in the class.

The youngest student in the class, John was expected to keep up with the rest of the class in all areas of the curriculum since he would be no less responsible than they for the care and management of his service dog. And Glory, after two years of careful preparation for her role with John, would be relying on him for her needs and safety.

Distinguished by a solemn composure and unemotional expression, John was not enthusiastically greeted at school. He had long since closed off the warmth and social vitality so much a part of boys his age. The invisibility he had experienced for several years was evident in his tight-lipped responses and unrelenting stoicism.

While that attitude might in some unknown way make his life bearable, unfortunately, it would not gain much responsiveness from a dog. And for his dog to do the intricate tasks required to give John some true independence, Glory would have to respond to him. It was evident that the school's instructors had their work cut out for them. John's emotive side had to be reached and freed to flourish.

Glory, the gently gregarious female Golden picked out for John by the instructors, could be counted on to be a help in this process, but John had so successfully sealed off his feelings, that even Glory would need some help. The instructors, aware of the need for John to emote with Glory, and experienced with the syndrome of disabled individuals' shutting off their emotional life as a means of coping with their unique minority status, began to strategize a method for awakening John's long-suppressed feelings. On that list were various strategies ranging from positioning him to succeed with Glory so they both could revel in the instructors' praise, to jarring him emotionally so that he would let go with some anger and frustration—the first step in breaking through the icy shell that separated him from the world.

John was harder than most to reach, so well

had he constructed his safety net of cynicism. It was painful to see in one so young, but understandable when recognizing how feeble a welcome society had shown him during his few years of life.

Day after day, John was told to praise Glory, to let her know he cared about her, to get her excited with the force of his emotion—and day after day John mumbled a dry "good girl" in Glory's direction. Glory was not to be dissuaded from her quest to get John's attention, as she pranced around him, placed her front paws in his lap, kissed his cheek, and cuddled up against him. The affection ma-

instructors, seizing this opportunity, pounced on John for allowing his dog to misbehave.

Since several passers-by were watching, John made an extra effort to get Glory's attention. It was futile. Glory was not buying. She had tried too, and been rejected. Now she was looking elsewhere for some feedback, some recognition. John found himself locked in battle with himself. He had two choices: one was to fail in front of the audience surrounding him; the other was to give in and show Glory some emotional energy to gain her interest.

Watching, it was easy to see the complexity of emotions creating havoc in John's mind. For

"Dyna" *(right)* is a star therapy assistance dog. She is sharing this warm moment with housemate **Quillmark's Pride-N-Joy CD** ("PJ").

nipulations so much a part of the Golden Retriever were fully at work as Glory tried to work her way into John's heart—in vain.

John was unmoved by it all. Too many times he had reached out to kids his own age for warmth and companionship only to be rejected in favor of the known, the familiar: able-bodied children. Even the neighborhood dogs preferred to run and romp with the physically mobile kids in the neighborhood. John was not ready to trust—not even Glory.

Field trips were a part of the school schedule, and John, whose management of Glory was still questionable, was required to attend along with the rest of the class. At one point, Glory, whose attentiveness to John was finally beginning to wane, ignored John's command entirely. The

years he had submerged his emotions beneath an impassive, noncommittal attitude. His determination to succeed was seen only in the seriousness of his approach. Now success could only come through a willingness to release the emotional ties that held him in check. What to do.

Glory stood out at the end of the leash, ignoring John entirely, focusing on the group of people surrounding the two of them. Her Golden antenna was desperately searching the group for a responsive, loving face to attach to her emotional needs. The crowd, curious and interested, let her know that they were empathetic. And that empathy acted like a magnet, attracting her attention even more.

At odds with one another, Glory stood facing away from John, while John was facing an internal turmoil with the potential to change the direction of his life. To succeed in this situation required a major revamping of his approach to life, a loss of his current identity. He would be risking a part of himself for an unknown—a life partnered with Glory. Was she worth the risk?

Determination to succeed won out! John put a forced smile on his face and with a barely discernible lilt to his voice called Glory to him. Glory, whose willingness to please was so much a part of her generous nature, responded instantly. The quick sincerity of her response so surprised and gratified John that his long pent-up emotions burst forth in a torrent of tears.

Sobbing uncontrollably, his body trembling with the release of years of sorrow and loneliness, John held tightly to the dog at his side. Glory, agitated by John's tears, but comforted by his touch, whined softly as she pressed even closer to John, feverishly licking the sorrow off his face.

The class, instructors and students alike gazed in silent reverence—the breakthrough had occurred.

From that point forward John and Glory were model students. Not only did they master all the commands required of them but they won the confidence of the class and were voted valedictorians. In the spotlight on stage on graduation night, John and Glory shared with the audience the humorous, painful and purposeful experiences of the two weeks of training. John's smile was soft and gentle; Glory's steady gaze at John while he spoke said more than any words could have relayed.

Later, John's parents wrote CCI about the changes that had taken place in his life. He had become one of the most popular boys at school, full of laughter and fun. He had emerged, not just a friend to many, but a leader as well. Glory went with him everywhere. In school she waited under his desk until called upon to pick up something he dropped, or retrieve something from the teacher. She played ball with the kids at recess under John's direction and with Glory pulling his wheelchair, he raced with the other kids around the playground.

Glory blossomed too. She had no doubt whose dog she was, whose life she was dedicated to serve and share purposefully. She and John slept together, ate together, worked and played together. She recognized that she was a vital member of this unit, and gave her whole life to it. She loved his family and friends as well, and enjoyed romping and playing with them when the opportunity arose, but when John called—she was there in a flash.

Glory, the gentle Golden, John, the solemn young man, came together to create a team stronger and more capable than each was alone. It is impossible to know who benefits more from this relationship, and that is as it should be.

ABOUT THE AUTHOR:

Bonita M. Bergin founded the concept of the service dog in 1975. Subsequently she founded and directed the first service-dog program, Canine Companions for Independence, building it into a major nonprofit organization with five centers throughout the United States and affiliates in Canada, Holland, and France. Currently she is president of The Assistance Dog Institute, an educational institute dedicated to research and development of assistance-dog work. Through the development and sharing of this knowledge, she hopes to ensure that more and more people with disabilities can benefit from an assistance dog.

The Assistance Dog Institute
421 East Cotati Avenue
Cotati, CA 94931

The Birth of the Service Dog

COURTESY OF CANINE COMPANIONS FOR INDEPENDENCE

In 1971, Dr. Bonnie Bergin began a journey which resulted in a vision that is impacting the lives of disabled people and dog worldwide. She left the United States to accept a one-and-a-half year teaching contract in Australia. Upon completion of that assignment, she spent a year traveling through Asia and Europe, ending up with another teaching assignment—this time for the Turkish government.

In Turkey, she coached a boys' basketball team to second in the nation, and confirmed what she had viewed many times in her travels through Asia—that disabled people in developing countries had to make do for themselves, oftimes using burros as helpmates.

Returning to the United States mid-1974, she entered a master's program in special education where, through class discussions, it became evident to her that something was needed to give disabled individuals more freedom of opportunity. Rejecting the concept of burros, Bonnie envisioned a dog to serve this population and it was realized.

Motivated by this vision, Bonnie left teaching to work in a dog kennel for $2 an hour in order to learn more about dogs. Armed with this knowledge and a determination to help disabled individuals live more fulfilled independent lives, she began the experiment which has resulted in the internationally acclaimed *service*-dog concept.

She initially developed the program from her home, working at two part-time jobs to support it, placing dogs locally, and as far east as Sacramento and as far south as San José. Bonnie initially started by placing puppies, expecting them to grow up with more understanding of the disabled individual's limitations. This did not work, since caring for a pup is so strenuous.

Bonnie then shifted her attention to rescuing dogs from local humane societies, but found that some unknown quality in the dog would appear at the most inopportune time. She returned to her original idea of breeding for the quality dog needed, but implemented a puppy-raising program to fill in the gap between puppyhood and a trained service dog placement.

Initially recipients were not asked to take much responsibility. Since the program was to help them, it was hard at first to make too many demands on them. After several calls from them asking for help, illustrated by a 3:00 a.m. call from San José asking Bonnie to come immedi-

ately to clean up a dog mess (which she did), she began to learn that in order for the program to work, it was necessary to hold the recipient responsible. The recipient of that dog had been told to toilet the dog prior to bedtime and had failed to do so.

Brent, a former retriever field-trial trainer, and his service dog **Finnigan**. Finnigan opens the mall door for partner Brent; holds it open while Brent enters; Brent praises Finnigan for his help. Support Dogs of St. Louis photographed by the author.

Bonnie and her husband were in the process of building a house and had framed two rooms, with sheetrock nailed to the walls, and a cement slab as flooring. There was no outside fencing as yet, so at one point they had as many as 18 dogs living inside that abode. To top if off, Bonnie's mother died and her two teenage brothers came to live with her. It was not easy.

In 1981, with the basic program outline in place, and *service* dog concept incorporated as Canine Companions for Independence (CCI), Bonnie wrote and received her first grant, and was thrilled to move CCI out of her home. CCI was moved into a small kitchen, one-car garage on Seventh Street in Santa Rosa. At the time, Bonnie knew nothing about kennel permits, nor about employing staff. The first individuals hired were minimum-wage, and acted accordingly.

In October of that same year one of the recipients of a dog offered to purchase a location for CCI to use. Bonnie was grateful, but had modest, unassuming expectations and would not let the recipient spend much money. Thus the recipient ended up purchasing and leasing to CCI an old broken-down warehouse on Sebastopol Road which, almost upon moving into it, was condemned by the county.

Bonnie had to launch a building campaign immediately—of which she knew nothing at the time. The county generously allowed CCI to use the structure while working to build a new building. Daily, staff would walk through the building, falling through the rotted wooden floor or being horrified by the rats that scurried comfortably around the area.

Since a breeding program was essential in order to produce the quality animals needed in this work, puppies were a part of the CCI reality. Almost immediately parvo hit, and CCI staff did round-the-clock attendance attempting to save some of the litter.

Despite the numerous setbacks, the successful placements kept adding up. Bonnie's innate business acumen saw a need to market this concept so that more disabled people could be served throughout the United States and abroad. Consequently, she worked toward expansion, risking the opening of centers in order to position CCI in the major metropolitan centers of the country—LA, NY, Ohio, Florida, along with the San Francisco bay area.

She also risked by paying higher salaries, expecting to attract better quality staff which would provide a return on the investment, ultimately covering the increased costs.

Increased and more expensive campaigns were also launched, which also paid for themselves.

The approach with the disabled recipients also changed over time. Students were required to pay fees in order to get a dog. This was a way of ensuring more accountability on their part. The program was essentially restructured, making the recipient carry the responsibility. The disabled person and his/her dog had a lifetime

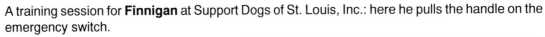

A training session for **Finnigan** at Support Dogs of St. Louis, Inc.: here he pulls the handle on the emergency switch.

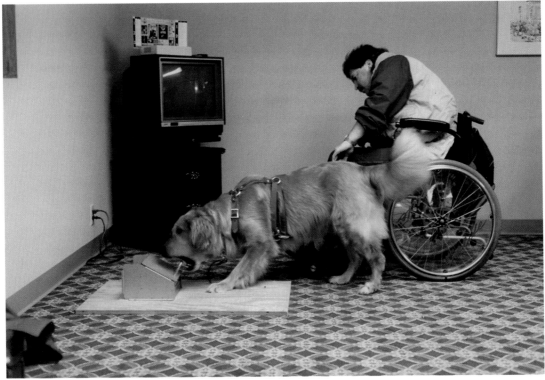

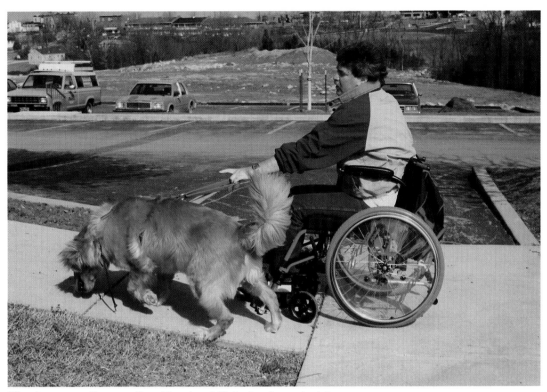

Finnigan practices pulling Brent uphill during team training.

working partnership for which no third party could be responsible—it needed to be between the two of them.

The process, a litter bred and placed out in homes in the community to be raised according to CCI's training methods, came into being. This was followed by a return of the pups to a CCI training center at approximately 16 months of age for six months of advanced training, in two three-month semesters. In that time, each dog was taught a total of 89 working commands, designed to prepare them to work in varied circumstances and situations with a multitude of disabilities.

The recipient, who had by then applied to CCI, provided medical information and references from friends and community contacts, arrived at CCI to begin a two-week intensive training. This training, dubbed "bootcamp" by the students, taught the recipients the 89 commands already known to the dog, as well as dog psychology, dog-training concepts, and dog care and grooming techniques.

Working in groups and on his own, each recipient was required to demonstrate his knowledge and abilities at every step in the process. Both written and practical tests were a part of the curriculum. And a welcomed formal graduation ceremony followed the successful completion of the training program.

Not every student who attended bootcamp

graduated. The serious responsibility of dog ownership required that only those who learned and could apply the necessary information and handling methods could be entrusted with one of the precious Canine Companions.

Developing CCI was definitely an entrepreneurial effort. Bonnie was developing administrative procedures, fund-raising, and doing PR, simultaneously with developing and implementing the training program.

She sought advice from the most successful, knowledgeable people in the profit business field. All the successful people with whom she spoke said, "Do it." Less successful people appeared to be more cautious, but those who were truly successful seemed to operate under the assumption that it could be done if one were willing to put out the necessary effort to do it.

With the concept proven, and with five centers across the United States and three foreign affiliates, Bonnie then worked to open communication between CCI and other assistance-dog programs. She co-founded and served as founding president of Assistance Dogs, Intl., a coalition of assistance-dog programs which included dog-guide programs, hearing-dog programs, and Bonnie's service-dog program. Membership was world-wide.

This exposure, along with media coverage by such prestigious programs as 20/20, Disney, and ABC, NBC, and CBS morning shows and

Helping Paws Golden Retriever **Honey** pushes the button to open the electronic door for her owner Charlene Maki.

news magazines, and print coverage by *LIFE* magazine, *Reader's Digest, National Geographic World,* and others began an awakening which caused many programs to emerge emulating this concept. Today there are at least 30 programs providing *service* dogs to individuals with disabilities.

With CCI launched, Bonnie has moved on to found the Bonnie Bergin Assistance Dog Institute, dedicated to the research and development of new and better assistance-dog methodologies. Results of this work will be shared with all assistance-dog programs so that more disabled individuals can benefit from the independence

resulting from this unique working relationship with a dog.

Listed in many *Who's Who* publications, the recipient of the prestigious Giraffe award, recognized by former President Reagan and former Surgeon General Koop, awarded the Distinguished Service Award by the California Governor's Committee on Employment for the Handicapped, and most recently named Grand Marshall of the Santa Rosa Rose Parade, Dr. Bergin has made a contribution to the lives of both disabled individuals and dogs by expanding the capabilities and role each is able to assume in society.

COMMONLY ASKED QUESTIONS ABOUT CANINE COMPANIONS FOR INDEPENDENCE

Q. What is Canine Companions for Independence?

A. Canine Companions for Independence (CCI) is a 501(c)(3) nonprofit organization that trains assistance dogs to serve people with disabilities other than blindness, providing them with greater independence.

Q. What types of dogs does CCI train?

A. CCI trains four types of dogs:

Service Dogs work for people with physical disabilities, performing such tasks as turning on and off light switches, pushing elevator buttons, retrieving items, and pulling a wheelchair.

Signal Dogs are trained to alert people who are hearing-impaired to crucial sounds, such as a telephone, alarm clock, smoke alarm or baby's cry.

Social Dogs work for people with developmental disabilities by providing the loving interaction known as pet-facilitated therapy.

Specialty Dogs are trained to help meet the needs unique to people with multiple disabilities, such as a hearing-impaired individual who also uses a wheelchair.

Q. What does it cost to receive a Canine Companion?

A. There is a $25 application fee and a $100 class registration fee, which includes the necessary canine supplies. These are the only charges to a CCI participant, even though the actual cost of breeding, raising and training each dog is over $10,000.

Q. How is CCI funded?

A. CCI is funded by donations, group and service-club contributions, grants, and ongoing fund-raising activities.

Q. Who can apply for a Canine Companion?

A. Any person with a disability wanting increased independence through the use of a dog, or a facility that wishes to institute a pet-therapy program may apply for a Canine Companion.

Q. What are the responsibilities of the person or facility receiving a Canine Companion?

A. The proper care, feeding, housing and medical needs of each canine must be met. The dog must be used in the working capacity for which it was intended.

Q. What breeds of dogs does CCI use?

A. CCI uses primarily Golden Retrievers, Labrador Retrievers, Border Collies and Pembroke Welsh Corgis.

Q. Where are CCI dogs trained?

A. CCI dogs are trained at one of CCI's four regional training centers across the nation.

Rosie Benecke and **Clancey**. Courtesy of Support Dogs of St. Louis, Inc.

Q. What type of training does the recipient of a Canine Companion receive?

A. Each participant must complete a two-week training course known as Boot Camp held at a CCI regional training center and pass a series of written and working tests before returning home with his or her new Canine Companion.

Q. Where does CCI get its dogs?

A. Most dogs come from CCI's selective breeding program. Occasionally donated dogs are accepted if they meet the strict qualification requirements.

Q. When does the training begin?

A. Puppies are placed with volunteer puppy raisers at approximately eight weeks of age and are returned to the training center for six months of advanced training at age 17 to 19 months.

Q. How long does each Canine Companion work?

A. The average service life of each dog is ten years. After that time the dog is retired and may become a household pet of its master or be returned to its puppy raiser.

National Headquarters: P.O. Box 446, Santa Rosa, CA 95402; (707) 528-0830.

Paws with a Cause: Home of Ears for the Deaf

When Golden Retriever Randi hears the alarm clock ring, she jumps up onto the bed and goes to work. Her owner, Bill Kerr of Grosse Pointe Woods, Michigan, with 65 pounds of persistent retriever pawing gently at his chest, has no choice but to awaken and begin his day.

Randi is a certified Hearing Dog owned by Bill and his wife, Rhonda. Bill is severely deaf, and Rhonda wears hearing aids in both ears for moderate hearing impairment. Trained by Paws with a Cause, Home of Ears for the Deaf, Inc., Randi has given the Kerrs the freedom they could otherwise not enjoy because of their hearing deficiencies.

Randi will respond to seven alert sounds: the telephone, an alarm clock, door bell or knocker, the smoke alarm, a baby's cry, and the more subtle sounds of a twisting doorknob or window raising or breaking... the threatening sounds of an intruder. At any of these noises Randi turns deadly serious. She will run to Bill or Rhonda, stand and stare demandingly until she makes eye contact, then take them to the source of the sound. Prior to Randi's training, the Kerrs were dependent on remote-controlled equipment hooked up or carried from room to room.

In 1990 about 50 hearing dogs were trained by Paws to help families like the Kerrs. Since its inception in 1979, the agency has trained and placed over 500 hearing dogs with hearing impaired people in seven states. Like many large or national assistance organizations, Paws originated with one man's singular effort to help another man with his problem: profoundly deaf Martin Jansen, his pet Cairn Terrier, Crystal, and the man who trained that dog to be his master's ears.

When Jansen in 1979 applied to hearing dog agencies for assistance, he was turned away. Existing agencies would not train family pets, dogs who were already part of the family. They insisted instead that an applicant give up his pet and use a pre-trained animal, and Jansen loved his dog too much to part with her.

That's when obedience trainer Michael Sapp offered to see if Crystal was up to the job of hearing dog.

As an obedience instructor, Michael questioned the existing hearing dog programs that trained and placed a dog after only two weeks of training the dog and one week spent training the dog and recipient together.

Hearing Dog **Randi** owned by Bill and Rhonda Kerr, Grosse Pointe Woods, Michigan.

"The deaf culture is totally different from ours," he said. "Their comprehension of the English language is much lower than the norm. There were too many factors that set up for failure after the hearing dog was placed. Since I had a hard time in eight weeks teaching normal, able-bodied people to teach their dogs basic obedience com-

and Rhonda already had successfully completed an obedience class, her course did not include the basic four to six weeks of obedience training included in the standard program.

Randi completed her last six weeks of training with a Paws field trainer who came to the Kerr's home twice a week to train the dog for the specific

Randi resting her paws and ears.

mands, I couldn't accept a program that claimed to successfully teach the deaf to handle a dog in less than that."

Michael spent two months training Crystal and another two months teaching Jansen how to understand and maintain that training. In February 1980, Crystal was officially certified as a Hearing Dog, and Ears for the Deaf was officially born.

Randi, like Crystal, was the family pet before she earned her status as a Hearing Dog in 1989. She was temperament tested before she was accepted into the training program, and attended hearing dog school at Paws headquarters and training center in Grand Rapids, Michigan, for four weeks of sound training. Because she

sounds and situations within the household. Once certified, she was issued an ID card, an orange collar and a short orange leash with "Hearing Dog" on it. Like Leader Dogs in 48 of the 50 states, Randi has legal access to public buildings and transportation, restaurants, hotels and shops that normally exclude dogs.

About 95 percent of Paws Hearing Dogs are obtained from animal shelters. Each year Paws representatives and volunteers give educational programs to organizations, clubs and other groups to solicit funds to train Hearing Dogs to help disadvantaged people like Bill and Rhonda Kerr. Martin Jansen and his willing Cairn Terrier Crystal had no idea . . . .

Helping Paws of Minnesota

Helping Paws of Minnesota began in 1985 as a pilot program at the University of Minnesota's Center to Study Human-Animal Relationships and Environment (CEN/SHARE). Through Helping Paws, CEN/SHARE planned to explore the use of trained Service Dogs to further the independence of people with physical disabilities.

The human-canine team is a can't-fail combination, and Helping Paws was no exception. They have since incorporated as a nonprofit organization, the first service of its kind in the state of Minnesota.

The Helping Paws training program was developed by Eileen Bohn, director of training and one of the founders, and CEN/SHARE'S assistant director Ruth Foster, with help from Guide Dogs for the Blind in San Rafael, California, and Support Dogs of St. Louis, Inc., also a Service-Dog organization.

Eileen has two assistant trainers and a host of volunteers who donate their time for classes, dog care and private instruction. A former obedience trainer, she also raises Golden Retrievers and has donated pups to the organization. Six of the ten dogs in training in 1991 were Goldens.

All Helping Paws dogs are donated by private breeders. Puppies are selected on the basis of their eventual size, upkeep and grooming, retrieving instinct and willingness and aptitude. They are screened for genetic defects, and at seven weeks of age evaluated for suitability using standard temperament tests.

Selected puppies are placed in foster homes for one to two years. The foster parents are responsible for the physical care and welfare of the dog and must attend weekly training and canine behavior classes, participate in demonstrations and socialize the puppy to many different experiences. Helping Paws provides the puppy's food, equipment, training instructions and some veterinary care.

The Helping Paws staff checks regularly on each puppy's progress. At 12 to 18 months of age, the dog is re-evaluated for service qualities and its desire to become a Service Dog. Of the dogs who qualify for the program, some are trained as home helpers who work only in the home and non-public situations, and others become street-certified Service Dogs who go everywhere with their person.

Once the dog is matched to a recipient, the team is trained together at home and in the workplace. During the first two weeks of training the Helping Paws trainer takes the dog into the recipient's home for two to three hours a day to teach the new owner basic commands and handling skills. The dog then stays with its owner for a week, with no contact between dog and trainer, to bond the dog and owner in their new life together.

For the next month or more a second Helping Paws instructor comes to the home and workplace every day for periods of training tailored to meet each person's needs. A total of 60 to 70 hours will usually complete a Helping Paws Service Dog owner individualized training.

Golden Retriever Honey is a street-certified Service Dog who teamed with Charlene Maki in 1989. Charlene, who has rheumatoid arthritis, takes Honey to work, into restaurants, shopping and to classes at Metro State College. Charlene writes that her Golden has changed her life forever.

"As I go about my job (at the Hennepin Count Government Center) Honey is there to retrieve objects I drop, such as pens, papers, my cane or even coins. She carries things for me in her mouth or in her backpack.

"At home she has been trained to retrieve objects from kitchen shelves for me. She will pick up boxes and cans in the store and put them in the lower shelf of the shopping cart or carry them in her mouth.

"Best of all, Honey is also my good friend and companion who is always there to love me. In public she helps to start a conversation, making it easier for people who may feel uneasy about approaching a person who is disabled.

"Honey is a wonderful addition to my life and I can't imagine life without her."

Freedom Service Dogs

At Freedom Service Dogs, Inc., in Lakewood, Colorado, founder and trainer P.J. Roche states, "we teach the disabled to be able . . . differently." Using Golden Retrievers rescued from animal shelters, Freedom Dogs performs a life-saving service for the dogs as well as the people who desperately need their help.

During the first few years since its 1987 incipience, P.J. and her paraplegic husband, Mike, have trained and paired 15 dogs as helpers for the disabled and have two or three dogs in training year 'round. There is an 18-month waiting list of clients who have applied for Freedom Dogs.

Mike, a former paramedic whose spinal cord was crushed during an ambulance accident in 1978, discovered first-hand how valuable a dog can be when you can't move beyond the confines of a wheelchair. When P.J.'s obedience-trained Border Collie, Oreo, retrieved and picked up things Mike accidentally dropped, P.J. went on to teach the dog to do other simple tasks, like open and close doors, turn on lights, bark for alert. Later, in 1987, at a Denver Rehab Center, an occupational therapist asked the Roches if they would train a dog to help another paraplegic. Other requests followed, and the Roches decided to incorporate as a formal program to train dogs for the handicapped. P.J.'s story about Freedom Service Dogs follows:

"We started with the prospect that we would train dogs rescued from our local animal shelters. We looked for dogs one to two years old, fully matured, who had confident, outgoing personalities and could withstand the stress of long training periods. We may look at about 100 dogs, be impressed with perhaps four, and temperament test each one for: friendliness, fear, pain level, confidence, baiting with food, natural retrieving, submissiveness, aggression, startle reflex, and finally just our own gut feeling. We feel quite lucky when we find one who passes.

"Each dog is chosen with an individual person in mind, although we do occasionally switch a dog to another person as the dog progresses. We first used working breeds because they are easy to train, but through trial and error found that herding breeds became overly protective of their owners after a period of time. Because the dog has the same legal access as humans in restaurants, planes and other high-visibility places, we couldn't have a dog who guards the wheelchair from people who are wearing uniforms or hats or gloves. We didn't have a breeding program to breed out these characteristics, so we needed to find another breed that would give us all the qualities we needed but without that extreme. The logical choice was the Golden Retriever.

"Our first one, Friend, was a bitch about a year old, left at the shelter because she was too

Melanie and Freedom Service Dog **Micah.**

rambunctious, and the owner didn't know what to do with all that energy. We took her, as we do all our dogs, first to our veterinary clinic who has kindly donated all their services free for the past four years. They give a complete physical and all the shots, do a worm check and hip x-rays. Then we bring the dog back to our training center at our home for six months.

"The dogs are allowed complete freedom in our home during the day under supervision; thus we

Greg and Freedom Service Dog **Miki.**

are able to train them to stay out of the trash, off the furniture and kitchen counters, etc. The dogs have all the usual bad habits (jumping up, chewing, barking), so we teach them basic obedience and good manners, and finally, to retrieve.

"Because the dog will have to pick up, carry, push and take things, we always teach the forced retrieve, a very important aspect of the dog's training. Friend's owner has two children, and she suffers from multiple sclerosis. When Linda Storey had her second baby, Friend was taught a new command, "bundle," so she could gently nudge the baby out of danger or tug on his clothing or walker and slowly pull him toward his mother. Friend also removes laundry from the basket and gives it to Linda to put into the washer, then removes the wet wash from the machine and gives it to Linda to put into the dryer. With such minor tasks, this dog has truly changed and improved her owner's life.

"One of the most important things we teach the dog is to pull a manual wheelchair. None of our dogs do sustained pulling, and pull only about five percent of the time. Most dogs pull with a handle attached to their harness, and since each client has different abilities and disabilities, each harness must be designed individually for the dog and its particular owner.

"Jeremiah was 11 years old and suffered from muscular dystrophy. This young man called us on his own, and his interview proved him to be a very mature and exceptional boy. So we found

Peanut Butter, another Golden bitch. We trained her for three months, then Jeremiah came to us three times a week for three more months to learn how to work with the dog before taking her home. That way the new owner develops the skills to expand on the dog's training over the years to come.

"Jeremiah and Peanut Butter became the stars of his junior high school. The dog takes Jeremiah's books out of his locker and carries them to class, takes Jeremiah's coat off, and picks up dropped objects. Jeremiah has trained her to stand up to look in the windows of the teacher's door and knock on the door for him.

"We tell our young men that Service Dogs are a great way to meet girls—just go to the mall and park yourselves, and the girls won't leave you alone. We placed a wonderful Golden female with a young boy in high school who had cerebral palsy and a severe stutter. He was very shy, and the other kids ignored him because he was hard to understand. Later when I visited him at school, it was altogether different—he was surrounded by girls and was grinning from ear to ear. The girls were pleading, 'Can I carry your books? . . . push your wheelchair? . . . pet your dog?'

"Another client with cerebral palsy is a wheelchair-bound teacher with a class of able-bodied six-year-olds. During her first weeks at school, a little girl in her class fell off a playground swing

Jeremy and Freedom Service Dog **Peanut Butter.**

and skinned her knee. She sat crying on the ground, and the teacher was unable to reach her because she couldn't move her wheelchair across the gravel yard. Her dog could not pull the chair across the gravel, and he was getting very upset because the little girl kept crying. So the teacher released the dog, and he ran to the child, sat beside her and licked away her tears. The girl petted Micah and yelled to her teacher, "It's okay, Micah fixed me." That teacher has come to depend on her Golden to "fix" those children who are unhappy, and she is now working with abused children, using Micah as therapy for them.

"We continue to follow up on each Service Dog for its entire lifetime. Under Colorado state law, dogs must be recertified every year, which requires a complete health check-up by the veterinarian, and a four-page document from the client. Then we retest and recertify the dog. That makes it even more rewarding, since we can watch the teams grow and do more and more things together.

John and Freedom Service Dog **Aurora.**

Reneé and Freedom Service Dog **Chester.**

"The best part of my job is that when I give these dogs free of charge to their new owners, it's not the end of the story, rather it's a new beginning for them both."

Information about these Service-Dog organizations can be obtained from:

Freedom Service Dogs, Inc., 980 Everett St., Lakewood, Colorado 80215.

Support Dogs of St. Louis, Inc., 301 Sovereign Ct., St. Louis, MO 63011.

Helping Paws of Minnesota, Inc., P.O. Box 12532, New Brighton, Minnesota 55112.

Paws with a Cause: Home of Ears for the Deaf, 1235 100th St. SE, Byron Center, Michigan 49315.

Peter Poliey III and his beloved guide dog **Tabitha**…never another quite like her…

Future Leader Dog, **Jamie-New-Barker,** the second Leader puppy to join the Michigan Department of Corrections Puppy Socialization Program at the Women's State Prison. Truly a ray of sunshine inside dreary prison walls…

Guide Dogs

There is nothing quite as heartening as a Golden Retriever in working harness with its blind companion. The obvious bond between the human and guide dog is even more enhanced by the Golden's famous soft, "warm fuzzy" appeal.

However, that same disarming expression can also be a problem. According to International Guiding Eyes, Inc., it is not uncommon for people to try to pet a Golden while it's working. That seldom happens with a German Shepherd guide dog.

International Guiding Eyes is one of the ten guide dog schools currently operating in the United States. Most schools use Labrador Retrievers, Golden Retrievers and German Shepherds because they are willing workers, of medium size, and have dual coats that adapt to both hot and cold weather. The schools use both dogs and bitches, all of whom are neutered at an appropriate early age.

Most guide-dog organizations maintain their own breeding programs, with some acquiring dogs through purchase or donation. Every school utilizes puppy-raiser families, who raise each pup with love and concern, and encourage the development of normal household manners and social skills. In some states, local 4-H clubs participate in the puppy raising and training programs. The loving interaction between the puppy and its first human family lays the groundwork for the dog's adult career as canine eyes and caretaker for the blind.

Puppies in the program are continually evaluated for potential during their growing-up period with the puppy raiser. Serious training begins back at the school between 12 to 18 months of age. The young dogs are retested, and those that qualify enter a three-to-six-month training program with school instructors. Most schools begin with basic obedience training, then progress to street training, teaching the dogs to observe curbs, pedestrians, traffic and other hazards. Advanced training takes the dog into heavy crowds, noisy construction areas, public transportation and other busy and confusing situations.

Dogs that fail under the rigors of formal training are offered back to the puppy raiser as a pet or adopted out to a good home. Such career change dogs make ideal companion dogs, and most schools have a perpetual list of applicants waiting to adopt them.

A guide dog must be physically sound, friendly and intelligent, and must respond to people and situations without fear or aggression. Yet each dog is different and has its own personality. All schools consider the characteristics, physical and mental, of both the canine and the blind person when matching applicants with their future guide dogs.

Every school, except the Fidelco Guide Dog Foundation in Bloomfield, Connecticut, has an on-premises training program lasting three-and-one-half to four weeks. The guide dog and blind person begin with 24-hour-a-day togetherness, with formal supervised training interspersed with lots of getting acquainted, petting and playing and routine care. During that time the guide-dog user learns to trust his life and safety to the judgement of his new canine friend, establishing a bond that will grow stronger each day.

Leader Dogs for the Blind in Rochester, Michigan is the largest guide-dog training facility in

Opal is a gem of a Seeing Eye Dog®...this photograph donated by Ellen Hardin. Opal is by Am-Can. Ch. Timberee's Tenacious Token UDT, WCX, Can. CDX ex Am-Can. Amerac's Melody of Wallenway CD, WC, Can. CD. Is there any doubt that versatility runs in Opal's family? Opal works for the Seeing Eye® Inc. of Morristown, New Jersey.

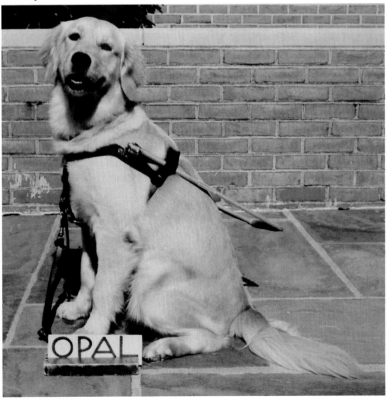

the United States and one of the largest in the world. Founded in 1939 by three blind members of the Lions Club, it has since trained over 8,000 Leader Dogs for teams in the United States and a dozen foreign countries. Each year Leader Dogs "graduates" over 300 teams of dogs and people. Approximately one-third of the guide-dog graduates are Golden Retrievers.

In 1989 Leader Dog expanded its puppy-raising program and added the women at the Huron Valley Women's Facility to the guide-dog army of puppy socializers. The noisy, busy prison environment provides an ideal arena for puppy socialization; in turn, Leader Dog puppies provide new growing and learning experiences for the prisoners, offering them unconditional love and an opportunity for responsibility and a rare positive experience.

Golden Retriever puppy Jamie-New-Barker was the second Leader Dog to enter the prison program. She spends her days at the prison with Carol Dyer, the project coordinator, who works with inmate trainers to socialize, train and care for the little Golden. Jamie reveled in her job as

Desert Guide Kirby CDX, Bda. CD delivers the dumbbell to Ed Eames during obedience training.

a puppy prison therapist, and snuggled up to everyone she met to offer an endless supply of tail wags and wet kisses. At day's end Carol took Jamie home with her.

The Huron Valley Leader Dog project is currently building a kennel on the prison grounds that will house ten puppies to be raised for various service organizations. Meanwhile, Jamie continued to capture the hearts of the inmates until she was old enough to begin training for her life's work.

About half of the Leader Dog puppies are donated by pre-approved private breeders. Others are bred and raised in Leader Dog's own puppy program. Michael Walrath, director of the breeding program, writes they have the highest success rate with Goldens from the Meadowpond line, which is the backbone of their Golden Retriever breeding program.

Of the 240 guide dogs issued in 1989 by Guide Dogs for the Blind, Inc., in San Rafael, California, nearly one-third or 75 were Goldens. Guide Dogs states that Golden guide dogs are known especially for their steady pace and friendly manner. From the California shores to the city streets of Tucson, Guide Dog's Golden graduates share their lives with computer operators, students, copywriters, homemakers and other blind people who have faith in the special trust that a Golden so easily evokes.

Ed Eames, a retired professor of anthropology at Baruch College in New York, obtained his first guide dog, Golden Retriever Kirby, in 1981 from Guide Dogs of the Desert in Palm Springs, California. His wife Toni, a psychiatric counselor and blind since birth, received her first guide dog, a Golden named Charm, from Guiding Eyes for the Blind in 1967. Today she relies on Ivy, her third Golden Retriever and current best friend.

Toni was a shy and retiring 22-year-old when she got Charm. Charm led her through graduate school at Hunter College in New York City and gave her the confidence to explore the outer limits of possibility for a blind person. Toni wanted to achieve, and what's more, she wanted to do it with her dog.

With help from experienced Golden breeder Laurie Doumaux, and permission from the training director at Guiding Eyes, Toni set out to train Charm for obedience competition. Laurie and Toni realized it was most important that Charm not confuse guide work with obedience routines. They kept the training gentle, used lavish praise and avoided use of the word "no."

Toni had to learn bare basics, like walking in a straight line for heeling patterns and how to navigate the "posts" on the novice obedience figure-eight exercise. (The stewards kept repeating "post" aloud.) On off-lead heeling, Toni learned to overcome the sense of insecurity she felt when not holding the leash, since the leash always assured her of Charm's presence beside her. Laurie and Toni discovered that with lots of constant vocal encouragement Charm would heel more energetically and begin to pant. Toni keyed off the sound of Charm's panting and relaxed.

Other adjustments were more difficult for Charm. She was reluctant to allow Toni to move across the ring alone for the recall exercise or to walk around her unassisted after the stand for examination. Weeks of gradual conditioning and practice helped her understand, and relieved her apprehension about Toni's welfare while doing their obedience routines.

In 1972 Toni and Charm entered the obedience ring, still under Laurie's watchful eye. They earned five qualifying scores in five straight shows, and Charm CD became the first obedience titled dog completely trained by a blind person. No one was prouder of them than Laurie Doumaux.

When Charm died in 1977, Golden Retriever Flicka stepped in to follow in her pawprints. Laurie had moved out of the state, so with help this time from Ann Strathern, a Golden Retriever field-trial and obedience enthusiast, Toni and Flicka earned their CD in 1982. In 1990, Ed joined his wife, Toni, in the obedience ring, and in November of that year both Kirby and Ivy became official CD-titled guide dogs.

Relocated once again to Fresno, California, the Eameses have continued their obedience training with help from trainer Jo Amenda. They reached even higher and started training for the CDX.

Despite the increased difficulty of the Open exercises, Ed and Toni found several creative devices to aid their training program. They use a beeping dumbbell, so they can tell where the dumbbell lands, and when the dog is coming back with it. A beeping device on the dog's collar also helps them find the dog; they use it on the drop on recall and on the long sit and long down.

Still, the road in Open class is a long and bumpy one. In five shows, Toni and Ivy had earned just one CDX leg, and Ed and Kirby, after four shows, were still trying for their first.

The breakthrough finally came in March of 1992 at the King's Kennel Club show in Hanford, California. Toni and Ivy qualified for their third leg with a first place award with a score of 193, becoming the first guide dog–blind handler team in obedience history to earn a CDX.

Saratoga's Edgecomb Ivy CDX, Bda. CD owned by Toni Eames, Fresno, California.

That same day Ed and Kirby followed suit and gained their first Open leg, and capped it with a fourth place award. In December they earned their third Open leg to become, appropriately, the second guide dog–blind handler team in the sport of obedience. Mission accomplished, Ed and Toni wouldn't consider resting on their laurels. In November 1992 they travelled to Bermuda and earned Bermudan CDs with Kirby and Ivy in one weekend.

Ed and Toni write a monthly column called "Partners in Independence" for *Dog World* magazine. Their columns reveal the steadfast trust of people who must depend on their devoted guide dogs for mobility and strength.

In 1980, Guiding Eyes also paired Peter Poliey III of Holbrook, New York with his first guide dog, a Golden Retriever named Tabitha. Three days after their graduation "Tabby" earned Peter's complete trust when in mid-street, she saved him from falling into an open manhole cover, and a short while later pushed him out of the path of a wayward bus. Tabby was Peter's eyes for seven years, accepting commands from only him and no one else until she died of cancer in 1987.

Peter now has another breed of guide dog, and

Saratoga's Edgecomb Ivy CDX, Bda. CD, owned by Toni Eames, returns the dumbbell in an open retrieve exercise.

when to play or just put her head in my lap to comfort me."

Jim Cunnin describes his Guiding Eyes Golden guide dog, Jade, in much the same way. "You would have a hard time distinguishing Jade from the humans in our household because of her almost human responses to various situations," he writes from his home in Winnipeg, Manitoba.

"On visits to our grocery supermarket, Jade quickly learned the geography of the premises and follows commands like 'deli,' 'bakery,' or 'produce' to take me to the right department. At the neighborhood liquor store, Jade goes right to the Bushmill's Irish Whiskey without a single word from me."

Jade proudly joined Jim's daughter's bridal party, and wore a matching bow on her harness as she led Jim and the bride down the aisle. Jim joked that his other daughter declined that arrangement when she married, afraid she might be referred to as the girl whose father walked his dog down the aisle!

"All dogs are wonderful," Jim conceded, "but in terms of devotion, friendship, and most of all, commonsense, the Golden is in a class all by itself."

The Guiding Eyes quarterly newsletter to their graduates included this author's request for information on Golden Retriever guide dogs. A very special thank you to the other kind people who responded: Neala Dawson, Pittsburgh, Pennsylvania; Finlay Herlihy, New York, New York; Kate Chamberlain, Walworth, New York; and Jocelyn Backston, Scarsdale, New York.

The names, addresses and telephone numbers of the guide-dog schools operating in the U.S. are listed here: Fidelco Guide Dog Foundation, Inc., P.O. Box 142, Bloomfield, CT 06002, (302) 243-5200; Guide Dog Foundation for the Blind, Inc., 371 East Jericho Turnpike, Smithtown, NY 11787, (516) 265-2121; Guide Dogs for the Blind, Inc., P.O. Box 1200, San Rafael, CA 94915, (415) 479-4000; Guide Dogs of the Desert, Inc., P.O. Box 1692, Palm Springs, CA 92263, (619) 329-6257; Guiding Eyes for the Blind, Inc., Yorktown Hts., NY 11375, (914) 245-4024; International Guiding Eyes, 13445 Glenoaks Blvd., Sylmar, CA 91342, (213) 362-5834; Leader Dogs for the Blind, 1039 Rochester Rd., Rochester, MI 48063, (313) 651-9011; Pilot Dogs, Inc., 625 West Town St., Columbus, OH 43215, (614) 221-6367; The Seeing Eye, P.O. Box 375, Morristown, NJ 07960, (201) 539-4425.

while Peter and his new dog Billy get along famously, he said Tabby will always be Number One. "A perfect example," Peter said from his home in New York, "is that while I sit here on the telephone, Billy is off somewhere else with my wife or the children. Tabby never left my side, not for one moment. She was completely devoted to me—I was her reason for living."

Billy is more protective of the family, however. Peter says Billy will automatically position himself between his children and any new person who enters the house. Tabby, on the other hand, welcomed every stranger she met like they were long-lost friends.

Guiding Eyes Golden Retriever graduate Farley is the third guide dog owned by Isabel Cortes of New York. Isabel said her Golden is by far the best of the three breeds who have been her eyes during the past 13 years. "She is much more sensitive and loving than the others," Isabel said. "She seems to know when I'm happy or sad, and

Therapy Goldens

"I believe the day is coming when doctors will sometimes 'prescribe' pets instead of pills . . . What pill gives so much love, makes one feel safe, stimulates laughter, encourages regular exercise and makes a person feel needed?"

This quote by Leo K. Bustad, DVM, PhD, was taken from his article, "The Importance of Animals to the Well-being of People." Dr. Bustad has been a pioneer in forging the human companion animal bond, and is the founder of the People-Pet Partnership program at Washington State University.

Dr. Bustad's words best describe the thrust of his dedication to implementing pet therapy into the whole of our society. In 1977 he helped establish the Delta Society, a national organization to study human–animal relationships and how they may be used to facilitate therapy. Today it is the leading professional organization conducting research on the effects of animals on human health; promoting animal programs for disturbed children, handicapped persons, prisoners, and patients in hospitals and nursing homes; and educating Americans about the benefits of human–animal interaction.

Research data on animal-assisted therapy can present astonishing numbers and statistics on the beneficial effects and results of human–animal interaction. But it is still the stories, the touching details about animals who penetrate the tragic worlds of the physically and mentally ill, the elderly and the lonely, that best present the case for animals as co-therapists in our lives.

Although many breeds of dogs are actively involved in therapy programs around the world, the Golden with its unique sensitivity and soft, trusting look is especially adept at making special connections with special people.

At the St. Louis State Hospital in St. Louis, Missouri, Golden Retrievers Alexander and Sonnet are the hospital's official therapy dogs. Equipped with their own identification badges, the two Goldens roam the hospital corridors, bringing smiles to hospital patients as well as personnel. They are the hospital's favorite volunteers, and staffers say these canine psychologists boost the morale of everyone they meet.

Alexander and Sonnet are owned by hospital psychologist Marty Russo. Alexander logged 400 hours of service during his first year of service in 1990, and Sonnet completed 200 hours after joining Alexander on the job.

The two dogs are on duty every Thursday from

Honey, a registered therapy and Delta dog, derives her name from her ever-sweet disposition and her color. A wonderful moment guided by Neva Sharlow, RN, OCN...Honey making the acquaintance of Justin at the Allen Park Nursing Center. Photograph by Karen Taylor.

7:30 a.m. to 4:30 p.m., and work primarily with mentally ill patients suffering from brain trauma or geriatric problems. Marty takes his Goldens with him on his rounds; the dogs may visit or just lie quietly at the patients' feet. He said the patients relate to him better when the dogs are there. People who are very withdrawn come out of their shells when the dogs are with them, and after a while they develop a therapeutic bond with the dogs.

Marty said his patients will often remember Alexander's and Sonnet's names, but will forget his name. "I'm just the man with the dog," he said, and that may be just what the doctor ordered.

This page and facing page: The work of therapy dogs cannot be capsulized in a few words—although a few photographs do an admirable job. **Honey** and Justin photographed by Karen Taylor.

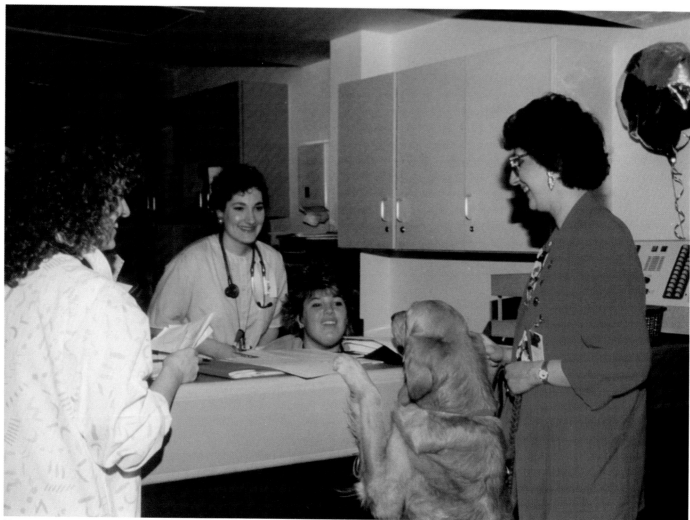

Honey signing in upon arrival at the Allen Park Nursing Center. Neva Sharlow with Kerri Vaughn, Lisa Berlasi and Maureen Valcke. Photo by Karen Taylor.

On the East coast, Ramson's Golden Dynamo CDX, TD, Can. CD, "Dyna," is affectionately known as the social director at the Medical Center Hospital of Vermont in Burlington, Vermont. Every other Friday Dyna, with her owner Gina Mireault, and two other therapy dogs and their owners, visits the hospital's two psychiatric wards (one for patients with temporary problems, the other a locked floor for acute psychiatric care). Patients in this second ward are more disturbed and more needy of the dogs.

Some of the patients cannot leave their rooms because of their medical status, and some refuse to come out because they are paranoid, withdrawn, schizoid, anti-social or extremely depressed. Because of her uniquely Golden character, trustworthy face and gentle style, Dyna is always singled out by the hospital staff to visit these patients in their rooms. It is during these times, Gina said, that Dyna does her best work, sometimes performing tiny miracles.

On one occasion, Dyna was asked to visit Hanna, a patient who was legally blind, severely withdrawn and incommunicative, and would not leave her room. Hanna was sitting on her bed when Gina brought Dyna in to introduce her. Dyna did the rest . . . Hanna's withdrawn behavior did not intimidate her. Instead she approached her gently, and began to lovingly lick her hands which were clasped in her lap. The lady unfolded her hands to receive Dyna's kisses, then reached out and softly patted Dyna's head. When she stopped petting, Dyna softly whined until the woman continued her attention. Hanna spoke only once, to say "She's soft." Before they left, Hanna smiled, and the nurse told Gina this was the first time Hanna had smiled since her arrival.

The next Friday when the dogs visited, Hanna actually requested that Dyna come to her room, and this time she made light conversation while Dyna sat with her. "Seeing Dyna with Hanna gave me a new appreciation of her sensitivity to special people," Gina said, and she recounted another Dyna story.

"Marcia was a young woman who was also very withdrawn when we first met her. She sat in the patient lounge, very quiet and avoided eye contact with me or Dyna. It's difficult to know if a very withdrawn person wants to be approached, so I visited with another patient who was more receptive. Dyna read Marcia better than I did, and occasionally went over to sit near her or lie across her feet. Before we left, Marcia softly told me she had been waiting since the previous day for the dogs to come.

"Dyna and I had to miss the next scheduled visit, hence a month went by before we returned. Marcia came into the patient lounge and sat on the floor. Dyna immediately sat close to her, but it wasn't until Dyna began licking her face that I realized Marcia was crying. 'You didn't come last time, Dyna,' she sobbed, 'I missed you.' Dyna, on her own choosing, stayed with Marcia for the remainder of our visit and laid across her lap until it was time to go."

Dyna made another connection with an elderly patient named Lindy. For three months Lindy had hostily refused when asked if he would like to pet the dogs. Dyna persisted in making advances toward him during every visit, but Lindy would shoo her away. She would stare at him from across the room while visiting other patients, and Gina continued to ask if he wanted to pet her. "I admit," she said, "I kept asking more for Dyna's sake...I couldn't stand to see her efforts rejected."

Finally the day came during one ordinary visit. After the routine question about petting the dogs, this time he said, "Yes," but Dyna was the

Therapy Golden, **Ramson's Golden Dynamo CDX, TD, Can. CD,** "Dyna," owned by Jay and Gina Mireault, Waterbury Center, Vermont, confers with psychiatrist Ellen Patterson before visiting "her" patients.

only one of the three he wanted to pet—the only Golden in the trio of pet therapists. Dyna's gentle persistence over the months had paid off.

One of the most touching connections Dyna made was with Joseph, who was severely withdrawn and apparently catatonic. He was sitting in the patient lounge, and Dyna saw him immediately. She approached him quietly, then wrapped herself around one of his legs and came out between his legs so that her face was peering right up into his. She sat there for about five minutes, panting calmly, with no attention from the man, as if he didn't know she was there. Just before Gina went to remove her, he reached out and rested his hand on her head, all the while staring into space. "I almost cried," Gina said. "In a way no one else could, Dyna had made contact with him."

"The man didn't undergo a personality change; he wasn't cured," she continued. "But pet therapy is not about amazing breakthroughs. When people ask me what therapy dogs 'do,' I say they wag their tails and make people smile. That's all, but it's enough, and it's sometimes the best medicine. Pet therapy is about making quality contact with people, and sometimes dogs are better at that than we are.

"It takes a very special dog to do therapy work, but an extra-special one to work with people suffering from mental disorders. Dyna adapted immediately to the strange gaits, postures, ges-

tures and vocalizations of the patients. She's taught me one of the best lessons I've learned, a sort of *Golden* rule."

This powerful bond between dogs and people has received a great deal of attention from the scientific community during the past decade. For the first time research has explored the canine's capacity for comprehension and emotion. Dogs have an uncanny ability to interpret human intention. When a handicapped person drops something on the floor, a working dog doesn't merely retrieve it, he also checks to see if the person wants the object back.

The dog's ability to respond to a human in need has also been recognized and researched. True to members of their own and to other species as well as man, dogs have also been known to protect injured or dying animals, bring them food and seek human intervention or assistance.

Science is simply now discovering what dog lovers have always known, that while the difference between people and other animals may be great, that difference is one of

Two of the author's reindeer convincingly disguised as Golden Retrievers dressed as reindeer...off to a holiday tour of the local nursing home. Nona and the deer visit the local facilities on a regular basis, when not training of course.

degree and not of kind.

Organizations: The Delta Society, P.O. Box 1080, Renton, WA 98057-1080, (206)226-7357; The People-Pet-Partnership, College of Veterinary Medicine, Washington State University, Pullman WA 99164-7010.

"Many humans benefit from the smiling face of a Golden Retriever. Touching, petting or just talking to a Golden can bring out the best in even the 'toughest' person", tells nurse Neva Sharlow. Not so tough at the Allen Park Nursing Center are *(top left)* Ruth Lezotte with **Molly**, *(top right)* Irene Pippin surrounded by **Molly** and **Honey**, *(bottom left)* James Lamb and **Molly**, and *(bottom right)* Mary Maynard with **Molly** and **Honey**. These photographs are the wonderful work of Karen Taylor of Taylor, Michigan.

Sandyhill's Hide'N Go Seek TD and Patricia Depp. "Seeker" is vested and ready to go.

Search and Rescue

Search and rescue (SAR) may be the least publicized area of canine heroics. While stories about "dog saves drowning boy/avalanche victim/lost child" seldom make newspaper headlines, such tales are prized by members of the dog community as shining examples of man's best friend in service to his master.

The skill of the SAR dog lies in his extraordinary scenting ability. The canine sense of smell is estimated at many hundreds of times greater than man's. Dogs trained in SAR can sniff out people buried under earth, snow, ice or other debris, and locate them in places that are dangerous or inaccessible to man. The trained dog can also indicate he has found more than one person, and if the victim is alive or dead. SAR dogs work for no reward other than the sheer pleasure of the work itself.

Official search and rescue work was introduced during the 1940s by the American Rescue Dog Association, a six-unit group of German Shepherd Dog-and-handler teams. In 1980 several units broke away from the parent organization to form an all-breed unit of SAR dogs. That split triggered the expansion of the SAR movement across the United States.

SAR groups are most likely to organize and operate in areas which are prone to natural disasters. In Juneau, Alaska, SEADOGS (Southeast Alaska Dog Organization for Ground Search) rescue dogs are invaluable in wilderness and avalanche searches. Tourists and hunters often lose their visual references in the thick Alaskan forest and get lost. SEADOGS can take their dogs through heavy underbrush and over rough, hazardous terrain that would be impassable for human searchers.

SEADOGS Golden Retriever Taco, owned by Riley Ritchie of Juneau, averaged 15 to 20 searches every year during her SAR career, many of them in Juneau's heavy forests. Before she

On Panama Canal Mission, at one-year-old, **Seeker** is already riding choppers.

retired in 1989, she spent eight years in wilderness and avalanche work. Certified at under seven months of age for wilderness search, she was the youngest dog ever to qualify for SEADOGS rescue work.

Riley and Taco also accompanied SEADOGS to Soviet Armenia in 1989, and spent ten days searching for victims of that tragic earthquake. Paired with another SEADOGS team, they typically worked three searches a day. Riley would walk Taco over areas of debris, and direct her through tunnels and into places too small for people or larger dogs.

"Retrievers are very obvious on a find," Riley said. "They get so excited, and their tails go like crazy. Taco is a very exuberant worker. She runs ahead, and after a find, sprints back and throws her body sideways against my legs. Then she races back at a dead run and barks and whines at the spot. Our obedience training was handy for me to keep up with her."

Initially in Armenia the dogs were very enthusiastic, Riley said. But as the search wore on, they became depressed at finding only dead people. With so many dead alerts, Taco became less and less enthusiastic in her body language. SEADOGS did live burials to bring the dogs' spirits up, but the effect was still very hard on them.

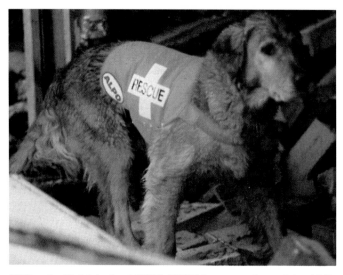

Hilltop's Rubble Lad UDT, WCX is a member of the U.S. Disaster Team Canine Search and Rescue Unit. He is a veteran of the earthquake in Soviet Armenia in 1989.

Taco's SAR training began at a tender 11 weeks of age. She and Riley joined the SEADOGS training group twice a week for puppy socialization, and Riley emphasized that for five months he was never more than a grocery store away from her. Their daily SAR training included several five-minute play sessions, with emphasis on obedience and verbal commands in a play environment.

The bond between Riley and Taco was strengthened during the initial disaster training. While Taco was restrained, Riley would run away, in an arc rather than a straight line, and partially hide around or behind an obstruction. The dog immediately would be released to run to her master.

For the dog it must always be a game, and the dog always receives a reward. The "game" progressed to a completely hidden Riley, longer distances and more difficult terrain, longer times before Taco was released, and finally to people other than her owner.

A dog in training must show consistent performance before the SEADOGS group will recommend testing for certification. Riley said their

requirements are rigid, and the final testing is very specific. SEADOGS uses an Alaska State Trooper and at least one SEADOGS handler with a certified dog.

An avalanche test involves the live burial of two people, one at least six feet deep, the other six feet or less, in an area about half the size of a football field, with the site tromped down to remove all visual clues. The test is tailored so that wind, terrain and other conditions will create about a four-hour search, although dogs can be successful in as little as two or as many as eight hours. The testers try to set up a sizable problem to make sure the new team can keep up on a two-to-three-day search.

In addition to the dog's capability, the handler must be proficient in first aid, CPR and radio commands; be in good physical condition and an intermediate-or-better skier; and be proficient on snowshoes, cross-country skis and in the use of maps and compasses. The testers also check the handler's backpack for proper rescue equipment.

These same standards also apply to the wilderness test. The dog and handler must work a fresh track about an hour old, a half-mile or less, with no known cross-tracks. The dog must be able to work out air-scenting problems, negotiate terrain, and in both test situations, the dog–handler team must display good chemistry and communication.

Taco worked the Juneau ski area for several years while Riley was a member of the ski patrol, and she has searched more for lost skiers than she has worked in avalanche. But Riley emphasized that the search dog, especially in Alaska, cannot be measured by the number of live or dead people found. "We take our dogs into very tough terrain and thick forests, and they will search the area more effectively than any ground searchers," he said. "Three or four dogs can do the work of 30 to 40 foot searchers, who can thus remain safely behind. The real measure of the search dog is more in the number of lives saved in searchers than in the number of victims found."

Hilltop's Rubble Lad UDT, WCX, was a ten-year-old SAR Golden Retriever from Pittsburgh, Pennsylvania, who, with his owner, Pat Depp, also assisted in the Armenian disaster search. A five-year veteran of search and rescue, Rubble was the only member of the U.S. Disaster Team to make a live find.

Rubble made his one live alert at night. With the only light source a generator-powered floodlight, 25 native Armenians followed hopefully after the dog, watching him pick his way across a mountain of broken concrete and twisted steel. After a second dog verified Rubble's live find, the handlers marked the alert site and sent for the U.S. Heavy Rescue Team. The dog's job was done, and he and Pat moved on to another search area. Rubble also made over 15 dead alerts during his work at the Armenian earthquake site.

The Soviet search was one of Rubble's last. He died of cancer the following year. During his rescue career, he and Pat had searched for dozens of flood and tornado victims, and missing and murdered persons. In five years he had made at least five live finds and over 35 dead alerts.

Rubble's father, Pooh Bah of Betyar UDT, WCX, Can. TD,

Working in Puerto Rico in 1985, this is **Pooh Bah of Betyar UDT, WCX, Can. TD,** making a find in beneath the mountain of concrete debris.

"Bear," was Pat's first SAR Golden. Father and son often worked as a team, and during one of their more challenging searches, they located a body buried for two years beneath a Beaver County landfill.

The Beaver County police authorities suspected a murder victim had been hidden under the local landfill and recruited the two Goldens to aid in the search. The dogs had to scale high mountains of debris, so the police instructed the bulldozers to strip off two feet of landfill at a time, then sent the dogs in to work each layer of newly exposed debris. After about ten feet of fill had been removed, the dogs gave a slight turn of the head in one particular area and then moved on. Pat noted their indication, and on the next pass the dogs made a

definite alert at that same site. Rubble started to dig . . . the woman's body was found at that location.

Two years earlier, in 1985, Bear and Pat had joined 21 U.S. Disaster Teams, and rescue teams with disaster dogs from England, France, Italy and Switzerland, to help search for victims of the landslide in Puerto Rico.

Armenian building where **Rubble** made his live alert—the only dog on the U.S. team to do so.

Rubble and Pat Depp in front of their sleeping quarters in Soviet Armenia. Temperature was five degrees.

qualify for disaster work. Both dog and handler must meet rigid requirements to be accepted into the program. They must have thorough obedience training and be proficient in tracking and agility work. They must function as one, and the dogs must get along with strange dogs and remain obedient at all times. SAR dogs are granted the same access as guide dogs for the blind, and when en route to search sites, remain with their handlers while on planes, railways or buses. The dogs and handlers represent the U.S. at all times, and have to show respect for the people and cultures in other countries.

It's a tough program, Pat said, but the pleasure the dogs get in finding someone alive makes it all worthwhile. What better reason could there be?

Pat's SAR puppies begin training at seven weeks of age. She does simple "play" training so the puppy will enjoy it. If the dog enjoys his work, she said, he'll do a much better job when under stress.

While in San Juan, Pat and Bear worked with five rescue teams composed of four German Shepherds and one other Golden. They searched from 5:30 a.m. until 6 p.m. for seven straight days, in temperatures of 90 degrees with 85 percent humidity. The ground was still shifting, and the search area was littered with jagged pieces of metal, broken glass and nails. The extreme conditions necessitated work periods of only 15 minutes followed by 15-minute breaks.

Bear made over 15 dead alerts. There were no live finds; the mud had cut off any air supply to the buried victims. When the job was finished, both dogs and handlers were honored at a ceremony and banquet in San Juan.

Finding only dead bodies had a negative effect on the rescue dogs, and they became depressed, irritable and aloof. After the San Juan operation, Bear was very dejected and out of sorts. Pat called her local police department for help, and they used their own search and rescue people to provide live bodies for the dog to find. After a few live alerts, Bear was soon his playful, happy self again.

It takes a special dog to

On a search in Indiana **Bear** found a seven-year-old boy.

Pooh Bah of Betyar UDT, WCX, Can. TD owned by Patricia Depp, Pittsburgh, Pennsylvania—search and rescue dog known as "Bear."

As the dog grows and matures, Pat starts him on agility work, e.g., teeter-totters, ladders, and planks raised about one foot above the ground. As the dog masters these obstacles, she moves up to a 20-foot extension ladder and raises the planks up to five feet. Pat works the dog very slowly over each obstacle, so he won't fall and lose trust in her. "That trust is very important, since so much of the dog's work is on unsteady surfaces," she said.

During the SAR agility training Pat also begins tracking and obedience work. Tracking teaches the dog to use his nose, and Pat tacks on tracking titles by one year of age. The obedience titles follow tracking. Pat stressed that the Golden's agility-tracking-obedience versatility is what makes the breed so perfect for her work in SAR.

Sandyhill's Hide 'N Go Seek TD, "Seeker," is Pat's newest SAR dog and by far her best, she said. Born in April 1989, Seeker made his first live find in training at five and one-half months old. He had made over five dead alerts on search operations before he was two years old.

In Snowmass, Colorado, Honor's Cogan in the Rockies UDTX, WCX, TDI was an SAR Golden specialist in avalanche rescue work, trained to find victims buried under up to 20 feet of snow or ice. His owner Ron Buksaitis was a longtime member of the Aspen Highlands Ski Patrol, and Cogan rode the chair lift up the mountain every day to work at the ski patrol station.

Cogan's story of avalanche rescue training is enhanced by the fact that he is himself a rescue Golden, a dog no longer loved or wanted, who came into Ron's life at eight and one-half months old. Shortly afterwards he and Ron began serious training in avalanche rescue work.

Ron began with simple games of hide-and-seek atop the mountain, simple exercises with Ron's disappearing into pre-dug holes in the snow. They progressed to shallow burials of Ron and co-workers on the mountainside, then advanced to a single person buried in gradually deeper snow with larger search areas. Ron's most effective training tools were large doses of praise, play and positive motivation. Keep it simple; keep it a game. Build the dog's confidence—the dog always wins. In 1978 Cogan, in a variety of tests, passed the scrutiny of Ron's peers, his superiors and the U.S. Forestry Service for certification in avalanche work.

In March 1991, at 14 years of age, Cogan and Ron's younger Golden Retriever Courage worked a back-country avalanche site a half-mile wide with a vertical fall of 2,200 feet. For three days Ron and a fellow patrolman handled the two dogs over the search site in zero-degree temperatures and a minus-twenty-degree wind-chill.

"Of all the dogs in the area, Cogan and Courage were the only ones to go back every day," Ron writes. "Despite the size of the deposition zone and hazardous weather conditions, they never quit on me." For motivation, the rescue team did a live burial of 45 minutes for both dogs.

Just one more measure of a search and rescue dog. Ron stressed that when one dog puts out a commendable effort, everyone associated with SAR benefits. They ALL win.

For further information contact:

National Association of Search and Rescue (NASAR), P.O.Box 3709, Fairfax, VA 22038.

This page: **Honor's Cogan in the Rockies UDTX, WCX, TDI** and owner-trainer, ski patroller Ron Buksaitis, during a training session for avalanche search and rescue work.

Above left: **Rubble** home from Armenia and very tired. *Above right:* **Cogan**…if you bury a frisbee, I'll find that too. *Below:* **Cogan** and **Courage** sleep well after a day's work at the Aspen Highlands Ski Patrol station.

Drug Detection

The Golden Retriever is part of the growing army of canine super-sleuths serving in America's war against drugs. From airport to seaport, from post office and school buildings to posh corporate offices, dogs trained in drug detection scour their drug beats in search of narcotics and other contraband substances.

The U.S. Customs Service Canine Enforcement Program was one of the first agencies to take advantage of the canine nose. From four dogs trained for drug detection in 1970, U.S. Customs in 1990 had grown to a task force of 218 canine enforcement teams nationwide. Since that first year, Customs detection teams have made almost 73,000 drug arrests. In New York State alone, the region's canine teams' sniffers have led to over 25,000 narcotics seizures since the 1970 inception of the Canine Enforcement Program.

Golden Retriever **Pete** works for the Interquest Group in the Contraband Detection Canine Program. Shown here with handler Mac McIntosh, Pete knows where and how to sniff out a wide variety of contraband substances.

Detection dogs more than earn their keep and have proven themselves a bargain for the U.S. government. In 1990 Customs Canine Enforcment teams made 3,287 seizures of narcotics and illegal drugs with a street value of over 815 million dollars. Statistics show more than a 91-to-one return in terms of drug seizure street value to dollars spent on the canine program. Now that's cost effective!

German Shepherds, Labradors and Golden Retrievers are the breeds most commonly used by the Customs Service. About 98 percent of their dogs come from animal shelters. Customs feels that shelter dogs adapt well to detection training because they are street dogs and survivors, familiar with real-world sights, sounds and smells, who have had to fend for themselves.

Canine instructors from the Customs training center at Front Royal, Virginia make several procurement trips a year through the Midwest, Northeast or Southeast evaluating animals at shelters. About one out of every 50 dogs tested may be suitable to enter the program.

Scott Zeitner, Customs instructor and course developer, said he looks for physically fit dogs about one to three years old, with a high energy level and a "maniac" desire to retrieve. Scott will throw a rolled-up towel in an open area on the first retrieve, then play tug-of-war to test for a possessive response. Because of the confined and elevated areas which the drug dog has to search, the towel is then thrown under a car, into an open car and up onto a bench or platform. Dogs who enter the program but later wash out will be returned to the shelter or placed in a pet home, according to the shelter policies.

The Customs canine corps is thorough and efficient: one dog working a post office can process approximately one parcel every two seconds, compared to the many hours spent checking packages manually. The mail is dropped on the conveyor belt, and the dogs work the treadmill on the conveyor.

One of Customs's most productive canines is New York Detection Golden Retriever Tommy. Trained at Front Royal in 1984, he was responsible for approximately 120 seizures during his first years on the job. Tommy made New York headlines when he led his New York Seaport handler to a 500-pound stash of cocaine valued at 40 million dollars, hidden in bales of paper shipped in from Colombia.

Golden Retrievers are also one of the primary breeds used for contraband detection in Houston, Texas. The Interquest Group, Inc., a private organization, trains the dogs to detect marijuana, heroin and cocaine, as well as alcoholic beverages, firearms, ammunition, and numerous commonly abused medications.

The dogs accompany Interquest handlers on inspections for school districts, and at commercial sites such as petro-chemical plants, oil

months of daily training, depending on the individual dog.

Debbie said a detection dog is trained to show its handler the exact location of contraband through either an aggressive or passive response. The passive-alert dog is trained to sit the instant it smells a contraband odor, and the handler must know how to read his dog to identify the location of the dog's interest just prior to the alert.

Topper *(left)* and **Bucky** *(right)*. Bucky is a contraband detection canine owned by Interquest Group. Bucky works with Carl Naylor of Bastrop, Texas. Topper (officially **OTCh. Fox Creek Topper MH**) is a professional hunting dog.

refineries and nuclear power plants. They also star in educational programs to teach school children about the dangers of substance abuse.

Like the Customs Service, Interquest uses a rolled-up towel to train their detection dogs. President Debbie Farmer explained that during early training the dogs are taught to associate the odor of contraband substances with a "toy."

A towel scented with a narcotic odor is thrown progressively farther, which allows the dog to learn an odor and seek it out as its own reward. As the towel is thrown out of sight, the dog must use its nose to find the toy. The towel can then be placed in harder-to-find places such as lockers, cars, desks or boxes. At the end of the training period the dog will be able to find the substance itself and will be rewarded with its own scented towel. The entire process can take up to three

The majority of dogs utilized by Interquest are aggressive-alert trained. Their response to a "find" is to paw at the object closest to the source of the contraband odor, which allows the handler to pinpoint the exact location. Both responses are widely accepted and utilized throughout the industry.

A Golden Retriever named Bucky is typical of the Interquest-trained contraband detection dog. Bucky works an eight-hour day, five-day week for the Bonham, Texas Police Department. Every year this busy Golden sniffs in excess of 180,000 lockers, 6,000 vehicles and 1,000 offices. Bucky also logs over 20,000 miles a year on search assignments and annually averages more than 900 confirmed alerts.

Bucky is still a typical Golden, however, and is a popular visitor at Bonham businesses and schools. According to his fans, he wags his tail over 40 times a minute.

In Michigan, eight-year-old Golden Retriever Goldie is a regular visitor at the maximum-security Michigan State Prison. Her welcome there, however, is far from warm or cordial. Rather she is greeted with hisses, hoots and threats, sometimes an object thrown at her from the bars of a cell door.

Goldie is not the typical therapy Golden who visits institutions. She is the state of Michigan's busiest and most successful drug dog, and comes to the prison to roam throughout the cell blocks looking for hidden drugs. The fact that she is good at her job is the reason some of those prisoners will spend most of their lives behind bars.

Goldie has been working drug detection since 1984. She works an average of 20 drug calls every month, and because of her skill and success record, both federal and local agencies often ask specifically for Goldie and her handler, state police officer Pat London.

Interquest's **Pete** on the job.

Pat and Goldie have been a team since 1988. Goldie lives with him and his wife and infant son, but spends 24 hours a day with Pat. Pat said the bond they have developed is the heart of the team concept and an important part of their success together. "I can tell the minute we walk into a room if Goldie's keyed on something or if something sparks her interest; little cues no one else would be aware of," he said. Powerful communication...the essence of working with drug detection dogs.

On call 24 hours a day, every day, it's not unusual for Goldie to run up to five drug searches a day. "We go into some extremely dangerous places," Pat said. "In the prisons, on the catwalks several stories above ground level, I'm always looking out for her, for someone trying to hurt her or stab her. One good kick from between cell bars, and my girl is ruined. They hate Goldie. I can hear them calling...'There's Goldie'...... shouting at the dog."

Crack and dope houses are equally dangerous, Pat conveys. For Goldie's safety, he always goes in first to check around. "I find a lot of poisons set out for the dogs...rat poison is a big problem. I also find drugs deliberately scattered around the floor, and since our dogs are trained to go to an odor, my dog could sniff cocaine up her nose." Some places are so foul Pat won't allow Goldie to go inside.

Goldie travels in a special canine four-door station wagon equipped with a cage in the back, customized fans for circulation and individual compartments for equipment. She has a special collar she wears only when she works—she learned in school that the collar means it's time to go to work. Her only identification is a tattoo in her ear that identifies her as a drug dog, and includes her training school and year of graduation.

All Michigan narcotics dogs attend a 12-week school where they are taught to identify six different odors: marijuana, hash, cocaine, heroin, crack and methamphetamine. Dogs must pass a state exam and be certified in all six odors before going to work for the Michigan State Police. Out of 40 new dogs, typically only five may make the grade, the others dropping out at various levels for a variety of reasons.

Pat said the school uses a box system to introduce the first odor, and all training is based on reward and play. The reward depends on the individual dog—with Goldie it's a tennis ball, her favorite object to retrieve.

"At the start it's very basic," Pat said. "With three or four boxes on the floor, only one will contain a drug. When the dogs gives an indication they smell the odor, they get their reward. After they progress, there will be several odors in the boxes. Next they go up in height, then in depth and plant the odor in the back, behind or buried underneath something. Training will also include various packing techniques and materials used in previous drug raids, so the dogs can get actual field experience. All the dog's activities and progress are charted, and they must be able to sniff out certain amounts at certain heights and depths before certification."

Additionally each dog and handler train together one day a week for the entire working life of the dog to ensure the dog's credibility in a court of law.

Michigan dogs are taught an aggressive response, to paw at the odor they have found. How to teach it? "Hands on training," Pat said. "You get right down there with the dog and dig away, and eventually the dog will understand and imitate you."

In 1988 Goldie pawed at two large blue suitcases at the Capital City Airport in Lansing, Michigan, and uncovered 11 million dollars in cocaine, the biggest drug bust by a canine in Michigan history. State Police Officer Jack Peet, Goldie's handler at that time, said Goldie's success rate has been essentially 100 percent: she never gives a hit unless something is there or previously had been there.

Michigan uses German Shepherds, Labradors and Goldens in its drug-dog program. Both Jack and Pat are impressed with the retriever as a narcotics dog because of its disposition and strong desire to retrieve. A drug dog also must be smart and possess a lot of drive . . . and, Jack said,

Interquest Canine, Golden Retriever **Jags** checks out a drinking fountain in a school. Jags's handler was Mary Maurer, who also owns and trained AFC Topbrass Gifford of Valhaven to his field title in 1990.

retrievers have more heart.

Goldie obviously fits that description. At eight years of age, she's still hitting 100 percent, but is entering the twilight of her career as a narcotics dog. Pat looks forward to the day when she retires and can live safely at home with his wife and son.

Pete continues his locker search.

Arson Detection

Following closely on the hocks of the drug-detection dog, Goldens also serve the public in arson detection work. Arson dogs frequently amaze state fire investigators by identifying accelerants in amounts too minute for laboratory tests to confirm, sometimes locating them beneath 12 inches of water or ice.

Golden Retreiver **Dudley,** arson detection dog, owned by the Maryland State Fire Marshal, is a handsome Golden…who proves good-looking dogs can also *work!*

Even modern science has difficulty competing with the canine nose. Although man has a large nose, his olfactory cells occupy only about one and one-half cubic inches and are located high in the top of the nose. This same organ in a German Shepherd or Golden Retriever has a volume of up to six cubic inches, with up to 200 million olfactory cells compared to man's paltry five million cells. Further, that part of the nervous system, called the rhinencephalon, which forms the link between the brain and the nasal cavity, is more highly developed in the dog than in the human. Is it any wonder the canine nose finds drugs and kerosene where human efforts fail?

Golden Retriever Dudley has been working for the Maryland State Fire Marshal since April 1989. Like Michigan's drug dog Goldie, Dudley is on 24-hour call and goes to work every day in a fully equipped police cruiser. The entire back seat has been removed, and bedding and grates installed for Dudley's comfort and complete security. He lives full-time with his handler, Deputy Fire Marshal John Brazil.

Dudley's duties extend beyond those of the typical arson dog. He has been trained to detect drugs and explosives as well as accelerants; and while the bulk of his work is arson, he and John occasionally work with the police bomb squad or conduct a drug search if state drug dogs are unavailable.

Although arson or other jobs may occur only two or three times a week, John and Dudley must train every other day because the dog is trained to do so many different things.

Dudley goes to work when given the command "seek," and will also take hand signals and other verbal commands. He is trained to search a materials line-up, where various fire debris is placed in a series of cans for the dog's inspection, and for a clothing line-up, where the dog inspects clothing taken from an arson suspect, mixed with clothing from the fire investigators.

In 1990, John's district lost a full city block to arson. Dudley tracked the building where the fire began, and working in a foot of water, searched for the origin of the fire. John said he was shocked when the dog plunged his head under water and pulled up a piece of soggy wood. Lab tests later confirmed an accelerant at the site of Dudley's hit.

John calls Dudley his "little Hoover" when he goes to work because he turns on like a vacuum cleaner, and you can hear his nose working like a small motor. His tail rides high, and when he's onto something, the Hoover sound grows stronger and his tail starts to wag.

Dudley was a rescue Golden when the Maryland Fire Marshal's Office took him in for training. At the Atlantic City, New Jersey Canine Training Center, while the Maryland fire investigators were looking for an arson-dog prospect, a woman brought in an 11-month-old, 75-pound Golden Retriever who had grown too big and

rambunctious for her and her two children. One look at the wild, rangy Golden bouncing at the end of the leash, and the Maryland agents said to each other, "That's our dog."

Dudley hasn't changed much. John describes him as a fearless alpha Golden whose courage occasionally gets him into trouble. Dudley has fallen halfway through collapsed floors and would leap from balconies and burned-out ledges to search the next room if John didn't keep him in check.

Dudley must be a hit with John's department because Maryland recently obtained their second Golden Retriever arson dog, a female named Misty who was rescued from a shelter by the New Jersey Canine Training Center. John Brazil is not the least bit surprised....

"Dudley" at work with his handler John Brazil at a fire scene, searching for the accelerant that caused the fire.

The things mom can teach you. **Amberwood Persimmon Charade** *(left)* and **Ch. Persimmon's Hat Trick CDX, WC** *(right)*, owned by Kristen Kothe. Photograph by Susan S. Rezy.

Golden Girls and Boys: Selection

BY CHRIS WALKOWICZ

A Golden puppy might grow up to be a good pet. Or he can be much more than that: a blue-ribbon winner, a helpmate, a Master Hunter, a Canine Good Citizen, a marvel of ability and, certainly, a beloved companion. The pup's future possibilities are restricted only by the owner's goals for him and enhanced by knowledgeable selection of this future Superdog.

Choosing to share our lives with a dog is only the first step of a decision-filled time. We must determine if our chosen breed really suits us and our lifestyle. It's wise to be prepared for several questions that will arise: Male or female? Adult or puppy? Did we select the Golden for its special qualities and abilities or simply because we like its appearance or temperament?

Within a breed—even within a litter—personality differences are found, and buyers should specify whether they want the one who bounces off the walls or the one who sleeps 23 hours a day. Other preferences, such as size or hue, might be stated. A potential exhibitor should say whether competition in obedience or achieving a championship is a priority.

MAKING CONNECTIONS

When a serious fancier chooses a dog to fulfill hopes and dreams, more is involved than simply finding a litter of the chosen breed and picking the pup with the waggiest tail or the lickingest tongue. First, a breeder with an impeccable reputation must be found. For those who are already involved in the dog world, it's less difficult to make connections because they are aware of preferences in structure or in ability and have an idea as to which lines produce well in these respects.

The recent enthusiast may have to overcome a few more obstacles, but the goal is worth the trouble. When people want the best, they haunt the places where the best are found. When Cape Cod tourists crave a fresh clam bake, they go to the beach, not the all-night grocery. The finest wines are found at first-class restaurants, not at a lunch counter. And the same is true of dogs. According to various interests, the superior dogs will be at shows, trials or tests.

While studying the dogs who are esthetically pleasing and who perform in the manner admired,

At five weeks this is **"Murphy Brown"** with five-year-old Patrick Bopp. Photo courtesy of Neida H. Bopp of Prairie Village, Kansas.

Never too young to start, this is **Farm Fresh Jersey Blue** at seven weeks retrieving for his proud mistress Leslie Dickerson of Riegelsville, Pennsylvania.

make notes on the kennels that boast the winners. Which sires and dams produce consistently? Their owners are the blue-ribbon breeders. Even if these kennels do not have puppies available, they are the places to start. Most owners are willing and able to recommend other breeders, and these people usually refer you only to places that they would buy from themselves. Giving a poor reference reflects on their own reputation; therefore, they stick to those with a four-star rating.

Starting at the root with a quality breeder allows a buyer to branch off if necessary. Show kennels have a monetary as well as an emotional investment at stake and seek excellence in the handlers, groomers and veterinarians with whom they do business. These professionals are additional sources of referrals. They often know who has litters, as well as who has top-notch ani-

mals and a squeaky clean reputation. Handlers, vets and groomers have a stake in the matter, too, because they might gain a client from someone who follows their lead and is pleased.

Dog clubs can supply reliable contacts as well. Many have a breeder index or answering services for just this purpose. The American Kennel Club can furnish the secretaries' names of sanctioned all-breed and specialty clubs, both locally and nationally. Often clubs are listed with the Chamber of Commerce or in the telephone book. The Kennel Club of Great Britain is the appropriate source for British residents, as is the Canadian Kennel Club for Golden fans in Canada.

Some local or regional clubs have a code of ethics which the breeders must sign and adhere to in order to be recommended. Money-minded profiteers are seldom found within the ranks of clubs because they have no interest in supporting and working at shows, seminars or canine charity fundraisers.

Ads in canine magazines and newspapers are costly, and kennels who advertise are usually secure, well-established businesses with owners who have a reputation to maintain. It is up to us to determine just how fine that reputation is. "Brag" ads trumpeting the kennel's latest Field Trial Champion or Best in Show Winner can give

A proud male puppy by Kyrie Ayodele ex Gala La Monique, bred by Suzanne Russ, Merced, California.

Learning the ropes. Early socialization by breeders is in part responsible for the dog's desire to please and enthusiasm to respond to human instruction. Photograph by Susan Rezy.

clues of success within a specific field of interest.

Published breed books display photos of top-winning dogs and descriptions of the kennels that produced them. The motto, "Records live, opinions die" is a truism. Any kennel that claims winners numbering in the double digits or above has begun its own records.

Of course, the professional breeder who is just starting up the ladder offers advantages as well. Because he doesn't have the widespread reputation, he is less likely to have waiting lists. Frequently, the person from whom he bought his bitch or who owns the stud he used will refer inquiries to him.

Although cost should not be number one on our list when searching for a companion, it is a consideration for most of us, and a beginner seldom can demand the prices of the established breeder. If the dedicated newcomer has bought his foundation stock from a reputable kennel, very likely he will have animals for sale that are comparable in quality to his mentor's. Not everyone who looks for a new, snazzy car can afford to buy a Mercedes. Some of us have to be satisfied with a well-built Chevrolet. And that Chevy can be attractive and dependable too. We don't always have to buy top-of-the-line to obtain quality, as long as we stay away from the junkyard.

NETWORKING

In conducting any type of research, one lead suggests another. A contact list mushrooms and grows, giving the buyer several options.

When contacting a well-known kennel and finding no puppies available, it is helpful to ask, "Can you recommend someone?" Or, "I just love your stud Alf (or your bitch Tigger). Does anyone have puppies with those lines?" Who can resist a compliment like that?

Ask breeders whether they belong to a local club and the national breed club. Club membership shows a sustained interest in the breed and in dogs. Ascertain whether they have signed their club's code of ethics. Puppy mill owners don't have time for "such nonsense."

Backyard breeders usually love their pets—which is a major reason they breed them. "Let's breed Snowy, so we can keep one of her pups, huh, Mom, huh?" And Mom gives in, not knowing how much work it's going to be, how costly the puppy shots and food will be, and how difficult it can be to place pups when you haven't developed a reputation.

It's not impossible to find a good pet at one of these homes. In fact, it's not impossible to find a good pet at an animal shelter or even a pet shop,

The "B" litter at Aquatico Goldens milling around before their first meal. Sire of this handsome litter was Ch. Jayba Jenlyn Fifth Avenue ex Harmony's Limerick Ginger Ale. Owners, Bruce and Donna Thompson of St. Louis, Missouri.

but it's a risky proposition at best, and nearly impossible to find a show-quality animal at any of these places. Among pet or show seekers, however, the highest percentage of satisfied customers are those who have researched their purchase wisely and bought from a breeder. The proof of this lies in the fact that, even though many people buy their first dog on a whim, they seldom buy their second in the same way—especially if the first was a lemon. "We loved Puddles, but we never could get her housebroken." Or, "We sure miss Jaws, but he left his mark on our house forever."

It is agreed that the problem with the backyard breeder does not lie with a lack of love, but with a lack of knowledge and, frequently, the use of animals with congenital defects, of which the average pet owner is unaware.

SEARCHING FOR SUPER DOG

Finding the ideal dog is not a whit easier than looking for the ideal mate. This search is about finding a buddy, a companion, one who appeals to us in every sense and will still do so when he's old, gray and pot-bellied.

When it comes to welcoming a new member into a family, spending the time to find the right addition is well worth the effort. It can't be done by placing an ad in the personal want ad section: Tall, athletic man of 40 desires a jogging companion who is cute, fuzzy and has floppy ears.

How then? Buyers should look at several examples of the breed before plunging into a ten-to-fifteen-year commitment. Many who have experience and have developed an "eye" know immediately whether or not a particular litter is going to offer promise. But those who are buying a dog for the first time or who are engaged in an initial search for their special pup need to see more than one specimen to make such a decision. And it's best not to base a choice on a picture in a book or a television commercial, unless you've had the opportunity to see the dog in reality and in action.

Certain questions arise that can only be answered through a one-on-one session. Can I live with the energy of this breed/individual? Is this dog too aloof for me?

Even if the dog of our dreams lives 2,000 miles away and it's impossible to make a speculative jaunt, buyers can observe the breed at shows or

Was it any wonder to owner Nick Kohn that this Superpuppy grew up to be Superdog? This is **Chances R Wisconsins Big Jake CDX**, bred by the author. Big Jake is an ace obedience dog, a born hunter as well as a delightful, loving family companion.

An eleven-month-old **DD's Made From Scratch** (now OTCh., TD, JH, WC) being loved by two-year-old Kevin Anderson. Photo courtesy of DD's Dog Training owned by the Andersons of Redwood City, California.

by tracking down a specimen that lives within 200 miles. Two hundred miles is too far? How far should you travel to find someone who is going to inhabit a corner of your life, your home and your heart for the next dozen years?

When the selection is narrowed down to one or two breeders and litters, and it comes to making a choice of the individual, this can be done even if the 2,000-mile trek isn't feasible. Of course, we have already ascertained that the breeder is reputable, so relying on his expertise and experience with the lines is helpful. Matchmaking is his business. He has everything to gain by ensuring the happiness of the new owner (and thereby the pup's) and everything to lose if it turns out to be a match made in hell.

Photos are a necessity in making a long-distance selection. Some modern-technology breeders offer videos to prospective buyers, demonstrating each puppy's movement, structure, attitude and interaction with littermates. A few think to film the sire during the nuptial visit and the dam prior to the loss of her willowy figure.

Precious moments with **Alderbrooke's Kelsey CD**. Owner, Carole Kvamme, Alderwood Manor, Washington.

Professional handlers can assist in the search in return for a finder's fee and the promise of a new client. If the pro appears at the door with a scraggly hag instead of the voluptuous vamp of our dreams, it's no thank you.

ONE ON ONE

If we're fortunate enough to live in the same vicinity as the kennel, we can conduct our own evaluation and perhaps participate in a temperament or aptitude test of the litter. Certain other subtleties can be assessed as well, such as the breeder's rapport with his dogs. An unspoken but obvious bond should be present, passing from one to the other. . . a look of devotion when the dam looks at her owner. . . pride shining on the face of the breeder and soft affection for the dogs in his eyes. . . an almost automatic caress of a velvet ear during the buyer's interview. . . a wet nose nuzzling under an arm.

Happy, healthy dogs greet visitors at the door. Firm but gentle corrections are given and obeyed—

at least partially, during the excitement of having guests. Needless to say, the sire and dam must be sound in mind and body as well as typical of the breed. Although the sire is seldom a roommate of the dam, the breeder should have photos and pedigree of the dog available for viewing.

Buyers should be prepared to ask questions as well as to answer them. Does the breeder belong to a club, has he ever shown, and do any of his dogs have titles? Does he linebreed, inbreed or outcross? Negative answers do not necessarily mean "Buyer Beware." The breeder should have answers, however, to educated questions and not say, "Huh?" or "Got no time for such foolishness."

It is our duty to discover whether any problems exist in our breed and whether the breeder has taken steps to avoid them. For instance, are his breeding animals OFA certified for good hips and CERF cleared for normal eyes? Also checked and cleared for vWD, SAS and OCD, in addition to other conditions that are hereditary and should not be present in breeding stock. If we're interested in becoming breeders ourselves, a free-whelping line and superlative foundation stock are pluses.

When appropriate, ask about and examine for entropion, incorrect bites and missing teeth, as well as other problems that may be known to appear in the line. If we've done our homework, most defects and improper coats should be apparent, but one should be aware of less obvious breed faults also.

MAKING THE GRADE

Those who wish to conduct formal temperament tests should do so when the puppies are seven weeks of age. These tests not only help breeders and buyers determine which pups are over-aggressive or horribly shy (hopefully none) but they show the range of good temperaments and obedience aptitude.

Pups should be tested separately, preferably on new turf by someone unknown to them. When the tester or surroundings is familiar, tendencies may be hidden or exaggerated.

In each instance, note whether the pups are bold, shy or curious. If a pup is startled or hesitant, does he recover and respond to the tester positively?

Social tests:

1. Observe the pup's reaction to the strange place and to a stranger. Is he bold, shy or curious? Note whether he bounces around immediately confident, hides in a corner or takes a moment to gain his composure and then begins to explore.

2. The tester should bend or kneel and call the puppy

Ruffian to his pals and playmates, this if **Sunfire's Kinetic Ruffian CD, WC.** (FC-AFC Ch. Kinike's Oro de Rojo ex Tanya du Shanka WC, Am-Can. CD). Born, March 10, 1979. Breeder, Michael A. Book. Owners, Michael A. Book and Barbara F. Biewer. Special element in the Sunfire breeding program: very smart and talented but difficult to train; grandkids are exceptional in obedience and field; excellent hips and good structure have been passed on.

to him in a friendly manner, clapping or whistling if he wishes.

3. The tester stands and walks away, calling to the pup.

Ch. Asterling Austin Healey ("Gunnar") and **Laurels Reingold Serenade**. "Sera" is pictured at eight weeks of age—she is from Gunnar's first breeding.

Dominance tests:

4. Rolling the pup on his back, the tester holds him in place for 30 seconds.

5. A stranger pets the pup on his head and looks directly at him, putting his face close to the pup's.

6. Pick up the pup with hands under the belly; hold elevated for 30 seconds.

Alertness/obedience tests:

7. Crumple noisy paper or rattle a stone inside a can.

8. Toss the paper or a toy to see if the pup retrieves and returns the object.

9. Drag a towel or similar object in front of the pup. Does he show curiosity and follow?

Responses:

The bold, naughty or aggressive pup reacts immediately, sometimes barking or biting. This pup struggles during the restraint or dominance tests. He might grab at the tester's clothing. A top dog such as this one needs a dominant owner, a person who is willing—and able—to train, discipline and maintain control.

At the other end of the scale is the pup who shrinks away, shows disinterest or hides. He might cry or give in immediately during the restraint and dominance tests. The underdog takes a patient owner, one who is willing to encourage and socialize.

In between is the pup who is friendly, accept-

Many breeders subscribe to socialization exercises to boast the pup's confidence. This eager pup bred by the author is mastering a cardboard box tunnel. Photo by the author.

Now what? "Bravo" at eight weeks...the future **OTCh. Aureo Kyrie Standing Ovation Am-Can. UD, Am. WCX,** owned by Lyle and Elba Heusinkvelt. Photo courtesy of Neida Bopp.

ing and rather middle of the road. He might be hesitant, but is cooperative in most efforts. This one should fit in almost any home!

The ideal obedience prospect would willingly follow and come. He'd also be alert and show curiosity; he'd run after the toy, pick it up and return it to the tester.

NARROWING IT DOWN

Breeders have the additional advantage of living with the litter for eight or more weeks. They are the best ones to know which pup is the pack leader, which one follows docilely and which one tries to topple the king of the mountain off his perch. Notes should be made on eager or picky eaters. Individual descriptions using such adjectives as rowdy or laid-back, outgoing or aloof, and independent or willing to please are helpful during matchmaking.

When initial contact is made with the seller, we should specify what type of personality is desired in our future pet. A "type A" perfectionist or

Bruwin's Carmel Kiss rolls over for new friend, the young **Pinecrest's Linebacker**. Owners, Ginger and Susan Rezy. Photography by Susan Rezy.

workaholic will find it difficult to live with a rough-and-tumble, devil-take-care livewire who is trying out for the next *Rambo* sequel. Nor would the 78-year-old gent who likes to snooze by the evening fire want to go home with the canine yo-yo. (But this pup would be perfect for the athletic man wanting a jogging companion in that personal ad.)

The one absolute no-no is picking a dog because you feel sorry for him. Sorry lasts a long time. Rarely does a new home cure timidity, illness or anti-social behavior.

An owner who intends to field trial or hunt with his dog wants to find one who has a good nose and high energy. Toss a duck or pigeon wing and see whether the pup charges after it and says "It's mine." Marked timidity shown during household pan rattling or door slamming wouldn't fare well for a dog who's expected to join in the hunt. A bold, independent dog who shows curiosity is desirable.

SELECTING THE FLYER

Those of us who have visions of red, white and blue Best in Show rosettes dancing in our heads look at type, structure, movement, and a certain indefinable quality called presence. The best way to do this is to view the pups two or three at a time, ideally in a place which allows free movement and play: a fenced yard or a large room.

Any pup who exhibits disqualifying or serious faults should be eliminated from choice and from the examination site immediately. We can't take the chance of a sweet face turning us from our goal. Dogs of every breed who are blind or deaf, display viciousness or cryptorchidism (undescended testicles) as well as those that are neutered are specifically disqualified from conformation competition. Most breeds have additional disqualifications or serious faults—for example, size, color, coat or bite—and potential show buyers must be aware of these.

While the puppies are playing, look for the

Pine Run's End of the Rainbow CD, JH, WC owned by Gerry and Karen Badesso of Allentown, Pennsylvania.

the blueprint standard in mind. Feel coat quality, taking into consideration the puppy coat. Is it fine or dense as required? Harsh or silky? The color, of course, should be acceptable. There is no sense in battling upstream with such an obvious fault which is so easily eliminated from selection.

Although personalities differ in dogs, sometimes with a wide normal range, temperament should be typical of the breed. Golden girls and boys are happy and responsive—some are more serious, some are more frisky—all are unique and loveable. The pup who displays confidence is always a better choice than one who cringes and shrinks from human touch.

Puppies are usually blessed with an innocent sweetness, a characteristic that makes them a delight to their family even if they grow to adulthood and snub everyone else (not at all likely with a Golden). Whether the affection is demonstrated by a glow in the eyes, a single thump of the tail or bounding ecstasy at our approach, our dogs should like us . . . even if they don't like anyone else on earth.

Puppies *bounce*, puppies *boinnng*, puppies *galumph*. But, given enough time, the one who is put together in the proper way will demonstrate a baby version of exciting adult movement. We must be prepared to catch a glimpse into the future.

strut of canine royalty. Some dogs are born to show and they know it. They exhibit the panache of Clark Gable as Rhett Butler or sparkle like opening night at the opera. Given the choice, the ring-wise will opt for the pup with a less elegant neck and more charisma than for a dead-head swan.

Buyers should use the breed standard as a blueprint and study the pups, using heads and eyes rather than hearts. First on the list is a "typey" litter, followed by the pup that is most representative. Pretend Great Aunt Minnie has seen only a picture of this breed. Which one could she look at and say, "Ah ha, *this* is a Golden". Ideally, this pup will also possess the other physical requirements and have the spirit that makes him or her a special dog.

While examining bone, topline, shoulder and rear angulation, breadth and depth of chest, and length of body, a person should compare this to

At eight weeks old, this is **Julius** and **Zachary** working it out. Julius is owned by Don and Judy Jennings and Zachary is owned by James and Karen Taylor. Photo by Karen Taylor.

Ch. Toasty's Jordan and **Toasty's Grand Prix** at eight weeks of age.

BUYING A PIECE OF THE FUTURE

Some buyers place a deposit for a puppy sight-unseen, sometimes even before the litter is born or bred! When we find a breeder who is producing the style, type and temperament we want, it might be necessary to make a reservation long before our future dream pup sets paw on the ground. After all, if we admire what is trotting out of this kennel's gates, we should realize a few others might have recognized its quality as well. Breeders who consistently produce well often have long waiting lists.

Before selecting a kennel to honor with the purchase, other factors can be discussed with the seller in advance. Be aware of the guarantee offered, what the contract covers and whether this kennel has established a reputation for standing behind its dogs.

Certain minimal records should accompany every pup: a pedigree, a registration blank, medical records, feeding and grooming instructions, a sales contract and some type of guarantee.

Registration papers are a necessity for the serious fancier who wishes to show and breed. ILP (Individual Listing Privilege) may be shown in obedience as can Limited Registration dogs who may also participate in a few instinct tests. They may not, however, be exhibited in the conformation ring. The American Kennel Club requires ILP dogs (other than those in the Miscellaneous

give an indication that the pup's family demonstrates trainability and intelligence. Likewise, several championship titles are encouraging. Quality begets quality.

An eight-week-old pup should not have a lengthy medical record, but this paper should note a physical exam and at least one combination inoculation. If the litter has been wormed, this should also be noted.

A good age to pick a puppy is when the litter is from seven to ten weeks old. By this time, they have learned canine socialization skills from their dam and littermates. With plenty of TLC given by the breeder as a background, sound puppies easily transfer their affection to a new family.

Lines and breeds vary, but many knowledgeable breeders prefer to pick their show and field prospects between eight to twelve weeks of age. Follow the breeder's advice: nobody knows the lines better than he does.

Occasionally the subject of co-ownership arises. The results may vary: it certainly forges the members of a paper relationship into the best of friends or festers them into the worst of enemies. An offer of co-ownership does signify that the breeder has faith in the dog. After all, he wouldn't want to co-own a poor specimen.

Golden puppies are not a little photogenic, as Karen Taylor effortlessly proves with this beautiful portrait.

Classes) to be spayed or neutered, and the Limited Registration stamp, begun in 1990, prevents the limited dog's progeny from being registered. These steps were taken by the AKC to discourage indiscriminate breeding practices.

A pedigree should contain at least three generations, with four to six being preferable. Pedigrees tell us more than the names and titles of ancestors. The knowledgeable dog person can see whether a pup is linebred, outcrossed or inbred, and health certifications such as OFA and CERF numbers are often included. A pedigree strong in obedience and field titles should

A decision can be made depending upon the strings of the co-ownership and whether the two parties can work together. Simple co-ownership agreements may require one puppy back from a breeding or stud rights. More complicated contracts demand half a litter—or half of every litter, exhibition requirements, hiring an expensive professional handler, or more. If breeder and buyer are congenial and willing to bend when situations not covered in the contract arise, a co-ownership can be an opportunity to purchase a dog or bitch normally beyond our price range.

Suppertime for three over-achievers: *(Left to right):* **Am-Can. Ch. Timberee's Tenacious Token UDT, WCX, VCX, Can. CDX (HOF)**; **Am-Can. Ch. Beaumaris Timberee's Tessa Ann UDT, WC (OD, HOF)** and **Ch. Timberee's Right On Target CDX, WC** owned by Bob and Sandy Fisher of Grand Junction, Colorado.

Sandy Sue Sunshine, owned by Ron DiMarco, and **Sexton's Kona Gold**, owned by photographer Karen Taylor and Jim Taylor, pose with their litter.

PAPER WORK

Sales contracts should cover the information listed on the registration blank, along with various requirements.

Following is a sample show contract:

Sales Contract

WHEREAS _____ ,
hereinafter called "Seller(s)," is the owner of a _____ show/showable
_____ (breed) bitch/dog, further described as:

Registered Name of Dog _____
Call Name of Dog _____
Color/Variety _____
Date of Birth _____
Place of Birth _____
Litter-AKC/Foreign Reg. No. _____
Name/Reg. No. of Sire _____
Name/Reg. No. of Dam _____

WHEREAS _____ ,
hereinafter called "Buyer(s)," is desirous of purchasing the animal described above: NOW, THEREFORE, in consideration of the sum of _____
payable _____ , the Seller hereby conveys one _____
(quality & breed) bitch/dog_____
to Buyer(s) under the following warranties and conditions and no other warranties or conditions either expressed or implied.

1. That the above-described animal is a pure-bred dog registerable with _____ kennel club within 180 days following the date of purchase and that a registration application has been given to Buyer(s) as of the date of purchase.

2. That the above-described animal may for any reason be returned to Seller(s) within five days of the time of purchase, and Seller will refund to Buyer(s) the full amount of the purchase price. Buyer(s) shall assume full responsibility for the health, anatomical make-up, appearance and temperament of the above-described animal following said five-day period.

3. In the event severe or disqualifying faults as listed and defined in the attached breed standard, and/or crippling congenital faults are found to be present in the above-described animal, on or before one year of age, the Seller(s) agrees to replace said animal with one of equal quality. In the instance Seller(s) is no longer in the business of breeding dogs, 50% of the purchase price shall be refunded.

4. In the event the Buyer(s) feels he must dispose of or sell the above-described animal for any reason, Buyer(s) will notify Seller(s) for first option.

5. That this contract is null and void except for dog of above registered name.

6. Further,

7. This writing constitutes the full agreement of the parties.

WHEREFORE, the Seller(s) and Buyer(s) have executed the foregoing contract of sale at

_____ a.m./p.m. on this _____ day of

_____ .

Buyer's Signature _____

Address _____
_____

Phone _____

Seller's Signature _____

Address _____
_____

Phone _____

Aureo Oahu Show Me the Wings CD, WC ("Tara") at ten weeks. Owner, N. Bopp.

Guarantees usually cover a short period of time until the buyer can take the puppy to a veterinarian. If there is a problem at that time, a full refund should be given. Most reputable sellers also give a health guarantee covering various congenital defects which arise by the age of one year (one year, because most have appeared by that time; congenital, because the seller cannot be expected to cover injuries or illnesses). Should a congenital defect appear after this age (such as failure to OFA certify at two years of age), the seller should still be willing to discuss a replacement.

Sellers' show puppy contracts usually cover serious and disqualifying faults as stipulated in the breed standard. All contracts and guarantees should be read carefully by the buyer. If any clauses are objectionable or questionable, ask for an explanation before signing.

Although the pup won't come with an operator's manual that directs you to "Put tab A into slot A" or have a bag attached with extra nuts and bolts, instructions should be part of the package. This will cover suggested puppy food, feeding schedule, housebreaking suggestions, and grooming particulars. Written advice on crates, training classes, and recommended reading material may have more than one use. It helps fill the wee morning hours when the pup misses his warm, fuzzy siblings and wails his loss to the world.

The purchase is only the beginning of a long relationship between buyer and seller. There are questions to be answered, pleasant stories to be shared and fears to be calmed. Photos of the little guy opening his Christmas presents, bathtime, the teenage uglies, entering his first puppy match and finishing his championship are treasured keepsakes for the breeder.

Sounds complicated, but puppies have an advantage over most purchases with moving parts. They come ready to use, all wound up and ready for action—no batteries needed. Nor is it necessary to plug in the pup to make him wag his tail or wash your face. In case of power failure, we don't even miss the electric blanket.

BENEFITS OF OWNERSHIP

The benefits of owning a pet are many, among them pride, social, educational, acceptance, responsibility. We are often proud of owning a beautiful animal (remembering that beauty is in the eye of the beholder) whose coat shines with health and whose eyes sparkle with glee at our approach. We can make friends and establish relationships through our dog. Kids and adults both learn responsibility through caring for the pet. We educate ourselves to provide physical care and, if we so desire, the intricacies of the dog world—as far as we want to go. Our dog doesn't care at what stage we stop learning. Acceptance comes because our dog always greets us with affection, no matter what our age, race, creed, size or abilities.

But probably the most important benefit is psychological. No matter what happens in our day-to-day life, there is always someone who cares, someone who asks little in return. Our dog provides us with a reason to rise in the morning, a reason to exercise, a reason to prepare food and, in some cases, a reason to live. We're never alone when we're in the company of a good friend.

One of the author's kids, this is **Chances R This Bud's For Me**, belonging to Clary and Lois Busse. Photo by the author.

Above left: Pretty tame for a **"Cougar."** *Above right:* Glenhaven Goldens awaiting St. Nicholas's visit. *Below left:* **Dusty** denying the accusations of queerly smirking orange vegetable. *Below right:* Ready for Wall Street, it's **Pinehurst Multimillion Air.**

Top: **Sharmels Jo-El Indian Summer CD, WC, TT** snacking out with two favorite pals. *Bottom:* Sweet dreams for **Timberee Tonga.**

Amberacs Persimmon Pudding—puppy—owner Kristen Kothe. Pepper was participating in the "costume class" dressed as Raggedy Ann in the semi-annual "Old Oaken Bucket" competition between the White River Golden Retriever Club and the Evansville Golden Retriever Club. A good time was had by all! Photo by Susan Rezy.

Right: **FC-AFC Right-On Dynamite John**, amateur trained by owner Elaine Klicker of Billings, Montana, is a tribute to all "non-pros" in the fancy who want to win big. *Below:* **Windy's Meadowpond Brydee CDX, WC** owned by Diane Schoenbach, photographed by Karen Taylor.

Versatile and strong, **Windy's Meadowpond Brydee CDX, WC** not only is a healthy working dog but is trained for drug and weapons detection, employed by several police departments. Owner, Diane Schoenbach. Photograph by Karen Taylor.

Prevention and Cure = A Healthy Life

BY CHRIS WALKOWICZ

Every owner hopes that his dog will live a long healthy life. Nowadays, this desire is enhanced through careful selection of puppies and breeding animals, modern technology and veterinary care and the family's care and concern—all of which aid in prevention and cure.

Dogs today are so much more fortunate than their ancestors. Regulations which were originally passed to protect property, livestock and humans actually ensure a dog's safety as well. Licenses and the accompanying taxes provide shelters for lost or abandoned animals, and a tag may prove to be a lifeline to home. Because leashes and confinement are now required by law, fewer families allow Rover to rove, and have his life ended by a bullet or highway traffic.

Many diseases commonly fatal in the early to mid-1900s are now prevented through inoculation. An old-time exhibitor understood that if he took his dog to enough shows, the animal would contract distemper sooner or later. It was common to lose entire litters to the dread disease, which plagued canines for hundreds of years. Now, thanks to nearly universal vaccination, most breeders have never even seen a case.

As recently as 1978, parvovirus swept the canine world, decimating kennels. As with all diseases, it was the very young and the very elderly dogs that succumbed in great numbers. Thanks to modern research laboratories and pharmaceutical companies, this time within two years a preventative vaccine was available.

GENERAL MEDICAL CARE

Before a puppy is sold, he should have received at least one full set of inoculations, protecting him from distemper, hepatitis (adenovirus), leptospirosis, parainfluenza and parvo. Many breeders vaccinate against corona virus and bordatella as well. Among the puppy's stack of official papers that are turned over to the expectant parents should be a list noting the ages when

The irresistible **Elysian Image of Oakshadows (TD)** is the spitting image of good health. Photo by breeder Jeannette S. von Barby of Evergreen, Colorado.

additional shots will be needed. Although the schedule varies from breeder to breeder, or one veterinarian to another, all agree distemper combination (DA2PP) and parvo vaccinations should be continued every three weeks until about 16 weeks. Some veterinarians may elect to give the parvo vaccine with the combination, or separately, a week apart. Rabies can be given at about 16 weeks with the last parvo-combination shot.

Before the puppy goes to his new home, he should be examined by a veterinarian and pronounced healthy and free of major congenital defects. Most bite, eyelid, testicular, cardial and esophagael problems can be detected before eight weeks, as can luxated patellas and open fontanels. From that point on, it's up to the new owners to continue examinations and veterinary care to keep him healthy. Routine health care, of course, includes yearly vaccinations and heart-worm checks, followed by administration of the preventative.

GROOMING

Even shorthaired dogs need grooming and a dog as long-coated as the Golden Retriever needs much time and attention. Twice weekly brushing, combing, occasional bathing, nail trimming, as well as teeth and ear cleaning help keep him in good condition. In addition, these sessions are ideal times to check him for any lumps, sores, rashes, parasites or other external signs of a health threat.

Brushing and combing the hair eliminate painful mats, as well as stimulating the natural oils and hair growth. Regular grooming also minimizes the amount of hair wafting and floating through the house.

Animals don't perspire the way people do, and unless they make contact with dirt or smelly substances, they don't require frequent bathing. Most exhibitors spruce up a dog before a show and this often includes a bath. Pet owners who keep their dogs clean may only have to face that chore a couple of times a year, usually during the hair-shedding season.

Nails must be kept short for comfort. The inner quick, containing the nerves and blood vessels, grows with the nails and makes them more difficult to trim the longer they become. Long nails are unattractive (forbidden in a show dog) and can actually curl around to cut into the foot. Besides, nails' clicking on floors is annoying!

Clean your dog's ears every week or two by using a quality product obtained through a veterinarian or pet-supply store. Or you can use baby oil and gauze. Owners of longhaired dogs often pluck the hair from the inner ear to help keep it clean and free of impacted wax. Medicated powder or ointment is recommended after pulling the hair.

A dog who shakes his head or rubs his ear may already have earmites or an infection, which must be treated only by a prescribed otic medication. A red, inflamed or odorous ear also indicates a problem which should be treated by a vet.

Feeding and nutrition are essential to the proper development of the growing puppy. This six-and-a-half-week-old litter by Ch. Adagio's Shoot-Em-Up Cowbot ex Ch. Ashford's Shine-On-Sharron is owned by Peter H. Welch and Colette Agresti.

Beauty begets beauty: **Classics Golden Caeser** and his son **Julius**. Owners, Don and Judy Jennings. Photo by Karen Taylor.

DENTAL CARE

Dogs can't be fitted with dentures ... yet ... so it's up to us to assure that their teeth last them as long as possible. Dry foods or a mixture of canned and dry help the teeth and gums remain healthy. Feeding only moist or canned dog food can allow food to stick around the gumline, causing gums to become inflamed or teeth to decay. Even with a diet of dry food, tartar (plaque) can accumulate.

Cleaning our dog's teeth with a veterinary dentifrice, or a mixture of baking soda and water, is suggested and should be done at least once a week. The act of rubbing with a toothbrush and/or cleaning plaque with a dental tool is more important than the product used.

In this area, as well as others, never substitute your own products for those specifically made for animals without asking a veterinarian. Human toothpaste or shampoos, for example, can actually be detrimental to his care.

PARASITES

Taking stool samples to the vet should be part of the annual examination or when observing symptoms such as diarrhea, bloody stools or worm segments. Dogs, especially puppies, may vomit and lose weight when infested with parasites. Hookworms, roundworms, tapeworms, whipworms, coccidia and giardia are common. They can be eradicated with the proper medication but could be dangerous if left untreated. An over-the-counter drug may not be the right one for the particular parasite which your dog is harboring.

With her basket of springtime sunshine, **Am-Can. Ch. Clark's Easter Bonnet UD, WCX, Can. CDX, WC** coddles her litter.

FLEAS

Bugs bug us and our pets. Fleas cause itching and carry tapeworm eggs. The resultant scratching can irritate the skin so that rashes and hot spots develop. Dogs lose hair, scratch and chew at themselves and are miserable. In attempting to exterminate the pests, owners tear their hair, scratch their heads, chew their nails and are also miserable. Better to prevent than to cure, but for everyone's sanity, once the invasion has occurred, the sooner the evacuation, the better.

Talk to your veterinarian about the proper products to use, then arrange a regular reconnaissance to prevent a losing battle with fleas. During the warm months of the year, many people spray or powder animals (including other pets who may pass fleas to your dogs) once a week and premises (house and lawn) once a month. In between, owners keep up flea surveillance. At the slightest scratch, they look for telltale evidence—skittering teeny bugs or flea dirt, which looks like a sprinkling of pepper. It's usually easiest to see the freeloaders on the less hairy groin, belly or just above the root of the tail.

Among the products used to combat flea pests are dips, collars, powders, sprays, tags and internals—drops or pills. Instructions should be followed implicitly as some of these products contain ingredients which may cause problems themselves if used carelessly or combined with each other.

If the critters are found, shampoo or dip all dogs (cats, too, with a product labeled safe for them), and spray living and sleeping quarters. It doesn't do any good to treat the animal without debugging the environment or vice-versa. One flea who escapes will happily reinfest all over again. If the infestation is heavy, it may be necessary to fog your house and to repeat the procedure a few weeks later. All animals must be removed from the premises for the period of time specified on the fogger can.

In addition to the regular regime, many owners spray their dogs before walking them in areas where they are likely to pick them up, e.g., woods, pastures, training and show grounds. Most flea pesticides also kill ticks, and daily grooming sessions should include running your fingers through the dog's coat to find engorged ticks. Natural, non-insecticidal products can safely be used on a daily basis in the on-going war on fleas.

Debbie Platt and retired obedience star **Arthur**.

LYME DISEASE

One species of tick, *Ixodes dammini,* the tiny deer tick, is the culprit which transmits the germ that causes Lyme disease in humans and animals. Deer ticks are found on mammals and birds, as well as in grasses, trees and shrubs. They are rarely visible because they are so small (as minute as the dot above an i), but the damage they can cause is magnified many times their size.

Lyme disease can damage the joints, kidneys, heart, brain and immune system in canines and humans. Symptoms can include a rash, fever, lameness, fatigue, nausea, aching body and personality change among others. Left untreated, the disease can lead to arthritis, deafness, blindness, miscarriages and birth defects, heart disease and paralysis. It may prove to be fatal.

People should cover themselves with protective clothing while outdoors to prevent bites. Repellents are helpful for both dogs and humans. Examine the body after excursions and see a doctor if symptoms appear.

Every good hunter understands the art of camouflage: at eight weeks of age, **Teddy Carr** blends in well with his picturesque setting. Owners, Felita and Brian Carr of Wellesley, Massachusetts. Teddy is by Ch. Twin Beau D Hi Speed Chase ex B. Bop'n Amber Royale Jubilee.

SKIN DISORDERS

Dogs, just like people, can suffer from allergies. While people most often have respiratory symptoms, dogs usually exhibit their allergies through itching, scratching, chewing or licking their irritated skin. These irritations often lead to angry, weeping "hot" spots.

Allergies are easy to detect but difficult to treat. Medications and topical substances can be useful, in addition to avoidance of the irritant, if possible.

CERF/OFA/VWD CERTIFICATION

Good breeders want to produce healthy, sound animals. The best way to do this is to start with healthy, normal animals judged to be free of hereditary conditions which can cause lameness, blindness and other disorders.

In the early years of dog shows, when symptoms of disease appeared, owners asked the opinion of experienced local breeders and veterinarians. As time went on, more specifics were learned about these various diseases and their heritability. Veterinarians took x-rays, performed

299

Barbara Branstad of Fort Collins, Colorado, with **Sunclad Streaker's Jupiter UD, *****.

OFA, 2300 Nifong Blvd., Columbia, MO 65201.

Eye problems can be detected by veterinary opthalmologists available at teaching hospitals, private specialty practices (in larger cities) and at eye-screening clinics hosted by kennel clubs. These specialists examine for cataracts, entropion, pannus, retinal dysplasia, luxated lens, progressive retinal atrophy (PRA), central progressive retinal atrophy, and other hereditary eye conditions. The Canine Eye Registration Foundation (CERF) may be contacted at CERF Veterinary Medicine Data Program, South Campus Courts, Bldg. C., Purdue University, West Lafayette, IN 47907. The age of the dog at first testing depends a great deal on the breed and the specific area of concern. A few diseases are apparent in puppyhood. Golden puppies can be examined for some problems as early as seven to eight weeks of age, although CERF will not certify eyes until one year of age. CERF requires annual examination for certification of freedom from some diseases.

Before you breed, determine whether or not your dog is free of these and other hereditary diseases. Although the tests involve some cost, they are not as expensive as attempting to replace faulty pups. And they are certainly much less costly than a broken heart or a damaged reputation.

blood tests and diagnosed symptoms. Now we are fortunate to have experts in various areas. Due to their specialized training and the numbers of cases these experts see, they are more likely to be accurate. Some have formed organizations which register clear animals and certify dogs free of hereditary disease.

Probably the first organization of its type, the Orthopedic Foundation for Animals (OFA) certifies dogs free of hip dysplasia upon clearance of an x-ray by three board-certified radiologists. Dogs must be two years old for lifetime certification. The OFA also reads and gives opinions of radiographs with evidence of other heritable bone disorders such as craniomandibular osteopathy (CMO), osteochondritis dessicans (OCD), ununited anchoneal process, and fragmented chronoid process. The organization's address is

BONE DISEASE

Many canine bone diseases have gained nicknames—albeit not affectionate—due to the unwieldy medical terminology. For instance, canine cervical vertebral malformation/malarticulation syndrome is referred to as "wobbler" syndrome; panosteitis is shortened to pano; and canine hip dysplasia is often simply called CHD or HD. The first symptom is usually a limp. Diagnosis is made through a radiograph of the affected area.

Craniomandibular osteopathy (CMO) affects the growth of bone in the lower jaw, causing severe pain. Spondylosis is the technical name for spinal arthritis.

Hip dysplasia is a poor fit of the hip joint into the socket, which causes erosion. Wobbler syndrome affects the neck vertebrae, causing weakness in the hindquarters and eventually the forequarters. Osteochondrosis dissecans (OCD) affects joints, most often the shoulder, elbow or stifle. Ununited anchoneal process, commonly referred to as elbow dysplasia, is a failure of the growth line to close, thereby creating a loose piece in the joint. Kneecaps which pop out of the proper position are diagnosed as luxating patellas. They all result in the same thing: pain, lameness and, left untreated, arthritis.

The exception is pano, which is a temporary affliction causing discomfort during youth. Pano may be visible on x-rays, showing up as a cloudi-

ness in the bone marrow in the long bones, particularly in fast-growing breeds.

ORGANIC DISEASE

Heart disease affects canines much as it does humans. A dog suffering from a problem involving the heart may exhibit weakness, fainting, difficult breathing, a persistent cough, loss of appetite, abdominal swelling due to fluid retention, exhaustion following normal exercise, or even heart failure and sudden death. Upon examination, an abnormal heart rhythm or sound

Legend's Rufus and **Brandywine's Golden Amaretto** owned by Vicki Rathbun, Saratoga, California. Rufus was Vicki's first Golden, an abused and abandoned three-year-old, who introduced her to the gentle world of Golden Retrievers. Rufus was extremely patient with all children and other animals, and was Vicki's constant shadow, fearful she would disappear and leave him alone again.

or electrical potential might be detected, or changes in speed or strength noticed.

Some heart murmurs may be due to SAS (Subvalvular aortic stenosis), a heart defect sometimes found in Golden Retrievers. Examination and follow-up by a board-certified cardiologist is recommended.

Chronic renal disease may first show up in vague symptoms—lethargy, diarrhea, anemia, weight loss and lack of appetite—as well as increased thirst and urination. Kidney disease is more common among geriatric canines. It may be compensated to some extent through diet. Diagnosis is most often made through blood and urine tests.

rapidly fatal. Torsion—medically termed gastric dilatation and volvulus (GDV)—is an emergency. Experienced owners, particularly of large breeds, know there is no time to waste whether it's the middle of the night, a holiday or vacation time. It is urgent to reach a veterinarian who can treat the shock, followed by surgery to reposition the twisted organs. During surgery, the veterinarian may tack the stomach to the abdominal wall to prevent recurrence.

AUTO-IMMUNE DISEASES

Auto-immune disease, like cancer, is an umbrella term that includes many diseases of similar origin but showing different symptoms. Liter-

The family Smithhaven on a trip to Canada.

GASTRIC TORSION

Because a dog's stomach hangs like a hammock, the ends are effectively shut off if it flips over. Nothing can enter or exit. The normal bacterial activity in the stomach causes gas to build with no release through vomiting or defecating. The gas expands and, just like a balloon filled with helium, the stomach bulges and bloats.

It's physical torture for the dog and mental anguish for the owner who sees his dog moaning in agony and retching in a futile attempt to relieve the pressure.

With the veins and arteries to the stomach and spleen also closed off, shock sets in which can be

ally, the body's immune system views one of its own organs or tissues as foreign and launches an attack on it. Symptoms depend on which system is the target.

For instance, hypothyroidism symptoms can include lethargy, musty odor, temperament change, decreased fertility or unexplained weight gain, in addition to the more suggestive thin dry hair, scaliness of the skin, and thickness and darkening of the skin. Testing for hypothyroidism (which can be from causes other than auto-immune disease) may be conducted as early as eight to twelve months, using the complete blood count, blood chemistry, thyroid T4, T3 and free T4 tests.

Ch. Pinehurst Traveling Goldust CDX, WC, VCX owned by Janet Schaadt of Quincy, Illinois.

(Addison's disease.)

The same reaction in the thyroid gland soon has the dog exhibiting symptoms of hypothyroidism. Auto-immune diseases of the skin are called pemphigus, while those of connective tissue are termed lupus. Many other varieties exist, and each requires specialized testing and biopsy. Most respond to treatment once a diagnosis is made.

ALTERNATIVE TECHNIQUES

During the 1970s and '80s, acupuncture, chiropractic and holistic medicine became part of the canine health picture. Veterinarians who have received special training in these fields now practice their techniques on patients who do not respond to or cannot take previously prescribed medical treatments. Patients have responded favorably to these methods, especially when done in conjunction with medical supervision. Certainly, when it comes to a much-loved animal, the most recent up-to-date techniques should be tried before resorting to euthanasia.

Owners should be aware, however, that practitioners must have a veterinary degree to practice on animals and that the holistic, chiropractic and acupunctural treatment should not take the place of standard veterinary medicine, but enhance it.

Rheumatoid arthritis is a result of an auto-immune reaction to the joint surfaces. The resulting inflammation and swelling causes painful deformed joints. If the red blood cells are perceived as foreign invaders and destroyed, the rapid onset anemia (called auto-immune hemolytic anemia) can cause collapse and death if diagnosis and treatment are not quickly initiated. Often an auto-immune reaction in an organ causes destruction of that organ with subsequent loss of function. Auto-immune disease of the adrenal gland leads to hypoadrenocortissism

Ch. Asterling Austin Healey at eight years enjoying the good life.

loss, increased water consumption and a dry thin coat are warning signs to seek medical attention. Many aging patients can be made comfortable and sustain a quality life.

Although our dogs will never live long enough to satisfy us, we can extend their lives through our precautions, specialized nutrition, exercise and routine veterinary care.

EMERGENCIES

The get-your-vet-on-the-phone-drive-there-as-quickly-as-is-safe emergency situations are few, thankfully. But they do occur, and that's why all owners should be aware of symptoms. Veterinarian numbers for day and night calls should be posted prominently near the phone.

Occasions that are well worth a middle-of-the-night payment are: shock, anoxia (choking), dystocia (labor and whelping complications), hemorrhage, gastric torsion, electric shock, large wounds, compound fractures and heat stroke. In addition, neurological symptoms such as paralysis, convulsions and unconsciousness indicate an emergency. If your dog has ingested poison, been severely burned or hit by a car, for instance, call an emergency number for help.

EUTHANASIA

Most owners dread facing the decision of euthanizing a pet. But as hard as it is to make that decision and drive a beloved animal on his final journey, it is more difficult to watch a dog who has lost all quality of life struggle through a day-to-day fog of pain. Of course, it's also more stressful for the animal, and don't we love him enough to spare him that trauma? Certainly, eyes that plead "Help me" deserve a humane response.

Euthanasia is a fact that most breeders and pet owners must eventually face if they do not wish their animals to suffer. Ask your veterinarian to administer a non-lethal anesthetic or tranquilizer, literally putting the dog to sleep while you hold your pet and caress him gently. The dog will drift off to sleep peacefully and without fear, no longer suffering. At that point, the veterinarian injects a lethal overdose of

Chance R Milady, "Mollie," (OTCh. Topbrass Rocky Mountain High ex Bonnie Brooks Golden Nugget). Chances R foundation bitch … exceptional producer … exceptional friend. Owned and missed by the author and husband Phillip Bauer. Photo by the author.

GERIATRICS

As dogs age, problems are more likely to occur, just as they do in their human counterparts. It is even more important to examine your dogs, noting every "normal" lump and sag, so that if a new one occurs you are aware. Owners should make appointments for veterinary check-ups at least once a year.

Elderly canines suffer the same infirmities as we do when we age. Deafness, arthritis, cancers, organ disease and loss of vision are common. Symptoms such as a cough, bloating, weight anesthesia which instantly stops the heart. Death truly comes as a servant in peace; euthanasia is a kind, quiet death.

Arrangements should be made for the disposition of the body prior to the euthanasia. Some owners wish to bury the remains themselves (be aware of local regulations, however, which are becoming more stringent) or to have the dog cremated. Others want the veterinarian to handle the arrangements. Planning ahead saves more difficult decisions during the trauma of losing your friend.

VETERINARY SPECIALISTS

With a surplus of small animal veterinarians expected in the latter part of the 20th century, and a surging volume of knowledge and medical technology, many veterinary school graduates elect to specialize with additional courses and training. These include surgery, dentistry, oncology, radiology, neurology, cardiology, dermatology, ophthalmology, theriogenology (reproduction) and internal medicine.

This "overpopulation," naturally, is a boon to pet lovers. If your dog has one of these problems, your veterinarian may refer you to a board-certified specialist or contact one for advice on specialized treatment. Any concerned, caring veterinarian will be happy to do so and assist his patient to live a healthier, fuller life.

Everyone who owns dogs for very long begins to build a canine medical chest. Basic supplies should include cotton, gauze, tweezer, ipecac, muzzle, styptic powder, cotton swabs, rectal thermometer, petroleum jelly, hydrogen peroxide, ear medication, anti-diarrhea preparation, ibuprofen pain killer and one-inch adhesive tape. Include first aid instructions and a poison help sheet with a hotline number.

ETHICS

In all diseases, symptoms may vary from mild to severe. In the most extreme cases, victims may have to be euthanized. Many do live, however,

Goldwing Gala Lalique, owned and loved by Suzanne Russ, in Yosemite National Park, after camping out in the high country.

under veterinary care and supervision, occasional medication and owner TLC. Nevertheless, it's important to know which diseases are known to be inherited. Our dogs can carry the factors which transmit hereditary conditions and pass on their afflictions to a higher than normal percentage of their progeny. Affected dogs should be spayed or neutered and never allowed to transmit their discomfort to future generations. Owners should also be aware that AKC and KC regulations specify that surgically corrected dogs may not compete in the breed ring.

Above: Here's **HR CH Ronakers Wildwood Flower MH** ready for home after a hunting test. The folks at Quartermoon Goldens tell us that newcomers to the tests are ever so impressed by Wildwood when she instantly responds to the command "Go back to the truck" than they are to any other command execution of the day. Photo by Bobbie Christensen.
Bottom: **Am-Can. Ch. Beaumaris Timberee Tessa Ann UDT, WC, Can. CD (OD, HOF)** fairly galloping through the water like the professional she is. Owners, Sandy and Bob Fisher.

Above: An all-star lineup from DD's Dog Training. **Am-Can.OTCh. Splashdown Tess of Culynwood WCX; OTCh. DD's Nuggett of Gold TD, WCX; OTCh. Tagalong Thumper TD, JH, WC, Can. CDX; OTCh. DD's Calaveras Sparklin' Gold WC; DD's Tagalong Miles to Go CDX; OTCh. DD's Culynwood Cotton Lace; OTCh. DD's Cher** and **DD's Marathon UD.** *Below:* **FC-AFC Mioak's Main Event…**"Rocky" bringing one in.

Mioak's Smoke 'n Zeke *** (FC-AFC Topbrass Windbreaker Zap ex Mioak's Golden Torch) bred by Mickey Strandberg, owned by Bill and Mary Glenn, Jackson, Wyoming. Zeke stacked up 28 Derby points, and had two Qualifying wins and an Amateur first by age two and one-half.

The lovely **Kona** pauses picturesquely for photographer Karen Taylor. Owner, James Taylor of Taylor, Michigan.

HR CH Ronakers Wildwood Flower MH— Wildwood is the foundation of the Quartermoon Goldens. She is a GRCA Hall of Fame OD having produced three MH (2 of those with **) and another ** dog who died before the advent of hunting tests. Photo by Bobbie Christensen.

AFC Sungold T-Bill Sunsplasher MH, "Splash" is photographed by Bobbie Christensen at 12 years of age. A hunter all his life, it didn't require training for Splash to win his MH title, instead it took relaxation therapy. After learning to relax and enjoy, this exceptional over-trained Golden breezed through his tests. A duck pro for years, Splash has learned pheasant, quail and grouse.

Above left: **Malcairn's Firebrand Molly CD**, goes by Molly, is owned by Sally Jenkins of Santa Rosa, California.
Below left: **HR CH Holway Vodka***** is an English import who goes appropriately by "Brit" (Osmington Victor ex NFC Little Marston Chorus of Holway) bred by June Atkinson, owned by Mercedes Hitchcock.
Above right: **Sunclad Streaker's Jupiter UD, ***** owned by Barbara Branstad.
Below right: **Ch. Parkerhouse Rise and Shine CDX, WC** and **Farm Fresh Apple Cider CD, TD, WC** owned by Leslie Dickerson, photographed by Bill Keyte.

OTCh. Benno Duckdown Duckbuster (HOF) (Mayfair Adam CD ex Holly Dee II) (1980-1989), bred by Tom and Carole Carter, owned and trained by Gary and Louanne Williamson, San Bernadino, California. Benno was a leftover puppy, always in trouble, ate everything in sight. He took instantly to obedience training, and gave Louanne 100 percent effort and attention at all times. Shown on a limited basis, Benno captured a second and a third in Gaines competition at his only times shown there, and claimed *Dog World* awards, many HITs, and Southern California Top Dog awards with frequent scores of 199 and 199.5. But more than winning, he made Louanne laugh. Unlike most other Goldens who love everyone, Benno belonged to her and her alone.

Above left: **Quantock's Sacajawea CD, TD,** owned by Eileen Bohn of Cattail Goldens.
Above right: **Chances R Mollie's Geronimo CD,** bred by the author and owned by the author and husband Phillip Bauer.
Below left: **FC-AFC Sangamo Red (HOF)** (AFC Son of Red ex Ben's Enchanted Micalaub).
Below right: **Windfall's Quantock Joshua CD, Can. CDX** owned by Eileen Bohn.

Above left: At ten years of age, this is "Curry"—officially **Am-Can. Ch. High Farms Jantze of Curaçao CDX, TC, WC, Can. CD, Can. TDX (OS).** Bred by Ruth Worrest Soule; owned by Barbara Tinker; photographed by Paul Korker.
Below left: Howdy "Pardner": this is **FC-AFC Tangelo's Sidekick (OS-HOF)**, owned by Bill and Terry Woods. Bred by Ted and Pat Gross.
Above right: Beware the "Bandit"…this is **Can. OTCh. Brownards Benjamin Brittan UD, JH, WCX, TT, Mex. PCE, TT, GRCC OBHF**. Winner of 16 HITs, Bandit has robbed the heart of Brenda Radcliffe of Orangevale, California.
Below right: **Ch. Smithaven's Magic O'Merlin CDX** and **Ch. Smithaven's Jazz Jeneration** owned by Debi Hanson and June Smith. The bitches are half-sisters and live in Alamo, California.

That the Golden Retriever be a structurally sound animal is the concern of all owners, whatever their pursuits. *Above:* **DD's Especial Triever** moves with power and grace into the water. Triever is by AFC, WR Glenhaven's Devil's Advocate UDT, MH, WCX, *** ex OTCh. DD's Calaveras Sparklin' Gold WC, bred by O. D. Anderson and Janet Naylor, owned by Glenda Brown. *Below:* **OTCh. Sunfire Spontaneous Combustion JH, WCX,** aptly nicknamed "Flash," demonstrates the importance of sound construction for the obedience dog. Flash is owned by Karen Price.

Genetic Diseases

According to Dr. George Padgett, Professor of Pathology, College of Veterinary Medicine, Michigan State University, every breed of dog carries an average of 14 genetic defects, with several breeds having up to 30 or 40. These statistics are the fodder of nightmares for the serious dog breeder or prospective puppy buyer.

There are no accurate estimates on the number of defective genes in the Golden Retriever, but the most obvious genetic problems prevalent in the breed today are reason enough for serious concern among the responsible breeders and fanciers who hope to preserve a healthy future for the Golden.

This chapter will address only genetic diseases, the ones confirmed and common in the breed today. It will not even attempt to discuss genetic "faults" or "defects," seen all too often in the general Golden population, e.g., undershot/overshot, oversize, aggression, etc. Those are matters best left to experts on the subject, and detailed studies can be found in several excellent books on dog genetics, some of which are listed at the conclusion of this book.

CANINE HIP DYSPLASIA (CHD)

Simply stated, CHD means bad development of the hip joint. The current accepted veterinary concept holds that it is a complex inherited polygenic disease, meaning that many genes affect the character or clinical expression of dysplasia.

CHD affects most breeds, but it is more common in larger breeds of dogs such as the St. Bernard, Newfoundland, Bernese Mountain Dog and most of the retriever breeds. Studies have shown that CHD's heritability factor in all breeds ranges from 25 percent to 85 percent, which indicates a significant genetic contribution. Environmental factors such as calorie intake, physical stress and excessively rapid growth can also influence the manifestation of dysplasia in a dog that is genetically predisposed, but will not alter the genetic structure of the dog.

The hip joint of a newborn pup is reportedly normal at birth, but in affected dogs, changes occur in varying degrees some time after two weeks of age. Extreme cases can be detected as early as seven weeks, while others may not become apparent for two or more years. The only accepted diagnostic tool is radiographic evaluation; CHD cannot be diagnosed by observing how the dog runs, jumps, lies down, etc. The most

widely accepted screening agency is the Orthopedic Foundation for Animals (OFA).

OFA is a not-for-profit foundation established in 1966 through the dedicated efforts of the Golden Retriever Club of America (GRCA), with help from the German Shepherd Dog Club of America. It operates as a voluntary diagnostic service and registry of the hip status for dogs of every breed.

Producing clinically clear, healthy puppies epitomizes the goal of all Golden breeders. These Hartzheim puppies sparkle with promising futures.

Located in Columbia, Missouri, OFA accepts and evaluates hip x-rays obtained and submitted by the attending veterinarian. Dogs under two years of age receive a preliminary evaluation, and dogs two years of age or older with clear hips are assigned a permanent OFA registry number.

Each x-ray of dogs 24 months or older is reviewed by three independent Board-certified veterinary radiologists, and their consensus determines the hip category and eligibility for an OFA breed number. The first three listed here are eligible for assignment of an OFA breed number. (1.) Excellent hip joint conformation: Superior, as compared with other individuals of the same breed and age. (2.) Good hip joint conformation: Well-formed as compared to other individuals of the same breed and age. (3.) Fair: Minor irregularities, as compared to other individuals of the same breed and age.

The following categories are not eligible for an OFA breed number. (4.) Borderline: Marginal hip joint conformation of indeterminate status . . . at this time. A repeat review is recommended in six to eight months. (5.) Mild: Radiographic evidence of minor dysplastic changes of the hip joint. (6.) Moderate: Well-defined radiographic evidence of dysplastic changes. (7.) Severe: Radiographic evidence of marked dysplastic changes of the hip joints.

The OFA publication, *Hip Dysplasia: A Guide For Dog Breeders and Owners* (second edition 1989) prepared by E.A. Corley, DVM, PhD, Dipl. ACVR, and G.G. Keller, DVM, explains and details the current theories on CHD, its cause and

effect, statistics for each breed and guidelines for combating the disease. An important booklet for every dog owner, copies can be obtained by making a donation to the Orthopedic Foundation for Animals, 2300 Nifong Blvd., Columbia, MO, 65201, (314-442-0418).

OFA and the GRCA strongly recommend that a dysplastic dog should not be used for breeding. And it goes without saying that anyone buying a Golden puppy should insist on an OFA clearance on both sire and dam. A "vet-cleared x-ray" is not acceptable, nor is the fact that either or both parents "can clear our six-foot fence without missing a step."

The GRCA maintains a list of over 26,000 Goldens that have received hip clearances from OFA. Over 35,000 Golden hips have been evaluated from January 1974 through March 1989, and over 23 percent have been declared dysplastic. Because x-rays submitted to OFA are generally first screened by the attending veterinarian and the obvious cases of CHD are not submitted, we cannot know the actual frequency of CHD in

Richland Kyrie Liberty Belle Am-Can. UD, WCX, Can. WC (OD) (Can. Ch. Kyrie Gesundheidt CDX, TD, WC, Can. CDX, TD ex Duckflight Tawny Owl CD), (July 1976–October 1990) "Bruiser's" mother, also owned by Neida Heusinkvelt Bopp. Throughout her lifetime, "Libbe" was a consistent obedience worker and Gaines placer, with two *Dog World* awards. Libbe even scored 199 and 198 in Veteran Obedience classes during her senior double-digit years. An exceptional producer, she achieved Outstanding Dam status from only two litters, with eight titled get to her credit; two OTCh., several UDs, four multiple-HIT achievers, and seven with titles in two or more areas of accomplishment. Most important of all, Libbe was a dedicated jogging partner and constant companion...still missed beyond words.

the overall Golden population.

A dysplastic dog may easily lead a happy and productive life, but exercise and weight control are critical factors in deterring and managing the arthritis often associated with a senior dysplastic dog. Several surgical procedures developed over the years, such as hip joint replacement, BOP Shelf Arthroplasty (remodeling of the hip socket, a still controversial procedure), and other specialized procedures, have proven successful in relieving the pain often associated with severe CHD, while allowing the affected dog to lead a normal active life. It is important to remember that surgery may eliminate the symptoms, but cannot cure the disease or remove the genetic presence.

The veterinary community agrees that the only current means of controlling and reducing the incidence of hip dysplasia is selective breeding. Dysplastic dogs should not be used for breeding, and the offspring of normal dogs who have dysplastic parents should be tracked and monitored for hip development. Until better controls are available, the fate of the Golden Retriever's hips rests with the conscience of the breeder.

ELBOW DYSPLASIA AND OSTEOCHONDROSIS

On January 1, 1990 OFA announced the formation of an Elbow Registry to provide a standardized evaluation of elbow joints for canine elbow dysplasia (ED), whether due to an ununited anconeal process (UAP), fragmented cornoid process (FCP) osteochondrosis (OCD) or any combi-

Ch. Elysian's Lil Leica Reprint UDT, JH, WCX, VCX (HOF), "Kacia's" daughter by Ch. Wingwatcher Reddi to Rally CD, WC. Leica earned her TD by seven months, and sped on to finish her championship from the puppy and bred-by classes. The same day she finished her championship, she completed her CD with a Dog World award and tied for HIT! She won BOB at two specialties while working toward her CDX and JH titles. Ten months later, in one owner-breeder dream weekend, she took Group I, Group II and a Best in Show, entering her in the Show Dog Hall of Fame. Leica is the first Best in Show Golden bitch to also hold these working titles.

Lake Tahoe's Princess, bred by the author, in 1982 with her litter by Ch., OTCh. Meadowpond Dust Commander. Two of these pups became OTCh. and one a UD, earning Tahoe Outstanding Dam status. One pup, **OTCh. Duster's Amber Starburst**, grew up to become the dam of Bernie Brown's record-breaking OTCh. Tanbark's Bristol Creme.

nation thereof, and to serve as a data base for control of elbow dysplasia through selective breeding.

ED is defined as a developmental disease of the elbow and is a major cause of front-end lameness in many large breeds of dogs, including Golden Retrievers. Occurring before the bones are completely ossified, clinical signs appear between four and seven months of age when most pups experience a rapid growth spurt. Symptoms can vary from apparent and recurring lameness to a "throwing out" of the elbow or forward rotation of the paw when gaiting. The classic case is the young dog that develops a sudden limp which can be intermittent and vary from severe to slight.

ED can be diagnosed only through radiographic examination. Some cases can be relieved by imposing complete crate rest and confinement. Many others can be surgically corrected with excellent results. Current research indicates that males are twice as likely as females to be affected.

OFA accepts that ED is an inherited disease, probably due to multiple genes, with the exact mode of inheritance not yet established. Most veterinary orthopedists also suggest that, as in HD, environmental factors such as excessive calorie intake, trauma and physical stress and rapid growth may also influence the manifestation of ED in those dogs who are genetically predisposed. Studies at veterinary universities in Sweden, Norway and Australia, and by the Guide Dogs for the Blind Association in Australia support a degree of heritability for ED, and question whether affected dogs should be considered for breeding.

Rainbow protecting himself from the dangers of ultraviolet. Owners, Gerry and Karen Badesso.

EYE DISEASE

A number of inherited eye disorders affect today's Golden Retriever. Briefly, the most common are covered below.

Cataracts are a leading cause of blindness in dogs. Defined as a partial or total opacity of the crystalline lens of the eye, they can be hereditary or non-hereditary. Unlike the case in humans, "old age" cataracts constitute a minor portion of the cataracts seen in canines. In Golden Retrievers at least one type of hereditary cataract appears before two years of age.

The genetically caused cataract most commonly found in Goldens is a triangular opacity that is bilateral (that is, affecting both eyes). Some may not interfere with the dog's vision, while others can progress into severe loss of sight and total blindness. Examination by a Board-certified veterinary ophthalmologist is necessary to establish the genetic origin of a cataract.

Cataracts are not painful. While they do not constitute a medical emergency, cataracts often can be removed successfully. Dogs with hereditary cataracts should never be bred, nor should the parents of affected dogs be bred from again.

Progressive Retinal Atrophy (PRA) is an hereditary eye disease that affects the retina and inevitably progresses into total blindness. There is no surgical solution as in cataracts, and all PRA affected dogs and the dogs who produced them should be removed from breeding programs. While the incidence of PRA is relatively low in the breed, some families of Goldens are known to carry the genes for this disease.

Retinal dysplasia (RD) is an inherited defect of the lining of the retina and is more common in Goldens than is PRA. It can seriously reduce vision and can render a working dog worthless in the field. Present at birth, RD does not progress or result in eventual blindness. Pups should be screened at six to eight weeks of age because RD lesions may be present in young pups and later disappear. As with PRA, RD-affected dogs should not be considered for breeding.

Several less serious eye problems exist in Goldens, but still render the dog ineligible for showing under AKC rules and undesirable for breeding. Entropion is an "in-rolling" of one or both eyelids, allowing actual facial hairs to rub against the surface of the eye. The opposite is ectropion, where the lower lid turns out, preventing normal drainage of the tear duct. Distichiasis involves extra eyelashes, on either eyelid, that rub against and irritate the eye. All three conditions are easily corrected with minor surgery, but affected dogs cannot be shown and should not be bred.

Profile of an eight-week-old puppy—**Amberwood Persimmon Charade**, owner, Kristen Kothe. Photo by Susan Rezy.

Because some hereditary eye problems don't develop until later in life, any Golden considered for breeding should be examined annually from one year old until at least eight years of age. Only a Board-certified veterinary ophthalmologist has the special equipment and training necessary for a correct and thorough examination. The ophthalmologist provides each owner with a written report of the evaluation, and dogs found to be free of hereditary eye disease can be registered with the Canine Eye Registration Foundation (CERF), who will then assign the dog a clearance number. As with hip certification, a puppy buyer should require an ophthalmologist report or CERF clearance on the sire and dam before deciding on a pup.

EPILEPSY

Epilepsy or recurring seizures or convulsions is a neurological disorder caused by abnormal electrical patterns in the brain. Seizure activity can be inherited, or idiopathic, meaning cause-unknown, or acquired due to a number of environmental factors, including viral and infectious diseases, nutritional disorders, toxic reactions and cerebral trauma.

The Golden Retriever is one of more than a dozen breeds predisposed to hereditary epilepsy.

The increased frequency of the disease has become a major concern for Golden breeders in the United States and abroad, and has also caused some guide-dog and service-dog organizations to discontinue use of the Golden as a canine helper and assistant.

The clinical signs of epilepsy depend on the severity and duration of the seizure. An affected animal may experience shaking or mild to severe muscle spasms, a loss or disturbance of consciousness, abnormal behavior and/or involuntary urination and defecation.

Onset of heritable epilepsy usually occurs between six months up to three years of age. With nocturnal attacks being the most common, it is easy to overlook mild cases for a considerable length of time. Seizure activity often can be controlled with medication, but there is no cure, and treatment is directed at controlling the seizures. In cases of very frequent or extreme attacks, some veterinarians feel the kindest treatment is euthanasia.

The exact mode of inheritance has not yet been determined, but most authorities agree one or more recessive genes is probably responsible. Currently there is no diagnostic process to identify hereditary epilepsy other than ruling out every other cause. Unless the cause positively can be identified, dogs subject to recurring seizures should not be bred. Several experts further suggest that the parents and normal relatives of epileptic dogs also be removed from breeding programs.

SUBVALVULAR AORTIC STENOSIS (SAS)

SAS an inherited heart defect known to exist in the Golden Retriever breed. It is caused by a

stricture in the left ventricle, causing a symptomatic heart murmur. Severity can range from slight to severe. There is no known cure, and the mode of inheritance has not yet been established, although the occurrence of the disease is due primarily to intensive linebreeding.

SAS can be diagnosed as early as eight weeks of age, although 16 weeks is the preferred age for initial examination. Screening must be conducted by a Board-certified veterinary cardiologist. Dogs should be re-evaluated at 12 and 24 months of age, and all dogs should be cleared before they are considered for a breeding program. Experts further suggest that normal relatives of affected dogs should not be bred, as they could also produce affected pups.

This page: Moving with ease is **UD, Am-Can. OTCh. Beckwith's Hennessy Five Star Am-Can. TDX, WCX, Can. WC** owned by Nancy Light. Hennessy takes the high jump and the broad jump.

HYPOTHYROIDISM

This is a breakdown or malfunction of the thyroid gland. Symptoms may include obesity, lethargy, coat problems, and/or reproductive problems, such as irregular estrus (heat cycle) and sterility in both the male and female.

This disease can be diagnosed only by laboratory blood tests which measure the levels of serum T3 and T4 produced by the thyroid gland. Affected dogs can be successfully treated with medication or thyroid supplementation, although supplementation should be administered with caution as it can cause side effects and other problems.

Golden Retrievers, like several other large breeds, have a high risk for hypothyroidism. Some forms may be inherited, while others can

The GDC shares the belief that elbow and hip dysplasia are heritable, with the mode of inheritance as yet unknown. GDC will certify "normals" at the minimum age of 12 months. Using studies and experience in Sweden and Norway as models, GDC maintains that any difference between evaluations at one year or older is balanced with

The young **Amberwood Persimmon Charade** with **Ch. Persimmon's Hat Trick CDX, WC,** owned by Kristen Kothe. Sharing toys—sort of. Photo by Susan Rezy.

be environmental and secondary to other disorders. Some experts suggest that dogs requiring supplementation should not be bred.

In June 1990 the University of California School of Veterinary Medicine at Davis announced the opening of the new Institute for Genetic Disease Control in Animals. A non-profit organization funded through private donations, GDC will operate as an open registry for canine hip, elbow, shoulder and hock diseases, the first registry of its kind in the United States.

In an open registry, all information about a dog and its relatives is shared, thus helping breeders determine more about the genes that a prospective sire or dam will pass on to its offspring.

The veterinarian radiologists for GDC will evaluate radiographs at 12 months of age, will not charge for the evaluation or registration of affected animals and will help to evaluate the genetic health of a purebred animal by evaluating its relatives.

increasing numbers of evaluations along with the selection of dogs with more than the breed average of normal relatives.

More information on GDC services, procedures and fees can be obtained by contacting them at P.O. Box 222, Davis, CA 95617, (916-756-6773).

The rate of occurrence for some of these hereditary diseases in Goldens has risen disproportionately during recent years as "backyard" and for-profit breeders have capitalized on the Golden's popularity. Even experienced breeders sometimes "overlook" a problem because of other "virtues" in the dog(s) to be bred. Only an objective evaluation of every dog and bitch, and the potential quality—or problems—it may produce, will help eradicate the genetic diseases afflicting the twenty-first-century Golden Retriever.

Ashford's Murphy Brown owned by Gil and Sara Merckel of Hillsborough, California.

Inherited and Acquired von Willebrand's Disease

BY W. JEAN DODDS, DVM

W. Jean Dodds is from the Wadsworth Center for Laboratories & Research, New York State Department of Health, P.O. Box 509, Albany, NY 12201-0509.

Von Willebrand's disease (vWD) in humans and dogs is now recognized to be congenital (present at birth) and inherited and/or acquired secondary to familial autoimmune thyroid disease. Presently, 44 of the 54 dog breeds known to have vWD also transmit this form of thyroid disease which results in hypothyroidism. The Golden Retriever is one of these breeds. The prevalence of both diseases has increased rapidly over the last decade despite the collective efforts of conscientious breeders to test and screen out carriers from their breeding programs.

INHERITED (CONGENITAL) vWD

The most common mild inherited bleeding disorder of man and animals is vWD. The disease in Golden Retrievers is classified as Type I vWD and is an autosomal (non sex-linked) incompletely dominant trait, which means it has variable expression within affected families. Both homozygotes who have inherited a double dose of the gene, one from each parent, and heterozygotes that carry a single dose of the gene from either parent can manifest a bleeding tendency. However, homozygosity is rarely seen because affected puppies usually die during fetal development or shortly after birth.

VWD affects many animals, although few have severe problems and even fewer die. The bleeding episodes are worsened by physical, emotional and physiological stresses as well as other diseases. Typical clinical signs include: recurrent gastrointestinal hemorrhage with or without diarrhea; recurrent hematuria; nosebleeds; bleeding from the gums, vagina, or penis; lameness that mimics eosinophilic panosteitis; stillbirths or neonatal deaths ("fading pups") with evidence of bleeding at necropsy; prolonged bleeding at estrus or after whelping; bruises or blood-filled lumps on the surface of the body, limbs or head;

A dam with her healthy brood of puppies photographed by Karen Taylor.

excessive umbilical cord bleeding at birth; and excessive bleeding from toe nails cut too short, or after tail docking, ear cropping and dewclaw removal. Affected dogs may even bleed to death from surgical procedures. Diagnostic tests require specialized assays. Screening coagulation tests (APTT, PT and TCT) are nondiagnostic. Affected individuals have long bleeding times, and definitive diagnosis is classically made by finding reduced levels of von Willebrand factor antigen (vWF:Ag) [<1-60%].

We have seen a dramatic increase since 1985 in the number of Golden Retrievers having low levels of vWF:Ag (<50%). (See Table 1). This increase is real because the number of dogs tested each year continues to be large enough for statistical validation. There are several possible explanations for this increase. The first invokes a shift in the measurement of vWF:Ag; this possibility is ruled out because our assay has been standardized over time and so varies less than ±5% of the actual value. Secondly, the prevalence of inherited vWD is increasing because tested or untested carriers continue to be bred as the popularity of the breed has increased. Lastly, the increasing prevalence of thyroid disease has produced a parallel increase in acquired vWD. The most likely explanation is a combination of the last two possibilities.

ACQUIRED vWD

In dogs, vWD becomes more clinically severe if the dog also has hypothyroidism. Thus, symptom-free carriers of the vWD gene may exhibit a bleeding tendency if they subsequently become hypothyroid, a situation commonly seen in the Golden Retriever breed. The relatively high incidence of both vWD and hypothyroidism and research on the synthesis and metabolic regulation of thyroid hormones and vWF have confirmed this link. Furthermore, hypothyroid dogs may exhibit low platelet counts (thrombocytopenia) which can cause mucosal surface bleeding. *It is generally impossible to distinguish between the inherited and acquired types of vWD in an individual patient with currently available techniques.*

RECOMMENDATIONS TO BREEDERS

The following recommendations are offered to reduce the prevalence of vWD in Golden Retrievers:

1. Blood-test animals for vWD that are related to those bloodlines known to have the problem, as well as other top-producing or winning foundation stock. Pedigrees can be sent to the Wadsworth Center for evaluation as to whether or not the animals are closely or distantly related to or unrelated to known affected families. 2. Ideally, all vWD-affected dogs and even carriers of the gene should not be used for breeding purposes. However, it may not be feasible to remove all carriers from a breeding program, especially if they are desirable for temperament, type, conformation, and free of other known hereditary problems. Therefore, if breeding vWD animals is necessary to preserve important bloodlines or type, breed symptom-free vWD carriers to normals and blood-test the pups. On average, one-half of the litter should be normal and the other half will be carriers. This is the best alternative to preserve bloodlines. 3. Do not mate carriers of vWD because one-quarter of the litter on average will be affected "bleeders." 4. Never breed an affected animal as its puppies are likely to be carriers of vWD. Also, severely affected females may not survive the pregnancy.

Puppy sleeping like a brick. Photo by Laurie Doumaux of Clifton, Virginia.

Looking like a professional from the onset, this is the future **Pekays Goldstorm Top Gun CD, WC** at five months of age. Owner, Diane M. Mueller.

BLOOD TESTING FOR vWD

The accuracy of the testing program in detecting the vWD genotype has been evaluated by retrospective analysis of the results to date for all three mating types (normal X normal; normal X carrier; and carrier X carrier). The rate of misclassification of genetic status by this test is only two to three percent, which means that in 97% or more cases the test is a reliable predictor of vWD genotype. However, we should remember that misclassification either way is always possible. Some of the reasons are that: 1. The animal belongs to the two to three percent not identifiable by this test; 2. The animal has some other health problem such as hypothyroidism or is receiving thyroid supplementation; 3. The bitch was in heat, pregnant or lactating when tested; 4. The offspring has one or both parents incorrectly identified as being the true parent or as having been tested as normal for the vWD gene; or 5. A collection, processing, or laboratory error was made. This last reason accounts for most of the misclassifications involving any type of genetic screening program.

Our laboratory issues vWD-tested clear certifications for results obtained by us or by other qualified laboratories. If you plan to breed to another person's stud dog, to lease or buy a tested animal or to buy a pup of tested parents,

be sure to see a copy of the certificate(s) indicated the test status beforehand rather than rely on the memory or word of the owner. This is an added precaution and should not imply dishonesty or mistrust.

Table 1. Prevalence of the vWD Gene in Golden Retrievers*

Year	No. of Valid vWD Tests	vWD Gene Prevalence
1982-85	1,783	11
1986	555	16
1987	652	20
1988	582	27
1989	708	31
1990**	642	32

* A total of 5,846 tested through January 1991.

**A total of 642 valid tests were performed in 1990. Of these, 193 (30%) had values at or above 70% vWF:Ag and were considered normal; 244 (38%) tested between 50-69% which is considered borderline (50-59%, possible carriers) or lower end of normal range (60-69%); 205 (32%) tested below 50% and were either carriers or affected with vWD. Another 39 tests were invalidated because of sample problems.

Over-zealous as usual, Golden Retriever **"Kona"** has *five*-times as much play energy as the next dog. (Photographer Karen Taylor assures us that this trickster actually has five tennis balls in her mouth!)

Let's Play Ball!

BY CHRIS WALKOWICZ

When we're young, our imaginations can carry us to faraway lands, and we can pretend we're princes slaying dragons, or cowboys, or ballerinas, or whatever we want to be. Somehow, as we grow older, the magic of imagination fades in the face of the real world. We lose the ability to create fun whenever we wish.

We turn to material stimulation such as VCRs, CDs, RVs and ATVs for our amusement. Sometimes the best entertainment is the D-O-G lying right at our feet. One of the best reasons for having a dog is that they're so much fun!

When a dog owner wants to spend quality time with his dog, the first thing that comes to mind is tossing a ball or a stick. Oftentimes, the entertainment doesn't go much further than that and maybe a walk around the block. Even those recreational activities are better than none, but with a touch of our youthful sense of adventure, we can escape the humdrum.

TOYS

Dogs chew—especially puppies. Let's face it. When the eruption of needle-sharp puppy teeth stimulates the urge to sink them into something, better a toy than the table leg . . . or yours. Believe it or not, they really need to chew in order to develop strong, healthy teeth and jaws.

Chewing on some toothsome object also fills long, boring hours when the master is busy or away. Six thousand dollars later, after repairs to the family room, owners realize toys—proper toys—are less expensive. It's always better to prevent bad habits before they occur than to try to retrain and repair and retaliate after the damage has been done.

Knowledgeable parents recognize that children's toys can be useful as well as entertaining. So can animal toys. Knucklebones obtained from the butcher provide exercise and chewing release, but can be messy. Prolonged chewing on these can also cause wear of the teeth. Rawhide products are popular but can prove dangerous if swallowed in chunks which can cause blockage in the intestines. All toys should be discarded when broken. A new toy is much more reasonable than a veterinary bill for surgery.

Articles made from super-tough nylon and polymer (a soft rubber) are safe and good for dogs, and—as with nutritional, but good-tasting cereal for kids—your pet will never complain. Many are hambone scented and flavored.

Given one of these toys, old dogs seem young again in their play. Sedate, dignified dogs act silly. And young, silly dogs go "bonkers" for toys such as the Gumabone® and other "pooch pacifiers." The hambone scent probably has a great deal to do with the attraction for the dogs, but the long-lasting durability appeals to owners. Nylabone® products are also a big hit, at the same time serving as teeth cleaners and furniture-savers. When dogs need to vent some serious chewing, they grab a Nylabone®. These resilient, durable products, found mainly in pet shops, last at least five times longer than the cheap plastic or latex toys found at the grocery stores and knowledgeable owners know they're a good investment.

When leaving the dog in his crate, a Nylabone® and a Gumabone® will make the hours pass

Ready when you are. This is **Quapaw's Royal Lukas of Britt CD** owned by Terry and John Hanley of Chesterfield, Missouri.

327

more quickly until you return again to be the main object of his affection. These toys can be washed and sterilized, and they are non-abrasive.

The Gumadisc® is a flying disc, made for sailing in the air so that the dog can leap and catch it. Nylaballs®, too, are popular retrieve objects. Although their scent is unnoticeable to humans, it enables dogs to find toys hidden in deep grass.

Because dogs don't eat candy, they suffer few problems with their teeth. They can usually brag after a dental check, "Look, Mom, no cavities!" It's gum disease that plagues our canine friends and results in tooth loss. Research shows that 90 percent of dogs over the age of three years are afflicted with periodontal disease. We can help our pets by brushing their teeth, scheduling regular examinations and by supplying good dentifrice toys.

Nylafloss®, particularly, is conducive to maintaining healthy teeth and gums. The nylon strands rub between the teeth and at the gum line, removing plaque and tartar, much like our own dental floss. Nylabone® products are sold in pet shops and by veterinarians.

RETRIEVE

Almost anything can be the object of a retrieve: a ball, a stick or a flying saucer disc. The purpose is to train the dog to bring back what you throw. Some dogs are naturals. Others need to be encouraged through praise and enthusiasm.

Start with throwing favorite toys small distances. Use a call phrase such as, "fetch" or "get it." If the dog does not return to you with the object, run in the opposite direction so he'll be enticed to follow. Train the dog to release the object by pressing his lips against his teeth, holding the object and saying, "drop" or "give."

"Retrieve" is in my genes. **Bruwin's Carmel Kiss**, at six months of age, has been rescuing this stick all morning. Owner, Ginger Rezy; photo by Susan Rezy.

If the dog needs further encouragement, a food treat might be given in return for his hard-earned treasure. Soon he'll learn that if he releases his precious object, you'll throw it again and again.

FLYING DISCS

Tossing a disc dates back to the ancient Olympics and the discus throw. Playing catch with a disc and a dog is much more recent.

The first time the event was seen in public, in 1974, it created a sensation. A man named Alex Stein and his dog, Ashley Whippet, leaped from the stands during a Dodger's baseball game and gave an impromptu demonstration of Ashley's amazing ability to fly through the air and catch the tossed object. Stein and Ashley were also tossed—out of the game and into the slammer. Nevertheless, the uninvited guests accomplished their purpose. Dog lovers soon took up the craze with competitions which Ashley dominated for years.

Anyone interested should first practice throwing the Nyladisc® or Frisbee® correctly. It's no fun for the dog if we sling the toy straight up or in the wrong direction.

Whet your dog's interest by rolling the disc along the ground. Encourage him to retrieve it. If you want him to leap into the air and make a spectacular "Ashley" catch, teach him to jump up and grab the Nyladisc® while you're holding it, increasing the height until he has reached his full potential.

Finally, you're ready for some throws. Start with short ones, so that your dog will keep his eye on the disc. Two people's tossing the toy back and forth creates a keepaway situation, but allow the dog to catch it every third or fourth cast to keep up his enthusiasm.

SCENT HURDLE AND FLYBALL

Dogs compete in relay teams, usually four to a team, racing over four jumps scaled to the shoulder height of the smallest canine participant. Minimum jump height is ten inches, with maximum at 16 inches. The continual jumping demanded by this event puts additional stress on

Mid-air, this is **Ch. Timberee Right On Target CDX, WC (OS)** right on as usual. Owners, Bob and Sandy Fisher.

the dogs, thus the lower height than obedience competition. Hurdles are placed ten feet apart.

The handler stands behind the starting line, shouting encouragement to the dog—who actually appears to need little. In fact, handlers of the other dogs waiting their turn often have to restrain their over-exuberant animals.

In scent hurdling, a platform holding four dumbbells (one with his owner's scent) is placed at the end of the jumps. The dog must find the right one, pick it up and race back over the jumps. If he's wrong or he misses a jump, he has to return to the end of the line and run again.

Flyball adds another twist. After jumping the hurdles, the dog hits a pedal on the front of a box. The pedal activates a lever on which a cup holding a ball is attached. As the ball flies into the air, the dog catches it and races back over the hurdles.

329

The most successful teams are composed of breeds who excel in obedience, but many breeds are seen. Dogs love these games, as do owners and spectators, evident by the cacophony that explodes as soon as the starting whistle blows. Handlers shout, dogs bark and the crowd cheers.

HIDE AND SEEK

Everyone knows how good Goldens are at following their noses. Sometimes they follow them into trouble, but more often they put them to good use by following them to lost or injured people, drugs, bombs, contraband and even termites.

Owners can take advantage of their dogs' skill by training them for tracking, Search and rescue and other canine occupations, or just for fun. These games can be used as a preface for advanced training or as an end in themselves.

Begin by hiding a short distance away indoors and calling to your dog. When he finds you, show your excitement. Distances should be increased and finds made more difficult until they're finally moved outdoors. Objects can also be hidden, favorite toys or tidbits, with a command such as "seek" or "find." Kids love this one, but it's fun for adults too!

Bruwin's Carmel Kiss, owned by Ginger Rezy, and **Pekay's Drambuie CDX,** owned by Mary Owens. The dogs are enjoying a friendly game of frisbee with their friend Bernie Rezy.

WEIGHT PULLING/CARTING

Several breeds were bred to haul and use their strong backs in order to save ours. It didn't matter whether their loads were humans or produce, the dogs were willing. Notions, bakery and dairy products, fresh fruit and vegetables all filled the carts hauled by Bernese Mountain Dogs, Rottweilers and other large, sturdy draft dogs. Nordic dogs, too, threw their shoulders into the harness, pulling loads and people on sleds, the only transportation available to the northern civilizations.

It was natural for competitions to grow out of necessity. In those days, people were hard pressed for entertainment. No Nintendos®, Cinema 11 or even a Monopoly® board. It often came down to, "My dog's better'n your dog." Who can forget Buck throwing his heart and his mighty strength into the pull that thrilled readers of London's *Call of the Wild*?

Nowadays, it's not just the working breeds who put their shoulder to the wheel or the runner; any dog is eligible. Sporting breeds like our Golden Retriever participate and often do well. Bouviers, German Shepherds and American Staffordshire Terriers join St. Bernards, Alaskan Malamutes and Newfoundlands in competitive pulls. Even members of the Chinese Crested, Bichon Frise and Pekingese breeds have pulled at the International Weight Pull Association (IWPA) competitions.

Entrants have one minute to pull weights over a distance of 16 to 20 feet. Great care is taken to avoid injury, and none has ever occurred at the IWPA competitions. When the dog shows difficulty pulling a load, assistance is given. An entry is never allowed to experience failure—even if someone lends a hand. According to the 1989 *Guinness Book of World Records*, the heaviest load ever moved was an amazing 6,400.5 pounds, heaved by a St. Bernard.

Carting is also becoming popular. Almost any dog can participate, towing a little red wagon with a doll riding, drawing a sulky with a couple of kids in a parade or hauling a four-wheeled cart loaded with wood.

A few clubs offer carting or drafting tests. The Newfoundland Club of America awards a Draft Dog title to those who perform well on a course with hills and obstacles.

It's important for the leather or nylon web harness to be fitted properly so that there is neither restriction nor discomfort. Acclimate the

Bama Bran Muffin on the sliding board with Justin. A healthy outing.

dog to the weight and the noise of the cart by having him wear the harness around the house, then pulling an empty cart. Weight can gradually be added.

Carting can be practical too. Exhibitors might pack a harness and hitch up the dog to pull his wheels, crate, tack box and accompanying show paraphernalia from the car to the site!

More information on weight pulling can be obtained through IWPA, 503 East Street, Spokane, WA 99203.

JOGGING

The jogging/running craze that hit the world some years ago has made exercise a way of life. Jogging suits, latex clothes and name-brand shoes are all part of the coordinated look. But your dog doesn't need a thing to join you. He already has weather-protective covering and built-in footwear.

The best pace for most dogs is a steady trot. Always consider the dog's physique and stamina when including him in exercise. People know their limitations. When they're reaching exhaustion or feeling overheated, they'll stop. A dog's will, particularly when accompanying his master, may drive him beyond the safety point. Although the point is to build his stamina, as well as enjoying his companionship, we need to set the dog's limits, or he'll keep running as long as we do. Just as when setting up our own exercise routine, we need to increase speed and distance gradually.

Events such as the Purina Fun Run®, hosted in several cities around the United States, recognize that pairing with a pal makes exercise and competition more fun.

HIKING

Hiking differs from the everyday walk because it's often goal-oriented, usually done in scenic areas and sometimes continues for more than one day. Just as we enjoy a change of scenery, our dogs will too. Whether it's local, state or national parks or a dream vacation in the Alps, it's wise to check the regulations, if any, regarding dogs. What a nasty surprise to arrive at our destination only to find that Phydeaux must remain in the motel room all day—or worse yet, isn't welcome even there!

Doggy backpacks may be purchased at pet stores or through mail order catalogs. The packs can be loaded with the pet's necessities: food,

Golden Retrievers are aptly labelled water dogs. After exploring the coral under the sea, **Mioak's Golden Torch (OD)**.

Rocky and **Luna**. Two "desert" Goldens, raised in the California desert for five years, enjoy their first taste of snow. "What have we been missing all these years?"

bowl, extra leash, first-aid kit. Keeping the pet on leash at all times eliminates the possibility of loss, and also makes dog owners less obtrusive to others enjoying the area. A collar with I.D. tags is additional insurance. Clean-up is part of owner responsibility as well, paving the way for other dogs and owners.

BE A SPORT!

In addition to those mentioned, dog lovers have no end of ways to enjoy being with their pets and teaching them new skills. There are water rescue tests, square-dancing dogs, and, of course, hunting,

Play is for puppies, and adult Goldens are far too sophisticated, as aptly demonstrated by **Can. Ch. U-UD Amberac's Gaety at Honeycomb Am-Bda-Can. UD, JH, SKC-UD, Am-Can. WC, TT, CGC**...and with that many titles, who has time for games?! Gaety's busy owner is Patricia O'Brien of Lakewood, New Jersey.

as well as any other place inspiration takes you and your dog. In most areas, courtesy, regulations and common sense require that the animal be under control and understand basic obedience.

Many of these sports require some training and equipment, but once the initial paraphernalia is purchased, cost is relatively low. The most important ingredients, however, are the owner and his dog.

Naturally, before performing any exercise, your dog should be examined by a veterinarian and passed as healthy. It doesn't hurt for the owner to be in good shape as well, since the whole idea

is to accompany your dog. Training often includes building endurance through roadwork, brisk walks or jogging. Exercising with our dogs provides bonuses. It increases their stamina and muscle tone, and it can't hurt us either!

Many of the above events are hosted by dog clubs at parks, malls or in conjunction with their shows. Whether competing formally, staging an impromptu demonstration for neighbors or simply having a good time with your dog, everything's more fun when you're doing it with your best friend! As in any other relationship, the dog–human bond is strengthened through quality time.

Left: **Cloverdale Ice Princess** in the field. Bred by Jane and Richard Zimmerman and owned by Felita and Brian Carr.
Top: **Wildtrout's Golden Oprtunity UD, WC**. "Chan" was bred by Joan Armentrout Jung and owned by Rita Robins.
Bottom: Two professional noses: **Honor's Cogan in the Rockies UDTX, WC, TDI** and **Honor's Who's On First? CDX, TDX, JH, WCX, TDI**, owned by Ron Buksaitis.

Top: All aboard…a summer day in Texas with **Gallo Gold Cool Cotton Khaki WC** owned by Terry Thornton; **Jamaica** (a Labrador Retriever); **Bonham's Rockhaven Raygon CD, JH, WCX** owned by Vida Bonham and **Gallo Gold Classic Renegrade WC** owned by Cindy Vinzant.
Bottom: **FC-AFC Tigathoes Kiowa II** at the 1980 Golden Specialty in California. Photo by Dave and Cindy Traylor.

Top left: Mom and daughter, **Quantock's Sacajawua CD, TD** and **Cattail's Seasan Opener** owned by Eileen Bohn.
Bottom left: **Farm Fresh Hasty Pudding** content with her pigeon retrieve, owned by L. Dickerson.
Top right: **Aquatico's Winsom Lusom**, "Lucy," owned by Melinda Petty.
Bottom right: **Ch. Asterling Austin Healey** adrift! Owned by Donna and Susan Nyberg. Photo by Missy Yuhl.

Some day! This is **Wynwood Dream Spinner CD** photographed by owner Susan Kluesner of Lakeville, Minnesota.

Tessa gone fishin' (owned by the Fishers).

Above: One of Lucille Sawtell's Yeo Goldens flies over a fence after retrieving its pheasant.
Below: **Yeo Leading Lady**, bred by Lucille Sawtell, Somerset, England.

The English Golden Retriever

BY LUCILLE SAWTELL

The development of the Golden Retriever, since 1938 when I had my first Golden Retriever bitch, has not been, in my opinion, very promising for the breed.

Although conformation has improved enormously over the years, much has been lost in true Golden temperament and purpose as it was laid down when the breed was first recognized and standardized in Great Britain in 1913. I am afraid the breed has become so popular as pets that the current soft temperament and glamorous coat have been its undoing as a working dog. Unfortunately it has become fashionable to encourage pale, glamorous dogs that have yet to prove themselves as tireless workers in the field.

The Goldens I remember from pre-war and post-war decades had a better working attitude. I do not mean they were more obstinate, but they had a strong enough character to accept a reprimand without sulking and did not crumple up and fall upon their backs as soon as a harsh word was spoken.

The style of coat has also suffered. Instead of the rich, gold wavy coat with thick water-resisting undercoat, we now see a fine silky coat—some of which is almost white—in both Britain and many other countries around the world. The cream Golden Retriever has taken over in Australia, New Zealand, and the Scandanavian countries where it is not used primarily as a shooting or hunting dog.

In Britain, as in other countries, there is a dividing line between the show dog and the field dog, the latter being finer in bone, generally darker in color and faster in the field. These dogs do very well in the field, but are a far cry from the top-winning show dog. Breeders who breed primarily show stock are encouraged to gain work-

Yeo Mastermind and **Yeo Leading Lady**, bred and owned by Lucille Sawtell, Somerset, England.

ing certificates with their dogs since this is required to become a full champion. Otherwise the dogs are titled as only show champions.

Toward that end, working tests and training classes are held in almost every area in Britain. Although this is a move in the right direction, it is rare that a genuine dual-purpose Golden hits the high spots in field trials.

Field trials in Great Britain are completely different from trials held in most other countries. Those generally correspond to our gundog working tests which are held during the closed season from February until October.

Our field trials take place during the shooting season and are run naturally as a dog would work on a shooting day. Game is either walked up or driven up by beaters. Usually six dogs walk in the line, the three judges walking with them. As the birds are shot, a dog is sent to collect them. If the first dog fails to do so in a certain time, then the next dog is sent. All dogs must walk off lead, and should any dog run in without being sent, he is immediately dropped from the stake. He can also be eliminated if he is hard mouthed or whines on the line, for chasing live game while working, or refusing to obey the whistle to return to his handler.

Each dog must have two retrieves under two different judges, but will probably have more if game is plentiful. Game is varied, and a dog must be prepared to retrieve from land and water, picking up ducks, pheasants, woodcock, partridge, snipe, hares or rabbits.

The number of dogs allowed to compete is limited, varying from 12 to 24, in which case the trial is run over two days. As a result, trials are always over-subscribed, with perhaps as many as 50 or more applicants, so you are lucky to get

In England as in America, the Golden Retriever must be bred first for utility. Owner, Mrs. Pounds Longhurst of Staplehurst, Kent, England. Photography by Robert Smith.

that your success in the show ring, or in the field for a field-trial judge, renders you knowledgeable enough to judge other people's dogs. Later, having judged a sufficient number of breed classes at Open shows, you may be asked to judge the breed at a Championship show and award Challenge Certificates. Championship show judges can award Challenge Certificates to the same breed and sex only once every nine months, and some societies demand a year's abstinence.

In time and with experience, you may be called upon to judge other Gundog breeds and award Challenge Certificates in those also, but only after the respective kennel clubs have given their approval. Once you have given Challenge Certificates in three different Gundog breeds, one of which should be the short-legged variety (i.e., Cocker or Springer Spaniel) *then* you may be asked to judge the Gundog Group. It is a long process, and many of our judges are also exhibitors and breeders. Therefore, they are familiar with many of the dogs presented to them in the ring.

in when the draw takes place. It is therefore extremely difficult to make up a field champion.

To become a full champion, a dog must have won three Challenge Certificates (wins) under three different judges and obtained a working certificate. The working certificate can be an award from a field trial or from a special qualifying trial held specifically to grant certificates to show dogs who have won a first place at a Championship show.

At some breed club shows, there is a class reserved for champions only, but this is rare. Champions usually have to compete with aspiring champions in the Open class which makes show competition much harder. If well-known champions are shown repeatedly, many promising young dogs may be held back, sometimes until it is too late.

In Britain, first is not always best; second and third place are also very creditable, especially when the classes sometimes have 50 or 60 entries. This is not true in other countries where a first place or group win are what counts. Goldens seldom win the Gundog Group or Best in Show here, because, I believe, the best do not measure up as well in sound conformation as in some other breeds.

Judges in some countries are required to attend lectures and take a written examination to qualify for judging. Not so in Great Britain. In order to judge here, one must be invited by a committee who thinks

English-bred Golden with retrieved dove. Photo by Robert Smith.

Two lovely Goldens from the home of Mrs. Pounds Longhurst. Photo by Robert Smith.

It is a rule here that no dog should be shown under its breeder for one year after it has been sold. There is also an unwritten rule which most exhibitors follow that no dog bred by a judge is ever shown under him or her. A judge may be judging one day and exhibiting the next. The majority of judges are successful breeders with a lifetime of experience behind them.

All Championship shows are benched, and some of the bigger Open shows as well. Goldens are so popular here that, unlike in other countries, they usually have a good classification in

ons with a commentary.

The system of judging in Scandanavia and on the Continent is different. Scandanavians use a grading system of first class, second class and third class, and in the Scandanavian countries, a critique is written on each dog while it is in the ring. This can be a very long process, especially if there are a lot of dogs in the class. Once all the dogs have been critiqued, the first class dogs are called back and judged as a normal class.

In Britain, the judge makes a critique of the first and second place dogs only. His critiques

In order to gain full championship status, breeders of show dogs must also attain working certificates. Photo by R. Smith.

the schedule. We have many classes not held in the United States: Maiden, Debutante, Graduate, Post Graduate, Mid Limit and Limit. They all have a different definition relating to the number of first prizes the dog has won. To qualify for Crufts, the British equivalent to Westminster in the U.S., a dog must win a first place at a Championship show in Puppy, Junior, or Yearling class, or a first, second or third in Post Graduate, Limit or Open. This can change slightly from year to year. You may enter as many classes as you wish, and frequently the same dog wins two or three classes on the trot. At Breed Championship shows there are usually Veteran and Progeny classes as well as a Parade of Champi-

are published in the weekly dog papers, which are avidly read by those in the fancy.

The Kennel Club Challenge Certificate is awarded to the Best Dog and Best Bitch, who then compete for Best of Breed. As Golden Retrievers have a separate judge for dogs and bitches, the two sometimes do not agree, and a referee is called in to decide.

Dog shows here are much more relaxed than elsewhere. It is considered a day out to meet friends and enjoy. Field trials are relaxed occasions, and gundog tests even more so. We have very few professional handlers in either field or show; many owners do a very competent job and are equal to any professional.

Steady and patient, the working gundog and companion. Photos by R. Smith.

Dog breeding is generally regarded as a hobby, not as big business or a status symbol. Some of our top winning dogs are, in fact, family pets who have never lived in a kennel. Many of our best-known breeders keep only a few dogs.

When we do kennel our dogs, they are usually kept in groups of three or four and never in single runs. We like to feel our dogs will mix freely with other dogs, which they will have to do when working on a shoot picking up. It is not the practice here to crate our dogs at any time. Some of the very small breeds may be transported to shows in crates, but never a Golden Retriever.

At present no license is required to keep a dog, although this is controversial, and the govern-

Job well done...returning with the pheasant.

ment may adopt new regulations. However, a breeder's license is required to keep three or more breeding bitches, and the premises must be inspected annually. Dog food must be kept in bins away from the family living quarters. Heating, lighting and fire precautions are also required.

Due to our more temperate climate, our kennels are often composed of converted outbuildings or wooden kennels with fairly large runs. I believe we attach more importance to daily exercise and free ranging than most other countries. Road exercise is considered essential to form good tight feet and firm muscles. Although straw is used as kennel bedding, the most popular is Vet bed, a synthetic material which looks like lamb's wool and allows all moisture to pass through while keeping the surface dry.

For easy cleaning, we spread the kennel floors liberally with sawdust, which also helps to keep the bedding dry in our very wet climate. Except during very bad weather, my dogs are only shut in at night.

Breed standards differ widely, which seems to me a pity, particularly if the dogs are to be imported from other countries. The U.S. breed standard for the Golden Retriever calls for a bigger dog, an inch higher than in Britain. Heads in particular are quite different.

While the U.S. shows are generally sponsored by professional dog-show superintendents, ours

345

hidden dummies. Finally they may be introduced to a dead bird, probably a pigeon. Live birds, such as shackled ducks or pigeons are never used in this country, and it is illegal to do so. Electronic equipment, spiked collars or similar training gear are also forbidden.

In the spring, dogs may occasionally be tested on cold game, that is, pigeons or rabbits that have been shot a few days before. Otherwise, all tests are run on dummies. When sufficiently proficient, the dog and handler may be invited to pick up at a shoot. This is valuable training for future field trials as well as being a most enjoyable pastime.

THE HOLWAY HALLMARK

In the English Golden Retriever, the name Holway has become synonymous with excellence and achievement. The pedigrees of many of today's titled and influential Golden Retrievers are linebred on important Holway dogs or carry pedigrees heavily influenced by a Holway connection.

Holway Golden Retrievers originated in the early 1950s with Golden Retriever fancier June Atkinson and her first home-trained Field Champion, Musicmaker of Yeo. The Holway legend was born in 1954 when F.T.Ch. Mazurka of Wynford, Musicmaker's two-year-old son, bred, trained and handled by June, won the National Retriever Championship.

Almost three decades and a dozen field champions later, June's son Robert, following in his mother's footsteps, won the 1982 National Retriever Championship with F.T.Ch. Little Marston Chorus of Holway. Chorus thus became the second Holway Golden and the third post-war Golden to achieve that success. It's not mere coincidence that Chorus's pedigree includes many of the 13 Field Champions June had made up since 1950, and carries four separate lines back to the famous Mazurka.

By the late 1980s, June had bred and trained more than 18 Field Champions, and had bred numerous others who were trained and handled to their titles by their owners. During the last decade, Holway Goldens . . . field champions plus several who won championship stakes but never titled . . . have won over 100 field-trial stakes and claimed more than twice that number in total field-trial awards.

As a member of the Kennel Club, June sits on the Field Trial Committee and has judged the Retriever Championship five times. Her contribution to the retriever world was honored in the *Golden Retriever Book of Champions*, 1946-1985, compiled by Valerie Foss and Graham Cox. Gra-

AFC Holway Barty (Eng. FTCh. Holway Westhyde Zeus ex Eng. FTCh. Holway Flush of Yeo) is the all-time field trial producer in breed history and was bred by June Atkinson of England. Barty is the sire of NAFC-FC Topbrass Cotton. He is lovingly remembered by owner Barbara Howard.

are always run by clubs and societies who form their own committees to handle each event.

Obedience classes have gained importance with Golden Retriever owners during recent years. While they do not match the popularity of gundog training, obedience classes are enjoyed during the winter months when they are held indoors.

Gundog training classes and tests begin in April and continue throughout the summer. Dogs attending these classes are expected to have some primary training and be able to sit, stay and walk at heel. The dog and handler must be prepared to take their place in line with others and learn to retrieve a dummy or bumper. They progress to directional handling and retrieving

Six field trial champions from England, all bred by Mrs. June Atkinson: **Chorus, Gem, Dollar, Grettle, Chanter** and **Trumpet**. The Holway dogs can be found in the pedigrees of the top field dogs in the U.S. as well as England.

ham states, "June . . . has a record as a breeder, trainer and handler of Goldens that is unlikely ever to be paralleled in any retriever breed."

Yet even more amazing than their field-trial record is the lifestyle of the Holway Golden. Several live in the house with June, and all are trained on her own property on "rough shoots and walk rounds." June's trial dogs are also her full-time companions, and they all generally accompany her on trial outings. When people at trials inquire about her kennels, she replies her kennels are with her, and directs them to the five or six Goldens lounging in the back of her estate car .

With obvious pride, June related a common observation on the Goldens she has bred: "People say they can tell a Holway Golden Retriever, they have that certain hallmark."

Among the English Field Trial Champions that June Atkinson has bred and/or owner-handled are F.T.Ch. Mazurka of Wynford, F.T.Ch. Musicmaker of Yeo, F.T.Ch. Holway Lancer, F.T.Ch. Flush of Yeo, F.T.Ch. Holway Bonnie, F.T.Ch. Holway Zest, F.T.Ch. Holway Westhyde Zeus, F.T.Ch. Holway Gaity, F.T.Ch. Holway Barrister, F.T.Ch. Holway Jollity, F.T.Ch. Holway Chanter, F.T.Ch. Holway Gem, F.T.Ch. Holway Dollar, F.T.Ch. Holway Grettle, F.T.Ch. Holway Trumpet, F.T.Ch. Holway Corbiere, F.T.Ch. Holway Denier, and F.T.Ch. Little Marstan Chorus of Holway.

These four American Master Hunters are linebred on Holway and bear a remarkable resemblance to their English cousins. "The Girls:" **Sparkle**, bred and owned by Kaye Fuller, DVM, and her three daughters; **China**, owned by the author, **Spirit** and **Dazzle**, both owned by Kaye. Sparkle, China and Spirit are also qualified All-Age in the U.S. and Spirit boasts an Amateur second place.

Canada's pride and joy. **Dual Ch., AFTCh. Carolee's Something Special II Can. CDX, Am. CD, Am-Can. WCX**, bred by Shirley Goodman, Carolee Kennels, Don Mills, Ontario. Finished in the field in 1981, "Bumper's" career accomplishments all were achieved at the hand of his owner, George Stewart of Campbellville, Ontario.

Goldens in Canada

In 1990 the Golden Retriever Club of Canada (GRCC) celebrated its thirtieth birthday. One of Canada's largest and most active breed clubs with nearly 700 members and six affiliate regional clubs, the GRCC annually hosts a variety of activities to promote the breed's diversity in show, obedience, field, tracking and agility, and service and companion dog.

In addition to a national specialty show and obedience trial, the GRCC sponsors a two-day field trial, working certificate tests and training classes, a sanctioned match, regional specialties and educational seminars. Their annual health clinic helps club members screen their dogs for genetic disorders, and a genetic improvement committee collaborates with various professionals to research genetic problems such as hip dysplasia, inherited eye disorders, epilepsy, heart disease and von Willebrand's disease.

The increased popularity of the Golden Retriever in Canada is creating some of the same problems found wherever the breed has multiplied: poor temperaments, aggression, lack of soundness and natural ability. On the upside, the achievements of Goldens throughout the Canadian provinces reflect the serious effort of dedicated breeders to preserve the quality and working abilities of the breed.

In British Columbia, Ainslie and Barrie Mills have raised Oriana Goldens for about 20 years. A past president of the GRCC, Ainslie strives to breed sound Golden Retrievers who excel in performance as well as the breed ring. From a modest ten litters over the past two decades, she has produced 27 conformation champions, seven obedience-trial champions, High-in-Trial dogs, and Puppy Group and Best in Show winners.

Ainslie's foundation bitch, Ch. Beckwith's Fancyfree Calypso Am-Can. CDX (Am-Can. Ch. Laurell's Especial Jason Am-Can. UDT, WC ex Am-Can. Ch. Beckwith's Apricot Brandy Am. UDT, Can. CDX), (1976-1988), purchased from Ludell Beckwith in Washington, was Canada's top brood bitch for 1981, 1982, 1983, and 1984, a record for GRCC. A member of the GRCC Hall of Fame and an Outstanding Dam, "Calla" has produced 14 bench championships, 26 obedience titles including one Can. OTCh. and one Am. OTCh.; numerous awards and working certificates, and added yet two more generations of Golden over-achievers.

Ch. Beckwith's Fancyfree Calypso Am-Can. CDX, (Am-Can. Ch. Laurell's Especial Jason Am-Can. UDT, WC ex Ch. Beckwith's Apricot Brandy UDT, Can. CDX) (1976-1988), bred by Ludell Beckwith, owned by Barrie and Ainslie Mills, Surrey, B.C. "Calla" holds a GRCC record as Canada's top brood bitch for four consecutive years, 1981 through 1984. She is here sitting with **Am-Can. Ch. Goldenquest's Oriana Kian, Am-Can. CD**, (1978-1985), the GRCC 1984 top stud dog, bred by David Hilliard and owned by the Mills.

One Calla daughter, Can. Ch. Oriana A Capella Can. CDX, WCI, TD, TT, Am. CD, TD, WC is a second-generation GRCC Hall of Fame and Outstanding Dam and was the GRCC top brood bitch in 1986. "Megan" was trained and handled to all her working titles by Eileen Battley, Ainslie's mother, who is a senior citizen.

Megan has followed her mother's example. Her first litter, by Am-Can. Ch. Alderbrooke's Rush-Hill Rebel Am-Can. TD, produced four Can. Ch., two Can. Ch. OTCh., and one Am-Can. Ch., one Certified Avalanche Search and Rescue Dog, and a host of working titles and awards.

One of those offspring, Can. Ch. OTCh. Oriana Felicia's Brittany Can. WC, Am. CDX. was Canada's Number One Obedience Golden in 1988, Number Three in 1987, and the GRCC Top Open B and Utility Dog in 1988. Owned by Craig and Julie Simon in Alberta, Brittany is their first competition Golden and was home-trained by Julie.

Ainslie's Am-Can. Ch. Goldenquest Oriana Kian Am-Can. CD, (1978-1985), GRCC Hall of Fame and Outstanding Sire, was a multiple-BOB winner in the U.S. and Canada, with Group placements in Canada, and the GRCC Top Stud Dog in 1984.

The top-winning conformation Golden in Canadian breed history (through 1990) is a typical Cinderella dog. Am-Can. Ch. Gretchen's Chivas Regal Can. CDX, and GRCC Outstanding Sire and Hall of Famer, was "just a pet" purchased by Anne and Byron Brown, who had never trained or shown a dog. Friends convinced them to take this special puppy to a match or two.

"Turk" developed into a champion and true showman who never stopped showing in the ring. He became the top conformation Golden in Canadian breed history, amassing more Hall of Fame points than any other Golden through 1990. He was Canada's Number One Golden in 1982 and 1984, and Number Two in 1981 and 1983, and during his career collected 14 All-Breed BIS awards, three BOBs, and 75 Group Firsts, over 80 Group placements and over 200 Breed wins.

At six years old "Turk" retired from the bench and entered the obedience ring. Within six months and in six consecutive shows he earned his CD and CDX with two High-in-Trial awards. His attitude and exceptional movement were always evident in the obedience ring.

Can. Ch.-OTCh. Oriana Felicia's Brittany Can. WC, Am. CDX, a "Megan" daughter by Am-Can. Ch. Alderbrooke's Rush-Hill Rebel, Am-Can. TD, was Canada's Number One Obedience Golden in 1988, Number Three in 1987, and is a member of the GRCC Obedience Hall of Fame with multiple High in Trials in Canada and the U.S. Bred by Barrie and Ainslie Mills, owned and home-trained by Julie Simon, Peace River, Alberta. She is shown here with Julie going High in Trial with a Novice B score of 198½ at the 1987 Evergreen Golden Retriever Club in Washington state. Judge Sharon Fulkerson, Show Chairperson Sandra Hourigan.

In Nova Scotia, Frances Walker proved the Canadian Golden is truly a retriever who can do it all. Her "Morgan," Ch. OTCh. Cedarcroft Nature Boy UDTX, WC (Ch. Rancher of Yeo ex Ch. Shadywell Eternal Mist) (1974–1989), obtained from Shadywell breeder Clive Taylor, was the first Golden in Canada to earn those combined titles.

When her second Golden arrived at seven weeks of age from breeders Mike and Val Ducross, Frances's goals were already set: conformation and obedience trial championships, a Tracking Dog Excellent and a Working

Certificate Excellent. "Bracken," Ch., OTCh. Ambertrail's Dreamweaver UDTX, WCX (Am-Can. Ch. Ambertrail's Flatbush Flanagan CD ex Ch., OTCh. Val's Dolly UD, WC) turned out to be a natural, and scored another Canadian first when she accomplished all of those goals. Along the way she also won High in Trials, a *Dog World* award, and in 1986 and 1987 received the GRCC J.P. Crawley award for Grand Champion Golden Retriever, an award for outstanding achievements in all fields of competition.

In Ontario, Shirley Goodman's Carolee Goldens have been making GRCC history for 25 years. From a limited breeding program of one or two litters a year, Shirley has bred many show champions, including Specialty winners with achievements in obedience and the field, High-in-Trial obedience Goldens, and excellent hunting and home companions.

A fierce advocate of the multi-purpose Golden, Shirley realized a breeder's dream in 1981 when Ch., FTCh.-AFTCh., Carolee's Something Special 2nd CDX, WCX Am. CD, WCX. (Ch. H.G.L.'s Golden Pine Gibson Solo Am-Can. CD, WC ex Ch. Carolee's Cafe Au Lait Am-Can. CD, WC), (1977-1990), earned his dual championship. "Bumper" was Canada's fifth dual champion, and the first to achieve dual status since 1960; only four other Goldens had accomplished this extraordinary feat.

A dual retriever championship is as prized in

"Calla's" daughter, **Can. Ch. Oriana A Capella Can. CDX, WCI, TD, Am. CD, TD, WC, (HOF, OD)** by Am-Can. Ch. Beckwith's Viking for Dasu UD, Can. CD. Owned by Barrie and Ainslie Mills and Eileen Battley, "Megan" is also an Outstanding Dam, having produced seven champions and two obedience champions from her first litter. Photo by Linda Lindt.

Canada as in the United States. It takes an exceptional animal, a dedicated and goal-oriented owner, and a very special something between the two of them. Bumper's owner, George Stewart of Ontario, apparently had that touch . . . he handled Bumper through each of his bench, field and obedience titles.

George finished Bumper's championship at 17 months, then quickly changed into his field

Am-Can. Ch. Gretchen's Chivas Regal CDX (OS, HOF) "Turk," owned by Byron and Anne Brown, Campbell River, B.C. This outstanding Golden collected more Hall of Fame points during his six-year show career than any other Golden in Canada through 1990. His true showman attitude coupled with his exceptional movement helped propel him to the top. Turk's last time in the show ring was at the 1988 GRCA National Specialty where he went second in the Veterans Dog Class.

attire to get serious about their field career. By 1981 Bumper was placing consistently in the major stakes, still collecting a bench award or two as time allowed. In June 1981 Bumper finally claimed that big blue-ribbon first to complete his field championship.

Shirley's next frontrunner, Ch. Beckwith's Carolee's Gamble (Am-Can. Ch. Beckwith's Justatuckerbear ex Am-Can. Ch. Beckwith's Whirlaway Dust) was purchased from Ludell Beckwith in 1986 at seven weeks of age. In Toronto in November 1990, Gamble thrilled the spectators with a Best in Show win over a 1,000-dog entry. Gamble also visits two major Toronto hospitals with a Pets in Therapy program. Shirley said his temperament is superb, and he is especially good with the disabled.

Ontario is also home to Clint and Vera McEvoy of Gloucester, welcome and familiar faces in the Canadian dog obedience world.

Dedicated to helping dog owners help their dogs, the McEvoys have trained over 10,000 dogs in classes for all levels of obedience since 1970. Between students and classes, they have succeeded in training five of their own Golden Retrievers to obedience-trial championships, with all five placing in Canada's top-ranked obedience dogs every year.

Clint's OTCh. Shadywell Mr. Rip WC, Am. CDX (1971-1981) and OTCh. Shadywell Kalon Kimberlin, Bda. CDX, Am. CD (1980-1984) were All-Breed winners in 1979 and 1983 and earned top-ten placings 12 times. From 1979 through 1987, the McEvoy Goldens claimed Canada's top obedience Golden Retriever eight times, placed Number One *and* Number Two twice, and placed in the top three 13 times.

In 1987, Clint's OTCh. Taygold Elsa Am-Bda. CD (1983-1990) was Canada's Number One Obedience Golden. She was ranked Number Two Obedience Golden in 1988, and Number Three in 1989.

But perhaps Elsa's greatest accomplishment was outside the obedience ring. Every year the McEvoy Goldens give obedience demonstrations for nursing and retirement homes, schools and centers for handicapped children and adults and other groups. Elsa visited over 100 institutions during her short life. Clint would often look around and there would be Elsa, leaning against a wheelchair or nuzzling a wrinkled hand. She blessed everyone who met her with a wagging tail and a quiet sense of knowing who most needed her attention and affection.

Quebec holds the distinction of being home to Canada's Number One All-Breed obedience dog, Golden Retriever OTCh. Sandy 9ieme (French for 9th), (Cidor Champ Sooner CDX ex Chanel-Daisy), bred by Denis Belhumeyr and owned by Rosanne Chayer of Pointe-Fortune. In 1986 Sandy shattered Canada's previous record of 637 points accumulated in one year by earning 1,095 points! That memorable year she competed in 101 Open B and Utility classes, with 24 Open High-in-Trials and four in Utility.

Her path to fame and glory began in 1984 with a CD and a litter of eight puppies, then a CDX and UD in 1985, with two *Dog World* awards, for Utility and for earning all three degrees in nine consecutive trials.

At ten years old, Sandy retired from competition to swim all summer and spend her winters as Rosanne's number one bed-and-foot warmer and best friend.

Ch. Beckwith's Carolee's Gamble, bred by Ludell Beckwith and owned by Shirley Goodman. Shown here with his handler Alan Goodman going Best in Show at the Caledon KC Show in Toronto in 1990.

Clint and Vera McEvoy shown here winning back-to-back High in Trials with **OTCh. Taygold Elsa Am-Bda. CD**, and **Can-Bda. OTCh. Shadywell Pride of Dan Am. CDX.** Elsa also won a Memorial Challenge trophy.

This page: **Ch., OTCh. Ambertrail's Dreamweaver UDTX, WCX** (Am-Can. Ch. Ambertrail's Flatbush Flanagan CD ex OTCh. Val's Dolly UD, WC) bred by Mike and Val Ducross, owned and trained by Frances Walker, was the first Canadian Golden to earn those combined titles, and she did it in grand style, with first placements, High in Trials and a *Dog World* award. She was the recipient of the GRCC 1986 and 1987 J. P. Crawley Memorial trophy for the Grand Champion Golden Retriever for outstanding achievements in all fields of competition.

Megan as a pup…looks like a winner already!

An Oriana Golden birthday party. When **Megan** turned ten on May 11, 1991, three litter-brothers and several of her kids turned out to help her celebrate. The birthday girl is center, third from left.

Can. Ch. Legend's Pride of Madera, "Bailey," bred by Catherine Boches and owned by Vicki Rathbun. Bailey lives in the U.S.—it is not too uncommon for American dogs to gain Canadian titles before finishing their American ones.

Ch. Freule Dutch Van Jalhay CD, WC at the 1980 GRCC National Specialty taking Best Brood Bitch, with two of her daughters, **Ch. Jalhay River Lady** and **Van Jalhay's Royal Dutch Mocha**. Joseph and Philo Jalhay of Ontario, Canada, owners.

Meet **"Morgan"** owned and trained by Frances Walker, Dartmouth, Nova Scotia. Morgan is officially **Ch. OTCh. Cedarcroft Nature Boy UDTX, WC** (Ch. Rancher of Yeo ex Shadywell Eternal Mist) (1976–1989) was the first Golden in Canada to earn all of those titles.

Meana and **Machi**. "…whither thou goest, mom."

CANADIAN FIELD TRIAL GOLDENS

Canadian retriever field trials are identical to those in the United States, except that, as mandated by Canadian law, only dead birds are allowed to be used at any trial. The Junior stake is the same as the U.S. Derby stake, that is, for dogs under two years of age. Placements earn the same number of points as in American trials, with the Certificate of Merit (CM) being the equivalent of the American Judges' Award of Merit (JAM).

Canadian field champions running trials in 1990 were bitches, and the ones who had been bred proved they were also worth their weight in pups.

In Ontario, FTCh-AFTCh Brasdor's Razzl Dazzl AFC Smoke'n Red Devil ex FC Windbreaker's Razzmatazz, bred by Pat DeNardo and owned by Dr. Tom Glen, took the lead by winning the Canadian National Amateur Championship Stake at Kamloops, B.C. in July 1991. She is the second Golden and only female to win a National in Canada since CNFCh.– AFTCh.–AFC

FTCh.-AFTCh., OTCh. Kipp's Cotton Jenny in 1990 was the only living Golden female in North America to claim championships in both field and obedience. She was bred by her owner, Ron Bischke of Lethridge, Alberta, was owner-trained and handled to all of her titles. She has qualified for every Canadian National since 1985. Ron feels that many of Jenny's obedience exercises provided a sound basis for her advanced field training. Jenny is a full-time house dog and is hunted on everything from geese to pheasants.

A number of American field trialers run the Canadian trial circuit, and approximately half the entries in the annual Canadian National Open and Amateur Field Trial Championship Stakes are U.S. dogs. Only one placement is required to qualify for a Canadian National; a dog must earn a first, second, third or fourth place, compared to the U.S. requirement of one first place and two additional points.

The male retriever usually dominates the field trial scene, but in Canada, the ladies of the '80s have outrun most of the boys. The majority of

Oakcreek's Van Cleve's win in 1952. The Canadian National Amateur is a new event, added to the Canadian agenda in 1988.

Razz was ranked among the top three Canadian field Goldens in 1990. She claimed both of her field titles as a three-year-old, the youngest Golden in Canada ever to earn both titles. In 1988 Razz was Canada's High Point Amateur dog with 11 points and placed second in Open and Amateur points in 1989. Through 1990 she had accumulated over 40 combined Open and Amateur points. Bred once to Shurmark's Split Decision***,

From a duck blind or a field trial blind, **FTCh.-AFTCh. Barty's Sunshine Express** will find it and retrieve it. Through 1990 she had accumulated 28½ Open and Amateur Lifetime points, and has qualified for the Canadian National every year since 1985. A superior hunting partner, "Sunny" also starred with Burt Reynolds and Cliff Robertson in a pheasant hunting scene in the 1986 movie, *Malone*. Bred by Brian Pratt and owned by Dennis and Linda Daley, Prince George, B.C.

who became FTCh.–AFTCh. in 1991, five of her eight puppies in 1990 amassed over 75 Junior or Derby points.

Razz has been trained and handled by Dave Thompson of Nilak Kennels, but plays the part of house dog when at home with Tom. Together she and Tom have bagged over 100 geese, 200-plus ducks, and countless pheasant and grouse. Tom said despite her talent, even after winning the National, her most outstanding quality is still her tremendous loyalty; she is a true companion and best friend.

Another female, FTCh–AFTCh, Can. OTCh. Kipp's Cotton Jenny, (NAFC–FC Topbrass Cotton ex FTCh. Windbreaker's Khaki Kipp CDX) earned all of her titles at the hand of her owner Ron Bischke of Alberta. As a Junior dog she was

CNAFC-FTCh. Brasdor's Razzl Dazzl, bred by Pat DeNardo and owned by Dr. Tom Glen of Maxville, Ontario, made Canadian field-trial history when she won the 1991 Canadian National Amateur Retriever Championship. She is the second Golden Retreiver to win a National, the last being CNFC-AFTCh. AFC Oak Creek's Van Cleve in 1952.

even handled by Ron's ten-year-old daughter to three Junior points and her WC/WCX.

Jenny is the only living Golden bitch in North America to earn both field and obedience championships. By 1990, she had qualified for every Canadian National for five consecutive years, and competed in five Nationals and two National Amateurs. She completed eight series of the 1990 National, just one week after being weaned from her recent litter of pups.

Ron also owns the only Golden male to hold the same combined titles, FTCh.–AFTCh., OTCh. Windbreaker's Bulrush Buddy, AFC Smoke'N Red Devil ex FC Windbreaker's Razzmatazz, bred by Pat DeNardo. Buddy completed his Canadian FTCh.–AFTCh. by winning the Open at the Edmonton trial in 1989. By 1990 he had earned a total of 26 Open points. His obedience career was highlighted by a High-in-Trial with a 198 from the Open B class.

A Buddy son, Aquaterra's Bulrush Bear Am-Can.***, out of Aquaterra's OK Katie, is owned by Ron's training partner, Al LaPlante. Bear placed third on the 1988 All-Breed Derby list and finished his Derby career with 42 points. By 1990 Bear had earned Open placements in both Canada and the U.S. Like his father, Bear has a typical Golden temperament and loves everyone he meets.

Another Canadian Golden female who made field trial headlines during the '80s is FTCh.-AFTCh. Barty's Sunshine Express (AFC Holway Barty ex Kona Sand Pebbles***), owned by Dennis and Linda Daley in Prince George, B.C. "Sunny" was Canada's top Junior Golden bitch in 1983 with 27.5 points. She earned her field championship as a four-year-old in 1986, and finished her AFTCh. in 1987. Sunny is a three-time recipient of the GRCC Frank Morley Memorial trophy for the top Canadian Golden with the most points in licensed field events, a two-time winner of the GRCC Challenge trophy for the top Open field dog, and through 1990 she had qualified for six Canadian Nationals.

Also from British Columbia, another Golden bitch who has distinguished the female of the breed is John Gunn's FTCh.-AFTCh. Osmington Anya (Whistledown Tally ex Eng. FTCh. Treunais Strathcarron Alexa). Retired after the 1988 Canadian National, Anya earned a career total of 75 All-Age points, a record for a Golden Retriever in Canada.

Anya qualified for every Canadian National from 1981 through 1988. She completed eight series at her first National at Williams Lake, B.C., ran through nine series at the '82 National at Winnipeg, and was a finalist at the '83 National

FTCh.-AFCh., OTCh. Kipp's Cotton Jenny shown with Ron Bischke at the 1986 Canadian National Retriever Championship Stake.

at Sudbury. She became a member of the exclusive "double-header" club when she won both the Amateur and Open stakes at the 1982 Kamloops B.C. trial.

John imported Anya in 1977 from English breeder Valentine Cadell. He said willingness and a love of water were her strong points; find a pond half-covered with ice, and she would be in it "doing donuts" to cool off.

In Acton, Ontario, FTCh. Goldendale's Maggie O'Tay (FTCh.-AFTCh. Goldendale's Rufus ex Rideau Riverside Tracy O'Tay) is the only female Canadian field champion completely trained and handled by a female. Maggie was never sent to a professional trainer, and was always run exclusively by her owner Diana Beatty, who admits to being a novice trainer who didn't know what to do or how to do it. She said Maggie took nine years to get her title because it took the dog that long to get her mistress trained. Maggie qualified for and ran the National in Sudbury in 1983 at age five. She was, in Diana's words, her "first, still and always, most wonderful Golden and best friend."

Ron's young field-trial hopeful, Jenny's granddaughter, **Moka**, at home in her family's training fields.

FTCh.-AFTCh. Mioak's Shake'N Jake, bred by Mickey Strandberg and owned by Charles Howard, has qualified for at least one Canadian National every year since 1987. Jake is the sire of FTCh.-AFTCh. Shurmark's Split Decision.

professional trainer, David Thompson, who continues to oversee his career.

Jake is Charlie's first field-trial Golden, and gave him a thrill by qualifying for and finishing the Canadian National Amateur Stake in 1989. Charlie was so excited when Jake returned with the last bird that he patted him and told him he was a "good boy." In Canadian trials you are not allowed to touch your dog until the last test is over and you have left the line . . . and this last test was not over, as there was still an honor. The judge asked Charlie if he would mind finishing the test, but Jake was so excited from the praise that he would not sit down, and stood through the guns and sending of the next dog. Surely a trial worth remembering.

The following year he earned his AFTCh. and took Charlie through seven series of the 1990 Canadian National Amateur. By 1990 he had a amassed a total of 61.5 combined lifetime points. Jake hunts with Charlie in the fall, and enjoys being a full-time house and bed dog when he's not working.

Another field champion picked up his titles in the fast lane. FTCh.–AFTCh. Shurmark's Split Decision, "Sprint" owned by Ambertrail breeders, Mike

FTCh.-AFTCh. Mioak's Shake 'n Jake (FC-AFC Mioak's Main Event ex Mioak's Katie), bred in the U.S. by Mickey Strandberg, is owned by Charles Howard, also of Ontario. Purchased from Mickey as a started dog, Jake placed second on Canada's 1986 All-Breed Junior list. He earned his field championship while only two years old under and Val Ducross of Maxville, Ontario, won an Open, an Amateur, and placed second in another Amateur in 1991 in just three weekends of trialing, earning 13 field points for the year. He topped it off on May 19 with an Open win at the Montreal RC trial in Quebec to claim the coveted titles, FTCh.–AFTCh.

Top: **FTCh.-AFTCh. OTCh. Windbreaker Bulrush Buddy** owned by Ron Bischke *(left)* and his son, **Aquaterra's Bulrush Bear Am-Can.***** (out of Aquaterra's OK Katie***) owned by Al LaPlante. In 1988 Bear earned 41 Derby points, becoming the Number Three Derby Dog in Canada that year.

Bottom: **FTCh. Goldendale's Maggie O'Tay** took nine years to train her owner, Diana Beatty of Acton, Ontario, before she titled. She ran the Canadian National Open in Sudbury in 1983, qualified for the 1987 National Open in Victoria and for her first National Amateur in 1988 at ten years of age.

or female, animal or human. He was bred by Dave and Barbara Beacock, and was sired by FTCh.–AFTCh. Mioak's Shake'N Jake, out of Sun Fire Sure Mark Tess***.

Five other Canadian Goldens who titled during the 1980s were: Dual Ch. and AFTCh. Carolee's Something Special II CDX, WCX, Am. CD, WCX, owned by George Stewart; FTCh. Twin Pine's Donna Lyn Kelly, owned by Rich Condratto; FTCh. Windbreaker's Khaki Kipp, owned by Glen Selwyn; FTCh.-AFTCh. Goldencol Amy's Ginger, owned by Beverly Fowler; and FTCh. Topbrass McCaffrey, owned by Sharon Selwyn.

Additional High-Combined Points Goldens entering 1990 were AFTCh. Anya's Cotton Candy, owned by John Gunn, with 17 points, Shurmark's Split Decision***, owned by Mike and Val Ducross, with 11.5 points, Kiowa's Colorado Sandstorm***, owned by B. Pratt, with nine points, and FTCh.-AFTCh. Goldencol Amy's Ginger, owned by Beverly Fowler, with ten points.

This page: **OTCh. Sandy 9ieme** (French for 9th) topped her obedience career with a record of 1,095 obedience points earned in one year, skyrocketing past the previous record of 637 points. Bred by Denis Belhumeyr, owned and coddled by Roseanne Chayer of Pointe-Fortune, Quebec. *Above:* Sandy scales a ladder in an agility exercise. *Below:* Sandy shows her spectacular style flying over the broad jump.

As a two-year-old "Sprint" was Canada's Top Junior Golden and second Top Junior dog with 48½ points. In 1989 he earned All-Age status with two qualifying firsts, one second, a third and fourth, three CMs, and qualified for the 1989 Canadian National.

Sprint is the dog Mike and Val Ducross have been searching for. He is intense, fast and accurate, with a very competitive spirit in his work, yet he is sweet and easygoing at home, and gets along with anything that moves, male

FTCh.-AFTCh. Shurmark's Split Decision (FTCh.-AFTCh. Mioak's Shake 'n Jake ex Sun Fire Sure Mark Tess***), known appropriately as "Sprint," is owned by Mike and Val Ducross, Maxville, Ontario.

John and **FTCh.-AFTCh. Osmington Anya** ran several Canadian National during Anya's field-trial career. Anya's 75 lifetime All-Age points are still a Canadian record for the breed.

Ch.-OTCh. Val's Dolly***, Am. WC, "Cory," owned by Mike and Val Ducross, Maxville, Ontario. Cory produced many of Canada's top Goldens of the '80s, multiple show and obedience trial champions, including Frances Walker's multi-titled Ambertrail's Dreamweaver, and in the U.S., Barbara Tinker's magnificent record-setting Ambertrail's Bargello Stitch.

367

John Gunn and his first field champion **FTCh.-AFTCh. Swell Duke**, shown after running the Canadian National Championship Stake.

Clint and **OTCh. Kaylon Kimberlin Bda. CDX, Am. CD** take High in Trial at the Lakeshore show in Montreal. Kaylon Kimberlin was the McEvoys' first female Golden; her name means "the beautiful newcomer." Kim was Canada's Number One Obedience Dog in 1983.

Recording another first, Ron Bischke trained and handled **FTCh.-AFTCh., OTCh. Windbreaker's Bulrush Buddy**, bred by Pat DeNardo, to the same titles, making Buddy the only living male in North America to hold those combined titles in 1990. Buddy lives in the house and is hunted on upland game and waterfowl.

Above: **Aus. Ch. Queenlee the Diplomat CD** (Aus. Ch. Billeira Beau ex Aus. Ch. Meykel) bred by Noelene Bolton and owned by Jennifer Farquhar. "Hamish" gained his championship at 16 months old. Two months later he earned his CD in three trials with three first place wins. *Below:* **Aus-N.Z. Ch. Brygolden Oatley Tyrone** (Ch. Balanora Delta Darius UD ex Ch. Brygolden Madonna Mist CD) owned by Mick and Pauline O'Sheehy of New South Wales. "Ty" has nine Royal Challenges, is a multiple All-Breed BIS and specialty winner, a multiple Group winner as well as a Royal Group winner. He is believed to be Australia's highest scoring Challenge Winner, with over 3,400 Challenge points.

Goldens in Australia

The first Golden Retriever in Australia was documented in 1937 with the registration of Grakle of Tone, an import bred by F. Newton-Deakin of Dorset, England. However, there does exist reliable information on two trained field Goldens brought from England to Australia in 1914.

Since that time the Australian Golden population has increased slowly, to 2,910 registered nationally in 1989, small compared to U.S. figures, but large enough to concern those breeders who strive to maintain and improve their own families of Golden Retrievers.

Breed fanciers today support five Golden Retriever clubs, one in each of the five Australian States, some with membership of 400-plus and growing. Each club must operate under the guidance of the Kennel Control State Council, which governs all breeds and reports to the Australian National Kennel Council (ANKC).

Rose Odell, breeder of Strelyna Goldens since 1964, also a founding member of the Golden Retriever Club of Victoria (GRC of V) and a member of the Golden Retriever Club of Queensland, graciously shared the following information about breed activities in Australia today. Rose credited John Lawton, a judge and participant in working trials, and obedience exhibitor Ruth Nichols, for supplying her with much of the information she sent.

Alarmed over the rising popularity of the Golden during the past 20 years, Australian GR clubs strive to educate their members on the do's and don'ts of proper breeding. They emphasize the importance of screening breeding stock for hereditary disease.

Hip dysplasia is a primary concern. The Australian Veterinary Association uses a scoring system to assess hip x-rays submitted to them for evaluation. PRA and von Willebrand's disease are rare; however, the GRC of V secretary reports several cases of epilepsy, apparently in dogs bred by non-members with limited knowledge of hereditary disease who are newcomers to the breed. Cases of poor temperament are few, and most Australian Goldens are friendly with everyone—people and other dogs.

Little change has occurred in the show Golden over recent years, although at the 23rd Annual Championship show of the GRC of V in 1990, the majority of entries appeared to be stockier and shorter in leg. The Best Exhibit and Runner-up in Show were both winners of longer standing:

six-year-old Ch. Tahmero Charming Kazar, bred in Victoria by owners A. and P. Kewish, and Challenge bitch, Ch. Alubyc Autumn Arwen, owned by F. Dyer and P. Heslop.

Points for the title of Australian Champion can be gained only at Championship shows where Challenge Certificates (CC) are awarded. A total of 100 challenge points must be earned under four different judges; five points for the Challenge, plus one point for each dog of the same sex entered for the breed to a total of 25 points per show. A Best in Group earns 25 points, but may not be added to the total already gained in breed judging. There is no Specials class, so titled dogs may continue to compete against the hopefuls and the also-rans.

The road to a field championship is a tougher route. While the abundance of wild game, such as rabbits, ducks and quail, is ideal for training a dog to hunt naturally, there are still only about 20 Goldens seriously working in field trials in Australia.

The first of two Australian field events is the Spaniel and Retriever Trial. It is conducted in the cooler months, June through August, as the dogs are required to work from 7:30 a.m. to 4 or 5 p.m. The game is seasonal, usually wild rabbit or quail, and the terrain consists of rolling hills covered with heavy grasses and coarse vegetation.

At the start of the trial, the names of competing dogs are drawn from a hat in pairs, and a Golden may draw any spaniel or retriever breed to compete against. The handlers, carrying loaded shotguns and walking with the judges, send their dogs forward. The dogs must cast 30 meters ahead and to each side, and the judges critique their air- and ground-scenting abilities. When a dog locates game, he must flush it, then sit immediately and allow the game to run or fly so the handler can raise his gun and shoot. Upon the kill or wound, the dog is sent for the retrieve and is judged for style of find and efficiency of retrieve.

At the shot, the opponent's dog must acknowledge the shot by sitting instantly and remaining steady until called in by its handler. It usually takes four or five finds for the judge to decide which dog to eliminate and which to elevate into the next round. In the last round, the two final dogs run against each other for first place and runner-up.

The Novice stake, which is the first level of the

Spaniel and Retriever Trial, is for dogs who have not yet won a Novice stake or placed first or second in an Open stake. Open stakes are for all Gundogs regardless of title or wins. A Novice first place earns two points, the runner-up, one point. An Open first earns four points, runner-up two points; a Championship first, eight points, and walk-up, with dogs picking up one bird at a time. Dogs must win two Restricted stakes before graduation. In the All-Age stake, a dog must complete three three-bird, 100-meter runs consisting of a double rise and blind, picking up the blind first, then a double blind and mark, any combination, picking up one bird at a time. The

1980s' Australian field trial champion, **RTCh. Arawmai Tangaroa CD** (Strelyna Shenendoah ex Cambronza Genevieve), whelped January 30, 1979. Owned by John Lawton.

the runner-up four points. A total of eight points with one Open win is required for the title of Australian Field Trial Champion.

The second field event called the Retriever Trial, which is open to all breeds of Gundogs, and simulates a typical duck shoot. Trials consist of five stakes with graduated degrees of difficulty and eligibility requirements for the dog. The first level, or Beginners stake, includes two short runs on marks, one across water and one on land over natural obstacles.

The Novice stake has three single-mark runs about 80 meters each, one on land, one across water, and a third in water, with natural obstacles to test marking ability. Dogs must win two Novice stakes before it becomes mandatory to compete at the next level of work.

The Restricted stake includes three two-bird runs of about 80 meters and 90 degrees apart, consisting of a double rise, a mark and blind

All-Age is open to all gundogs from Novice winner to RT Champion, and the winner receives four championship points.

The fifth or Championship stake has five three-bird runs, any combination, judged by two judges. Dogs must win a Restricted or All-Age stake to enter, and the winner earns eight championship points. To become a Retriever Trial Champion, a dog must have earned eight points.

There are few Goldens working in these trials today. Australia claimed her first field trial champion in 1975 when Dual Ch. Sweet Water Courage, owned by David Hands, succeeded in both the field as well as the show ring. The current dual champion, Tiptree Timothy CD, worked by owner John Lawton, is a Courage grandson. "Timmy" is also placing in the Retriever Trials, and the two required wins in the All-Age stake would make him Australia's first triple champion.

FTCh. Ferndarra Game Seeker, (Ch. Leegolden Valley King ex Ferndarra Sea Shanty), whelped March 9, 1986. Bred by J. Dusting, owned and trained by J. W. Lawton of Victoria, Australia.

In Victoria, five Goldens are working in both field and retrieving trials, with FTCh. Ferndarra Game Seeker NRD, another Lawton Golden, earning her title in 1990.

South Australia has about eight Goldens working, with two of them retrieving trial champions; RTCh. Goldberg Arron and RTCh. Goldberg Brookly, both owned and worked by John and Chris Kersley.

Aside from field trials, Goldens have been lighting up Australian obedience rings since 1965 when the ANKC adopted its first set of rules and exercises for obedience trials. They hit the big time in 1974, when two Goldens earned the first UD titles in the breed. The bitch, Ob. Ch. Aspley Golden Lady owned by George Nicholls and trained by his daughter Ruth, after completing her obedience titles through Utility, pressed on with her career, and in 1976 became Australia's first Golden obedience champion when she earned the TD and TDX required to achieve the Ob. Ch. title. In 1990 she was still the only Golden in Victoria to have earned an obedience trial championship.

Lady didn't stop there, however. She went on to compete in retrieving trials, and later added a QC certificate to her list of achievements.

Under ANKC rules, both UD and TDX titles are required for application for an obedience trial champion certificate. Since Lady titled, eight Goldens have earned their UD and we hope to see more. Ob. Ch. Tiptree Timbarra, also owned and trained by Ruth Nicholls, has continued Lady's tradition and has become an Ob. Ch., with a subsequent QC in the field.

In 1988 ANKC launched a new concept for working dogs, gundog obedience. Designed for gundog owners who want to work their dogs, but are not ready or able for trials in field, retrieving or obedience, it offers the zest of competition and provides a stepping stone to greater achievements for the handler and his dog. Tests are held on grassed areas sufficient in size to allow for retrieves of about 50 meters.

The goal is to pass against a standard by gaining an overall score of not less than 75 percent with at least 50 percent in each exercise, similar to the scoring in U.S. hunting tests. A passing dog receives a certificate, and when a dog has gained three passes in Novice tests or won a Novice test, it qualifies to compete in Open Tests. There are also prizes for winners and placements in each event, although no titles are awarded.

The Novice gundog obedience test consists of four tests: In the first three the handler must walk the dog at heel for 20 meters; put the dog on

Dual Ch. Tiptree Timothy CD (Ch. Queenlee Debonair AOC ex Ch. Tiptree Trushka CD) whelped February 15, 1983. A grandson of Australian Dual Champion Sweet Water Courage, "Timmy" was bred by James Moore and is owned by John Lawton of Victoria.

Rose Odell's "veterinary-assistant" Golden, "Smuggler," **Ch. Strelyna Shikaree** (Gyrima Xcliver Sunbronze ex Strelyna Sierra Star), in April 1990, at nine years old.

that combines tracking and retrieving. Goldens have placed as winners in every gundog obedience trial held thus far.

GRC of V also maintains a highly successful Recovery Service which finds homes for abandoned and neglected Goldens, and more recently, for those who sadly outgrow their welcome once they are fully grown. Club members provide homes and loving care for even the most difficult or hopeless cases during the interim periods of assessment and veterinary care, and they proudly boast that in 15 years only two Goldens have been euthanized. There have been some difficult cases when even the vet has been doubtful about recovery, but tender nursing has restored these Goldens back to health, and the dogs have finished their years knowing about love.

Australia also has its own share of Golden tales that warm the heart and stir the mind. Breeder Rose Odell told of Sean, an obedience-trained Golden, firm on the command to "stay" whenever his mistress went into a shop. Except for that one day when she was shocked to see him fly at her through the open door of the furniture store, knocking her soundly to the ground . . . as a huge roll of linoleum fell from the

sit or down, then walk 20 paces away and call the dog to heel; again sit or down the dog, move 20 paces, but stop the dog during the recall before ordering the dog to heel. The fourth test, for breeds other than setters or pointers, is a 50-meter, single-marked retrieve with a shot fired at the game while it is airborne. The dog is sent to retrieve and should return to deliver in front of the handler.

The Open gundog test repeats the first three Novice tests, with some added difficulty, adds a fourth retrieving test that combines a double retrieve with a blind, and a fifth test

Ch. Goldsirius Desert Sheik (Gaylon Aristocrat/UK import ex Goldsirius Bubbles) shown here with handler Melissa Aspinall. Melissa was the Victoria State Top Junior Showman in 1988 and the Melbourne Royal Top Junior Handler in 1989.

Aus. Ch. Jindabo Gentle Tell (Aus. Ch. Goldog Alpine Columbo ex Aus. Ch. Goldog Alpine Serenade), owned by Mr. and Mrs. R. Hawes and handled by V. and W. Pearson of Jindabo Kennels, went Best of Breed at the Royal Melbourne Show in 1990.

shelf directly above where she had been standing. Had Sean seen that movement above his mistress, or was it instinct that told him she was in danger?

Then there was Oscar, over-indulged in every way, who had a standing order at the butcher for his morning breakfast bone. Each morning when the butcher heard the familiar thump against his door, he opened it and handed Oscar his paperbound delicacy. The dog then carried it home, where his owner unwrapped and presented it to the very patient Oscar. The aging butcher sold his shop, but stayed on with the new owner for a bit. Upon hearing Oscar's thump, the new proprietor was surprised to see a Golden seated at the door. Upon instruction, he gave Oscar the fresh meat bone set aside for him, but the dog promptly spit it out and sat there. The old butcher scolded, "You can't expect him to take it when it's not been wrapped." Oscar finally accepted the wrapped package, and with a wag of his tail, set off for home.

Rose describes her own Golden, Smuggler, as

the dog who beat her vet at his own game. Rose's 14-year-old bitch Shari had developed a large hematoma on her ear flap, and, worried about the effect of anesthesia at Shari's advanced age, Rose asked her vet about alternatives to surgery. The vet had none, but suggested they wait about two weeks until the swollen mass was fully ripe to better ensure the success of surgical removal.

Back at home, Smuggler had his own ideas and began to gently lick the old dog's ear. At first Rose scolded him, but then decided to let the old bitch do the chiding, while Rose monitored the ear for further damage. Under Smuggler's gentle massage, the ear seemed to improve, and when the two week appointment arrived, Shari's ear was completely normal. Her unbelieving vet requested they keep the cure a secret lest Smuggler put him out of a job. Then he commented on the gentleness of the Golden Retriever breed as a whole. Of course, Rose reminded, that's something we've all learned from the Golden teachers in our own lives.

Top left: **Aus. Ch. Tahmero Golden Duke** (Aus. Ch. Sunlodge Hereo ex Aus. Ch. Danoi Kasia CD), owned by Tahmero Kennels of Victoria.

Top right: **Aus. Ch. Miaura Moon Shadow** (Aus. Ch. Carlsden Sansoo Bobby ex Aus. Ch. Miaura Candy Callunar), bred by W. Dalton, owned by Seawye Kennels.

Middle left: **Aus. Ch. Tahmero Golden Charmer** (Aus. Ch. Sunlodge Hero ex Aus. Ch. Danoi Kasia CD), bred by A. and P. Kenish of Victoria.

Middle right: **Aus. Ch. Tahmero Charming Cujo** (Gaylon Aristocrat ex Aus. Ch. Tahmero Golden Charmer), bred by the Kenishes.

Left: **Aus. Ch. Goldog Alpine Columbo** (Aus. Ch. Goldog Alpine Giles ex Aus. Ch. Goldog Alpine Heather), owned by Jindabo Kennels in Victoria. Columbo is a multi-Best-in-Show winner and in 1984 took the GRC Dog Challenge Winners award.

Above: **Aus. Ch. Goldog Alpine Maestro** (Aus. Ch. Glenessa Ingot ex Aus. Ch. Gunarryn Anthia), owned by Jindabo Kennels. Maestro's wins include—1985: GRC Champ. Show—Best Intermediate Dog, 1983: GRC Puppy Of The Year, 1983: Melbourne Dog Club—Best In Parade, 1984: Frankston & Peninsula—Best In Parade, and 1990: GRC Champ. Show—Best Veteran Dog and multiple Best In Show winner.
Below: **Aus. Ch. Jindabo Gentle Able**, (Aus. Ch. Goldog Alpine Columbo ex Aus. Ch. Goldog Alpine Serenade) owned by Jindabo Kennels. Able won the 1987 Melbourne Royal—Reserve Challenge Dog and 1988 GRC Champ. Show— Best Intermediate in Show.

New Zealand's top field trial dog in his day, **Moorfield Gambit QC, CDX** (Ch. Moorfield Ambros QC ex Moorfield Emma QC) (1978–1988), owned by Miriam Dobson of Christchurch. During his career Gambit earned three field trial Challenge Certificates (All-Breed wins), 19 All-Breed championship placings and 22 placings in Retriever Championships, with a total of 142 field trial awards in nine years of competition, more than any other Golden in New Zealand since 1973.

Goldens in New Zealand

In New Zealand the Golden Retriever is bred against the English standard for the breed and judged accordingly. Breeders in that country emphasize their Goldens are quite different from the U.S. Golden, who would not be given a second look in the New Zealand, Australian or English breed rings.

Barbara Dick of Charterhall Golden Retrievers in Auckland has judged in the breed ring since 1985 and recently passed the examination for championship judging status in Gundogs. She states that while New Zealand Golden show champions speak for the breed, their breeders feel the true quality of the dog is in the progeny it leaves. In New Zealand there is little future for a Best-in-Show winner that has no puppies following at its heels.

Barbara said that Goldens in New Zealand "are all one breed—no three-way splits here." Breeders also will not tolerate bad temperaments, and quickly remove any breeding stock with poor or unstable temperaments.

The first noteworthy Charterhall litter was whelped in 1977, but the real power behind the name arrived in 1982 when Barbara traveled to England to import Pinecrest Trooper. Trooper has sired 180 puppies in his stud career and has champion progeny in New Zealand, Australia and the United States.

In Christchurch, Miriam Dobson with Moorfield Goldens is one of only two women ever appointed as Approved Start Field Trial Judge. Miriam explained that New Zealand has two types of field trials at the championship level for retrievers, including the Labrador, Golden, Curly-Coat and Flat-Coat, with the Labrador most commonly used. In the Retriever Championship, for retrievers only, game must be retrieved over land and water.

In the All-Breed Championship, open to any breed of Gundog, all dogs are expected to retrieve over water. The land section is a spaniel-type test where dogs must range over ground and retrieve planted dead game as well as live pigeons flushed from electric traps. Blank shot is fired at the pigeon's release, as New Zealand has very strict live game laws which prohibit the shooting of live game.

The All-Breed Championship Trial is very difficult, and few dogs of any breed make the grade.

Barbara Dick and some of her Charterhall team. Front, **Pinecrest Trooper**; left to right, Trooper's 15-month-old granddaughter, **Cariston Clair de Lune**; Trooper son, 10-month-old **Vanrose Welcome Home**, and another grandson, 11-month-old **McIlroy Hexachord.**

Since 1954 only six Golden Retrievers have earned their field trial championships in New Zealand.

Miriam's Moorfield Gambit QC, CDX (Ch. Moorfield Ambros QC. ex Moorfield Elma QC), 1978–1988, was one of only nine Golden field trial Challenge Certificate winners (All-Breed wins) since 1954. Gambit was New Zealand's top field-trial Golden, amassing three CCs, 19 All-Breed Championship placings, and 22 placings in Retriever Championships, with a total of 142 field-trial awards in his nine-year career, more than any other Golden since 1973. Although field

379

trialing leaves time for little else, Gambit also managed to become a Test C obedience dog during his field career.

Miriam recalls one of Gambit's greatest field achievements, in 1988, shortly after he was diagnosed with bone-marrow cancer. Already entered in the New Zealand All-Breed Team Championship stake, Miriam was not permitted to withdraw, and Gambit was never one to complain. Despite his illness, he plunged into the trial and showed the heart that made him such a superb field-trial contender. In a final 70-meter swim, he battled high winds, with heavy waves breaking over his head, to complete a swim to an island on the lake. He was exhausted, but he was doing what he loved best. Of the 70 entries, only 20 dogs completed this test, and Gambit's was the only team with all dogs finishing. He worked until the week before he died.

Gambit was a credit to Ambros, his sire, who had also been an Open field-trial winner and placer in All-Breed Retriever Championship stakes, a Best-in-Show Golden, and winner of the New Zealand Golden Retriever Club Best Dual-Purpose Dog award for seven consecutive years. Further preserving the tradition of retriever excellence, Gambit's son, Moorfield Larikan QC, CDX, is a third-generation overachiever and Miriam's current challenge and field-trial companion.

Miriam has also bred two obedience champions, Ob. Ch. Moorfield Holly QC, CDX, and Ch., Ob. Ch. Moorfield Dwayne QC, CDX., who is the only show and obedience champion in New Zealand. Only about 15 New Zealand Goldens have earned their championships in obedience.

Sally and Peter Scales with Banbury Goldens in Christchurch also believe in the dual-purpose Golden. Their "Nick," Ch. Banbury's Gingerbread Boy QC, CDX, (Ch. Markman Aaron QC ex Ch. Samantha of Reneg'at QC, CDX), 1979-1990, did it all for them. A multi-Group and Best-in-Show winner and obedience qualifier, Nick reached his career highlight in 1988 by winning

Charterhall English import, **Pinecrest Trooper,** owned by Barbara Dick of Auckland, New Zealand. Born July 12, 1982, Trooper has sired over 180 puppies, among them multiple Best-in-Show winner, Ch. Charterhall Home Rule (dam: Charterhall Enigma); another multiple Best-in-Show winner, N.Z. Ch. Charterhall Gaelic Gold (dam: Charterhall Enigma); Am. Ch. Charterhall Ivanhoe (dam: Charterhall Baroness); Am. Ch. Charterhall Titan (dam: Tamarley Silver Fern—U.K. import). Although not a big winner in the show ring, Trooper has passed on his fine attributes of dark pigment, good bone and deep body, as well as his "soppy" temperament.

Ch. Charterhall Gaelic Gold, "Sean," (Pinecrest Trooper ex Charterhall Enigma) bred by Barbara Dick and owned by Margaret and David Hean, is proof of Trooper's great strength as a sire. Sean took Best-in-Show awards at the 1989 Auckland and Southern Golden Retreiver Club shows, as well as Best-in-Show awards at Gundog and All-Breed Championship shows. In 1990 he pressed on, winning two more Best-in-Show and four Reserve Best-in-Show awards. The Heans are proudest of Sean's accomplishments as a sire. To date he has produced six champions, Group and in-show winners, 13 Challenge winners and has offspring working in obedience and the field. His production record has challenged Jamie's, and Sean was runner-up stud dog in 1988 and 1989. Margaret said his absolute best, however, is as a true Golden gentleman who gives his all just to please.

the All-Breed Retriever Championship Trial at the Championship trial hosted by the Southern Golden Retriever Club. He became the third Golden All-Breed winner in 17 years and joined that select group of nine Challenge Certificate Golden Retrievers.

In Wellington at Speyside Golden Retrievers, Pat Grieg agrees the majority of New Zealand breeders are still trying their best to breed pups who can perform in show, field and/or obedience, whichever discipline interests the new owner.

Pat's foundation bitch, Ob. Ch. Leacroft Golden CDX, (Aus-N.Z. Ch. Leacroft Logan ex Ch. Moorfield Emma), "Isla," proved the breed's endurance and eternal eagerness to work when she earned her obedience championship at eight and one-half years of age and after two litters of pups. Not one to rest on her laurels, she later won a Test C at the New Zealand Dog Assembly in 1990, beating all the best obedience dogs in the country.

Isla subscribes to the New Zealand breeder philosophy on quality offspring. Of her nine puppies, two are breed champions with CDX titles, another has breed challenges and obedience placements, and one has produced pups who boast breed challenges, have obedience titles and work in field trials.

Many New Zealand breeders promote the dual-purpose Golden by striving for a Qualifying Certificate (QC) during their dog's show or working

"Jamie," **N. Z. Ch. Lawnwoods Nocturn** (U.K. import) (Eng. Ch. Westley Munro of Nortonwood ex Lawnwoods Careless Rapture), one of the Heans' Goldens, retired from his show career to become an outstanding sire. His offspring boast one Grand Champion son and Grand Champion grandson as well as nine champion get, 22 challenge winners and many show and group winners. Jamie's kids also work successfully as shooting dogs, and he is the sire of the first New Zealand-bred Golden to earn a CD in the United States. His progeny also work well in New Zealand obedience and two have qualified for their CDX titles. Small wonder Jamie was Stud Dog of the year in 1987, 1988 and 1989.

career. A QC is earned during actual field-trial competition, and the dog must complete a two-bird Heel Retrieve over land and water with a minimum score of 75 percent in each section. The QC indicates the dog can retrieve game tenderly over land and water and is steady to shot.

At Arangold in Christchurch, Margaret and David Hean are the proud owners of the only Grand Champion Golden bitch in New Zealand. Additionally, Grand Champion Happy Donagh of Monterey QC (Ch. Markman Aaron QC ex Ch. Vanrose Morning Sun) is the only Golden Retriever Grand Champion to also hold a Qualifying Certificate as a working gundog.

In New Zealand eight Challenge Certificates (wins) are required to make up a show champion. In 1989 the New Zealand Kennel Club added the title of Grand Champion, requiring three All-Breed Best-in-Show awards under three different judges, and 50 Challenge Certificates, with one of those earned after January 1, 1988.

Donagh had retired from competition in 1986 after taking three consecutive Best-in-Show awards. In 1989, enticed by the new Kennel Club title, Donagh happily returned to the ring at almost ten years of age.

As always, she gave her very best, and culminated her career in true Golden style at the March 1989 Buller Championship Show. She scooped up the Bitch Challenge, Best of Breed, Best Gundog and then the Grand Champion frosting, Best-in-Show. Donagh has since re-retired and spends her time snoozing in the sun at Arangold.

Margaret's Golden boys have also made a name for Arangold. Their Ch. Lawnwoods Nocturn, (Eng.Ch. Westley Munro of Nortonwood ex Lawnwood's Careless Rapture), "Jamie," a U.K. import, has been a consistent top stud-dog winner, with his progeny winning the largest number of Challenge Certificates in 1987, 1988, 1989 and 1990. Her younger Golden, Ch. Charterhall Gaelic Gold, (Pinecrest Trooper ex Charterhall Enigma), "Sean," was runner-up stud dog to Jamie in 1988 and 1989, and in 1990 captured two Best-In-Show and four Reserve Best-in-Show awards.

Seven years old, Sean continues to show, while the retired Jamie oversees his career and comes out for an occasional veteran's parade.

Above: **Grand Champion Happy Donagh of Monterey QC**. (Ch. Markman Aaron QC ex Ch. Vanrose Morning Sun) is the only Golden Retriever Grand Champion bitch in New Zealand, and the only Golden Grand Champion to hold a Qualifying Certificate as a working gundog. In true "grand" Golden style, she earned her prestigious title at almost ten years of age, bringing her tally to nine Best-in-Show awards and 123 Challenges. Donagh's special qualities will live on in her progeny; of 36 offspring, 12 are Challenge winners, 10 are Group winners, and three have claimed All-Breed Best-in-Show awards. Owned and loved by Margaret and David Hean, Christchurch, N.Z. *Below:* Donagh is a credit to her sire, **Ch. Markman Aaron QC** (Ch. Falconhurst Anton ex Strathcarron Goddess), also owned by the Heans. Aaron is one of the most influential sires in New Zealand, having produced seven champions and 11 Challenge winners as well as the record-setting Donagh. He also sired Ch. Banbury's Gingerbread Boy QC, 1988 All-Breed Championship field trial winner. Six more offspring hold field trial Qualifying Certificates. During his own career, Aaron amassed 74 Challenge Certificates, achieved Open class status in field trials and was an outstanding rough shooting dog. He is photographed here at age 12-and-one-half-years-old.

Ch. McIlroy Alto Rhapsody CDX, owned by Barbara Kearney-Brown, is triple-purpose Golden who competes in all three specialties. "Sherry" qualified for her CDX by two years of age, is an Open field trialist, and has won three Challenges and two Reserve-in-Shows at the Golden Retriever Club specialty shows in 1987, 1988 and 1989. She is the dam of Ch. McIlroy La Boheme, a Best-in-Show and Best-of-Breed winner, and granddam of field trialist Ch. McIlroy Choral Symphony CDX.

Bottom left: **Banbury's Morning Glory QC, CDX.** (Ch. Keidrych of St. Germain ex Ch. Amberline Jemima QC, CDX), bred and owned by Sally and Peter Scales, Christchurch, New Zealand. At five years old, "Katy" had captured six Show Challenge Certificates and a Best Gundog Group. Having earned her CDX, she is currently working well in All-Breed and Retriever Championship field trials, having placed in both.

Bottom right: **Banbury's Dandy Lion** (Ch. Banbury's Gingerbread Boy QC, CDX ex Banbury's Morning Glory QC, CDX), 1989, bred and owned by the Scales. "Tim" has won six Puppy Championship field trials, and at his first Novice Obedience Championship, won handily with 190 (out of 200) points.

Above: **Gambit** on the Cornhill Shield Team at the Jubilee New Zealand All-Breed Championship in 1986; Gambit and his Labrador friends claimed Top Team status. *Below:* **Ch. Banbury's Gingerbread Boy QC, CDX**. (1979–1990) (Ch. Markman Aaron QC ex Ch. Samantha of Reneg'at QC, CDX) bred and owned by Sally and Peter Scales of Christchurch, New Zealand. "Nick" won the Retriever All-Breed Championship at the field trial championship trial hosted by the Southern Golden Retriever Club in 1988, thus gaining a field trial Challenge Certificate…one of only three Goldens to do so in New Zealand in nearly two decades. A true dual-purpose Golden, Nick is also a multi-Group winner, and went Best-in-Show at a Southern Golden Retriever Club Specialty. He has been runner-up at many other Championship field trials, and was Top Dog at both the All-Breed and Retriever Championship trials at Otago in 1988.

Dutch Ch. Aradias Apricot Whirl, "Lady," (Ch. Stolford Likely Lad ex Bryandstown Serenade). The foundation bitch at Henri and Thea Dekkers' v/h Wiekse Veld Kennel in Holland. Lady was BIS at the Golden Retriever Club Championship show in 1985. She has collected nine CCs and RCCs, and has passed her superior qualities on to her get, with several consistently placing at Championship shows.

Goldens on the Continent

SWEDEN

The popularity of the Scandanavian Golden Retriever has advanced rapidly during the past two decades, and many U.S. breeders are importing Goldens from Sweden and her sister countries to expand and improve their own lines. The pedigrees resulting from the breeding of those Goldens into American lines include Goldens who have accomplished a great deal in their homeland, but about whom little is known in the United States.

Henric Frykstrand, a Scandanavian championship judge who has bred Golden Retrievers for 25 years under the Dewmist kennel prefix, has written a book about the breed in Sweden and has supplied many authors with historical information about Goldens in his country. His account of the breed in Sweden, Norway, Finland and Denmark follows, and may shed some light on 1990 pedigrees that include Goldens imported from those countries. The author extends her deepest appreciation to Henric for his valuable contribution to these pages on the international Golden Retriever.

The foundation of the Golden Retriever in Sweden began in earnest in 1950 when Borghalla kennels imported Barthill Fanny, in whelp to Strelly Starlight, from the United Kingdom. A second U.K. Golden, Ch. Stubblesdown Tinker, was imported and used by Hedetorpet kennel. Count Leo of Little Compton, born in 1954 at Apport kennel, whose foundation bitch came from Borghalla, joined these two Goldens to lay the 1950's groundwork for the Swedish Golden Retriever.

In the late 1950s, Stubblesdown Begay was imported to Sweden in whelp to FTCh. Stubblesdown Larry. From their litter of six pups, Apports Larry Jr. and Ch. Apports Joy made important contributions to the further development of the breed. Later Ch. Apports Larry II also became a prominent stud dog in his own day.

In 1960 Hedetorpet kennel imported an English Golden (from the Netherlands), Int. Ch. Azor v d Kruidberg, who was popularly used along the west coast of Sweden. Hedetorpet mated Azor to another of their imports, Int. Ch. Whamstead Jess, producing Int. Ch. Hedetorpets Honey, who was a top winner in her day.

At Sandemar kennel, one of Larry's daughters,

Int. Ch. Sandemar's Azurra, became the Sandemar foundation bitch as well as the first bitch to finish. Sandemar also imported Int. Ch. Stubblesdown Shaun and Stubblesdown Argus, who continued to produce the type already established by earlier imports.

More Golden imports arrived during the mid-60s. At Sandemar, Int. Ch. Glenessa Waterbird of Stenbury produced a somewhat different type of offspring, many of whom went on to continue his line. His best known daughter, Sandemar's W. Grandezza, became the first bitch to gain the title of Int. and Scan. Champion.

Another famous U.K. import joined the Sandemar Goldens, Ch. Cabus Clipper, who was a younger brother to Christopher Caleidoscope. Cabus is also well known for one of his famous daughters, Int. Ch. Francisca.

Imported from Denmark, Ch. Wessex Timmy Tinker sired many champions of yet a different type. Bred to Joy, he produced the famous Int. Ch. Apports Country Boy, and a winning daughter, Int. Ch. Daisy, who was later one of the top ten dogs of all breeds in 1969 with numerous Group and BIS awards.

The Hedetorpet imports continued to impact the breed through the 1960s. Int. Ch. Stolford Seabird went BIS in Gothenburg in 1965, but unfortunately died at the age of four. His sister, Stolford Larkspur, became a great brood bitch, and her best known daughter, Int. Ch., FTCh. Hedetorpets Bijou, became the first bitch to win that title.

Hedetorpet enjoyed more success with Int. Ch., FTCh. Coxy, whose career on the bench and in the field earned him Sweden's top awards for Dog of the Year in 1972 and 1973. As a sire, Coxy contributed to champions in all categories. Most of the champions made up at Hedetorpet also had won their field trial awards.

English imports also marked the foundation of kennel Twinkle. Golden Wings of Petrina, a Tallyrand daughter, produced well for Twinkle, with winners like Twinkle Gentle Granny, and littermates Twinkle Night Cap and New Chapter. They were inspiration for Petrina's Magic Moment, a later import from the United Kingdom.

In the late 1960s, Apport kennel imported from Denmark, Goldstone Es, a son of Int. Ch. Honeyat the Viking, whose stud career heavily influenced several large kennels in Sweden.

Two more important dogs of the '60s' era came from Sandemar: Ch. Glenessa Helmsman, a BIS winner at the prestigious Stockholm Show in 1968, and Int. Ch. Synspur Iona, who won her way to Top Dog of the Year in 1970 with many BIS awards.

Sandemar later imported two famous dogs of interest. In 1971 they brought in Ch. Calpih of Yeo, whose importance as a stud dog was obvious through his many titled offspring. Ch. Glenavis Barman came to Sandemar in 1974 and became a top winner throughout his lifetime. His good looks and strong personality earned him top awards as a veteran, and in 1976 he was a contender for Top Dog of the Year.

In 1971 kennel Dainty imported Davern Fergus, who was a brother to Ch. Davern Figaro. Fergus became a valuable stud dog, especially in the south of Sweden.

Imported from the United Kingdom, **Moorquest Mandarin** (Ch. Meant to be at Moorquest ex Moorquest Maid of Honour) bred by Shirley Crick, United Kingdom, imported and owned by Chantal LeFeivre, Switzerland.

Other important imports at Dainty were Ch. Alseras Capello, a BIS winner and runner-up for Top Dog of the Year in 1981. Littermates Ch. Stenbury Sealord and Ch. Stenbury Seamusic also did a great deal of winning and represented a very extreme type. Sealord won the Group at the Stockholm Show as a veteran, and Seamusic had numerous BIS awards.

A new era began in the 1970s with the arrival of Ch. Deremar Donald and his sisters, Ch. Denise and Ch. Deborah, who were out of Figaro and Ch. Deremar Rosemary. Donald's value as a highly respected stud dog was well known, and he helped establish breed soundness and temperament. Donald was owned by kennel Knegaren, who had bred numerous winners in the field as well as the ring. A few of Donald's most prominent progeny are Ch., FTCh. Teacher's Melvyn; Int. Ch. Kimbalee Colonel Peron; brother and sister Ch. Earl Dinwiddy and Ch. Dancing Elinda; Ch. Knegaren's Go Go Girl and Int. Ch. Knegarens Heidi. These dogs, along with many other Donald progeny, have continued to produce typical Goldens of high quality.

Another famous Donald son, Ch. Mjaerumhogdas Limelight, has countless BOB and BIS awards. One more top dog of that era, owned by kennel Pallywood, was Int. Ch. Pengelli, whose winning ways earned him BIS awards throughout his lifetime.

The working side of the Golden has always been well tended by the experienced breeders in Sweden. Many dogs of the early decades were used as gundogs, and a few also started at field trials. Today Sweden has breeders with strong backgrounds for training Goldens for field work.

FTCh. Duckflight DikDik arrived at kennel Duvkullan in the early 1970s, and she has produced a long line of field winners at this kennel. Duvkullan also imported FTCh. Rambler of Maar, who proved to be a great dog and sire. Imports from Holway, Ardyle and Standerwick have also contributed to the development of the Swedish Golden in the field.

Kennel Respons started in 1971 with a dual champion bitch and has since succeeded in campaigning many dogs to their dual championships. Kennel Pickup has also produced a number of field-trial champions.

In the 1980s Ch. Gyrima Zacharias came to kennel Dewmist and was finished at 18 months. His value as a stud dog is legendary, with every pup from his first five litters earning BIS awards. The winning continues with his grandchildren.

Another famous Dewmist Golden owned by kennel Knegaren was Int. Ch. Dewmist Chrysander, who at 18 months of age was the

The Dekkers' Golden family: **Charlie** (an Alyss son), **Fellow** and **Simon** ("Lady" sons), **Boris**, **Evelyn**, **Lizzie** (English import Moorquest Music for You) **Lady**, **Kimberly** and **Alyss** (Lady daughters), and **Annebel** (Alyss daughter).

first Swedish bred Golden to go BIS at a Kennel Club show. One famous Chrysander son is Int. Ch. Moviestar's Buster Keaton, who for many years won not only at shows but at field trials, obedience trials and working tests.

In 1982 Knegaren and Dewmist imported Styal Samarkand who proved to be a superb stud dog, producing the best in hips and many winning dogs. Another famous Knegaren-Dewmist dog of the '80s is Int. Ch. Sansue Golden Arrow, a top winner and sound producer with many winning and titled progeny. One outstanding Arrow litter produced four Dewmist champions, one of them a three-time Challenge Certificate winner.

Wedford Gingerbread Man, owned by kennel Moorlac, was also a superior field-trial dog who produced many working champions.

Kennel Ringmaster has produced champions since 1966. They started a new line with the introduction of Ch. Enterprise of Yeo, and through her, they produced field-trial winners as well as show champions. Ringmaster's Checkpoint of Yeo and Goldfinger of Yeo were also widely used at stud.

Nortonwood Secreto, who came to kennel Dream Max in 1984, has sired a number of winners throughout the Scandanavian countries. One of his best known offspring, Ch. Dream Max Never Say Never Again, has claimed 10 CCs and many BIS awards. In 1988 Dream Max was the top-winning kennel of all breeds in Sweden, having completed winning Breeder Groups consisting of five even dogs of highest quality all over Sweden, certainly a great achievement.

Kennel Dainty has continually imported high-quality dogs from the United Kingdom and has bred some lovely individuals. Their Christopher Caleidoscope and Commander of Nortonwood have won Gundog Groups as well as BIS, and Dainty's Pretty Face has been a top brood bitch for many years.

Farbank Scotch Mist, owned by kennel Fairfax, has been successful at stud as well as in the ring, having produced a large family of CC winners. One foundation bitch at Fairfax, Ch. Precious Gold of Petrina, also started her own chain of winners over time.

Kennel Guldklimpen also has produced winners

who excel in the field. Ch. Guldklimpen Tarzan has won several BIS awards and sired winners such as Ch. Guldklimpens Ruffel o Bag, who also holds three Challenge Certificates. Perhaps this kennel's most outstanding bitch is Ch. Guldklimpens Olga the Comtesse, who has taken top awards all over Sweden and Norway. In addition to her numerous BOBs, with BIS and Group awards, she is the dam of five different CC winners.

Another Challenge Certificate winner who produced well is Noravon Lucretia, who holds two CCs and is a sister to Norway's Ch. Noravons Lucius. Lucretia has three champion offspring and many more winning progeny. Pinecrest Byron, owned by kennel Trisoblue, holds three CCs and was a popular stud dog during the late '70s and early '80s. His progeny include two champions as well as many other accomplished offspring.

Eva Johnsson is a Swedish veterinarian whose husband Filip breeds Golden Retrievers under the Dainty kennel prefix, and is also a championship judge.

Eva has studied inherited diseases in Goldens Retrievers. She writes that the Swedish Kennel Club keeps an official data register with open results on all examinations for hip and elbow dysplasia and eye disorders, so it is possible for everyone to learn the status of an individual dog or its progeny by requesting a computer reading. The Kennel Club, together with the breed clubs, veterinarians and genetic experts, offer recommendations on how to deal with problems, but the individual breeder must still decide how and what to breed.

Dogs can be x-rayed for hip dysplasia at one year old, and the results are written into the pedigree as well as the computer. The frequency of dysplasia presently runs about 20 percent. Most breeders also now check elbows on their breeding stock as well as their progeny. The present rate of elbow dysplasia is relatively high, probably because the majority of dogs x-rayed are those who display front-end lameness, so the percentage should drop when breeders begin to x-ray all their dogs.

All breeding stock receives annual eye exams. The frequency of total cataracts is very low, and while cases of PRA are still few, the incidence has increased over recent years. Eva said the recessive trait of PRA places great demand on breeders to voluntarily exclude suspected carriers from breeding, and some do not always comply.

Epilepsy is one of Sweden's most problematical inherited diseases, and there is no official way to register known cases. Certain bloodlines are more affected than others, and the Swedish Golden Retriever Club is investigating how to best attack this problem.

There are no known cases of von Willebrand's disease discovered thus far, and very few dogs with heart problems.

In 1989 a new association was organized called the European Golden Retriever Association (EGRA). The EGRA aims to improve international contacts with other Golden Retriever organizations by exchanging views and information on all aspects of the breed. The chairman is from Sweden, the secretary from Switzerland, and the treasurer from England. National correspondents write articles for the EGRA publication called *The Golden Express.*

Scarlet and **Brit** visit in Holland. Photo courtesy of Mercedes Hitchcock.

NORWAY

The Norwegian Kennel Club recorded its first Golden Retrievers in 1954 with the registration of four imports from the U.K.: Pennard Golden Tosca, Mellowgold Jester, Prinmere Alistair and finally Somerscot Timothy.

Tosca had one litter by Jester. But it wasn't until the 1962 breedings of Redstead Belinda and Seaspel Boyers . . . both imported in 1959 . . . that the breed really established itself in this country. Both bitches were mated with a Danish Golden, Int. Ch. Philips Tais Flapore, who was visiting Norway at the time.

In 1964 another import, Ch. Drexholme Chrysler Venture, became the first Golden to earn a championship in Norway. The following year Ch. Camrose Una led the female Golden population and became the first bitch to finish in that country. During this period, another fine import, Ch. Boltby Brigand, a Ch. Cabus Cadet son, was also widely used at stud.

Imports from the kennel Tais in Denmark and Hedetorpet in Sweden joined Norwegian Goldens in the ring. In 1966 Ch. Hedetorpets Guy became the first Golden to take BIS at a kennel club show. Inevitably, more Hedetorpet imports followed.

The Norwegian Retriever Club was founded in 1960, but only a handful of its members had Golden Retrievers. Gradually this changed. Golden owners researched and contacted good breeders in other countries in order to establish a foundation of valuable imports.

During the late '60s Brambledown Harvester was imported, and he is behind many Norwegian Goldens of today. Ch. Cabus Clarion, a younger brother to Christopher, was imported in 1968.

Two bitches who heavily influenced the breed in Norway during this period are responsible for generations of many top-quality Goldens. Ch. Camrose Tudina, a Tallyrand daughter, is behind all the Gitle's Goldens, and Camrose Evensky, a Christopher daughter, became the foundation of the Kargul Goldens.

A number of top-quality Goldens were imported in the '70s. The most well-known and important dogs were Ch. Davern Lion Lotcheck, a Figaro son, and Ch. Camrose Voravey, who

This "Lady" son, **Happy Lad Charlie v/h Weikse Veld**, at 14 months had his Working Certificate and a first place at a Championship show.

both did a great deal for the breed in Norway; also Int-Scan. Ch. Sansue Sunlover, who was the first Golden to earn this impressive international title; and Ch. Styla Scimiter, Ch. Likely Lad of Yeo and Ch. Noravon Lucius.

Lucius, himself a top winner at shows, quickly proved his influence on the breed and produced a chain of winners in Norway as well as other countries. He is behind many top Goldens of today, and among his progeny, Ch. Chribas Crackerjack has probably won more than any other.

Norway has used artificial insemination successfully over the years, and through AI in 1974, Christopher produced ten puppies to a Norwegian bitch. This litter was star-crossed and contained many winners, most notably Ch. Spervikbuktens Philip, who was one of the top dogs of all breeds in Norway for several years.

In 1979 a granddaughter from this same litter was AI'd back to Christopher, producing yet another well-known litter of winning Goldens of that period, all with the Asebygardens prefix.

Since the early '70s, the top-producing kennel in Norway has been Mjaerumhogdas, who has finished over 40 champions. They have imported a number of high-quality stud dogs over the years.

One of their well-known Goldens of the '80s is Ch. Mjaerumhogdas Crusader, a superior show dog who has done a much to improve the breed. Crusader also spent some time in the U.K., where he was used at stud and shown.

Again it was AI in 1988, and again it was

Christopher who sired a large litter born at Mjaerumhogdas. Many of those pups were shown, and one dog, Mjaerumhogdas Top Hit, was retained. Top Hit started his show career with three CCs in a row as well as BOB awards. Another Mjaerumhogdas Golden, Ch. Mjaerumhogdas Limelight, a Donald son, owned by kennel Waterloo, has amassed wins all over Norway and Sweden.

Two more outstanding dogs from Mjaerumhogdas are Ch. Golden Look and Int. Ch. Classic Sound, both owned in Sweden by kennel Friendship. Look had a spectacular career, winning nine CCs and several BIS awards. Sound won seven CCs, but above all he has been a "sound" producer, and his many offspring have done very well.

A new star of the '90s has been Ch. Floprym Home Made Hotdog by Janward Dollar. Owned by kennel Floprym, she won over ten BOBs during 1990, several with prestigious Best-In-Show awards.

The Norwegian Golden population has prospered. In 1970 there were 243 registrations. In another ten years, annual registration had climbed to 1,672. By 1990 annual registration was well over 2,000 Goldens.

FINLAND

The first two Golden Retrievers registered in Finland, Holway Sweep and Woodbarn Autumnglint, were imported in 1959 solely for field-trial use. The following year Peter of Elvey arrived. He became the first show champion in that country, and propelled the Golden into Finland's show ring.

In 1962 Peter was mated to Autumnglint, and the first litter of native Golden Retrievers entered the Finnish dog fancy. The same year Rivertrees Larry arrived. When Larry finished, he happily joined Peter at stud.

In 1965 two Goldens were imported from kennel Apport in Sweden, Ch. Glenessa Waterbird of Stenbury and Ch. Apports Corinna. Corinna became the Woodhill foundation bitch, and when bred to Waterbird, produced Blond Boy of Woodhill, one of the top dogs of that era. Woodhill imported another outstanding bitch, Whitewater Patricia, who produced a long line of winners and is today behind many of the top-winning dogs in Finland.

Kennel Leavenworth, a famous Cocker Spaniel breeder, started its line of Goldens in 1970 with an imported bitch called Pride of the Morn of Petrina. Leavenworth's later imports include Deerflite Summer Storm and Ch. Deerflite Daffodil, later owned by kennel Reflect.

Reflect also owned a famous dog of the '80s, Ch. Noravon Cornelius, who was a great show dog and left his mark on the breed with his many winning progeny.

During the early '80s, Finnish breeders sometimes used artificial insemination, primarily live semen from Camrose Fidelio of Davern. Many of those progeny have been shown, and many of them used for further breeding at the Woodhill kennel.

Dogs are permitted and welcomed in restaurants and pubs in Holland...most Dutch dogs are well behaved and trained to sit or lie down. **Scarlet** (in foreground) appears surprised and somewhat subdued by this, while the Golden in the background has no trouble at all making himself at home.

Other imports who have been widely bred and have impacted the Finnish Golden are Ch. Thenford Hamish, who was a Christopher son, Ch. Mjaerumhogdas Your Choice from Norway, and Ch. Gildas Midnight Sun from Sweden of pure English breeding.

Two Goldens born in the mid-'80s and owned by the kennel Karvin have been good producers as well as top winners themselves. Both Ch. Linchael Ravel and Ch. Lovehayne Darter were imports from the United Kingdom.

In the early '70s there were about 120 Goldens registered each year. Ten years later registrations had climbed to over 1,000 annually, and by 1990, that number had doubled to over 2,000 Goldens registered every year.

DENMARK

Golden Retrievers first appeared in Denmark in 1957 with the arrival of Vagabond of Coldharbour and Empshott Charming Lady. These two produced the first litter of Danish Goldens and became the foundation stock for the Danish kennel Tais. One of those pups went on to become Int. Ch. Philips Tais Flapore, who was later widely used in Denmark as a stud dog.

The 1960s witnessed the arrival of Taddington Lady Smock, Corn Dolly, and stud dog Ch. Taddington Bellringer. Ch. Camrose Quixote was also born that year, and despite his death at the early age of five, he left an indelible mark on the breed.

During the early '60s, Anbria Laurel, Ch. Joriemour Lisbeth, and stud dog Ch. Anbria Tarlatan came to kennel Wessex, destined there to begin a long line of winning Goldens.

Other Goldens from Camrose, Anbria and Westley were imported to create a solid foundation for Goldens in Denmark. Later, other well-known dogs from the kennels Crouchers, Sansue and Lacons joined the ranks at the novice Danish breeding kennels.

During the mid-'60s, two outstanding show and stud dogs came to Denmark, Int. Ch. Honeyat

the Viking and Int. Ch. Byxfield Cedar. Although they began their show careers together, the two were so unlike that they never met in the ring, and their progeny reflect the vast differences in these two sires.

Two very well-known dogs of the 1980s are Int. Ch. Crouchers Xavier, a son of Ch. Stradcot Simon of Crouchers, and Int. Ch. Lacons Honey Lover, a son of Ch. Sansue Tobias. Both have been used extensively at stud and have produced a long chain of winning Goldens.

One Xavier son, Matthew, has already produced a new generation of winners of very high quality. Both Xavier and Matthew are owned by Tallygold, who imported another well-known Golden from Norway during this decade, Ch.

First Lady Alyss v/h Weikse Veld, a "Lady" daughter, earned three CCs, two RCCs, two BOBs and one BIS by three-and-one-half years of age. In this photo she poses with her biggest challenge thus far—eleven puppies sired by **VDH. Ch. Wyvan Midnight for Moorquest.**

Camillo, of pure Camrose breeding. Camillo has produced high-quality progeny, while still winning in the ring.

Because Denmark is a small country, one would think a close cooperation had existed between breeders in earlier days. This was not the case, partly because the distance between the Danish islands made travel complicated in those days. As years have passed and transportation improved, breeders with good foresight began to use dogs all over the country as well as

Netherland Ch. Westley Beedee VDH Ch. (Ch. Jescott Galahad ex Ch. Westley Martha). Born in 1985; owner, Mirjam en Bont van Maren.

from other parts of Europe.

Artificial insemination has been successfully used in Denmark, primarily with live semen from Sweden. The introduction of additional bloodlines in this manner has produced good results in many Danish breeding programs.

Goldens are very popular in Denmark, and by 1981 a total of 33,158 had been registered. In 1990 the annual registration was about 2,000.

HOLLAND

The first Golden Retrievers in Holland, imported from England in the 1930s, gained very little ground over the next 20 years and were bred and used mostly as working stock.

How times have changed! Today the Golden is Holland's most popular breed of dog, and the Golden Retriever Club Nederland (GRCN) boasts over 7,000 members. Yet of the almost 5,610 Goldens registered in 1990, only about 15 percent were bred by GRCN members.

Henri and Thea Dekkers are long-time GRCN members and raise Goldens under the kennel prefix "v/h Wieskse Veld." Eight of their ten

Goldens are house dogs, who share the Dekkers' bed and board like any respectable member of the family.

Thea writes that the GRCN stipulates all breeding stock should be checked for hereditary cataracts, PRA and hip dysplasia. Hips are scored on a schedule with five classifications: A1/A2 - No signs of HD; B1/B2 - Transitional case, approved in Holland for breeding purposes; C1/C2 - Mild, approved for breeding in Holland when the dog has an "Excellent" qualification in the breed ring; D1/D2 - Moderate and not for breeding; E1/E2 - Severe, most of these dogs have physical problems.

Only about 25 percent of the Goldens in Holland are screened for HD, and of those about 50 percent receive A/B ratings, the remainder receiving C/D or E. Despite pressure from the GRCN, indiscriminate breeding often occurs with little regard for hereditary problems, and with the unfortunate results of untypical appearance, lack of soundness and undesirable behavioral traits.

In an attempt to improve the breed, serious

breeders have imported Goldens from England and Denmark, bringing in the best known blood-lines. The result has been a steady improvement in the quality of Goldens who win in the show ring.

To become a Dutch show champion, a dog must win four CACs *(Certificat d'Aptitude au Championat,* similar to the Challenge Certificate in England) under two different judges, with one gained after 27 months of age. The show dog is evaluated and classified under four different qualifications: *Uitmuntend* (U) or Excellent, very close to the standard for the breed; *Zeer Goed* (ZG) Very Good or close to the standard with very few faults; *Goed* (G) Good, which is not typical with a few faults; *Matig* (M) which is Moderate, a very untypical dog with many faults. Henri's current Golden bitch, First Lady Alyss, has earned a U rating as well as a BOB award, a CAC and CACIB.

To earn the field trial champion title, a dog must earn two CACs at field trials in Holland and a "Very Good" or better qualification at a National or International Championship show.

The GRCN annually runs two amateur and two national field trials where the winner claims a CAC. It also runs three gundog tests on dum-mies, one on cold game and two working tests on dummies.

The Dekkers emphasize and support the work-ing Golden Retriever. Their foundation bitch, English import Dutch Ch. Aradias Apricot Whirl, "Lady," was the only Golden in 1986 selected among the overall best 20 dogs in Holland. She has her obedience GG1 (Behavior and Obedience certification), many Working Certificates and excels in the field as a hunting companion.

Most Golden Retrievers in Holland have only one specialty, with few competing in both show and field or obedience. In 1990, of the 77 Goldens who held Dutch Champion titles, four were inter-national champions, eight had become field cham-pions and one had achieved the coveted dual-champion status.

A Monday night class for retrievers held at a large public park near Amsterdam. **HR Scarlet O'Hara of Belvedere***** and **HR Ch. Holway Vodka*****, owned by Mercedes Hitchcock of Sugar Island, Texas, relax with the local Goldens before performing their retrieving demonstrations. Scarlet, "Brit" and Mercedes spent two weeks in Holland giving demonstrations and training sessions in different parts of the country.

SWITZERLAND

In Switzerland, Chantal LeFeivre has written many articles on the Golden Retriever. From her mountains of research material, she shared information about the breed in Switzerland.

All dog breeding in Switzerland is strictly controlled by the Swiss Kennel Club and the Swiss Golden Retriever Club. The first three litters bred by a new breeder must be first approved, then must be bred, whelped and raised under the guidelines and supervision of the breed and kennel clubs. Thereafter, one litter is allowed per year.

Every dog used for breeding must first have "one admission to breeding." This stipulates the dog's hips have been x-rayed and cleared for hip dysplasia by the Veterinary Clinic of Berne or Zurich, the eyes attested free of entropion by a veterinarian or judge, and the dentition complete and correct with a scissors or level bite. Males must be examined for descended testicles.

For those breeders who so desire, the judge or veterinarian will also conduct a "mental test" for temperament to check for shyness, aggression or other behaviors. At the breeder's request, a show judge will also evaluate the dog.

Breeders must send a card to the club breeding committee to announce a mating, and again announce, within 12 days of whelping, the number of pups born, how many kept and their date of birth. One member of the club breeding committee will visit the litter to see if the puppies are in good condition, if they are wormed and kept on a proper diet, and to inspect the kennel for cleanliness. If there are more than eight puppies, the breeder must have a foster mother also in attendance.

Puppies cannot be sold until ten weeks of age.

Lucerne 1989, the International All-Breed Show: Dog CAC–CACIB **Toby Woodrose**, judged by Mrs. P. Holmes of Great Britain and Bitch CAC–CACIB **Rossbourne Serene Vimy**, judged by Mr. R. Coward also of Britain. Photo courtesy of Miss Chantal LeFeivre of Colombier, Switzerland.

This trio represents three generations of Sevenhills Golden Retrievers bred by Chantal LeFeivre of Switzerland. Left to right: **Swiss-Int. Ch. Sevenhills Chesham** (Int. Ch. Catacombe Calibre ex Vimy Whinchat), **Sevenhills Kobha** (Reserve CAC) (Catacombe Carefree ex Sevenhills Chesham), both owned by Chantal, and **Sevenhills Maina** (Jucridor Endeavour ex Sevenhills Kobha) owned by Mr. and Mrs. Reichenbach.

They must be vaccinated, and the breeder must give a copy of the pedigree (supplied by the Swiss Kennel Club) to the new puppy's family. Chantal writes that Golden litters have increased from eight registered in 1971 to 100 in 1989. The population of Switzerland is only 6 million people.

The title of Swiss (show) Champion requires three CACs *(Certificat d'Aptitude au Championat)* under at least two different judges, with two of the shows international All-Breed shows, and at least 12 months passing between the first and third CAC. In 1990, 18 Goldens became show champions, five of them Swiss-bred.

An International Champion requires two CACIBs (won at an international All-Breed show) won in two different countries, plus a field-trial award. Field-trial wins are accorded the CACT or CACIT, as in show wins, with the "T" added for *"Travail"* meaning work. Of Switzerland's ten International Champions, five are Swiss bred, and only five Goldens hold both Swiss and International Champion titles.

Swiss Golden owners also do "Utility" dog work, training their dogs for *Sanitatshunde*, which is a kind of search and rescue work, and for tracking and avalanche work. Only a few train for retrieving, as field trials on live game are strictly forbidden by law. Working dogs can enter three or four cold game tests a year or several working tests, which use only dummies. Field trialers must go to France or Italy to compete.

Ch. Honor's Let 'Em Have It WC (OS), "Bang," an exceptional hunter who finished his championship with two five-point majors in two days. Bred by Ann Chase, owned and hunted by Bob Lund.

The Golden Retriever Club of America

The Golden Retriever Club of America (GRCA) was the brainchild of Colonel Samuel S. Magoffin, Golden Retriever owner, avid sportsman and gundog enthusiast. Magoffin not only founded the club in 1938 and acted as its first president but also set a shining example when he took his English import Am-Can. Ch. Speedwell Pluto on to become America's first Golden Retriever bench champion and first Best-in-Show winner. Pluto was hunted regularly and became an outstanding producer, a dog behind many of today's great Golden lines.

In 1939 Magoffin wrote about the formation of the GRCA in the September issue of the *AKC Gazette.* "The GRCA was formed primarily for the purpose of assisting, by selective breeding, the further development of the Golden Retriever as a gundog." In that article, Magoffin advised novice breeders not to become discouraged if all litters did not produce field-trial winners or Best-in-Show dogs. "What we have in the Golden Retriever is a grand hunting dog for both upland game and waterfowl during the hunting season, and the best companion imaginable for all the family for the balance of the year."

Magoffin had been quick to recognize the many talents of the Golden as having potential for exploitation by specialists in various breed activities. The first GRCA vice president, E.F. Rivinus, later wrote in the *Gazette* in 1940..."while the breed is still young as a breed here, let us resolve that there will never be one group of dogs for show and a totally different group for the field."

Rivinus's vision haunts us half a century later. In 1940 at the first GRCA National Specialty and Field Trial held at Theinsville and Mequon, Wisconsin, conformation entries totalled 45 and the field trial 44. Sharp contrast to the Fiftieth Anniversary National Specialty in Colorado in 1989, where 626 Golden entries sparkled in the show ring, while the field trial sported only 173 athletic contenders. Magoffin and Rivinus might have had some interesting observations about that.

Built on the foundation laid by those dedicated early founders and officers, the GRCA today is

Bracken at fourteen weeks with his first pigeon. Bruce and Donna Thompson are his breeders; Barb Roy, his proud parent.

5,000 members strong, one of the largest breed clubs in the world. Dedicated to the preservation and advancement of the breed through education and communication, it boasts a core of six officers, six regional directors and nine national committees that oversee the welfare of the breed and direct a myriad of on-going projects and breed activities.

Forty-eight member clubs in over two dozen states provide hubs of activity and information at

AFC Topbrass Super Trooper (NAFC-FC Topbrass Cotton ex Pacapooches Pandemonium***) bred by Robert and Sandee Peterson, owned by Darrell Frisbie, Waverly, Minnesota.

the local level to those owners and fanciers interested in training, exhibiting, breeding or just enjoying their Golden Retrievers. The clubs host specialty shows, hunts and working tests, sponsor lectures and seminars on all aspects of breed activity, hold clinics to promote a sound and healthy animal and publish newsletters to inform and educate their members.

The voice and thrust of national club is in the *Golden Reriever News*, the information link between GRCA members-at-large and the parent club. Published bi-monthly, the national magazine has grown into a 200-plus page magazine bulging with articles on breeder ethics, medical information and genetic issues, training techniques, and notice and advice on all aspects of breed activity and accomplishment.

Many efforts of the GRCA have benefited the purebred dog population-at-large. The GRCA Advisory Council on Hip Dysplasia during the 1950s was the driving force behind the formation of a national hip registry ultimately to benefit all breeds affected by HD. Born of the singular efforts of one dedicated GRCA member who was concerned about her litter of dysplastic puppies, the Council established the informa-

tion and procedures that eventually became the Orthopedic Foundation for Animals. Since 1974 OFA has evaluated over 300,000 hip x-rays of more than 82 breeds of dogs.

To honor that member's lifelong crusade against hip dysplasia and her many contributions to the breed, the GRCA in 1989 established the Vern Bower Humanitarian Award "to acknowledge exemplary contributions and selfless devotion to the Golden Retriever."

Over the years GRCA has developed and updated literature to further its emphasis on education. "Acquiring a Golden Retriever" is a 32-page pamphlet intended to educate potential puppy buyers. It offers information on how to choose a reputable breeder and pick a puppy or an adult Golden. It explains breed hereditary problems, the whys and why-nots of breeding, including time and cost factors, the advantages of spaying and neutering, plus the complete breed standard on the Golden Retriever.

"An Introduction to the Golden Retriever" is

OTCh. Pekay's Rocky Mtn. Skipper (HOF) (Ch. Captain Neil's Goldstorm CD, WCX ex Pekay's Pawprint CDX), owned and trained by Judy Lee, Pleasant Plains, Illinois. Skipper's tremendous joy and enthusiasm in his work always captivated spectators at the obedience ring. He garnered 16 HITs and claimed top-ten placings in the Gaines Regional and World Series.

Am-Can. Ch. Beaumaris Timberee Tessa Ann UDT, WC, Can. CD (OD, HOF) (Ch. Beaumaris Line Drive CDX ex Beaumaris Aspen Hill Tessa) owned, trained and adored by Sandy Fisher, Grand Junction, Colorado. Tessa Ann has repeatedly turned heads in both rings…show and obedience…as the only bitch in breed history to win both Best of Breed and High in Trial at a specialty. Her enthusiastic, tail-wagging happy heeling is her hallmark…she has several HITs as well as multiple BOB wins. Tessa topped her show career by going Best of Opposite Sex at the 1989 National Specialty…at seven and one-half years of age.

directed at the new puppy owner. It contains all the information in the smaller "Acquiring" booklet, plus additional chapters on the care and training of a Golden puppy during its first year.

The *Reprint Handbook: Selected Reprints from the Golden Retriever News* was published in 1988. It contains over 170 educational articles on Golden behavior and temperament, hereditary problems and other diseases, genetics, breeding and whelping, health care, puppy selection, field, obedience, conformation, tracking and rescue Goldens. GRCA plans to reprint the Handbook to update the articles and information.

In 1989 GRCA launched its most ambitious educational effort thus far, the PAL Program. The creation of GRCA officer Jeffrey Pepper, PAL is a Public Awareness Letter, a single sheet brochure of Golden Retriever breed information as found in the "Acquiring" pamphlet. Undertaken with the cooperation of AKC, PAL is sent to every new Golden owner registered with AKC, over 65,000 mailings every year, at an annual cost of over 20 thousand dollars. PAL hopes to educate the new owner and help curb indiscriminate breeding practices in the general population.

The club also publishes a bi-annual yearbook of breed statistics on specialty results, new title holders, competition wins, Outstanding Sires and Dams and Hall of Fame Goldens.

Since 1940, GRCA has hosted an annual National Specialty Show and Field Trial, consistently one of the largest events in AKC records. To recognize the Golden's versatility and accomplishments, the GRCA requires their national specialty offer every area of competition: a conformation show, licensed field and obedience

Ch. Birnam Wood's Show 'N Tell CD, owned by Bruce and Donna Thompson, St. Louis, Missouri.

the country to participate from a reasonable distance. Member clubs also volunteer to host regional and national specialties.

With the boom in Golden popularity threatening the welfare of the breed, GRCA has shifted its emphasis from breeder advocate to one of education and preservation of breed quality. Their commitment to the preservation of a sound, good-looking, functional Golden may best be expressed in the initial statement of the original GRCA Articles of Incorporation:

"Realizing that the Golden is a gundog, the purpose of the Club shall be to encourage the members to perfect, by selective breeding, the type most suitable for such work."

trials, Tracking and Tracking Excellent tests, plus the Working Certificate and Working Certificate Excellent tests.

GRCA support of the versatile Golden paid off. In 1988 the Golden opened a new era of achievement as one of only two breeds to earn all 12 AKC titles at the time. GRCA annual trophies are presented at every national specialty to recognize the achievers in so many Golden endeavors.

To further encourage and recognize Golden Retriever achievement in multiple areas, in 1991 GRCA Board of Directors formally approved the new GRCA Versatility awards. Developed by regional vice-presidents Marcia Schler and John Shannon, the Versatility Certificate (VC) and Versatility Certificate Excellent (VCX) are offered to Golden Retrievers who attain specific achievements in conformation, field and obedience, with the VCX recognizing more advanced levels of accomplishment.

The specialty host site rotates annually from East to West to Midwest to allow breeders from all corners of

For information on the GRCA, member clubs, or reputable Golden Retriever breeders in the United States, contact the American Kennel Club, 51 Madison Ave., New York NY 10010, or write to the Golden Retriever columnist, *Pure-Bred Dogs / American Kennel Gazette,* at the same address.

Ch. Beckwiths Justa Tuckerbear with two of his accomplished sons (*center*) **Ch. Golden Pine Scillian Sun (OS, HOF)** and (*right*) **Ch. Beckwiths Easter Celebrity**. He is also the sire of Ch. Pepperhills Golden Pine Trumpet, who belongs to Charlotte Gaynor of California. Owned by Ludell Beckwith of Washington.

GRCA HALL OF FAME

GRCA Field Dog Hall Of Fame requirements: Any Golden Retriever that accumulates a total of 25 points or more based on his performance in Licensed Field Trials will automatically be honored in the Hall of Fame. Any Golden that wins the National Field Trial or National Amateur Field Trial will also be included.

GRCA Obedience Dog Hall Of Fame requirements: Any Golden Retriever with a Utility Dog (UD) title that has accumulated five Highest Scoring Dog in Trial (or tied for HIT) will be entered in the HOF.

Regional Specialty Best of Breed 3
Independent Specialty Best of Breed 1

GRCA Outstanding Sire and Dam Program recognizes those Goldens whose progeny have achieved a level of excellence in one or more areas of performance and/or competition. In 1986 the GRCA Board of Directors began a revision of the standards in order to recognize a wider area of achievement. Effective January 1, 1988, the requirements for Outstanding Sire are: Sires must have at least five qualifying progeny. Progeny may qualify by earning either:

(1) one three-point or higher title, OR

Ch. Malagold Summer Encore (OD, HOF), a Malagold Outstanding Dam and member of the Show Dog Hall of Fame, a multiple Best-in-Show and Best of Breed winner, owned by Sandy Bator and Connie Gerstner.

GRCA Show Dog Hall Of Fame requirements: Any Golden Retriever who earns 25 or more points based on the following schedule will be entered in the GRCA SDHOF.

Best in Show 10
          (plus 5 points for Group I)
Sporting Group I 5
Sporting Group II 3
Sporting Group III 1
Sporting Group IV .... ½
National Specialty Best of Breed 5

(2) any combination of two two-point titles, except that no more than *two* progeny may so qualify towards achieving "Outstanding Sire" status. The qualifying progeny must have earned a total of at least 18 title-points among them. Effective January 1, 1988, the requirements for Outstanding Dam are: Dams must have at least three (3) qualifying progeny. Progeny may qualify by earning either:

(1) one three-point or higher title, OR

(2) any combination of two-point titles, except

that no more than *one* progeny may so qualify toward achieving "Outstanding Dam" status. The qualifying progeny must have earned a total of at least 11 title-points among them. Title points will be calculated according to the following schedule:

9				FC/AFC
6	OTCh			FC or AFC
4	UD	TDX	MH	***
3	Ch		SH	
2	CDX	TD	JH or WCX	**
1	CD		WC	

Points for titles may be added across from column to column, but not up and down within a column. Outstanding Sires and Dams will also include any dog or bitch which has produced:

Sam Silverman's **"Zap"** with a pheasant. Zap is a no-nonsense field champion with an unshakeable spirit.

Two field champions (FC or AFC) *or* one field champion (FC or AFC) *and* one show champion, or one Utility Dog, or one Tracking Dog Excellent.

VC/Versatility Certificate Dog must have earned points from all three areas, with a total of six points.

VCX / Versatility Certificate Excellent Dog must have earned points from all three areas, with a total of ten points. Points from two different categories are cumulative. Points within a given category are maximized at the highest level/title earned (are not cumulative).

CONFORMATION

Champion 4
Major points 2
Major Reserve or
Minor Reserve 1

OBEDIENCE

RING		TRACKING	
OTCh	6	TDX	4
UD	4	TD	2
CDX	2	CD	1

FIELD

COMPETITIVE		NON-COMPETITIVE	
FC/AFC	9	MH	4
FC or AFC	6	SH	3
***	5	JH or WCX	2
**	2	WC	1

Sunfire's Kinetic Cascade Am-Can. UD, MH, WCX (OD). (FC-AFC Kinike's Oro de Rojo ex Tanya du Shanka WC, Am-Can. CD (OD)). Born: March 10, 1979. Breeder, Michael A. Book. Owners, Michael A. Book and Barbara F. Biewer. Completed her Master Hunter title at age 10 and won the Shoreline Retriever Club Master Hunter trophy; obedience accomplishments include a high in trial and completion of all six legs of both UD titles within two weeks; offspring have excelled as hunting companions and in hunting tests; four offspring with Senior Hunter titles made her a GRCA Outstanding Dam.

Am-Bda. Ch. Twin-Beau-D Hi Speed Chase (OS, HOF), bred by Nancy Dallaire, owned by Donald and Sharon Beech of Rehoboth, Massachusetts, and Nancy Dallaire. A Best-in-Show winner and a top-ten Golden in 1989.

GRCA TROPHIES AND AWARDS

GRCA Perpetual and Challenge trophies are awarded annually for achievements based on accumulated points earned and for achievements at the GRCA National Specialty, and are awarded only to GRCA members.

FC RIP TROPHY Awarded annually to the member-owned dog winning the Open All-Age Stake at the National Specialty Field Trial.

CH. TONKAHOF BANG*** TROPHY Awarded to the member whose bench champion places highest in the National Specialty Field Trial.

FC PIRATE OF GOLDEN VALLEY TROPHY Awarded annually by a majority vote of the Board of Directors to the member-amateur handler placing highest in the National Specialty Field Trial.

GILNOCKIE CHALLENGE CUP Awarded to the GRCA member-owner whose Golden has the highest scoring field-trial record during the year.

ROCKHAVEN SPEEDWELL PLUTO CHALLENGE CUP Awarded by the GRCA Board of Directors to the member whose registered purebred Golden Retriever achieves highest honors in AKC-licensed or member dog shows. Calculated on the number of dogs defeated during the year.

PETER OF WOODEND PERPETUAL TROPHY Awarded annually to the GRCA member-owner whose Golden's performance in Derby Stakes is most outstanding, based on licensed trials only.

THE KINGSWERE CHALLENGE CUP Awarded by the majority vote of the Board of Directors to the GRCA member-owner of each successive Golden Retriever qualifying as a Dual Champion.

GRANAT BROTHERS TROPHY Awarded annually to the GRCA member-owner whose Golden earns the highest number of points in Amateur All-Age Stakes that year.

MAGOFFIN PERPETUAL TROPHY Awarded annually to the member-breeder of the Golden winning the most points each year in AKC licensed Open All-Age, Limited All-Age, and Amateur All-Age Stakes combined.

FORREST L. FLASHMAN MEMORIAL TROPHY Awarded to the member who wins the Qualifying Stake at the National Specialty Field Trial.

FC-AFC MISTY'S SUNGOLD LAD CDX TROPHY Awarded annually to the winner of the Amateur All-Age Stake at the National Specialty Field Trial, provided the owner and handler are members of GRCA. The stake must have sufficient Qualified dogs to carry championship points.

Ch. Aspengold's Semi-Tough CD, bred, owned, handled and hunted by Hugh and Linda Atwell, Albuquerque, New Mexico. "Guv" has 15 GRCA Show Dog Hall of Fame points and a Group win and placements from the classes. And never a whimper about brushing the burrs from his coat after a day in the field to prepare for tomorrow's show.

This page: **U-UD, Am-Can. OTCh. Beckwith's Hennessy Five Star Am-Can. TDX, WCX, TT, Can. WC** (Am-Can. Ch. Beckwith's Viking for Dasu UD ex Beckwith's Piccadilly CD). Owned by Nancy Light, Seattle, Washington. This very accomplished Golden is a role model of versatility and a portrait-perfect of the Golden clown. Hennessy's adolescence lasted "for years" and usually plagued Nancy in the obedience ring. He failed on-lead by jumping up on her and grabbing at her clothes, he jumped up to lick her face on the recall, rolled wildly on his back on the Open long down or between exercises, and would dash out of the ring to take a quick lap of water from his dish, returning with a devilish grin. He finally hit his stride at five years old, adding a bit of accuracy to his exuberance, earning 110 OTCh. points and the Obedience Hall of Fame. With his UKC UD, he became the first triple UD (AKC, CKC and UKC) Golden in the Northwest. Hennessy tracked with a level of concentration and intensity that won him many admirers. His trademark was rolling in joy on the final glove. Nancy believes Hennessy is the first Golden to hold an OTCh. and TDX in both the U.S. and Canada. Although retired in 1989, with a high in trial, of course, Hennessy continues to be Hennessy, stealing tubs of margarine, loaves of bread, cereal boxes, whole cantaloupes… sneaking 199 in Veterans Obedience, and blessing everyone he meets with howls of Golden greeting.

Ch. Alderbrooke's Raid O' Rush Hill UD, owned by Tonya Struble and bred by Carole Kvamme. 1988 Best-in-Show *and* High in Trial at the Yukon Kennel Club. *That's* versatility!!

JUMBEAU*** MEMORIAL TROPHY Awarded to the member whose Golden places highest in the Derby Stake at the National Specialty Field Trial, provided the member is the Amateur-handler of the dog.

CHRISTOPHER R. BURTON BEAU BRUMMEL TROPHY Awarded to the highest placing Golden Retriever owned and handled by a GRCA member in the Derby at the National Specialty Field Trial.

RALPH BOALT-STILROVIN MEMORIAL TROPHY Awarded to the Golden Retriever placing highest in the National Specialty Field Trial that is handled by a current GRCA member who is also the breeder and owner of the dog.

CH. WOCHICA'S OKEECHOBEE JAKE TROPHY Awarded to the member-owner whose Golden is named Best of Breed at the National Specialty.

CH. BECKWITH'S COPPER COIN CUP Awarded to the member-owner whose Golden is named Best of Opposite Sex to Best of Breed at the National Specialty.

JOHN ROGERS MAGOFFIN MEMORIAL TROPHY Awarded to the member-owner whose dog places first in the Bred-by-Exhibitor Dog Class and Bred-by-Exhibitor Bitch Class at the National Specialty.

CH. PEPPERHILL'S BASICALLY BEAR TRO-

PHY Awarded to the member-owner of the Golden winning the Stud Dog Class at the National Specialty.

LUCY WADE MEMORIAL TROPHY Awarded to the member-owner-handler who handled the dog winning the regular Novice A Obedience Class at the National Specialty.

MUD CREEK FLARE UD TROPHY Awarded to the member-breeder-owner-handler of the highest scoring Golden in any regular Obedience Class at the National Specialty, including Graduate Novice and Veterans. Qualifying score only to count.

CH. INDIAN KNOLLS COLONEL UD,*** TROPHY Awarded to the member whose dog is the highest scoring dog in the regular obedience classes at the National Specialty.

SAN FRANCISCO GYPSY JOY CD WC MEMORIAL TROPHY Awarded to the member-owner-handler of the oldest dog of either sex who earns his/her WC at the National Specialty. The dog must be eight years of age or older and never have earned a field title from any AKC, GRCA, NAHRA or any other registry.

CH. TOASTY'S ROYAL MERCEDES TROPHY Awarded to the GRCA member owning the Golden Retriever named Winners Bitch at the National Specialty. First offered in 1991.

OTCh. TOPBRASS RIC O SHAY BARTY WCX TROPHY Awarded annually to the member-owned dog who earns the greatest number of high-combined scores in Utility and Open B Classes during the previous calendar year, who also holds any AKC-recognized field title, WCX or WC. Awarded beginning with the 1992 National Specialty, based on 1991 statistics.

Ch.-AFC LORELEI'S GOLDEN ROCKBOTTOM UD TROPHY Awarded by the GRCA Board of Directors to the member whose Golden Retriever earned an AKC Championship in conformation and became Qualified All-Age (earned three stars) in AKC licensed-Retriever field trials.

TOBY/TRIGGER TROPHY Awarded to the Golden Retriever earning the highest number of points in AKC-licensed or member obedience trials during the previous year.

AM-CAN. CH. AMBERAC'S ASTERLING ARUBA TROPHY Awarded to the GRCA member owning the Golden Retriever winning the Brood Bitch Class at the National Specialty.

DICK SAMPSON MEMORIAL TROPHY Awarded to the member-breeder of the Golden Retriever Club winning the most points in AKC-licensed or member Open All-Age, Limited All-Age and/or Amateur All-Age Stakes.

CH. SENECA'S RIPARIAN CHIEF CD, TD, WC TROPHY Awarded to the member who is the breeder of the Rockhaven Speedwell Pluto trophy winner.

JEANNIE FOX MEMORIAL TROPHY Awarded to the member whose dog is the highest scoring dog in the Veteran's Obedience classes at the National Specialty.

GRCA BOARD OF DIRECTORS JUNIOR HANDLER OF THE YEAR TROPHY Awarded by the Board of Directors to the best junior handler of a Golden Retriever during the year. GRCA membership or member sponsorship required.

GOLDEN RETRIEVER CLUB OF ENGLAND BEST VETERAN TROPHY Awarded to the best veteran from the Veteran conformation classes at the National Specialty owned by a GRCA member.

Ch. Aspengold's Catch the Spirit, bred and owned by Linda Atwell, shown taking a JAM at the 1989 GRCA National Specialty. Spirit finished her championship by taking Best of Breed, then did it again her next day out as a special.

Taking Veteran Bitch at the 1987 GRCA National Specialty is **Bargello's Colabaugh Tansy UD, WC, TT, Can. CD**. Owner, Janine Fiorito of Croton-on-Hudson, New York.

MC's Flyin High in the arms of owner Mike Carlucci. Susan Rezy photographed this golden moment of ownership.

Owner Concerns

BY CHRIS WALKOWICZ

If something's worth doing at all, it's worth doing right. Behind the scenes of every gourmet feast, there's a lot of work, time and expense. Someone has to handle messy clean-up chores as well. The same is true of any worthwhile effort: a prize-winning novel, a community play, a good marriage, children, pets.

Conscientious owners know that there's more to raising a dog than picking one out, feeding it once a day and petting it if they feel the urge. Just as a fancy restaurant includes fine linens, flowers on the table and an attractive ambiance with the sustenance, being a top-quality dog owner means more than tossing a bone in the backyard now and then.

STRAYS

Although some people still have the mistaken idea that "a dog must be free," most are discovering that the world isn't what it once was. Loose dogs enjoying their "freedom" face all kinds of traumas: shotguns, poison, traps, oncoming semis, dog pounds and the resulting euthanasia.

A dog without a home can rarely find a handout or even a rabbit to run down anymore. Garbage forays don't go far enough to fill an empty stomach, and they anger the person who is left to pick up the mess. Cars take their tolls on the highways. To combat these and other problems, good owners are taking steps to make sure their dogs remain welcome in society.

When a breeder is first contacted by a prospec-tive buyer, the question is not simply, "Do you have a fenced yard?" but "Do you have a pen or a fenced yard—or do you plan to walk your dog on leash?" No option. If "none of the above" is the answer, it's bye-bye, buyer.

Children who are uncontrolled and unrestricted are obnoxious, cause damage and are a danger

A future obedience star, this is **Topbrass Supercharger** as a tot. Owners, Bonnie and Lew Baker.

to themselves. Responsible people know that when they tell their children "No," it really is for their own good and that of others. It's not just a power ploy to deny them a privilege. Although it is difficult, there are reasons parents deny complete freedom to children, and there are reasons to deny it to dogs.

Dogs will be dogs. Loose animals are, at the least, a pain in the posterior and, at worst, a threat to themselves and others. Stray dogs bite, poop, scare kids, chase people, strew garbage, ruin lawns and gardens, kill other animals and produce unwanted litters.

At 18 years of age, **"Dusty"** poses for owner-photographer Karen Taylor. Karen says that Dusty is the reason that she and her husband decided on the Golden Retriever as the breed of dog for them. Dusty moves a bit slower these days, but still he's active enough to have fun.

LICENSING

Dog licenses are not simply another means to extract more money from your pocket for the local government, but rather they are insurance for your dog. A dog license just might save your pet from euthanasia. Animal control officers compare the dog license to our own driver's licenses. It's an I.D. That tag hanging from his collar can be traced to the owner, which means a lost pet might be saved from the gas chamber. Licenses also contribute toward the care of the unwanted, forgotten and forlorn ex-pets who will pay the price for "freedom."

THEFT AND LOSS

It's terrifying when a dog owner first looks outdoors and sees the empty yard with the gate swinging open. When someone realizes his pet is gone, the heart takes a plummeting ride to the pit of the stomach.

Sometimes, no matter what precautions are taken, accidents happen—a child leaves a gate open or a well-behaved dog finds a rabbit on the other side of the fence too attractive to resist.

Owners should take action immediately to assure the pet's return. Don't wait a few hours to see if he'll come home. It may be too late.

To find a lost dog:

1. Posters—Have hundreds printed at a jiffy printer, preferably with a photo, and post every one. Someone who sees one poster may not retain the memory, but someone who sees twenty will remember. Describe the dog, always keeping in mind the fable of the blind men and the elephant. To a large man, a medium-sized dog may appear to be small; to a child, it may seem to be an elephant. In addition, a lost dog usually loses weight. Remember if the dog is gone for more than a few hours, a well-groomed animal can quickly become disheveled and appear unkempt.

2. Spread the word—Tell the mail carrier (who's always on the alert for stray dogs). Call the neighbors and schools (kids enjoy helping and love dogs). Call the police, veterinarians, pounds, shelters and humane societies not only in your county but in the surrounding counties. Dogs travel many miles in search of the cat they spied . . . or home. Not all dogs have the homing instinct of Lassie. As soon as possible, visit animal organizations with your posters. Don't take their word that there is no handsome Golden on the premises.

3. Advertise—Call the papers and the radio stations. Offer a reward (which should also be printed on the posters). Make it high enough to make it worthwhile for someone to return the dog, but low enough that it does not invite extortionists.

4. Search—Never stop searching. Use an answering machine or have someone stay by the phone to answer any reports of the dog being sighted. Dogs have been found as long as six months after their loss.

5. Humane trap—Set a familiar object (a blanket or a crate with a favorite toy) on your porch or in your garage, along with bowls of food and water. If he does come home while you're out searching, he'll have a reason to stay.

6. Prevention—Fences, kennel runs and walking on leash. If the dog is a jumper or climber, make the fence higher or plant shrubs around to increase the distance and top the run. I.D. your dog with *collar*, *tags* and a *tattoo*. Take photos, both *haute coiffure* and *au naturel*.

7. Be prepared—A lost dog is often terrified. Even those who are normally friendly can panic when called by a stranger, or even by someone they've known and loved all their lives. Use a lure: food, a kennelmate, an open car door, a bitch in season for a stud dog, a favorite toy or sound (like food pans, or a gunshot for a hunting dog).

Too often, also, dognappers are lured by a winsome face, easy prey, or the potential dollar signs flashed by a purebred. The dognapper's booty is sometimes sold to people who are unaware of the circumstances. Most times, however, they're marketed to dog brokers, who fake papers and resell the dog. Worse yet, they might be sold to dog fighters (as bait or fighters) or laboratories (for experiments). Stolen dogs are difficult, if not impossible, to trace unless they can be positively identified.

NO DOGS!

In Europe, dogs accompany their masters everywhere—to stores, on buses and even in restaurants. Because the dogs are accustomed to public acceptance, they're well behaved and sit or lie quietly. Or is it because the pets are well behaved that they are accepted?

In the United States, however, "No Dogs"! signs are popping up like weeds—all over and too many. Because of bratty canines and careless owners, landlords demand a no-pets clause in leases. Parks restrict certain areas for pets if they're allowed at all. Many motels and hotels no longer admit anyone with a dog.

Many cities have a poop-scoop ordinance. Owners are required to clean up after their dogs or pay a fine. For too long, people have had the mistaken notion that their bad habits are not offensive to others, or even if they are, that's tough luck. These people claim, "It's our right to leave doggy doo-doo (drive carelessly, be sloppy drunk, blow smoke in your face or you fill in the blank). We aren't hurting anyone." Wrong. It's our right to own dogs but not to turn parks, sidewalks and public places into doggy latrines.

McKensie Hollas with Belvedere puppies out of "Brit" and "Tory."

tions, worry for the owner, a frightened pet, even death of the animal—all of these are major concerns for the person considering air shipment of a dog.

Various precautions can help assure your pet's safety. Buy a shipping crate, available from airlines, pet suppliers and pet stores. The crate is two pieces made from durable, molded plastic, held together by nuts and bolts. Because these sometimes loosen, particularly after use, examine for tightness. Bungee cords can also be used to secure the crate in both directions. When shipping puppies, shredded computer paper makes a soft bed and is more absorbent and less messy than a blanket in case of a "goof." A favorite toy covered with your scent will be comforting. Acclimate the dog to a crate prior to the shipping date. Label the crate with the dog's name (in case of a mishap, calling a dog by name helps), owner's name, address and phone. A health certificate must be obtained within ten days of the shipping date. Most veterinarians do not advise tranquilizing the animal as it may disorient them.

"Blaze" owned by Laurie Doumaux of Clifton, Virginia, taking a photogenic ponderous moment from his tennis game.

Now we know our bad habits can be not only offensive but harmful to others, and we've got to straighten up and fly right, or we'll be flying solo. No Snoopy in our cockpits.

If we want to continue this special bond between dogs and people, we must scoop poop, walk dogs on leash and train them to behave in public. It's no longer a good idea but a necessity that we attend classes and practice good manners. That demands confining pets and curtailing barking. It means no destruction of motel rooms, no jumping up when uninvited and no disgusting piles left behind—in other words, cleaning up our act.

SHIPPING

Whether for a move, a dog show, breeding or vacation, owners occasionally must ship their pets by air. Loss, discomfort, missed connec-

Three handsome and talented Goldens: **Ch. Hunt's Yeoman of Smithaven CD, WC; Smithaven's Legerity CD, JH, WC** and **Am-Can. Ch. Smithaven's Firm Fav O'Rhet CD, WCX**, owned by June and Betty Smith of Alamo, California.

Toy dogs may be carried on board in a small (7.5 inch) crate which is placed under the seat. FAA regulations state that the dog must remain in the crate. Reservations must be made at least a week in advance for shipping, whether in cabin, excess baggage (accompanied by a passenger) or as air freight. Ship nonstop or direct, if possible, and avoid shipping on weekends or using two different airlines. If this must be done, check with the flight attendant at each stop.

The dog should not be fed for eight hours prior to shipment, and unless it's extremely warm, water should be withheld for the last couple hours before the flight. A bowl can be attached to the inside of the kennel door so that chips of ice, water or kibble can be dropped in without opening the door. Walk the dog immediately before placing him in the crate for loading.

Although airline regulations stipulate that no animals may be shipped when the temperature is below 10°F or -12°C (others say 35°F or 1°C) or above 85°F or 30°C, a warm rug is soothing during cold weather, and insulated cold packs under a damp towel help during warm spells.

Depending on the size of the airport, the dog must arrive at baggage one or two hours before the flight. When you arrive, buy additional insurance. It doesn't hurt for the ground crew to realize it's handling valuable cargo. Verify with the flight crew that your dog is safely on the plane. Check and double check.

Above: **Ch. Honor's Goldstorm Party Girl JH** having her way with a fuzzy duck. Owner, Diane Mueller.
Below: "Dash" for short, this intense and beautiful Golden is **Sunfire's Dashing Rapids Am-Can. CD, SH, WCX**, owned by M. Book and F. Biewer of West Suffield, Connecticut.

Breeders typically keep puppies until they are eight weeks of age, committing much time to the socialization and development of each individual puppy. Photo by Karen Taylor.

PUPPY MILLS

The best puppy mill or puppy farm cannot possibly offer the care and attention that a hobby breeder can. The sheer numbers prevent that. Puppy mill profiteers boast of placing 300 puppies a week! Adding the adult dogs, even with a staff of ten, that's less than three minutes a working day per dog—barely enough to feed and clean up. Socialization and cuddling must be sacrificed, even if the caretakers like dogs. Face it, would we like animals if all we did was put food in one end and clean it up from the other?

Certainly, niceties such as evaluating temperament and personalities, matchmaking new owners with pups, introduction to grooming and leash training cannot possibly be squeezed into the day. These "high-class" businesses occasionally have a veterinarian they work with. Other times, they diagnose and medicate dogs themselves. Breeding stock is never tested for congenital and hereditary conditions, i.e., hip dysplasia, cataracts or deafness.

Pedigrees are iffy. Registration papers are as good as the owner's word. Sometimes two males are with the bitch. Sometimes one male services everybody of that breed, daughters, sisters, mother. This is the best of the puppy mills.

The worst dispenses with the amenities. Dogs live in small pens or chicken coops their entire lives, with feet never touching the ground. Some, kept inside, never see light and go blind. Waste piles up underneath the grating which serves as a floor to the pens. When such premises are raided, the animals panic when they are touched or if they are placed on the ground. They're wormy, mangy, undernourished and full of fleas and maggots.

Water is scarce, ventilation poor and sanitation unheard of. They're fed the poorest food, sometimes scraps, sometimes nothing. In some circumstances, they have been forced to cannibalize each other when one starves. Carcasses lie where they drop until there is time or the inclination to haul them out and dispose of them.

Bitches are bred on the first season and every one thereafter. They pay their way or they die. When bitches stop producing or their litters decrease in numbers, they're killed, usually shot. Sometimes the first shot doesn't kill them. But since bullets cost money, sometimes the castaways lie there until they die.

Puppies are shipped as soon as they're weaned, so that no unnecessary expense is invested in the product. If they are weaned, it may be on bread

416

and milk or scraps. The only medication that is given is that which is required by law.

The problem with even the best of these operations is that they think of a dog as produce. Profit is the only motive.

On a farm, food stock such as cattle and hogs produce meat, milk, butter, eggs or leather. Dogs, however, are themselves the end product. The buyers have to live with all the psyches and physical conditions caused by the birth environment.

Animals who are kept in this environment don't live, they only exist . . . and not for long. Perhaps the saddest thing is that the great devotion and loyalty that is instinctive in dogs is never tapped. . . and certainly never returned.

Puppy placement is a sensitive matter with breeders. Knowing that a puppy from a line of field trial champions goes to a hunting home makes a difference to the committed breeder.

WHAT CAN WE DO?

1. Spay pets so that one of our pups will never end his days in a chamber of horrors.

2. Learn which questions to ask to determine whether the breeder is in it for love or money.

3. Examine the premises and ask to see the parents or at least the dam of the litter.

4. Don't buy on impulse—compare. Go on gut feeling. If you sense something is wrong, get out.

5. Educate yourself about the breed, then ask to see health certification papers for hips, eyes or specific conditions that appear in your chosen breed.

6. Don't think that just because a pup has registration papers and a pedigree that it is automatically quality.

7. Pet shop owners who deal in dogs should buy only from local breeders whose premises and animals can be checked out.

8. Demand stricter laws so that all animal abuse and neglect cases will be punished and put out of business. Join Responsible Dog Owners Assn. (RDOA) 73 Old Dublin Pike #13D, Doylestown, PA 18901.

Puppies live to play, especially with each other. **China** and **Buddy** at nine weeks. Bred by Kaye Fuller, DVM. Photo by author. (P.S. Buddy won.)

No doubt that **Farm Fresh Grade A Apple** has his instincts in tact at three-and-a-half months of age. Owner, Leslie Dickerson. Photo by Bill Jany.

FOSTER HOMES

One of the saddest facts about owning dogs is that we lose them so quickly, and those of us who love animals will face this sorrow over and over. What many owners fail to consider, however, is that their pets may outlive them.

Death is not the only thing that can cause separation. Illness, injury or extended hospitalization or nursing home care can mean that we're unable to care for our dogs.

Pet owners should name a caretaker who will take over in case of an emergency. Write all information about your dog in a booklet or type an instruction sheet, covering feeding, medication and medical records. Include a paragraph about the pet's schedule, likes, dislikes, allergies, favorite toys and so on. If there is more than one pet, note a description of each, preferably with a photo. Give a copy to the veterinarian, a neighbor, a relative and the caretaker. Inform the caretaker of travel plans. If you fall off a ski lift in Switzerland, it is unlikely anyone else will think to notify the boarding kennel where Pinkerton is awaiting your return.

Providing for your dog in case of your death is responsible ownership. Allot a sum for his care

and note the provisions in a statement of intent which should be attached to your instruction sheet as well as to your will. Waiting for the will to be read could mean a long spell before your dog's next meal.

The following is acceptable to probate courts, and relatives aren't as likely to battle a fair trust fund as they are a 400-acre estate given to Pinkerton.

"I bequeath my dogs Pinkerton and Holmes to my friend, Dudley DoRight, in return for the sum of one dollar. Dudley DoRight will act as guardian for my dogs and will provide care and maintenance for the rest of their natural lives. A trust fund in the amount of XXXX is established for their care. In return for a nominal fee, Dudley DoRight agrees to provide a home for Pinkerton and to find a good, loving home for Holmes. The trust fund will be divided to cover the care and maintenance of the dogs."

You may add further provisions, such as neutering or euthanization of an old or sickly pet who may have trouble adjusting or be too much care for another person. Notify your veterinarian of specific wishes. Have the statement witnessed and notarized.

Ta's Teddy Bear was surely a teddy bear of a puppy and growing fast at six months. Teddy is by Bda Ch. Twin-Beau D's Hi Speed Chase ex B'-Bop'N Amber Royale Jubilee. Owners, Felita and Brian Carr.

419

Two puppies who survive because of Golden Retriever rescue. **Victory** and **Max** are in the arms of owner Tamara Neff.

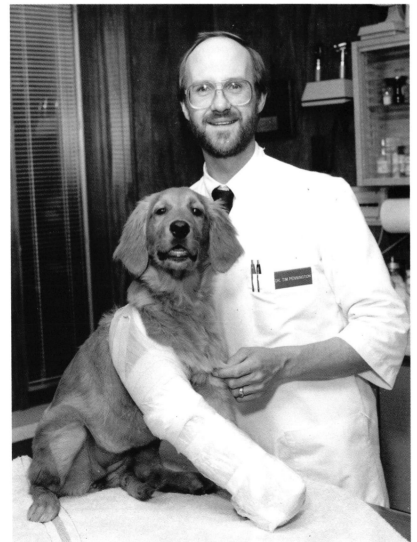

Dr. Tim Pennington is a veterinarian in St. Louis who donates his services to the care of Golden rescue pups.

Golden Retriever Rescue: Saviors of the Breed

In this day and age of disposable everything, our society looks for ways to rid itself of anything used or unwanted, inconvenient or unnecessary. Our highways, beaches and parking lots all bear abundant evidence of people bent on dumping their waste and surplus for others to trip over or clean up.

Sadly that same mentality often includes our society's pets. Throwaway dogs and other animals have become as common as discarded plastic bottles and fast-food containers.

In 1989 the American Humane Society estimated that 2,000 dogs, 3,500 cats and 415 humans were born *every hour* in the United States. It is not surprising then, in 1990 over 18 million dogs were euthanized at humane societies and municipal animal shelters. And according to the Humane Society of the United States, for every loved and cared-for dog and cat, there are nine others that are homeless and roam the streets at the mercy of speeding cars, freezing weather and abusive human beings. An estimated 20 to 25 percent of the dogs roaming as strays or received at animal shelters are purebred dogs. Shelter statistics show that less than one out of every four animals that comes in will leave there alive.

No breed is exempt. Dog lovers have searched diligently for ways to solve this heartbreaking and seemingly hopeless dilemma. Over the years arose a plethora of purebred-dog rescue services, each one dedicated to salvaging its own breed.

GRCA members were among the first to come to the aid of their breed. By January 1991 the GRCA had 32 Golden rescue services. Most are full-service and provide foster homes, health and other necessary care and permanent adoptive homes. A few, due to lack of funds or people, are referral services only and maintain a list of Goldens needing homes and a "want" list of people looking for Golden Retrievers.

This network of Golden rescue clubs represents the best and worst in dogdom. On the top side, the breed is blessed with a national cadre of dedicated volunteers who donate countless hours to the rescue and rehabilitation of thousands of abused and abandoned Goldens of all ages, sizes and character. Their only compensation, one that can't be measured in money or rewards, is a recycled Golden made happy and whole again.

At the bottom of the heap lies the fact that there is a need for rescue in the first place. The burgeoning Golden population, fattened by the puppy mills and backyard breeders who mass produce poorly bred puppies, many with unstable temperaments and serious genetic problems, provides a supply-side basis for rescue services. The problem is compounded by hundreds of well-bred pups who are placed with families or individuals who are unprepared or unwilling to deal with the vagaries of raising an untrained, rambunctious retriever. The common misconception that a Golden is a wonder dog, an easy keeper, a just-add-food, train-itself canine—coupled with society's impatience with anything that grows too big, costs too much, or _____ too much (*insert:* sheds, barks, eats, digs, chews, etc.) also adds to the dilemma of Golden abandonment.

Sunny is one of nine puppies given to rescue at two-and-a-half weeks of age. New owner is Maureen Witthaus.

Here's **Teddy** at age two-and-a-half months, now owned by John and Marijo Manestar.

Goldens arrive at rescue's door for a variety of reasons: "so many health problems, we just can't be bothered anymore," "don't have the time we used to have," "gets hair in the pool ...on the furniture...the new carpet," and other excuses that irresponsible pet owners feel justify the callous dumping of a friend.

Some Goldens just get passed along from one family or friend to another until someone gives that final ultimatum: no more dog. Ironically that same unwanted Golden would stand by them until death and willingly give up its life for theirs. But they have reasons, after all.

Prerequisites for any rescue service is an abundance of energy, time and money. Many services are abundant on the first two criteria; most are short on the last. Some operate dog-to-dog as available funds allow.

Rescue committees generally consist of at least four club members, although "a committee of one" is not unheard of in some outlying areas. The clubs are usually self-supporting, and several have incorporated as non-profit, and thus are eligible for tax-deductible charitable contributions.

Rescue members contact local animal control agencies (pounds, shelters, humane societies) to explain the work they are doing, and to learn about the holding period for stray dogs and owner turn-ins. They ask shelter personnel to call a committee member if a Golden is picked up or turned in by its owner. If a dog comes directly to a rescue, in most cases the owner must sign a release form giving the committee sole ownership of the animal.

Some rescue clubs routinely visit their area animal shelters to check for Goldens among the lost and lonely waiting out their time. They are usually there, one or two a week, curled up shivering in a corner or pacing frantically inside the run, brown eyes lighting up with hope at each new face....it might be Mom... lost, abandoned, abused, or just inconvenient.

Where funds and facilities allow, the rescued dogs are taken to a veterinarian for a check-up on condition, heartworm, parasites and other problems. Adoptable dogs receive a booster shot and are placed in a foster home for subsequent care and evaluation. All dogs are spayed or neutered before placement in permanent adoptive homes, and many veterinarians offer reduced rates on surgeries for rescue animals.

Foster homes provided by club members and other dog-loving volunteers care for rescued animals until permanent homes become available. The foster family may nurse a sick Golden back to health, evaluate temperament and other problems, or just provide a temporary loving home. Many foster parents fall in love with their Golden charges and find room for "just one more" in their own human and canine families.

Yankee Golden Retriever Rescue, Inc., founded in 1985, is one of the GRCA's largest rescue services and surely one of the busiest. Incorporated as a non-profit, federal-tax-exempt, charitable organization, it has grown to over 400 members and covers the six-state New England area (Connecticut, Massachusetts, Maine, Vermont, Rhode Island and New Hampshire). In 1989 they averaged three to five Goldens admitted

Here's **Sunny**, now owned by Maureen Witthaus.

every week, and in 1990 successfully placed 146 rescue dogs in loving homes.

Yankee GRRC has been a model for other Goldens rescue clubs organized during the past five years. Like all successful rescues, their operation depends on Golden people who give their time and effort and accept inconvenience as a way of rescue life.

All Yankee Rescue Goldens are first admitted to one of two animal hospitals, both located in Massachusetts. During the initial examination and testing, they are tattooed with a YGRR I.D. prefix number, which is then registered with the National Dog Registry. The dogs are also given all necessary medical care, which includes spay/neuter surgery. Those who need extended care for medical problems or surgery are placed in foster homes until they have recovered. Healthy dogs are transferred to one of the rescue's two boarding facilities for evaluation and further care.

Special dogs, such as the senior Golden or ones with extraordinary medical problems who are unlikely adoptees, are placed in Yankee "Long-Term Foster Care" homes. The Rescue provides the food and special medical care. While the dogs are still available for adoption, they continue to receive quality family living to support their special needs.

People requesting to adopt a rescue Golden from Yankee are sent an information packet outlining the adoption procedure. It also includes Golden statistics (size, grooming, etc.) and a questionnaire to be completed and sent to the adoptive home coordinator. The applicant receives an acknowledgement postcard and within two weeks a volunteer will visit the prospect to discuss what the potential owner is looking for in a Golden. If approved (about 15 percent are not), the new owner will meet an adoptee, then wait the prescribed 24-hour "cool-

ing off" period so the rescue staff and adoptive family can make sure the match is appropriate or decide they should see another dog. The new owner also receives a packet to prepare for the new dog, which includes a copy of Carol Benjamin's book *Second Hand Dog.*

Another winner from that litter of nine, this is **KC**, enjoying a flavorful rawhide treat.

Once the adoption is approved, the new owner signs an adoption contract releasing Yankee from any liability concerning the dog. If the dog is too young to be spayed or neutered, the contract stipulates it be altered by a specific date. If the family must give up the dog during its lifetime, it *must* be returned to the rescue program. If returned within 30 days, in as good or better physical and mental condition, a prorated, conditional refund may be granted, pending approval by the board of directors.

Yankee continues its responsibilities to the dog throughout the lifetime of the animal. They do post-adoption follow-ups and mail a home questionnaire annually to see how the dog and family are getting along

Operating funds come from membership dues, grants, donations, litter donations, auctions and the annual, and very popular, Yankee Rescue calendar which features pictures of rescue Goldens and monthly hints on canine care. Members also donate their time and suggestions in their personal areas of expertise.

Yankee's quarterly newsletter for members

423

"Chip" has too much white to be accepted as a Golden Retriever; fortunately he is a hamster, and the best friend of Magnum (**Windfall's Royale Frolic CD**), who accepts and loves Chip just the same. Owner, Robin Peoble.

contains valuable information on dog safety, behavior and training, and they encourage sharing these to promote responsible pet owners throughout every community.

While Yankee does not accept any Golden who has bitten or is aggressive to people, they will refer those owners to a battery of assistance programs, including behaviorists, trainers and medical evaluators. The club also sponsors tattoo clinics, periodic training and health seminars, and lost and found assistance.

One of Yankee's happy-ending rescue stories is of Otti, a bedraggled Golden found dazed and wandering during a rainstorm on a highway in Connecticut. He was taken to the local pound and put in a run with other dogs for the mandatory seven days.

During that time, due to the cold, wet weather, he became very stiff and could not move well. At feeding time he was too slow to get to the food, and the other dogs finished it off. He was scheduled for euthanasia when a Yankee Rescue member heard of him and arrived to pick him up. By now his eyes were sunken in, his body was one big mat, and he could not move. The pound staff thought Rescue was crazy, but Otti's eyes smiled and his tail thumped a feeble welcome sign.

When he arrived at the animal hospital, everyone sighed. Otti was so sweet, but looked so bad. Upon examination he was found to be infested with worms, was dehydrated and malnourished, but all his parts operated in good order. Otti just smiled at his new provider, and his tail thumped a little harder. He ate, was lovingly groomed and bathed, and he just thumped some more.

For the balance of his life, Otti shared his bed with two other Goldens in Theresa Yeager's home, in long-term foster care. He took ascriptin daily for his arthritis and led a comfortable life thumping his plume-like tail very hard. He was a very old Golden, about 14 years of age, and while the quantity of his life was not too long after his rescue, the quality of it was unbeatable. He was *loved!* (Story reprinted with permission from the Yankee GRRC.)

In another rescue journey, the Golden Retriever Rescue, Education and Training, Inc., (GRREAT) of Maryland and Virginia encountered what is undoubtedly a rescue club's worst nightmare.

It was February 1988, and volunteers from GRREAT accompanied the State Humane Officer to a farm whose owner had recently been committed to a psychiatric hospital. The officer was planning to confiscate dozens of abused and neglected animals, and asked several breed rescue groups to take in and care for some of the dogs.

At the farmer's property, dozens of dogs had been left starving in the most filthy and horrifying conditions. Over 60 dogs were found in the house and on the grounds, some locked in outbuildings and rooms filled with excrement piled two feet high. Many were beyond hope and had to be euthanized immediately, including several Golden adults and puppies who were near death.

Most of the remaining 16 Goldens were chained to trees with no shelter, food or water. Small amounts of dog food had been scattered around the dogs, some of it only inches from the starving animals straining at their chains—in desperation they had eaten the dirt around the trees.

Sixteen filthy, sick and starving Goldens at midnight on a frigid Friday night: rescue challenges don't come much bigger.

Rescuers loaded the dogs into their vans, took some to individual volunteer homes and 11 to a volunteer who offered kennel space. All the dogs were extremely people-shy, severely malnourished and infested with every variety of worms....hook, whip, round and tape. Rescuers worked into the night to worm and vaccinate all the dogs.

The next day the Goldens began their journey to rehabilitation with warm baths in an oversize horse trough. The veterinarian made a special house call to examine and evaluate all the dogs. Two were already in congestive heart failure from heartworm. And all were terrified of people and a human touch.

Human response to the plight of these poor animals was swift. Within several days they all went to special families who were prepared to deal with housebreaking and extreme fear responses to strangers or an outstretched hand. Some dogs took months to learn to trust again. But each one eventually blossomed under pa-

tient and consistent loving care, a tribute to the true gentle Golden spirit.

Today all 16 are well-adjusted and well-loved, many adopted by their foster families who couldn't part with them. One Golden rescued named Micro, tiny and terrified of humans, took six months to accept a gentle pat or scratch behind her ear, and now she begs you not to stop. Brandy, pregnant and full of heartworms, delivered four healthy puppies and then survived her battle with the heartworms. Her proud foster family couldn't let her go. Dogberry and Snackers were also adopted as a pair by their foster family, as were Sweetheart and Stinky, two Golden ladies who gladly share the attention of their adoptive master.

A GRREAT $2,000 journey led to health and happiness for 16 Golden Retrievers.

One of the tragedies emerging from the nightmare

Bruwin's Carmel Kiss owned by Ginger Rezy, resting with her best friend Nerm the cat. Photo by Suzy Rezy.

of Golden rescue is the Golden who is unadoptable because of aggressive or vicious behavior. Most Golden owners have read that Golden temperament is not what it used to be—Rescue knows it for a fact.

Pam Dahmen, member of the GRCA Educational Committee and former chairman of the GRC of Greater Los Angeles Rescue, can cite far too many examples of bad temperament encountered during a rescue career.

Becky was one of Pam's typical happily-ever-after rescues... found abandoned, then placed in a permanent, safe and loving home...... until 15 months later when she and another Golden mauled a teenage babysitter. Pam's veterinarian, who always talked her into giving the "old gold" another chance, agreed that Becky should be euthanized. He added he was seeing more and more Goldens with a vicious streak. In the end, Pam held Becky's trembling paw and cradled her head as she gently fell asleep.

Pam knows another dedicated rescue chairman who resigned after a rescue Golden she was

Cleo greets owner Mary Dewitt of Houston, Texas this way every evening.

trying to place attacked the child of a potential adopting family. Pam said too many cases of unexpected and unprovoked aggression warrant a closer look at making excuses for the dog; taking a ball away is *not* provocation; walking past a sleeping dog is not reason for the dog to lunge; holding a dog down for a tattoo is not cause for an attempted bite.

Pam is adamant about temperament for good reason. She does not want to comfort any more heart-broken familes, and she doesn't want to hold any more Beckys as they leave this world.

These frequent exceptions to the loving Golden temperament are not a recent product of the '80s. As early as the 1960s knowledgeable breeders realized the Golden's rapid rise in popularity would not enhance the positive qualities in the breed.

In 1982 Shirley Goodman wrote in *Dogs In Canada* magazine about the high price of Golden popularity, and recounted numerous cases of untypical and undesirable temperament, Goldens who bit their owners, groomers and veterinarians without provocation. Temperaments, good and bad, are inherited along with other genetic faults and blessings, she reminded her readers. A good look at the sire or dam will often reveal the future smiles or snarls of their offspring.

Environment too plays an important role in molding temperament, she wrote. Proper socialization is second only to proper selection of the puppy and its sire and dam. New owners need instruction on what to look for, the importance of positive early imprinting, and how to build a strong foundation for future learning experiences.

Untrained and poorly socialized dogs easily become statistics. Behavioral problems are the leading cause of death in dogs in the U.S., according to the Morris Animal Foundation. More dogs are taken to animal shelters and euthanized for bad behavior than for any other reason. An estimated ten million pets are surrendered to shelters every year because of behavior problems ranging from phobias to anxieties, many for outright aggression. So many could be saved if people only knew.

It is interesting to note that, given the problem of surplus Goldens and the burden faced by Golden rescues, many responsible and long-time breeders are restructuring, postponing, and in some cases, abandoning their breeding programs to make time and room for a permanent rescue Golden or two.

Breeding a Golden Retriever is a matter that demands expert guidance and advice, more than could adequately be addressed in a single chapter

Bruwin's Carmel Kiss wishes owner Ginger Rezy good luck before competing in a local horse trial. Photograph by Suzy Rezy.

of a breed book. The books listed in the bibliography at the end of this book cover all aspects of breeding, whelping, and raising a litter of Golden Retriever puppies. GRCA member clubs and individual member-breeders can also direct and assist a novice interested in properly breeding and raising Golden Retrievers. A prospective breeder must be well informed and should consult an army of experts before bringing new Golden lives into the world.

GOLDEN EDUCATION: HOPE OF THE FUTURE

Golden Education: Hope of the Future

Education is the key to saving the Golden Retriever and its "golden" personality. The opportunities are legion. Thanks to the over 65,000 Goldens registered annually in 1989 and 1990, we see ads for Golden puppies in every city and neighborhood newspaper, on grocery-store bulletin boards and in windows along busy and residential streets: "Golden puppies for sale..$75...$100," bargains waiting for the unsuspecting.

In an effort to counter the mass production of Golden puppies, the Golden Retriever Club of Greater Los Angeles Rescue prepared a letter to educate the casual breeders, the ones Golden people run into at dog shows, obedience trials, the vet clinic or pet-supply shop.

Since the GRC of Greater Los Angeles Rescue operation began, the number of homeless Goldens has multiplied from one or two dozen a year to sometimes a dozen in one week, a parade of barely weaned puppies to gray old timers, many of them destined for euthanasia because of their sheer numbers. The GRC-GLA breeder letter is reprinted here with their permission.

Dear Breeder or Prospective Breeder:

The Golden Retriever Club of Greater Los Angeles appreciates the opportunity to share the following information with you. We are a volunteer group of dog breeders, owners and exhibitors who are active in helping pure-bred Golden Retrievers in trouble. We are alarmed that, as this versatile breed has gained popularity, the number of homeless or unwanted Goldens, as well as the incidence of emotionally unstable and physically unsound dogs, has increased immensely.

Since you are advertising Golden Retrievers for sale or have asked for information on breeding, we hope you will share our concern for the breed's future.

Opposite: Photographer Karen Taylor captures **Sexton's Kona Gold** as only a Golden Retriever disciple can.

PLEASE HELP US HELP THEM! By placing your puppies carefully and following up on the dogs you sell, you can reduce the number of homeless Goldens. BEFORE you sell a puppy:

1. EVALUATE YOUR BREED. This is a large and hairy breed. They slop water on the floor and can eat forty pounds of food a month. They go through an active and often destructive adolescence that may last until the dog is two years old. They are intelligent and inquisitive (they shouldn't be bred any other way), so they bore easily and make their own fun. They dig, bark, and shed.

2. EVALUATE YOUR LITTER. Rate puppies by activity levels, noisemaking abilities and general pecking order. A rowdy, dominant puppy usually grows into a rowdy, dominant adult. It might not be the right choice for a family with young children. A quieter, more docile puppy might be more suitable. Try to match your puppies to their prospective homes. It is common and acceptable for a breeder NOT to allow a buyer to pick the puppy he wants.

3. EVALUATE YOUR BUYER. Ask questions and listen carefully to answers. Not every person who shows up with the purchase price is right for a dog...especially one as special as a Golden Retriever. It is a breeder's right to say NO, and by saying NO to unsuitable homes in the beginning, you prevent a homeless dog in the future. A breeder should ask these questions:

1. WHO will live with this dog? If it is a couple, listen carefully for the woman's attitude because she will probably become the major caretaker, and if she doesn't really want the dog to begin with, it will be homeless eventually. If there are children, remember a seven or eight-month-old Golden weighs more than many seven or eight-year-old children, so youngsters will be knocked down even if the dog is gentle. The dog will eat the kids' candy and their toys. If the children are undisciplined, the dog will be the same way...and people do not keep unmanageable dogs.

2. WHERE will the dog live? A dog without a well-fenced yard will live a short life. It will probably have a violent end, under a car or in an animal shelter. A Golden which is always kept outdoors will be frustrated and bored, and very apt to develop behavioral problems which cannot be cured. Require written proof of landlord

429

Joshua Armentrout Jung, at age four, with his nine-week-old pup **"Scottie."** Owners, Joan and Tony Jung, Lancaster, Texas.

approval before selling a puppy to buyers who rent....rescue puppies have come from people who believed they could hide the dog out indefinitely, but hiding elephants is easier than hiding Goldens. Remember, although some individuals adapt to apartment living, overall, the breed is not suited to it, and it requires tremendous commitment from the owner.

3. WHY do the buyers want a Golden? Will it be a pet, hunting companion, or show dog? If they are looking for an angelic lap dog....they aren't looking for a Golden Retriever. Be objective and realistic about the abilities of the dogs you have bred. If a buyer is looking for a show dog and the nearest champion in your pedigree is several generations back, the chance of your puppies being show quality are slim. If you've bred the hottest bird dogs in the swamp, they might not be a docile, patient pet. If you've bred show lines, the chances of producing the courage, nose and ability to be a hunter are small, even if the grandsire was a field dog. If you represent your dog's ability as more than it is, a disappointed buyer will probably part with the dog.

4. WHAT is the buyer's "pet-history"? Buyers who have had many pets for short periods of time, if they "gave them away" or they "ran away," or had a few hit by cars, they are not a good prospect for a permanent home. If they move and dump pets at each location, your pup will probably join their list of homeless ex-pets. Ask them if they are prepared to care for this animal for its expected lifespan of 10 to 12 years.

AFTER you sell a puppy:

1. Keep in touch with your buyers. A postcard on each of the puppies' birthdays will help you remain in contact for the dog's entire lifetime. As a breeder, you should have a wealth of information to share...a puppy's Dr. Spock. Your helpful advice could give new families the support necessary to keep their pets when they go through an especially difficult time in doggy development.

2. Most important, you will know if one of your pups is endangered. Sometimes even the best placements don't work out. Family situations and living arrangements change. It happens to the best of breeders. It is not a failure. What is a crime is not to care, not to be there, when one of the lives you profited from creating needs you. You, as a breeder, have the obligation to accept your dog back and find it a new safe home.

GOLDEN OVERPOPULATION

When our rescue operation began several years ago, the number of homeless Goldens was one or two a month. Now it is more often one or two a day. It used to be primarily older males, but now we handle weaned puppies to silver-muzzled veterans. Formerly, we rarely had to destroy healthy young dogs, but today we can no longer accept all the homeless...so many die.

Please do not be a breeder who turns his back on the problems. Don't fool yourself into believing that all your puppies go to "good homes" and stay there. We have helped puppies of the sweetest household pets and the most celebrated show and performance champions. Every breeder shares in the responsibility for the tragedy.

Please take an objective look at your breeding program and practices. Ask yourself if every breeding you undertake is absolutely necessary and if you are prepared to help the dog you have produced. Since there are not enough quality lifelong homes for dogs...even purebreds...we must breed only the best.

THE BEST BREEDER:

1. Clears all breeding stock for inherited defects. Poeple do *not* keep dogs with problems. Rescues cannot place them. Most die. Remember that even though your breeding stock may not show defects, most are internal and can only be detected by special testing. But these unknown

The very handsome and versatile **OTCh. Altair's Dune Mirage TDX, WCX, JH, Can. UDT (OS)**. Owner, Rosemary Chase, Bedford, Ohio.

There are some things that only a mom can explain. Puppies acquired from good breeders have the added advantage of the bitch's presence until the litter is eight weeks old or older. This mom-knows-best is **Quantock's Sacajawea CD, TD, Can. CD** and her puppies out of Ch. Jayba's Golden Cadillac. Breeder, Eileen Bohn.

defects can be passed along to the get. Several hereditary defects are now seen in Goldens.

Hip Dysplasia (HD) ... a crippling developmental problem in the pelvis and leg bones. Can be detected by x-ray. Cleared animals can be registered with the Orthopedic Foundation for Animals (OFA) if over 24 months old.

Opthamolic (eye) deformities ... including cataracts, eyelid deformities, retinal dysplasia and atrophy. Most can be detected by a veterinary opthalmologist. Cleared stock can be registered with the Canine Eye Research Foundation (CERF).

Circulatory disorders ... von Willebrands Disease (vWD) is a clotting disorder and can be detected by specialized blood testing. Sub-valvular Aortic Stenosis (SAS) and other coronary defects can be detected by a veterinary cardiologist. Neurological and behavioral problems ... seizures, epilepsy, unreliable temperaments, and viciousness seem to run in families. Although testing is not available for these problems, affected animals should not be bred.

2. Has a long-term goal for the improvement of the breed's structure, temperament and inherent bird-retrieving ability, and does not overproduce. We cannot breed solely for profit...the price of this fancy is in lives. We cannot breed as a way of extending immortality to a beloved pet. We breed only to produce *better* Goldens, not *more* Goldens. Spay or neuter any non-breeding-quality animals, and urge pet puppy buyers to do the same. It will prevent accidental breedings and lower the tremendous numbers of Golden mixes we see in the animal shelters.

3. Stands behind what he has produced for the dog's entire lifetime. Accepting payment for creating this life is accepting lifetime responsibility for this living thing. If you are not able to or ready to accept this obligation, please show the selflessness and foresight not to continue breeding.

Everyone loves the joy and excitement of new lives, and certainly puppies are one of the happiest events. But for those of us who love this breed and these dogs so much, there is no greater heartache than having to hold the unwanted, un-needed and unloved as their lives are taken away.

TATTOOS

Lost or stolen dogs can happen to anyone. A dog's best defense against such an occurrence is a collar and a tattoo. Without identification, the dog who wanders off, chases a rabbit into unknown territory, jumps over the fence or out of the car is a prime candidate for euthanasia at a dog pound or fair game for anyone who picks it up.

Collars are worthless without tags or owner identification. Non-choke-type collars should have a tag or brass plate bearing your name, address and both daytime and evening telephone numbers. Most professionals recommend against including the dog's name. Some further suggest including a line that states "Dog needs medication." After all, what thief or research laboratory wants to bother with a sick dog?

A tattoo is permanent legal proof of ownership and won't be forgotten after a bath or pulled off during a run in the woods. Tattoos are recognized and honored by all animal shelters, police agencies and rescue organizations. A lost tattooed animal is almost guaranteed eventual return to its owner.

Tattoos are best applied to the inside of a hind leg; ears can be too easily severed. There are several active tattoo registries in the United States, and most are recognized by any agency that handles dogs.

The most common and economical choice of tattoo number is the owner's social security number. It can be used to register an unlimited number of dogs with the same registry. The second most popular choice in tattoo numbers is the dog's AKC registration number; the AKC will aid in tracing the owner of the tattooed dog.

The tattooing process is uncomfortable, but relatively painless and takes about five minutes. Most veterinarians will tattoo a dog, some groomers offer that service, and many dog clubs hold

Pre-titles, this is **Am-Bda. Ch. Twin Beau D. Hi Speed Chase (OS, HOF)**, himself the sire of many beautiful Goldens. Owners, Donald and Sharon Beach and Nancy Dallaire.

Enjoying the snow like so many Goldens is **Pinehurst Traveling Goldust CDX, WC, VCX**, owned by Janet Schaadt.

annual tattoo clinics for less than half the normal cost per dog.

A number may be registered for a fee with the National Dog Registry (NDR), Box 116, Woodstock, NY 12498, 914-679-BELL or 800-NDR-DOGS. NDR also sponsors an organization for pets of the elderly or financially disadvantaged who have pets in need of emergency care. The NDR Rescue Fund is aided by donations.

Other registries are the Breeder's Action Board, 15870 Allen Road, Taylor, MI 48180, 313-285-6311; I.D. Pet, Inc., 74 Hoyt Street, Darien, CT 06820, 203-327-3157 or 800-243-9147; Tattoo-A-Pet, 1625 Emmons Avenue, Brooklyn, NY 11235, 718-646-8200 or 800 TAT-TOOS. The American Kennel Club contacts the owner of record for dogs tattooed with AKC numbers, phone 919-493-7396.

Another recent method of identification is implantation of a microchip. Information may be obtained from INFOPET, 5137 N. Clareton, Suite 110, Agoura Hills, CA 91301, 800-INFOPET.

The majority of lost Goldens who come to rescues are without a collar or tattoo. Using one or both might slow the rescue business down a bit, something Golden Retriever people would applaud.

Unfortunately rescue is a major part of the

Golden Retreiever world of the 1990s, and is a sad daily fact of life for GRCA rescue clubs. These dedicated "Golden people," and surely they are that, routinely go out of their way to do the out-of-the-ordinary to promote the welfare of their breed. Why do they go to so much trouble? Because, when you love dogs, particularly this special breed, to save even a single Golden puppy is a great deed. To save hundreds of Goldens is the stuff of dreams.

Ch. Llanfair Intrepid CD. "Peter."

Quartermoon Nighthawk SH photographed by Bobbie Christensen in Montana.

Above: **Sunfire's Kinetic Cascade MH, Am-Can. UD, WCX (OD)**, a bitch of many talents and titles, hits the water like a professional. *Below:* Taking a moment from the day's work to look picturesque, this is **Sunfire's Rowdy Rebel UD, JH, WCX**.

The swamp on a good day. Golden Retrievers photographed by Karen Taylor.

Drug-awareness cards issued by the United States Customs Service illustrate Golden Retrievers **Bandit**, **Benny**, **Bernie**, **Beto**, **Buck** and **Cody**. The cards are collected by children to whom the drug-free messages are directed. Courtesy of U.S. Customs Service.

BANDIT
NOGALES
SOUTHWEST REGION

BANDIT

1991 Series

Tattoo #: C-613
Breed: Golden Retriever
Age: 3
Weight: 75 Pounds
Year Started in Customs: 1989
Year Prior Ports Assigned to:

Largest or Most Notable Seizure:
Bandit was called upon to search an empty truck semi-trailer (18 wheeler). Bandit showed that it was not at all empty, but contained 1,488 pounds of marijuana beneath the floor of the trailer.

YOU CAN HELP BANDIT
STOP DRUG SMUGGLING
TO REPORT SUSPICIOUS ACTIVITIES, CALL
1-800-BE-ALERT

BETO
PORT EVERGLADES
SOUTHEAST REGION

BETO

U.S. CUSTOMS - PORT EVERGLADES FL

1991 Series

Tattoo #: C-380
Breed: Golden Retriever
Age: 7
Weight: 92 Pounds
Year Started in Customs: 1985
Year Prior Ports Assigned to:
1985 New York, NY

Largest or Most Notable Seizure:
Beto's best seizure was 2,200 lbs. of cocaine at Port Everglades Seaport inside container roof.

YOU CAN HELP BETO
STOP DRUG SMUGGLING
TO REPORT SUSPICIOUS ACTIVITIES, CALL
1-800-BE-ALERT

BENNY
CALEXICO
PACIFIC REGION

BENNY

1991 Series

Tattoo #: C-585
Breed: Golden Retriever
Age: 4
Weight: 70 Pounds
Year Started in Customs: 1989
Year Prior Ports Assigned to:

Largest or Most Notable Seizure:
Benny's most significant seizure was 195 lbs. of cocaine concealed in the trunk of a vehicle that contained a hidden compartment. The cocaine had a street value of $20,005,651.

YOU CAN HELP BENNY
STOP DRUG SMUGGLING
TO REPORT SUSPICIOUS ACTIVITIES, CALL
1-800-BE-ALERT

BUCK
SAN LUIS
SOUTHWEST REGION

BUCK

U.S. CUSTOMS - SAN LUIS, ARIZONA

1991 Series

Tattoo #: C-552
Breed: Golden Retriever
Age: 3
Weight: 58 Pounds
Year Started in Customs: 1988
Year Prior Ports Assigned to:

Largest or Most Notable Seizure:
Buck searched a 2 door sedan arriving from Mexico and began alerting on the side panels of the car. A total of 141 pounds of marijuana was discovered.

YOU CAN HELP BUCK
STOP DRUG SMUGGLING
TO REPORT SUSPICIOUS ACTIVITIES, CALL
1-800-BE-ALERT

BERNIE
PROGRESSO
SOUTHWEST REGION

BERNIE

U.S. CUSTOMS - PROGRESSO, TEXAS

1991 Series

Tattoo #: C-587
Breed: Golden Retriever
Age: 4
Weight: 62 Pounds
Year Started in Customs: 1989
Year Prior Ports Assigned to:
1989 San Ysidro, California

Largest or Most Notable Seizure:
Bernie's largest seizure occurred in August, 1989 and was 143 pounds of marijuana from Mexico.

YOU CAN HELP BERNIE
STOP DRUG SMUGGLING
TO REPORT SUSPICIOUS ACTIVITIES, CALL
1-800-BE-ALERT

CODY
HIDALGO
SOUTHWEST REGION

CODY

U.S. CUSTOMS - HIDALGO, TEXAS

1991 Series

Tattoo #: C-414
Breed: Golden Retriever
Age: 6
Weight: 70 Pounds
Year Started in Customs: 1986
Year Prior Ports Assigned to:
1986 Laredo, Texas
1987 Hidalgo, Texas

Largest or Most Notable Seizure:
Both of Cody's largest drug finds have been in big, 18 wheel trucks. Cody found 2,735 pounds of cocaine inside the walls of the trailer behind one truck and 1,701 pounds of marijuana inside the trailer of another truck.

YOU CAN HELP CODY
STOP DRUG SMUGGLING
TO REPORT SUSPICIOUS ACTIVITIES, CALL
1-800-BE-ALERT

Golden Retriever Fever

It's hard to believe that there are a few breeds that outrank the Golden Retriever in breed popularity. More than any other canine, the Golden has its soft, appealing image projected into every facet of our lives: Goldens promote cameras, cars and boats in newspapers and magazines; they accompany movie stars and politicians, assist the handicapped, guide the blind, and cheer the elderly. We all live next door or down the street from at least one Golden Retriever. Small wonder, then, the marketplace seems gripped by Golden Retriever fever, with breed collectibles and memorabilia available in gift shops, art galleries, book stores, and even the local grocery store.

Most popular among collectors are "sandcast" sculptures of the breed. These Golden likenesses represent a wide variety of type to please both pet fanciers as well as field and show folks. Small Golden images are also available in pewter for minimal cost or larger pieces in cold cast bronze that sell for a small fortune. Plate collectors can indulge in limited edition issues that feature appealing Golden puppies or entire families in a typical outdoor setting.

Additional Golden models adorn teapot stands, pocket

Dog patch from the collection of Officer Mike Bishop issued by the Lancaster County Drug Task Force of Pennsylvania.

puzzles and refrigerator magnets, postcards, bookmarks, and carved wooden letter-openers. Look in catalogs and novelty stores and you'll find Golden Retrievers on wastebaskets, coffee mugs and glassware, needlepoint pillows, lap throws and sweatshirts.

The Golden's scenting ability is highly respected and valued by narcotic agents and search-and-rescue teams. Some agencies recognize the Golden's contribution by depicting a breed likeness on their official patch. Officer Mike Bishop, K-9 trainer and handler for the Fairfax County Police Department in Annandale, Virginia, collects canine patches from organizations throughout the world. The dogs portrayed in patches from his collection attempt to honor the Golden as an integral member of their support team.

Despite the popularity of so many Golden collectibles, the most influential Golden image of the '90s may be that of the drug detection dog. In 1991 the U.S. Customs Service released a million-dollar series of canine drug-sniffer trading cards, similar to the ever-popular baseball cards. The face of each card features a portrait of a narcotics-sniffer dog, with the reverse side giving the dog's description, (breed, age, weight, tattoo number), its previous port assignment, and the dog's largest or most notable seizure.

The cards are distributed at schools after a U.S. Customs live canine demonstration. The dogs in action spread the anti-drug message to the students, and the cards become valuable reminders of the children's experience with the dogs. The cards not only build anti-drug camaraderie among the student collectors but also heighten the children's awareness of the drug problem and how effective the canine corps can be in stemming drug traffic into the U.S.

The cards also carry a 1-800 BE ALERT number young people can call to report activities or information about drugs, guns or money, thereby encouraging them to become partners with the Customs canine teams. If callers wish to remain anonymous, Customs will assign them a permanent reference number and never refer to them by name.

In 1992 distribution of canine corps trading cards spread to the breakfast table. Adults as well as children could collect the cards from their favorite cereal boxes.

With Goldens numbering among the most successful drug detection canines, dogs like Humphrey from Boston's Northeast Region may become as popular as baseball's top pitchers and batters. Humphrey hit on 72,000 pounds of marijuana buried beneath hundreds of tons of gravel onboard a cargo ship. Golden Retriever Cody from Hidalgo, Texas found 2,735 pounds of cocaine hidden inside the trailer walls of an 18-wheel truck. Bernie, Bandit, Goofy, Sandy, and dozens of other drug-sniffing Goldens are working with Cody and Humphrey and the U.S. Customs Service to stop the flow and demand for drugs, and help spread the drug-free message where it's most needed . . . the young people of America.

Golden Retriever paraphernalia-mania…dishes, coasters, pins, bookmarks, puzzles, etc.

Painted ceramic plates and "sandcast" sculptures depict the Golden Retriever. Notice the different types of dogs chosen for portrayal…from beautifully coated show-dog quality to the more racy field-type dog…all appealing to the various "races" of Golden Retriever lovers.

U.S. Customs Service drug cards honoring Golden Retrievers **General, Goofy, Humphrey, Money, Sandy** and **Tinton** and their miraculous records of merit. Courtesy of U.S. Customs Service.

GENERAL
ROMA
SOUTHWEST REGION

GENERAL
U.S. CUSTOMS - ROMA, TEXAS

1991 Series

Tattoo #: C-557

Breed: Golden Retriever

Age: 5

Weight: 65 Pounds

Year Started in Customs: 1988

Year   Prior Ports Assigned to:

1988 New York, JFK Airport

Largest or Most Notable Seizure:

General's largest seizure was 18,900 Pounds of marijuana in a large truck from Mexico. He has also found 9 pounds of cocaine and 2 pounds of heroin.

YOU CAN HELP GENERAL
STOP DRUG SMUGGLING
TO REPORT SUSPICIOUS ACTIVITIES, CALL
1-800-BE-ALERT

TINTON
SAN LUIS
SOUTHWEST REGION

MONEY

1991 Series

Tattoo #: C-546

Breed: Golden Retriever

Age: 5

Weight: 62

Year Started in Customs: 1988

Year   Prior Ports Assigned to:

Largest or Most Notable Seizure:

Money is one of the first Customs canines trained for passive response and is used to inspect international passengers arriving at our Customs ports of entry. In her first year alone, she was responsible for over 40 narcotic seizures.

YOU CAN HELP MONEY
STOP DRUG SMUGGLING
TO REPORT SUSPICIOUS ACTIVITIES, CALL
1-800-BE-ALERT

GOOFY
SAN YSIDRO
PACIFIC REGION

GOOFY

1991 Series

Tattoo #: C-594

Breed: Golden Retriever

Age: 3

Weight: 75 Pounds

Year Started in Customs: 1989

Year   Prior Ports Assigned to:

Largest or Most Notable Seizure:

Goofy alerted on a boat that contained 1,500 lbs. of marijuana at San Ysidro port of entry. Goofy also alerted on a volkswagon that contained 85 lbs. of cocaine in November 1990.

YOU CAN HELP GOOFY
STOP DRUG SMUGGLING
TO REPORT SUSPICIOUS ACTIVITIES, CALL
1-800-BE-ALERT

SANDY
EL PASO
SOUTHWEST REGION

SANDY

1991 Series

Tattoo #: C-537

Breed: Golden Retriever

Age: 3

Weight: 80 Pounds

Year Started in Customs: 1988

Year   Prior Ports Assigned to:

1989 Columbus, New Mexico

Largest or Most Notable Seizure:

Sandy found 140 pounds of marijuana in the double floor of a truck, 42 pounds of marijuana in the gas tank of a truck, 117 pounds of marijuana in the tires of a truck, and 184 pounds of marijuana in the false floor of another truck. Sandy enjoys working trucks.

YOU CAN HELP SANDY
STOP DRUG SMUGGLING
TO REPORT SUSPICIOUS ACTIVITIES, CALL
1-800-BE-ALERT

HUMPHREY
BOSTON
NORTHEAST REGION

HUMPHREY
U.S. CUSTOMS - BOSTON, MA

1991 Series

Tattoo #: C-312

Breed: Golden Retriever

Age: 9

Weight: 70 Pounds

Year Started in Customs: 1983

Year   Prior Ports Assigned to:

Largest or Most Notable Seizure:

72,000 pounds of marijuana buned beneath hundreds of tons of gravel onboard a cargo ship.

YOU CAN HELP HUMPHREY
STOP DRUG SMUGGLING
TO REPORT SUSPICIOUS ACTIVITIES, CALL
1-800-BE-ALERT

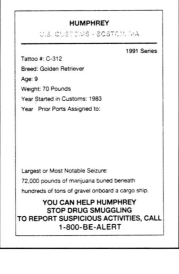

MONEY
LOS ANGELES
PACIFIC REGION

TINTON
U.S. CUSTOMS - SAN LUIS, ARIZONA

1991 Series

Tattoo #: C-595

Breed: Golden Retriever

Age: 5

Weight: 72 Pounds

Year Started in Customs: 1989

Year   Prior Ports Assigned to:

Largest or Most Notable Seizure:

Tinton searched a car and began to alert on the floor. Removal of the carpet revealed 45 pounds of marijuana in a hidden compartment beneath the floor.

YOU CAN HELP TINTON
STOP DRUG SMUGGLING
TO REPORT SUSPICIOUS ACTIVITIES, CALL
1-800-BE-ALERT

This page: Canine patches from around the United States and New Zealand for police dogs, search and rescue dogs, and drug K-9 teams from the collection of Officer Mike Bishop of Annandale, Virginia.
Opposite page: The very patriotic **Tejas Polo Player** (OTCh. Spicewood C Krystle of Tejas UD, JH, WCX, ex Ch. Daystar Tornado Warning) owned by Pat Cullum of New Caney, Texas. "Dozer" knows how important it is to be alert and nationalistic!

Left: Author Nona Kilgore Bauer's beloved field dog—this is **KC Chances R Walk'n on Sunshine MH, CD, WCX,*****. Sunshine is truly aptly named and brings that and much more to Nona and her husband Phillip…Sunshine lives for them and of course…the *hunt*.

Below: **Am-Can. Ch. Skilfor Butterblac Bisque Am-Can. UD, JH (OD)** earning her Junior Hunter title at 11 years of age. "Tea" was bred by Doug Windsor in Canada (Am-Can. Ch. Cal-Vo Starfarm Gambler UD ex Butterblac's Solar Halo). Gambler, Tea's sire, was Francine Shacter's first Golden. Francine, also the owner of Tea, brought Tea out of retirement (where she reigned as "chief couch potato") to earn her JH title in 1990. Five years previous, she won both UDs in the U.S. and Canada. Tea is truly a versatile, Golden over-achiever since very few bench champions go on to title in both obedience and field work, plus, as Francine says, she is "one of the nicest dogs I have ever known." Incidentally, Tea was BOS at the 1982 GRCA National Specialty.

Opposite page: Enter the Master Hunters…*Clockwise* are four star hunters from Quartermoon of Berthoud, Colorado…**HR Quartermoon Dixie Lilly MH, ** (OD)**, the dam of four Master Hunters; **HR Quartermoon Shelby MH; Quartermoon Nighthawk SH, WCX**; and **HR Quartermoon Dakota MH, ****. In the *center* is a young man, his young dog and their first goose!

444

Above: Truly picturesque! This is **AFC Sungold T-Bill Sunsplasher MH**. Photo courtesy of Quartermoon.
Below: Three littermates from Quartermoon.
Opposite page: The wonderful things about Tiggers…this is **Quartermoon Tigger MH**.

Above: "Krystle gems"…the first litter from **U-CD OTCh. Spicewood C Krystle of Tejas JH, WCX** by BISS Ch. Daystar Tornado Warning. Owner, Pam Cullum. Krystle eyeing her gems…wearily.

Opposite page: Puppies are introduced to decoys and wings at an early age to instill the natural hunting instincts. These puppies learning the ropes at Quartermoon.

Right: **"Blossom"** owned by Jane Hallie Schuldiner. Photo courtesy of Mr. and Mrs. Stanley Schuldiner.

Left: **Ch. Sassafras Batterys Not Incld** would rather pose with pumpkins than win National Specialties…but he's done both more than once! "Ready," as he's known, won the GRCA National Specialty BOB in 1990 and 1991. He is shown on a very limited basis and is owned by L. Rodolph of Marshfield, Massachusetts.

Below: Three field champions…one household…owned by Ron Wallace and Judy Rasmuson. They are **FC-AFC Valhaven Smoke'N Vindaloo, FC-AFC Topbrass Tyonek** and **AFC Deerhill Iditarod**. Photo by the author.

Above: **Golden Bear's Sweet Ashley** bred by James and Cindy Lichtenberger of Mt. Holly, New Jersey.

Below left: Litter of rowdy pups from the author's 1992 breeding…as with all the Chances R litters at the Bauers, every puppy found the "right" owner and is likely working on his MH already or at least a couple pheasants! From this litter Nona kept Ginnie "because she simply couldn't resist."

Below right: Obedience-titled guide dogs! Ed and Toni Eames with guide dogs **Ivy CDX, Bda. CD** and **Kirby CDX, Bda. CD**. Ivy is the first guide dog in AKC history to earn the CDX obedience title…and Kirby the second.

Above: Golden Retriever **Chelsea**, Kibbles 'n Bits and Ken-l-Ration 1990 Dog Hero of the Year and member of the Texas Pet Hall of Fame, with owner Chris Dittmar, Houston Texas.

On February 19, 1990, Chris chatted with a neighbor on his driveway, three-year-old Chelsea resting at his feet. Two strangers approached, asked the time, then suddenly pointed handguns at Chris and his friend. Without warning, Chelsea growled fiercely and lunged upward at one of the gunmen. Two shots were fired, one hitting Chelsea in the shoulder. Chris and the neighbor ran into the garage as the assailants continued to shoot. The gunmen fled, and after authorities arrived, Chris began searching for Chelsea. He finally found her two blocks from home, hiding in the bushes; she was limping badly and bleeding from the shoulder. He carried the wounded dog home and rushed her to an emergency veterinary clinic. Chelsea required two weeks of recuperative therapy before she could endure surgery to remove the bullet from her shoulder. "Chelsea attacked the gunmen because she smelled my fear and set about to protect her family," Chris said. "Without her, the consequences could have been severe."

Left: **NAFC-FC Topbrass Cotton**, pride and joy of the Golden Retriever field-trial world, sits pretty for photographer Julie Carothers.

Ch. Spicewood's Empyreal Tiffany UD, JH, WC, Can. CDX is a natural obedience achiever…*(above)* at ten weeks of age, Tiffany is sniffing out the high jump in her back yard *(below)* Tiffany doing her thing in the ring. Owners Barb and Fred McMorris deserve credit for recognizing talent from such an early age! Tiffany was bred by Carolyn Durway and is a third-generation Ch.-UD bitch, a breed first in Golden Retriever bitch lines. Her dam, Ch. Spicewood's Almond Joy UD, WC, owned and also bred by Carolyn, was out of Ch. Ginger Ballad of Spicewood UD, WC (OD), owned by Carolyn and bred by Ginger Gotcher.

Above: Top performers at the GRCA 1991 National Specialty Field Trial include: **FC-AFC Topbrass Windbreaker Zap, FC-AFC Windbreaker Mighty Mo, AFC Topbrass Super Trooper, FC-AFC Stoneybrooks Jersey Devil, FC-AFC Topbrass Dustbuster, FC-AFC Topbrass Tyonek** and **FC-AFC Valhaven Smoke'N Vindaloo.** Photo by author.

Below: Field trial stars line up during a training session at Blackwater Kennel, Centerview, Missouri, for the 1991 GRCA National Specialty in Kansas City. **FC-AFC Topbrass Windbreaker Zap** and **Mistfield Red Zinger***, "Rosie," both owned by Jane and Sam Silverman; **FC-AFC Windbreaker Mighty Mo**, owned by Jerrie Heiner; **Topbrass Comet***, "Halley," owned by Mary Maurer and Kim Martin; **Topbrass Abilene***, "Abby," owned by Torch Flinn; **Sundust Rom***, "Rome," owned by Mary Jane Wolk; **FC-AFC Topbrass Tyonek**, "Ty"; **FC-AFC Valhaven Smoke'N Vindaloo**, "Lulu"; and **AFC Deerhill Iditarod**, "Dede," all owned by Ron Wallace and Judy Rasmuson; and **FC-AFC Topbrass Dustbuster**, "Buster," owned by Barbara Howard. Photo by Rasmuson.

Above: **Am-Can-Bda-Jap. Ch. Laurell's Jiminy Crickett (OS, HOF)** (Ch. Hilltop's Pekay's Pistol Pete ex Ch. Laurell's Susie), owned by Ray and Judy Laureano. "Jimmy" was the Number One Golden, all systems in 1987 and 1988. He has eight U.S. Best-in-Shows, one in Bermuda and two in Japan, and was BISS four times. He has sired over 15 champion get, with son Stonehill's Wide Montana Sky (HOF), also a BIS and BISS. During his show career Jimmy claimed over 50 Group Ones and over 100 Group placements. A most loving Golden, he also claimed the hearts of everyone who met him.

Below: A prominent "Jimmy" son, **Ch. Stonehill's Wide Montana Sky (HOF)**, owned by Ray and Judy Laureano.

455

Above: **Ch. Goldenbear's Hot Shot**, known to all as "Shooter", was bred by James and Cindy Lichtenberger and owned by Kathy Martin and Cindy Lichtenberger.

Below: **U-CD, OTCh. Spicewood's C Krystle of Tejas JH, WCX**. Krystle earned her OTCh. at four years of age, claiming over 15 High-In-Trials along the way. She was a Gaines placer and is in the Obedience Hall of Fame.

Above: The very exclusive ladies' club for Master Hunters—mom and three girls all from the same litter! The girls have a MH brother who wasn't invited to this luncheon. They are **KC's Sparkle Plenty MH, WCX, *** (OD)**, the dam, and **KC's Chances R Walk'n on Sunshine MH, CD, WCX, ***, CGC, TDI, KC Spirit of Sparkle MH, WCX, *****, and **KC's Reflection of Sparkle MH, WCX, ****. The author is the owner of Sunshine. This is a very exceptional litter…four MHs from such a small brood…and most of all, these field dogs *look* like Golden Retrievers.

Right: **High Times Booker T MH, WCX, ***** (Chances R Cool Hand Luke CDX, MH, *** ex High Times Southern Comfort)…both parents were outstanding producers. Booker was a well-known field trial and hunting test participant who loved birds and his mistress very much (not necessarily in that order…unless it was hunting season). His mistress was Pat Dougherty. Photograph by the author.

Top left: **Holway Sunny Sage of Dunbar MH**. Top right: **Quartermoon I Am Reddi! JH, WC**.
Bottom left: **Ch. Spicewood Empyreal Tiffany UD, JH, WC, Can. CDX** owned by Barb and Fred McMorris.
Bottom right: **HR Quartermoon McKeag MH** with owner Dr. Mike Scott.

Above: **Ch. Spicewood's Cloud Nine CD, JH, WC** (BISS) (Ch. Salyran's Spider John CD ex Ch. Ginge Ballad of Spicewood UD, WC). Owners, Dr. and Mrs. William Treadwell. Breeder, Carolyn Durway.

Below: **Can. Ch. Bargello's Hit-a-Miss CDX, JH, WC, Can. CDX, TT**—or "Scatter"—owned by Barbara Tinker.

Above: A tender moment at the Allen Park Nursing Center with Molly and resident Mason Bagget. **Molly** is a registered therapy dog who enjoys visiting nursing facilities and what could be a better pick-me-up than a Golden's smiling face and wet tongue? Photograph by Karen Taylor.

Below: **Brandy's Champagne Mist**, owned by Carol Sprague, proud of her seven whelps sired by Ch. Pinehurst Traveling Goldust CDX, WC, VCX, owned by Janet Schaadt.

Opposite page: **HR Quartermoon Kermit MH** and owner Doug Koeppel paint the proverbial dog and hunter portrait.

460

To a Golden Retriever

Wendy: April — December 1927

You came to your first home only in June,
And changed the currents of our summer days,
When in your puppyhood your mistress found
New joy of life, and in your brown eyes' gaze
Read all your heart, so that the world went round
And filled it with a new tune—
Wendy, wooly baby doll that rolled
And ruffled a soft coat, waved a broad paw,
And heard from one loved voice all puppy law;
Golden Retriever Wendy, nine weeks old.
And so through August days to strength you grew,
Gay with your mistress, learning at her side;
Questioning, dancing, slender and light as she,
Following her by field and road and ride
And watching I would wonder which could be
The happier, she or you—
Day takes away the gift that day bestows;
Death called predestined through
December snows,
And laid you, young, obedient, to sleep.
So short, the life has passed.
The dream remains.
Still may I watch you with an inward eye,
Still may I love you with unwounded heart,
Forgetful for an hour that dogs must die,
Choosing of memory this small part,
So that by Surrey lanes
Wherever once you ran in rain and sun,
There still by row or ride your light foot falls,
Still from the summer lawn your mistress calls,
Still through the summer garden blithe you run.

A photograph worth a thousand poems. This dog is **Can. OTCh. Kelly of Queen Island UDT, WCX, TT**. Photograph by owner Susan Kluesner.

Abbreviations

TITLE ABBREVIATIONS

AKC PREFIX TITLES

AFC	Amateur Field Champion
Ch.	Conformation Champion
Dual Ch.	Ch. and FC
FC	Field Champion
NAFC	National Amateur Field Champion
NFC	National Field Champion
OTCh.	Obedience Trial Champion

OTHER PREFIX TITLES

AFTCh.	Canadian Amateur Field Champion
FTCh.	Canadian/Australian Field Champion
HR	UKC Hunting Retriever
HR CH	UKC Hunting Retriever Champion
WR	NAHRA Working Retriever
MHR	NAHRA Master Hunting Retriever
GMHR	NAHRA Grand Master Hunting Retriever
Eng. Ch.	English Champion
Am-Can. Ch.	American and Canadian Champion
Can. Ch.	Canadian Champion
Aus. Ch.	Australian Champion
Bda. Ch.	Bermudian Champion
N.Z. Ch.	New Zealand Champion
Int. Ch.	International Conformation Champion (European)
R.T.Ch.	Australian Retriever Trial Champion
CFC	Canadian Field Champion

SUFFIX TITLES

CD	Companion Dog, first-level Obedience degree
CDX	Companion Dog Excellent, second-level Obedience degree
UD	Utility Dog, third and final Obedience degree
TD	Tracking Dog
TDX	Tracking Dog Excellent
TDI	Canadian Tracking Dog Intermediate
UDT	UD and TD
UDTX	UD and TDX
WC	GRCA Working Certificate
WCX	GRCA Working Certificate Excellent
WCI	Canadian Working Certificate Intermediate
*	Dog has earned a Working Certificate
**	Placement or JAM in a licensed Derby stake 3rd, 4th, or JAM in a licensed Qualifying stake
***	Qualified All-Age status in licensed field trial, earned with JAM in Open or placement in Amateur or first or second place in Qualifying stake
JH	AKC Junior Hunter
SH	AKC Senior Hunter
MH	AKC Master Hunter
VC	GRCA Versatility Certificate
VCX	GRCA Versatility Certificate Excellent

AD ....Agility Dog
AAD ....Advanced Agility Dog
MAD ....Master Agility Dog
OS ....GRCA Outstanding Sire
OD ....GRCA Outstanding Dam
OBHOF ....GRCA Obedience Dog Hall of Fame
HOF ....GRCA Show Dog Hall of Fame
SDHOF ....GRCA Show Dog Hall of Fame
FDOH ....GRCA Field Dog Hall of Fame
TT ....Temperament Tested
CGC..Canine Good Citizen
TDI ....Therapy Dog International
Mex. PC ....*Mexican Perro Compañero* (CD)
Mex. PCE ....*Mexican Perro Compañero Excellente* (CDX)

TERM ABBREVIATIONS

AI ....artificial insemination
AKC ....American Kennel Club
ANKC ....Australian National Kennel Council
BIS ....Best in Show
BISS...Best in Specialty Show
BOB ....Best of Breed
BOS..Best of Opposite Sex
BOW ....Best of Winners
CC ....Challenge Certificate / conformation or field wins /
Great Britain, Australia, New Zealand
CAC ....*Certificat d'Aptitude au Championat* (wins)
Switzerland, Netherlands
CACIB ....international conformation CAC
CACIT ....field trial win / Switzerland, Netherlands
CERF ....Canine Eye Research Foundation
CKC ....Canadian Kennel Club
CM..Certificate of Merit / Canadian field trial award
FCI ....Federation Cynologique Internationale
GRCA ....Golden Retriever Club of America
GRCC ....Golden Retriever Club of Canada
GRCN..Golden Retriever Club of Netherlands
HD ....Hip Dysplasia
HIT...High in Trial / highest scoring dog in trial
JAM ....Judges Award of Merit / U.S. field-trial award
KCGB ....Kennel Club of Great Britain
NAHRA ....North American Hunting Retriever Association
NCDA ....National Club for Dog Agility
OFA ....Orthopedic Foundation for Animals
QC ....Qualifying Certificate, earned during
field trial competition, other than the U.S.
RCC ....Reserve Challenge Certificate
SAR ....Search and rescue
SAS ....Subvalvular aortic stenosis
SKC ....States Kennel Club
UKC ....United Kennel Club
UKC/HRC..........................United Kennel Club / Hunting Retriever Club
USDAA ....United States Dog Agility Association
vWD ....von Willebrand's Disease

Hunt Test Comparison

	AKC*	UKC/HRC†	NAHRA†
First level	Junior	Started	Started
Title	Junior Hunter/JH	None–points only	None–points only, certificate issued
Second level	Senior	Seasoned	Intermediate
Title	Senior Hunter/SH	Hunting Retriever/HR	Working Retriever/WR
Third level	Master	Finished	Senior
Title	Master Hunter/MH	Hunting Retriever Champion/HR CH	Master Hunting Retriever/MHR
Fourth level	None	Grand	
Title		Grand Hunting Retriever Champion/Grand HR CH	
Game birds	Dead or shot only	Shackled allowed	Shackled allowed
Scoring	Scored 1–10 on abilities. No ability less than 5, overall 7 or higher	Pass–Fail	Scored 1–10 on each test. Average score 80% or better

FIRST LEVEL	JUNIOR	STARTED	STARTED
Qualifying scores/points	Four	Five points per pass, maximum 15 towards HR CH	Two and one-half points, maximum five toward MHR
Tests	Two land singles Two water singles	Two land singles Two water singles	Five singles, land and water
Distances	100 yards maximum	75 yards land; 60 water	75 yards land; 50 water
Deliver to hand	Yes	No, to designated area of line	No, to designated area of line
Steadiness	May be held	May be held	May be held
Casts	Twice from the line	Twice from the line	Twice from the line

AKC titles appear as suffixes.

†*UKC/HRC and NAHRA titles appear as prefixes.*

	AKC	UKC/HRC	NAHRA
SECOND LEVEL	**SENIOR**	**SEASONED**	**INTERMEDIATE**
Qualifying scores/points	Five Four if dog has JH	10 points each pass, maximum 20 points toward HR title	Five points each pass, 20 maximum toward WR title
Tests	Four Land double, water double, land blind, water blind, walk-up recommended	Five Land double, water double land blind, water blind, walk-up, tracking, quartering	Five Land double, water double, water blind, tracking, quartering
Distances	100 yards maximum	Land, 100 yards; water, 75 yards; land and water blinds, 40 yards each. Dry shot recommended	land, 100 yards; water 75 yards; water blind, 30 yards
Deliver to hand	Yes	Yes	Yes
Steadiness	Controlled break allowed, scored accordingly	Controlled break allowed, scored accordingly	Controlled break allowed, scored accordingly
Casts from line	Twice allowed, scored accordingly	Twice from line	Once only
Diversion shot(s)	Yes	Yes	Yes
Diversion marks	Allowed	Yes	Yes
Honor	Yes	Yes	

THIRD LEVEL	**MASTER**	**FINISHED**	**SENIOR**
Qualifying scores/points	Six	20 points each pass, 100 total for title	20 points each pass, 100 total for title
Tests	Five Multiple land, water and land/water marks. Land and water blind, one a double blind. One walk-up required. Other situations allowed	Four Multiple land, multiple water, land and water blinds	Six multiple land and water, land and water blinds, quartering, tracking
Distances	Established by judges, 100 yards recommended	Land, 150 yards; water, 125 yards; blinds, 100 yards	100 yards, land and water marks and blinds
Steadiness	Must be steady	Must be steady	Controlled break allowed, scored accordingly
Diversion	Shot(s) and mark(s)	Yes, mark used	Yes
Honor	Yes	Yes	Yes
Casts	One allowed	One only	One only

Recommended Reading

The following works are recommended by the author and have been divided by appropriate chapters of this book.

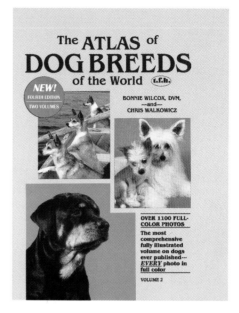

The Golden Comes of Age

De Prisco, Andrew and James B. Johnson, *Canine Lexicon*, T.F.H. Publications.

—. *Mini-Atlas of Dog Breeds*, T.F.H. Publications.

Walkowicz, Chris, and Bonnie Wilcox, DVM, *Atlas of Dog Breeds of the World*, T.F.H. Publications.

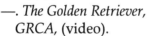

In the Conformation Ring

Elliott, Rachel Page, *The New Dog Steps*, Howell Book House.

—. *The Golden Retriever*, GRCA, (video).

—. *Dog Steps–A Study of Canine Structure and Movement* (video) American Kennel Club.

Fisher, Gertrude, *The New Complete Golden Retriever*, Howell Book House.

Golden Retriever Club of America, *Introduction to the Golden Retriever*.

Nicholas, Anna Katherine, *The Book of the Golden Retriever*, T.F.H. Publications.

Pepper, Jeffrey, *The Golden Retriever*, T.F.H. Publications.

Schler, Marcia, *A Study of the Golden Retriever*, Travis House.

Goldens in Obedience

Bauman, Diane, *Beyond Basic Training*, Howell Book House.

Burke, Lew, *Dog Training*, T.F.H. Publications.

Dunbar, Ian, *Dog Behavior*, T.F.H. Publications.

Front and Finish, P.O. Box 333, Galesburg, IL 61402-0333. Robert Self, ed.

Koehler, William, *Koehler*

Method of Dog Training, Howell Book House.

White, Angela, *Everybody Can Train Their Own Dog*, T.F.H. Publications.

The Field Trial Golden

Free, James Lamb, *Training Your Retriever*, Coward, McCann and Geoghegan, Inc.

Quinn, Tom, *The Working Retrievers*, E.P. Dutton, Inc.

Rutherford, Clarice and Cherylon Loveland, *Retriever Puppy Training*, Alpine Publications.

Spencer, James, *Retriever Training Tests*, Arco Publications.

Tarrant, Bill, *Hey Pup, Fetch it Up!* Sun Trails Publications.

Tri-Tronics, *Understanding Electronic Training*, Tri-Tronics.

Walters, D.L. and Ann, *Training Retrievers to Handle*, Interstate Book Manufacturers.

—. *Charles Morgan on Retrievers*, Interstate Book Manufacturers.

With Courage and Style—The Field Trial Retriever, AKC, (video) Cherylon Loveland.

Retriever Hunting Tests and the Hunting Golden Retriever

Hunt Test News, 1 E. 9th Street, Hutchinson, KS 67501.

Milner Robert, *Retriever Training for the Duck Hunter*, Junction Press.

Quinn, Tom, *The Working Retrievers*, E.P. Dutton.

Rutherford, Clarice and Cherylon Loveland, *Retriever Puppy Training*, Alpine Publications.

Spencer, James, *Hunting Retrievers: Hindsights, Foresights and Insights*, Alpine Publications.

—. *Retriever Training Tests,* Arco Publications.

Tarrant, Bill, *Hey Pup, Fetch it Up!* Sun Trails Publishing Company.

Walters, D.L. and Ann Fowler, *Training Retrievers to Handle.* Interstate Book Manufacturers.

Wolters, Richard, *Duck Dog,* Penguin.

—.*Game Dog,* Penguin.

—.*Water Dog.* Penguin.

Love 'Em, Hunt 'Em, Test 'Em — AKC Hunting Tests For Retrievers. (video). American Kennel Club, 51 Madison Avenue, New York, NY 10010.

Working Certificate Tests

Rutherford, Clarice, Barbara Branstad and Sandra Whicker, *Retriever Working Certificate Training,* Alpine Publications.

Rutherford Clarice and Cherylon Loveland, *Retriever Puppy Training,* Alpine Publications.

Wolters, Richard, *Game Dog,* Penguin.

—. *Water Dog,* Penguin.

Tracking

American Kennel Club, *Tracking Regulations,* AKC, 51 Madison Avenue, New York, NY 10010.

Brown, Wentworth, *Bring Your Nose Over Here,* ASAP Printing.

Canadian Kennel Club, *Regulations and Standards for Tracking Tests,* CKC, 100-89 Skyway Avenue, Etobikoke, Ontario, M9W 6R4 Canada.

Cree, John, *Nosework For Dogs,* Arner Publications.

Davis, L. Wilson, *Go Find!,* Howell Book House.

Johnson, Glen, *Tracking Dog.* Arner Publications.

—. *Tracking Trainers Handbook,* Arner Publications.

McCartney, William, *Olfaction and Odours,* Arner Publications.

Pearsall, Milo and Hugo Verbruggen, *Scent: Training to Track,* Alpine Publications.

Tracking Club of Massachusetts, *Tracking: A TD Field Guide,* 438 Lowell Street, Wakefield, MA 01880.

—. *Advanced Tracking: A TDX Field Guide,* 438 Lowell Street, Wakefield, MA 01880.

Agility

Front and Finish, P.O. Box 333, Galesburg, IL 61402-0333. Robert Self, ed.

Hobday, Ruth, *Agility...Is Fun,* USDAA.

Lewis, Peter, *The Agility Dog International,* USDAA.

USDAA, Inc. *Official Rules and Regulations,* P.O. Box 850955, Richardson TX 75085-0955.

NCDA, *Dog Agility Regulations,* 401 Bluemont Circle, Manhattan, KS 66502.

Therapy Goldens

Anderson, R.K.,B.L. Hart and L.A. Hart, eds. *The Pet Connection.* Censhare, University of Minnesota Minneapolis.

Bustad, Leo K., DVM, PhD, *Compassion: Our Last Great Hope. The Delta Society,* P.O. Box 1080, Renton, WA 98057-1080.

Fogle, Bruce, *Pets and Their People.* Collins Harvill, London.

Levinson, Boris, *Pet-Oriented Child Psychology.* Charles C. Thomas, Springfield, IL.

—. *Pets and Human Development.* Charles C. Thomas, Springfield, IL.

Search and Rescue

Bryson, Sandy, *Search Dog Training,* Boxwood Press.

Syrotuck, William, *Search and Rescue Dog Training Methods,* Arner Publications.

—. *Scent and the Scenting Dog,* Arner Publications.

Golden Girls and Boys

Bauman, Diane, *Beyond Basic Training,* Howell Book House.

Benjamin, Carol, *Dog Training for Kids,* Howell Book House.

—. *Mother Knows Best, the Natural Way to Train Your Dog,* Howell Book House.

Burris, Christopher, *The Proper Care of Dogs,* T.F.H. Publications.

De Prisco, Andrew and James B. Johnson, *Which Dog For Me?,* T.F.H. Publications.

Dunbar, Ian, PhD, MRCVX, *Sirius Puppy Training* (video), James and Kenneth, 2140 Shattuck Ave., #2406, Berkeley, CA 94704 .

Koehler, William, *Koehler Method of Dog Training,* Howell Book House.

Monks of New Skete, *How to be Your Dog's Best Friend,* Little, Brown & Co.

Rutherford, Carlice and David Hill, *How to Raise a Puppy You Can Live With,* Alpine Publications.

Vollmer, Peter, *Super Puppy, Super Puppy,* P.O. Box 3539, Escondida, CA 92025.

Volhard, J and G. Fisher, *Training Your Dog—A Step by Step Method,* Howell Book House.

Genetic Diseases

Corley, E.A., DVM, PhD., and G.G. Keller, DVM, *Hip Dysplasia: A Guide for Dog Breeders and Owners,* Orthopedic Foundations for Animals, 2300 Nifong Blvd, Columbia, MO 65201.

De Prisco, Andrew, and James B. Johnson, *Canine Lexicon,* T.F.H. Publications.

Holst, Phyllis, MS, DVM, *Canine Reproductions,* Alpine Publications.

Hutt, F.B., *Genetics for Dog Breeders,* W.H. Freeman and Co.

Lanting, F.L. *Canine Hip Dysplasia and Other Orthopedic Problems,* Alpine Publications.

Onstott, Kyle, *New Art of Breeding Dogs,* Howell Book House.

Richards, Dr. Herbert, *Dog Breeding for Professionals,* T.F.H. Publications.

Whitney, Leon, *How to Breed Dogs,* Howell Book House.

Inherited and Acquired von Willebrand's Disease

Dodds, W.J., A.C. Moynihan, T.M. Fisher, and D.B. Trauner. *The frequencies of inherited blood and eye diseases as determined by genetic screening programs.* Journal of American Animal Hospital Assoc. 17:697–704, 1981.

Dodds, W.J., *von Willebrand's disease in dogs.* Modern Veterinary Practice 65:681–686, 1964.

—. *Bleeding disorders, Handbook of Small Animal Practice.* RV Morgan, ed., Churchill Livingston Inc., 773–786, 1988.

—. *Contributions and future directions of hemostasis research.* Journal American Veterinary Medical Association 93:1157–1160, 1988.

—. *Bleeding and immune diseases, Parts I and II and acquired von Willebrand's disease.* Proc. 56th meeting AAHA, St. Louis, MO, 606–619, 1989.

The English Golden Retriever

Sawtell, Lucille, *All About the Golden Retriever,* Pelham Books, London.

Golden Education

Barrie, Annmarie, *Dogs and the Law,* T.F.H. Publications

Benjamin, Carol, *Second Hand Dog,* Howell Book House.

Campbell, William, *Behavioral Problems in Dogs,* American Veterinary Publications.

Fox, Michael, MRCVS, *Understanding Your Dog,* Coward, McCann & Geoghegan, Inc.

Miller, Louise, *Careers for Animal Lovers,* T.F.H. Publications.

Pfaffenberger, Clarence, PhD, *The New Knowledge of Dog Behavior,* Howell Book House.

Walkowicz, Chris and Bonnie Wilcox, DVM, *The Complete Question and Answer Book on Dogs.*

—. *Successful Dog Breeding,* Second Edition, Howell Book House.

Wilcox, Bonnie, *Things to Think About Before Breeding Your Dog.*

Index

*Page numbers in **boldface** refer to illustrations.*